AF804811

THE LOGIC OF FINANCIAL NATIONALISM

Using case studies ranging from cross-border bank resolution to sovereign debt, the author analyzes the role of international law in protecting financial sovereignty, and the risks for the global financial system posed by the lack of international cooperation. Despite the post-crisis reforms, the global financial system is still mainly based on a logic of financial nationalism. International financial law plays a major role in this regard as it still focuses more on the protection of national interests rather than the promotion of global objectives. This is an inefficient approach because it encourages bad domestic governance and reduces capital mobility. In this analysis, Lupo-Pasini discusses some of the alternatives (such as the European Banking Union, Regulatory Passports, and international financial courts), and offers a new vision for the role of international law in maintaining and fostering global financial stability. In doing so, he fills a void in the law and economics literature, and puts forward a solution to tackle the problems of international cooperation in finance based on the use of international law.

Federico Lupo-Pasini is a lecturer in international business and finance law at Queen's University Belfast School of Law. He studied at the World Trade Institute and at the National University of Singapore, and previously worked at the University of New South Wales. He has been published in numerous journals in the field of international economic law, and he has served as a consultant on international finance and international trade law for the Asian Development Bank, the EU, and various governments in Asia.

The Logic of Financial Nationalism

THE CHALLENGES OF COOPERATION AND THE ROLE OF INTERNATIONAL LAW

FEDERICO LUPO-PASINI

Queen's University, Belfast

CAMBRIDGE
UNIVERSITY PRESS

CAMBRIDGE
UNIVERSITY PRESS

University Printing House, Cambridge CB2 8BS, United Kingdom

One Liberty Plaza, 20th Floor, New York, NY 10006, USA

477 Williamstown Road, Port Melbourne, VIC 3207, Australia

4843/24, 2nd Floor, Ansari Road, Daryaganj, Delhi – 110002, India

79 Anson Road, #06-04/06, Singapore 079906

Cambridge University Press is part of the University of Cambridge.

It furthers the University's mission by disseminating knowledge in the pursuit of education, learning, and research at the highest international levels of excellence.

www.cambridge.org
Information on this title: www.cambridge.org/9781107189027
DOI: 10.1017/9781316986950

DAMAGED

© Federico Lupo-Pasini 2017

This publication is in copyright. Subject to statutory exception and to the provisions of relevant collective licensing agreements, no reproduction of any part may take place without the written permission of Cambridge University Press.

First published 2017

Printed in the United Kingdom by Clays, St Ives plc

A catalogue record for this publication is available from the British Library.

ISBN 978-1-107-18902-7 Hardback

Cambridge University Press has no responsibility for the persistence or accuracy of URLs for external or third-party internet websites referred to in this publication and does not guarantee that any content on such websites is, or will remain, accurate or appropriate.

Contents

Contents

Tables

Acknowledgments

This book is the result of my professional and academic journey into the fascinating field of international economic law. I started my career as an international trade policy advisor in South East Asia, and I have progressively switched my interests toward law and economics and financial regulation, which are now my main areas of research. The book reflects this trajectory as it combines my interest for the problems international finance, my appreciation for the analytical insights of economics, and a desire to investigate the political economy dynamics of international law.

The book would have not been the same without the precious mentoring and help of Professor Ross Buckley, with whom I had the opportunity to work at The University of New South Wales (UNSW) in Sydney. He helped me more than he had to in navigating the academic life, and I taught me a great deal on international finance law. I owe a very big debt of gratitude to Professor Claudio Dordi who has always been there as a mentor, friend, and colleague. I am very also grateful to Professor Thomas Cottier and Pierre Sauvè, who taught me when I was a student at the World Trade Institute, and constantly helped me in my professional and academic life afterwards. My year at the WTI as The Master of International Law and Economics (MILE) student has been probably the most formative moment of my academic life. The unique combination of law, economics, and political science at the core of the WTI's mission has shaped the way I think about the world and the law.

This book is partially based on my PhD dissertation, defended at the National University of Singapore in 2015. My deepest gratitude goes to my supervisor, Professor Jiangyu Wang, for his useful advices and the constant support throughout the entire PhD period. His suggestions and critiques were of fundamental importance for the development of the argument. I also appreciated the support of Professor Charles Adams, who acted as co-supervisor for the economic side during part of my PhD tenure, and

Professor Simon Chesterman and Professor Dora Neo, who have constantly helped me throughout my PhD. The three reviewers of my thesis – Professor Joel Trachtman, Professor Michael Ewing-Chao, and Professor Christian Hoffman – together with Professor M. Sornarajah gave me invaluable suggestions on how to improve the research. NUS was a great place to work. I benefitted greatly from the bi-weekly research seminars with the academic staff and junior researchers, where I could test my theses. I also wish to express my deep appreciation to the Singapore's Ministry of Education and NUS for their funding and financial support during the 3 years of my PhD.

At Queen's University Belfast I have found the perfect place to work and an amazing group of colleagues. My research assistant, Sayira Santana, helped me greatly in revising the manuscript for the editor. I also thank the editorial team at Cambridge University Press for their precious help. I owe a big debt of gratitude to Prisca Tami who helped me in designing the cover of the book.

Finally, I would like to dedicate this book to Thuy, my parents and family in Bergamo, for their love, dedication, and constant support.

Introduction

FINANCIAL INTEGRATION AND INSTABILITY

At the outset of the catastrophic East Asian financial crisis of 1997, Jagdish Bhagwati challenged, in a highly influential essay, the economic wisdom of free capital mobility at the core of the Washington Consensus' agenda for financial globalization.[1] As he succinctly pointed out in the title of his essay, trading in widgets and trading in dollars cannot be considered the same. While the benefits of the former have remained unchallenged for the last 200 years – supported by strong economic evidences – the virtues of the latter are questionable at best. From a purely historical viewpoint, it is difficult to challenge Bhagwati's view. The history of finance and the recurring financial crises unquestionably demonstrate that financial globalization exposes domestic economies to far more dangerous risks than free trade.

Eleven years later, indeed, the global financial system was embroiled in two even more destructive crises in the United States and Europe. Both events had major international repercussions and forced regulators and scholars to question once again how to reconcile the benefits of an integrated international financial market with the need to control its stability. As a lawyer, it is not my role to comment on whether financial globalization shall be maintained or dismantled in favor of a return to a situation of financial autarchy. I take financial globalization as a fact. For me, the question is how to manage it. In this regard, the discipline of law and economics offers very good insights on the power and limits of the law in addressing social problems. It shows how to use incentives and punishments to modify the behavior of individuals, companies, or states toward a desired outcome. It helps in understanding when and

[1] Jagdish Bhagwati, "The Capital Myth: The Difference between Trading in Widgets and Trading in Dollars," 77 *Foreign Affairs* 7 (1998).

to whom rights shall be allocated so that they can be used more efficiently. My contribution to the analysis of the difficult relationship between financial globalization and financial stability therefore looks at the role of international law in addressing the problem of global instability. It discusses whether the current international law of finance is actually efficient in reducing global spillovers and, if not, how it shall be changed.

Modern financial systems are structured as networks made by a constellation of diverse entities – banks, funds, traders, central banks, clearinghouses, and other intermediaries. The reason being that financial institutions are, for a variety of reasons, highly interdependent; they borrow, lend, and invest in various forms in each other. Their creditors too are subject to the same mood swings and, often, they influence each other. This means that a problem in one node of the financial network can easily transmit instability to others and therefore endanger the entire financial system; in financial jargon, we say that it can create *systemic risk*. Regulation plays a fundamental role in containing systemic risks.

In modern times, different solutions have been put forward to reduce the systemic impact of financial crises, from high capital requirements, to licensing rules, to concentration limits. Irrespective of their technical differences, these regulatory strategies rest on a common and simple principle – to participate in a common and interconnected financial system, financial institutions must internalize the social costs of their actions. The rationale behind this principle is to reduce the incentive that firms have in taking socially excessive risks, by imposing on them a price for participating in the financial system: a necessary sacrifice in terms of reduced freedom of action and potential earnings. I define this rationale as the *logic of externality*. The law plays a fundamental role in this regard, because by prohibiting financial market participants from engaging in risky (albeit lucrative) activities – such as the use of excessively high leverage – it can modify the behavior of individual financial institutions toward the socially optimal, and therefore minimize the risk of instability.

When we move to the role of international law in the international financial system, however, the music changes. From the great depression in the 1930s until a few decades ago, financial systems were predominantly national, with only limited cross-border interconnectedness between foreign financial intermediaries. In this situation, regulators largely developed their own national supervisory rules for financial institutions; they decided how to resolve them in the event of a crisis, and the level of protection accorded to depositors; and, crucially, they managed independently their monetary and macroeconomic policies. Since the 1970s, financial systems have progressively internationalized and become interdependent to the point that a problem in one country can now easily be transmitted across the global financial system and affect other states. The push for deeper integration was not, however, always accompanied by a parallel push for real international policy coordination. True, since the creation of the Basel Committee on Banking Supervision in 1974, regulators have increasingly engaged in regulatory cooperation through the various Transnational Regulatory Networks. Yet, in various circumstances, cooperation was not possible or did not lead to actual policy convergence. At times, cooperation failures actually increased global instability.

In an interconnected global financial system, one would expect international law to require states to take into account the global implications of their policies, and internalize the social costs of their actions. Surprisingly, however, the logic of externality does not fully apply to states. The very foundation of international law is based on the idea that states are sovereign in their territories. In principle, they do not need to answer to anyone for their policies, except their citizens. For instance, states can take up as much external debt as they want. They can, in principle, decide the rules that their banks will follow and how to restructure them.

More generally, states can decide their economic policies and legitimately refuse to coordinate them with other states. Even when states have agreed to reduce their sovereignty in favor of a more coordinated approach, they are, nonetheless, protected by various legal doctrines that have the ultimate goal of protecting the strict bond between the regulators and their citizens. For instance, most of the international rules on regulatory cooperation are in the form of soft laws. This means that, ultimately, states can renounce them at any time if they consider it necessary to protect their own political interests. Regulators cannot resort to international law to challenge another regulator's failure or refusal to cooperate, thus leaving the solution of regulatory disputes to pure power politics. In the few cases in which rules are binding, international law sometimes dispenses states with their obedience whenever doing so would impair an essential state interest. In sum, in the international law of finance what really matters is not the protection of social goals, but rather the safeguarding of national interests. In other words, in international finance, the logic of stability often gives way to its opposite: the *logic of financial nationalism*.

The goal of this book is to analyze the rationale underlying financial nationalism by looking at the economic and legal incentives that national regulators have to protect their own interests even when this is inefficient from a global perspective. In doing so, I will examine various policy areas, from bank supervision to derivatives regulation. I will show that financial nationalism is, ultimately, a very inefficient regulatory strategy in the long term. Over time, the interconnectedness between national financial systems has increased exponentially, and with it, the risk that wrong or otherwise socially suboptimal domestic policies in one country might impair the financial stability of others. This book argues that in an interconnected financial system, the protection of financial nationalism contributes to the creation of global systemic risk and, therefore, it is an unsustainable way to regulate global finance. It incentivizes states to adopt unsustainable domestic policies, and it transfers to the wrong side the costs of maintaining a stable global financial system.

This book also shows that, under the right circumstances, coordination is possible. The quest for a stable global financial system requires, however, a fundamental change in philosophy with regard to the way in which international law addresses financial stability. Addressing the moral hazard of nation states is no different from addressing that of individual financial institutions in a domestic financial system. In both instances, the law must force those subjects to internalize the costs of their actions and price correctly their participation into an integrated financial network. International financial law must therefore move from the logic of financial nationalism toward the logic of externality. What does that mean, precisely? In essence, an international law of externality focuses on addressing the social costs of stability policies, rather than simply enabling their adoption. On the one hand, the law must enable states to enjoy the benefits of market expansion, but on the other hand, it must also take into account the role of integration as a vehicle for global instability. Thus, it shall price adequately the externalities of economic sovereignty by making states wishing to participate in a truly integrating economic system responsible for the external effects of their domestic economic policies.

Most of the solutions proposed by the literature to the challenges of global financial stability focus either on a reduction in the level of financial integration, or on the entire dismantling of financial sovereignty in favor of a centralized international regulator. In contradistinction to these solutions, the strategy that I am proposing focuses on the role of (binding) international law and the correct attribution of rights and obligations among states, firms, and creditors. First, I argue that international agreements should increase the power of foreign stakeholders in driving international financial policymaking – for instance, by giving them rights and standing in international courts, similar to what international law does already in international trade or investment agreements. This should be complemented by the establishment of dispute settlement mechanisms to adjudicate or mediate financial disputes between regulators. Second, I propose to change the political economy bargain at the basis of financial integration in favor of a system that grants market access to foreign firms only when their home states agree to a binding code of conduct that guarantees regulatory and policy cooperation. I call this approach "Regulatory Passporting." By leveraging on the desire of nation states to access foreign markets, this strategy forces states to adopt a binding regulatory framework that reduces regulatory frictions and, therefore, global instability.

The book is ideally divided into three distinct parts. The first part comprises the first two chapters, which set out the theoretical analysis of the book. In Chapter 1, I will discuss the role of the law in national financial systems and I will analyze the logic of externalities. In Chapter 2, I will then proceed to the analysis of the role of international law in the global financial system. I will explain the logic of financial nationalism at the core of the current international law of finance, and I will develop all the concepts that will be fully explained in the subsequent chapters.

The second part of the book comprises four chapters, and presents four case-studies on financial nationalism. In Chapter 3, I will discuss the logic of financial nationalism in the context of home-host supervisory relations, with a particular focus on the question of home-country control. In Chapter 4, I will analyze the complex regulatory framework for cross-border bank resolution and the challenges of international policy coordination. In particular, I will analyze the bailout of a multinational bank, a cross-border bank insolvency, and an international bail-in. In Chapter 5, I will move my analysis to sovereign debt, where I will look at the question of sovereign defaults, and the coordination problems in sovereign debt restructurings. In Chapter 6, I will analyze the problems of regulatory convergence in the context of derivatives regulation. To do so, I will look at the recent EU-US regulatory war on the regulation of OTC derivatives and the supervision of central counterparties.

The third part of the book discusses the strategies that are currently adopted and could be adopted to address the problems of financial nationalism. In Chapter 7, I will discuss the centralization of regulatory and policy functions into a supranational financial authority, with a specific reference to the European Banking Union. In Chapter 8, I will analyze the question of compliance in international finance and propose a new theory that explains how it works in different areas of finance. In Chapter 9, I will propose a different mode of financial integration – which I address as "regulatory passporting" – that ought to achieve the goal of free capital mobility and market access while guaranteeing a more stable financial system. Finally, in Chapter 10, I will discuss the logic of adjudication in international finance, and the prospects for the establishments of international financial courts.

Before concluding, it is worth spending a few words on the limits of this book. Financial nationalism is, thankfully, not the only approach to international financial policy. The field of international monetary law, which is closely intertwined with international finance, is actually based on a well-functioning hard law framework with the International Monetary Fund at its center. Moreover, since the 1970s, financial regulators have been increasingly engaging in regulatory cooperation and financial standard setting through Transnational Regulatory Networks. In certain areas of finance, like terrorist financing and money laundering, cooperation has been extremely successful and based on a very effective sanctioning regime. Since the global financial crisis, regulatory cooperation has actually improved dramatically, thanks in particular to the efforts of the Financial Stability Board and the G20. Scholars, regulators, and practitioners are now much more aware of the need to address the international dimension of financial policies.

Yet, it is too early to call nationalism finished. Experience suggests that when a crisis strikes or when the domestic political equilibrium turns against globalization, the sirens of financial nationalism become way too appealing to resist for regulators. It is precisely in those moments that international law becomes necessary. Much of this book has been written before the decision of the United Kingdom to leave the European Union, and well before Donald Trump was elected as the new President of the United States. Unfortunately, from what transpires from the news, the world financial system is entering into a new phase of regulatory uncertainty due to the revamped appeal of nationalist policies and a disdain for international cooperation. In a meeting in early 2017, the Basel Committee failed to agree on a new stronger framework on capital adequacy owing to the division between the EU and the US regulators on the use of banks' internal models. In its election platform and in the early weeks of its presidency, President Trump has clearly stated its desire to reduce regulation for the financial sector and revamp – or even eliminate – the Dodd-Frank Act, one of the bedrock of global financial regulatory reforms. In various Eurozone countries, the criticism against the Euro is mounting and talks about a return to monetary sovereignty are now part of everyday's political discussions. Finally, in the context of the Brexit negotiations, Europeans authorities have repeatedly stated their intention to devise new rules that would impose EU controls on the Euro-clearing market, thereby forcing a repatriation of the operations from London into the European Union.

It is too early to say now whether financial nationalisms will increase in the future. My hope is that this book will serve as a warning on its dangers, and as a useful guidance for those who believe in the benefits of international cooperation.

1

The Logic of Externalities

Tommaso Padoa-Schioppa, the late Italian central banker and regulator,[1] used to say that only in finance do economists refer to a "system": the "financial system."[2] This is because the modern financial industry is largely structured as a network that relies on the interconnectedness between the different financial service providers to maximize its efficiency.[3] A financial institution, as opposed to a law firm or a car manufacturer, is never fully independent from its competitors. It relies on other financial institutions for funding, on central clearinghouses to settle payments and derivatives contracts, and on other intermediaries such as broker-dealers or stock exchanges to perform the functions that make a financial market work.[4] Crucially, the interconnectedness operates on both sides of the balance sheet, which makes the relationship between the financial institution and the broader financial system even tighter. For instance, banks borrow in various forms from other financial institutions but at the same time invest heavily in other firms' financial products. Because they often rely on the same source of funding, like deposits, stocks, loans,

[1] Tommaso Padoa-Schioppa (1940–2010) was an Italian central banker and economist. He is considered by many to be among the founding fathers of the Euro. His career spanned five decades and involved top positions in some of the most important national and international financial institutions. He was the vice-director general of the Bank of Italy (1984–7); President of the Basel Committee on Banking Supervision (1993–7); Chairman of the BCBS Committee on Payments and Settlement Systems (2000–5); Member of the European Central Bank Executive Committee (1998–2005); and Minister of Finance of Italy (2006–8).

[2] Tommaso Padoa-Schioppa, *Regulating Finance: Balancing Freedom and Risk* (Oxford: Oxford University Press, 2004), p. 97.

[3] See Nicholas Arregui, Mohamed Norat, Antonio Pancorbo, and Jordi Scarlata, "Addressing Interconnectedness: Concepts and Prudential Tools," IMF Working Paper WP/13/199, International Monetary Fund (2013).

[4] For a good overview, see Stephen Valdez and Philip Molyneux, *An Introduction to Global Financial Markets* (New York: Palgrave Macmillan, 2010, 6th edn.).

or securities, financial institutions are subject to the same market swings. At the vertical level, financial intermediaries are also strictly linked to the state, through the central bank, which operates as the *deus ex machina* of the whole financial system and conducts monetary policy.[5]

Financial institutions are no different from other businesses: their ultimate goal is simply to increase profits. Like other firms, financial institutions sometimes take excessive risks by overborrowing or investing in the wrong products. Like any other businesses, if their gambles fail, financial institutions may go bankrupt. What makes financial institutions, and banks in particular, different from any other firm is that when a financial institution fails or stops responding to normal economic incentives, the consequences necessarily transcend the destiny of that individual firm and its customers, to affect other subjects. When a financial intermediary is too interconnected or too big in terms of business size, there is a risk that its failure will produce systemic effects. This means that the contagion originating from a firm's collapse would either drive other financial firms connected to it through various linkages out of business or even spread to the real economy. Economists define this phenomenon as *systemic risk*.[6]

Thus, in an integrated system the overall social costs of a firm's failure are inevitably higher than those incurred by the individual firm. How should we deal with firms' natural necessity to take risks when the consequences transcend the destiny of a single institution? Should regulators accept interconnectedness and managers' risk appetite as a fact of life and let the market regulate itself, perhaps by progressively reducing funding to those firms that are perceived as unstable? Or should regulators try to reduce the interconnectedness between firms and let them operate as unit-banks that rely on their own source of finance and investment? Perhaps what regulators should do is

[5] Charles Goodhart, *The Evolution of Central Banks* (Cambridge, MA and London: MIT Press, 1988); see also, Richard Brealey, Alistair Clark, Charles Goodhart, Juliette Healey, Gelln Hoggarth, David Llewellyn, Chang Shu, Peter Sinclair, and Farouk Soussa (eds.) *Financial Stability and Central Banks: A Global Perspective* (London: Routledge, 2000).

[6] See IMF, FSB, and BIS, "Guidance to Assess the Systemic Importance of Financial Institutions, Markets and Instruments: Initial Considerations," Report to the G-20 Finance Ministers and Central Bank Governors (October 2009); Jean-Pierre Fouque and Joseph A. Langsam (eds.) *Handbook on Systemic Risk* (Cambridge: Cambridge University Press, 2013); Viral V. Acharya, "A Theory of Systemic Risk and Design of Prudential Bank Regulation," (2009) 5 *Journal of Financial Stability* 245; Douglas W. Diamond and Philip H. Dybvig, "Bank Runs, Deposit Insurance, and Liquidity" (1983) 91 *Journal of Political Economy* 401; Jean-Charles Rochet and Jean Tirole, "Interbank Lending and Systemic Risk" (1996) 28 *Journal of Money, Credit and Banking* 733–4; Franklin Allen and Douglas Gale, *Financial Contagion* 1–2 (C.V. Starr Center for Applied Econ., Research Report No. 98-33, 1998).

to focus on the firms by reducing their tendency to ignore the consequences of firms' behavior to their creditors and the market? All options present their pros and cons. Yet, the regulatory and policy framework for financial stability adopted in virtually all national financial systems is largely based on the use of regulation to force firms to modify their business strategy and corporate model to reduce the risk that a single failure would propagate across the network. This means that in order to protect financial stability, every entity participating in an interconnected financial system must be forced to internalize the costs of its actions to the point that is socially optimal. I define the philosophy that underpins this regulatory strategy as the *logic of externality*. Regulation is, however, not enough to make a financial system stable. Not all market failures originate from the business decisions of individual firms. A functioning financial system necessarily depends on a legal system. Therefore, against the backdrop of systemic risk regulation lies the powerful role of the state and the law, which allocate and distribute financial losses, legitimize and enforce contracts, and regulate market entry.[7]

The goal of this chapter is to discuss the structure of modern financial systems and the logic of externality underpinning systemic risk regulation. Understanding the role of the law in maintaining financial stability in a national financial system is of fundamental importance if we want to move on to the analysis of the international financial system. Only by understanding what the law can do, and which mechanisms it should adopt to address systemic risk, can we appreciate the role of international law in maintaining financial stability in an interconnected global financial market.

1.1. AN INTERCONNECTED FINANCIAL SYSTEM

"Banks are special!" This is a common mantra among commentators and policymakers that we recurrently hear, especially when government are forced to intervene to bail banks out. The fact that this alleged "uniqueness" is used to justify government support that would not be available to other commercial firms does not, however, erase a powerful truth: banks are indeed different from any other firms. What makes them so unique is that both their main outputs and their inputs are the same: debts contracts. This places banks in a unique and very critical position in the economy. More than any other commercial enterprise, banks absorb and transmit financial losses across the

[7] On the theory of financial regulation, see John Armour, Dan Awrey, Paul Davies, Luca Enriques, Jeffrey N. Gordon, Colin Mayer, and Jennifer Payne, *Principles of Financial Regulation* (Oxford: Oxford University Press, 2016), pp. 50–98.

system. To understand the origin of systemic risk and financial interconnectedness, we thus need necessarily to start from the very basics of banking: the bank's debts and its balance sheet.

Every commercial enterprise needs money to run its operations. In general, the sources of funding can originate from the equity of its owners, the firm's profits, or through debts. On average, corporations and commercial firms finance their operations largely through equity, retained profits, and only for a small part by borrowing. Debt is usually very expensive and often difficult to raise for medium-sized firms. For this reason, commercial enterprises are mostly financed through their owners' money. Equity holders take on the commercial risk of the enterprise with the hope that, if it succeeds, they will get to enjoy all the profits. On the other hand, if the firm loses money, the shareholders are the ones who take the largest losses. With the money available, commercial enterprises buy machinery and raw materials, pay staff, buy or rent the land or office space; in sum, they use the firm's financial inputs to sustain the production of the goods or services that constitute the firm's final output to be sold in the market, be it marketing services or microchips.

1.1.1. *A Typical Bank Balance Sheet*

Banks are in a very different line of business. The business of a bank and any other financial firm is to intermediate money between those who have it and those who need it. Thus, banks raise money from individuals and corporations to provide credit to those enterprises and individuals that need it and are willing to pay. The main outputs of a bank are therefore financial contracts in which the bank is the creditor of a certain amount of money. Those contracts take the form of long-term loans to enterprises or the public sector, mortgages to individuals, short-term loans to other financial institutions, investments in debt and equity securities, derivatives, real estate, or cash parked at the central bank. The money that is owed to the bank and the bank's various financial investments constitute the bank's *assets*. Like any commercial firm, the bank's assets need to be financed somehow, as the bank cannot create money out of thin air. Banks could, for instance, use their owners' capital. At the very beginning, banks were indeed joint-partnerships financed solely with the owners' equity. This model, however, had the limitation that it could rely only on a limited amount of money. This problem was solved when bankers eventually realized that they could use the money deposited at the bank by its clients. Essentially, they borrowed from depositors by offering them an interest and lent the money out for a higher price. The spread between the interest paid to the bank's creditors and the bank's debtors constitutes the bank's revenues.

The core business model of banks did not change substantially from then, except that now banks borrow from more diversified sources. Medium-sized commercial banks engaged in retail operations now largely finance their asset side by entering into various forms of debt contracts of which deposits constitute only 40/50%. The rest is made up of short-term financing obtained from other banks, bonds, and equity. The debt of the bank toward its depositors and financial creditors constitutes the bank's *liabilities* and is conventionally represented on the right side of the bank's balance sheet.

By looking at the bank's balance sheet, we can have a very good idea of the exposures of the bank toward other firms and individuals and vice versa. In other words, we can understand the financial interconnectedness of the bank. In this regard, a quick look at the evolution of a typical bank balance sheet over the last 100 years shows unequivocally how much more interconnected modern banks are. The financial industry that existed in the United States and in Europe until the early 1970s was very different from what it is today. Before the rise of mega banks and the process of progressive *financialization*, banks served primarily to channel funds to businesses or individuals. Credit intermediation to the real economy through the origination of loans and mortgages was thus the main function of retail banks. Other financial institutions such as merchant banks, investment banks, or clearing banks existed alongside the classical savings banks, but they occupied a relatively peripheral role in the financial system. In that environment, banks operated mainly as unit-banks; as entities with relatively limited financial interconnectedness within the broader financial system. Investment banks functioned as joint-partnerships in which the partners risked their own money. Savings banks funded most of their assets through retail deposits and invested in the real economy. In the United States, until the early 1990s, when the limits on banks' branching were relaxed, banks could only operate within one State. This meant that their funding model had to rely mostly on local credit. The unit-bank model kept banks quite insulated from systemic risks and financial contagion. The main channels of contagion during the nineteenth and early twentieth centuries were depositors' panics and bank runs, which nevertheless only rarely extended to the entire financial system. A banking crisis was, mostly, a problem for the depositors and financial creditors of that bank. In this unit-bank based system, credit was scarcer and more expensive as financial institutions could rely on smaller sources of credit. Consequently, also the revenues of banks and the compensation of bankers were much smaller.[8]

[8] See John Kay, *Other People's Money: Finance: Masters of the Universe or Serving the People?* (London: Profile Books, 2015).

From the 1970s, a process of progressive technological sophistication and globalization of the banking business changed dramatically the business models of banks and the very structure of financial systems. The demise of the Bretton Woods monetary system propelled the internationalization of finance and expanded the frontiers of finance. Banks could lend to (and borrow from) international markets, trade in foreign currency and invest abroad. Capital markets could rely on a much wider investors' base and diversify across many different assets classes. Over time, the increased availability of capital and the new investment opportunities influenced the shape of financial institutions, which grew dramatically in size and functions. At the same time, technological advancements enabled banks to streamline financial processes and process information in a very short time frame. With the use of automated systems, financial institutions could carry out millions of transactions in the same day and move money in a nanosecond. The vast availability of capital, the propensity of banks to invest in financial markets to increase returns, and the complexity of financial market nonetheless augmented the financial risks of firms. To address those risks, two financial innovations took place in the 1980s and 1990s: the rise of over-the-counter (OTC) derivatives markets, and the widespread use of securitization. Both inventions served to reduce the risks of banks, and rely on the creation and trading of financial instruments. Securitization, in particular, is the process whereby a bank repackages and sells its debts in the form of securities to investors through a special purpose vehicle. By doing so, it relieves its balance sheet from the burden of having debts and increases its liquidity. Banks eventually embraced these financial innovations as they increased efficiency and liquidity. However, it also meant that financial institutions became more and more intertwined through direct and indirect financial linkages, paving the way for the current network-based financial system.[9]

On the liability side, a combination of factors – an increased appetite of institutional investors for collateral, an erosion of the competitive advantage of bank deposits, and a special treatment given to securitized financing in bankruptcy law – changed the funding model of banks, which relied less on retail deposits and more on financial obligations.[10] At present, most systemically important banks get a large part of their funding from other financial

[9] On the evolution of finance in the last 30 years, see Emilios Avgouleas, *Governance of Global Financial Markets: The Law, The Economics, The Politics* (Cambridge: Cambridge University Press, 2012), pp. 21–89.

[10] Gary Gorton and Andrew Metrick, "Regulating the Shadow Banking System" (2010) 41 (2) *Brookings Papers on Economic Activity* 266.

institutions. This is via direct lending in the form of loans, but also other forms of financing such as sale and repurchase agreements (REPO) and asset-based financing that banks get from other banks, hedge funds, asset managers, and financial institutions specialized in short-term lending. For instance, REPOs are financial contracts whereby an institutional investor lends funds to the bank, which secures them by offering a collateral in return. At the end of the day, the bank repurchases the collateral at a slightly higher price. The operation then is replicated from the beginning every day. The direct financial interconnectedness on the liability side is probably not going to change in the future. At present, the new Financial Stability Board (FSB) resolution standards require that banks hold around 15% of their liability side in loss-absorbing capital instrument and bail-in liabilities. As a result, in the future, financial institutions will be even more interconnected on the liability side, as only other financial institutions can afford the risk that these instruments entail.

The dependency on financial contracts was mirrored in the asset side. Banks became increasingly eager to investing a large part of their money in financial instruments issued by other banks. For instance, banks entered into derivatives transactions whereby they insured Credit Default Obligations from other banks, or financed securities transactions. In this context, the use of derivatives and the broader process of securitization represents a core business of banks.[11] Second, banks often invested increasingly in the same types of assets, which created an indirect connection between all the asset holders through the market price of the asset. For instance, banks invested heavily in sovereign debt of OECD countries due to the perceived lower risk associated with sovereign debt.

1.1.2. *Financial Infrastructures*

The financial interconnectedness between financial institutions does not only arise from the bank's investments, but also extends to the infrastructures such as the payment system or central counterparties that enable and support the bank's business. Those infrastructures are made of a complex set of rules and standard processes that facilitate the movement of money or intermediate exposures between market participants to reduce financial risks. The payment system is a fundamental part of the financial system as it connects financial institutions and payment providers that need to process payment transactions for their clients; essentially, it provides the arteries through which

[11] See Kathryn Judge, "Fragmentation Nodes: A Study in Financial Innovation, Complexity, and Systemic Risk" (2012) 64 *Stanford Law Review* 657.

money flows. To function, the payment system relies on a complex network of clearing banks, with the central bank at the top, which process and settle transactions through various accounting methods. Importantly, the payment system is also used to clear and process securities transactions. In recent years, especially after the global financial crisis, central counterparties have become a critical node at the center of the financial network because they centralize the financial exposures of financial institutions trading in derivatives and other securities. Central counterparties are institutions financed by their members – mostly banks – that place themselves at the center of a financial transaction between a buyer and a seller of securities. Their role is to reduce the exposure risks of their members by assuming and guaranteeing the contractual obligations of the parties of a financial transaction. Because they are co-owned and financed by the very financial institutions that use them to reduce their risks, they connect banks that would otherwise simply be connected through direct financial exposures.[12]

1.2. SYSTEMIC RISK

Financial interconnectedness undoubtedly enhanced the efficiency of the system: banks could rationalize their business models and get cheaper credit. However, the tight interconnectivity between different parts of the financial network also undoubtedly increased the possibility to transmit shocks across the financial system: in sum, it increased system risks. To understand how systemic risk is directly dependent on financial interconnectedness, it is necessary to start from the very concept of financial risk.

Risk is a natural and unavoidable component of finance and, thus, of any financial system. It starts from the balance sheet of banks. Banks make money by investing the funds they have borrowed from their creditors. This process is called maturity transformation: using the bank's short-term debt to invest in long-term projects, such as financing a mortgage or a commercial loan. Essentially, banks use other people's money to provide their services. Nothing wrong with that; borrowing is not illegal. However, it is very risky indeed. The investments of the banks in the form of loans or debt securities have mostly a long-term timeframe during which anything can happen. Because the bank does not have the direct control on the investment, there is always a high risk that not all of the bank's assets perform satisfactorily. If a bank takes a loss on the asset side of the balance sheet, the loss must be met with an equal loss on

[12] See Julia Lees Allen, "Derivatives Clearinghouses and Systemic Risk: A Bankruptcy and Dodd-Frank Analysis" (2012) 64 *Stanford Law Review* 1079.

the liability side. This means that some of the bank's creditors will not receive their money back. Despite the risks inherent in the process of maturity transformation, lending bears positive effects for the entire economy that justifies the underlying risks. Indeed, it leads to the creation of new money through what economists call the multiplier effect. Let's imagine that Bank A receives a deposit of $100, of which it lends out 90% to a borrower. This borrower then uses this cash to pay a supplier, who then deposits the $90 into Bank B, which eventually lends 90% of those funds out to a new borrower. The new borrower then uses the $81 to pay another creditor who then deposits the cash in Bank C, which invests $73 (90% of the deposited funds) in a commercial loan to a new customer. This simple chain of transactions has created a monetary base of 344 out of only $100 originally deposited.

At the same time, however, this process has linked three otherwise independent financial institutions. Now, here comes the problem. Because each bank invests with borrowed money, an investment loss in one part of the financial chain means a direct equal loss for the bank's creditors, and an indirect loss for the bank that has originated the preceding loan. Following the same example, if the $73 loan originated by Bank C does not perform, the bank suffers a loss on the asset side of the balance sheet that is immediately reflected on its liability side. If the bank goes bust because of that loss, some of its creditors will not be able to repay their loans to their banks, which then will suffer other losses. Hence, a single loss immediately reverberates across the entire network. This basic example may help in understanding how systemic risk spreads across a financial network, in this case, a chain of banks. In reality, banks have thousands or millions of investments in their trading or loan books that dilute the impact of individual losses on the bank's solvency position; hence, the likelihood that a single loss would trigger a domino effect is minimal now, especially in light of the concentration and exposure limits that most regulators impose on banks. Nonetheless, because banks are directly connected to each other through various financial and psychological channels, the risks of the insolvency of a critical node in the network can become seriously acute.

Systemic risk is a hardy perennial of financial markets. The peculiar interconnectedness of banks and financial intermediaries makes systemic risk reduction a constant object of financial policymaking. For instance, the concept of central banks as lenders of last resort, already advocated by Bagehot in 1873,[13] the creation of central banks in the late eighteenth and early nineteenth

[13] Walter Bagehot, *Lombard Street: A Description of the Money Market* (New York: John Wiley & Sons, 1999, originally published in 1873).

centuries, and the use of depositor guarantee schemes are all examples of the struggle of financial authorities to limit systemic risk. Rosa Lastra accurately observes that systemic risk is not a specificity of finance. Indeed, it can also be identified with regard to epidemics or environmental catastrophes.[14] However, it is undeniable that the complexity of modern financial markets,[15] the pivotal role of finance in modern economies, and the unprecedented level of integration between markets and institutions[16] make systemic risk reduction a priority of financial policymaking. Behind the simplicity of the concept, the nature of systemic risk and its evolution has been highly debated by commentators. Indeed, in their conjunct report the International Monetary Fund, the Bank for International Settlement, and the Financial Stability Board state that at the outset of the global financial crisis of 2007–8 most G20 countries did not even have a formal definition of systemic risk to guide their regulatory intervention.[17] Economists and regulators have often disagreed over the causes of systemic risk and its transmission mechanisms, choosing to give prevalence to one element over the others.[18]

Until the global financial crisis of 2007–8, systemic risk was essentially synonymous with financial contagion: a cascade of defaults originating from the failure of one financial institution and transmitted to the system through direct inter-bank exposures, the kind of problem highlighted in the previous example.[19] During the global financial crisis, financial contagion was particularly severe for banks. This was partially due to the high volumes of intra-bank lending, but also to the large portion of banks' credit exposures to OTC derivatives. The OTC market grew dramatically in size in the year preceding the

[14] Rosa Maria Lastra, "Systemic Risk, SIFIs, and Financial Stability" (2011) 6 *Capital Markets Law Journal* 197–8.

[15] On complexity, see Dan Awrey, "Complexity, Innovation, and the Regulation of Modern Financial Markets" (2012) 2 *Harvard Business Law Review* 235.

[16] IMF, "Understanding Financial Interconnectedness," International Monetary Fund (2010); IMF, "Understanding Financial Interconnectedness – Supplementary Information," International Monetary Fund (2010).

[17] IMF-BIS-BCBS, "Guidance to Assess the Systemic Importance of Financial Institutions, Markets and Instruments: Initial Considerations," Briefing Paper for the G20 Finance Ministers and Central Bank Governors (28 October 2009).

[18] Steven Schwarcz defines systemic risk as "the risk that (i) an economic shock such as market or institutional failure triggers (through a panic or otherwise) either (X) the failure of a chain of markets or institutions or (Y) a chain of significant losses to financial institutions, (ii) resulting in increases in the cost of capital or decreases in its availability, often evidenced by substantial financial-market price volatility." See Steven L. Schwarcz, "Systemic Risk" (2008) 97 *The Georgetown Law Journal* 193, 204.

[19] See Robert Kollmann and Frank Malherbe, "Financial Contagion," in Gerard Caprio Jr. (ed.) *Handbook of Safeguarding Global Financial Stability: Political, Social, Cultural, and Economic Theories and Models* (London: Elsevier, 2013); Allen and Gale, above note 6.

crisis, up to an estimated US$35 trillion.[20] Since they are traded bilaterally between buyer and sellers, without the need for them to disclose information about their credit position, OTC derivatives prevent each party of the transaction from knowing the true solvency of the other party and thus to price the financial risk accordingly.

Recent analyses, however, almost unanimously agree that systemic risk cannot be encapsulated only in direct intra-bank exposures. The financial crisis of 2007–8 showed that systemic risk could also originate from common shocks simultaneously affecting many institutions through market channels. Banks and other financial institutions now operate in financial markets by purchasing and trading large amounts of securities. Often, financial institutions hold a large portion of their securities in the same asset class, such as Treasury Bills. These common exposures can exacerbate systemic instability as they subject financial institutions to the same market swings and price fluctuations, particularly during periods of financial turmoil, thereby exacerbating further their negative effects. From a balance-sheet perspective, the actual market value of those assets makes the final market value of the firm. This is because the changes in value are reflected directly in the credit position of the bank. During boom times, this system can inflate the balance sheet of the banks, but during crises it can lead to a perilous situation of insolvency.[21] One of the core problems in this regard is fire-sales. Sometimes banks are forced to raise liquidity. This might occur for a sudden liquidity problem or a capital shortfall. When they need cash, banks might be forced to quickly sell some of their assets at a fraction of the price at which it would have otherwise sold them. Sometimes, the fire-sale arises from the need for banks to sell the collateral pledged to them by a defaulting financial institution in order to cover their losses already incurred. In both cases, a decline in the market price of those assets nevertheless affects all other financial institutions that hold them in their balance sheet, thereby transmitting the contagion through the exposure to the same assets.

In other circumstances, systemic risk is transmitted through psychological channels. Banks are linked to each other not only through direct or indirect financial channels; they also have in common the fact that they are funded by the same class of creditors, be they depositors, repo lenders, or institutional investors. Because those creditors make their investment decisions based on

[20] Zijun Liu, Stephanie Quiet, and Benedict Roth, "Banking Sector Interconnectedness: What Is It, How Can We Measure It and Why Does It Matter?" (2015) *Bank of England Quarterly Bulletin* 2.

[21] Awrey, above note 15.

their individual perception of risk, they could be subject to irrational biases, uncertainties or false observations. For instance, investors might be tempted to follow in other investors' footsteps when they decide that it is time to sell their assets fearing that a bubble might burst, thereby leading to a sudden depreciation of their value.[22] Under certain circumstances, when the same class of creditors fails to distinguish the different creditor conditions of each bank because it perceives them as having the same problem, it might act irrationally. The clearest example in this regard is a bank run in which depositors rush *en masse* to their banks because of the news of the problem in another bank. When the fear spreads among creditors of different banks, the risk is that a bank run turns into a widespread panic. Panics are, essentially, bank runs on a broader scale motivated by an irrational fear that all banks might be unstable. The most important example is, perhaps, the panic during the great crisis of 1929. At the outset of the stock market crash, depositors rushed to their banks to demand the conversion of their deposits into cash, thereby forcing some banks to become insolvent. Those banks in turn stopped lending, which created a situation that inadvertently caused other banks to become insolvent, and ultimately led to the well-known credit crunch that paralyzed the US economy.[23] Bank runs motivated by depositors' panic are not as frequent nowadays as they used to be, although they occurred in Greece during the financial crisis, in Cyprus in 2013, and during the insolvency of Northern Rock Bank in the UK.[24] Gary Gorton has argued that a new type of bank run – this time, a run on the repo market – took place during the US subprime crisis, when repo lenders refuse to roll over the loans to banks on the fear that the collateral they pledged was not worth its declared value.[25] Panic can also take an international dimension. International bank runs might occur when the news of a cross-border bank failing in one country might lead to a bank run in one of its foreign subsidiaries or branches. Alternatively, they might occur when two countries share broadly similar economic conditions. Finally, information

[22] Gorton reports that since 1970 around 62% of financial crises around the world involved some kind of bank runs. See Gary Gorton, *Misunderstanding Financial Crises: Why We Don't See Them Coming* (Oxford: Oxford University Press, 2012), p. 32.

[23] Michael D. Bordo, Bruce Mizrach, and Anna J. Schwartz, "Real Versus Pseudo-International Systemic Risk: Some Lessons from History" (1995) NBER Working Paper No. 5371; Gary Richardson, "Bank Distress During the Great Contraction, 1929 to 1933: New Data from the Archives of the Board of Governors" (2006) NBER Working Paper No. 12590; Gorton, *ibid.*

[24] See Rosa Maria Lastra, "Northern Rock, UK Bank Insolvency and Cross-Border Bank Insolvency" (2008) 9 *Journal of Banking Regulation* 165.

[25] Gary Gorton, *Slapped by the Invisible Hand: The Panic of 2007* (Oxford: Oxford University Press, 2010).

failures can culminate in investors' panic and capital outflows bonanzas, as during the East Asian crisis of 1997.[26]

The preceding examples show that the risk that a banking crisis will turn into a systemic threat is a real possibility in an integrated and highly developed financial network. Experience suggests that serious financial crises have disastrous economic effects that might take years to subside, as we are still witnessing in Europe and United States.[27] From a regulatory perspective, the question then is how to address the need of financial institutions to be part of the financial network and reap all its benefits, with the concurrent need to reduce the systemic risks of financial interconnectedness.

1.3. THE LOGIC OF EXTERNALITIES

Systemic risk confronts financial institutions and their creditors with a classical problem of cooperation: how can a firm pursue legitimate financial targets without concurrently endangering other firms? Imagine a financial system with no regulator and no state – a perfectly free market in which a firm's actions depend only on the response of its competitors and clients. Because of the nature of the banking business, all financial institutions need to take risks in order to make profits. The risks start with the simple process of maturity transformation, but they could easily entail more dangerous behaviors. Banks may overborrow to reduce funding costs and increase profitability; they might engage in high-return but very risky lending and investments operations; or they might sometimes concentrate their exposures in a few but very promising assets. At the same time, financial institutions will decide autonomously whom to deal with and how to structure their business. Because borrowing from capital markets or financial institutions specialized in short-term lending is more efficient than simply holding retail deposits, banks might decide to borrow half of their assets from other financial institutions. When a bank needs more liquidity, it might decide to securitize its mortgages and sell them to investors through a special investment vehicle. Since the underlying value of the mortgages is not perfectly reflected in the market prices of the securities, banks do not have any incentives in selecting carefully their borrowers; on the contrary, their incentive is to lend as much as possible. Similarly, given the potentially

[26] Ross P. Buckley, "An Oft-Ignored Perspective on the Asian Economic Crisis: The Role of Creditors and Investors" (2000) 15 *Banking and Finance Law Review* 431; see Douglas Arner, *Financial Stability, Economic Growth and the Role of Law* (Cambridge: Cambridge University Press, 2007), pp. 22–5.

[27] See Carmen M. Reinhart and Kenneth S. Rogoff, *This Time Is Different: Eight Centuries of Financial Folly* (Princeton, NJ: Princeton University Press, 2009), pp. 222–47.

high return of derivatives contracts, banks might decide to devote a large part of their business and financial resources in selling them to companies or other financial institutions without disclosing the potential risks involved.

1.3.1. *Firms' Behaviors*

In all these examples, investment decisions depend entirely on the financial returns they produce for the firm and the firm's particular attitude toward risk. A firm might decide that concentrating the investments in a single asset class or borrowing heavily is not worth the risk of becoming insolvent. Conversely, the firm's managers might be incentivized to take extra risks in order to receive a higher bonus at the end of the year. This precise problem became particularly important over the last few years, when banks started to suffer the competition of the hedge fund industry, which was offering larger salaries often as a percentage of profits. Banks had to devise a strategy to retain their best staff. They responded by changing their corporate governance models from partnership to limited liabilities and by resorting to end-year bonuses to increase the final salary. This, of course, changed the incentives structure in place to contain the risk appetite of managers and ultimately ended up encouraging managers to take more risks.[28]

Irrespectively of the firm's individual investment strategy, financial institutions have very little incentive to take into account the impact of their actions on the broader financial system and, in more general terms, the firm's place in the financial system. Had the bank financed itself primarily with its managers' or shareholders' money, the losses would have been borne only by them, and thus contained to a few individuals. However, the time when financial institutions were structured as unlimited liability partnerships is long gone. This means that, if a modern bank fails, absent regulations, the costs of a firm's bad investment decisions would be borne by the bank's creditors. These creditors would be depositors, retail investors, institutional investors, repo lenders, and other short-term lenders. The managers who made the actual investment decisions do not incur any loss. Similarly, because of the indirect relationship that links financial institutions through the assets they hold, selling the assets at below-market price to achieve some liquidity, although it could save the selling bank from further problems, could nonetheless cause balance-sheet losses to the other firms. Furthermore, when a bank securitizes its loans and sells them to investors as Mortgage-Backed Securities (MBSs), it has limited

[28] James Barth, Gerard Caprio Jr., and Ross Levine, *Guardians of Finance: Making Regulators Work for Us* (Cambridge, MA: MIT Press, 2012), p. 66.

incentive in ensuring that the quality of the underlying loans does not deteriorate. Because the ultimate financial risks are transferred to the securities holders, the incentives for the originator to monitor the borrowers are diluted. Finally, a bank could also be on the receiving end of the loss, either because it has invested in other ailing banks or because it has purchased assets whose market value has dramatically declined.

These examples show that systemic risk does not merely originate from interconnectedness between firms. Inter-bank lending, securitization, or market operations do not create instability; they simply transmit it. The causes of systemic risk are, on the contrary, always inherent to the behaviors of individual institutions or the market as a whole.[29] In modern financial systems, financial institutions have very high incentives to become intertwined and operate within the existing network of financial firms to increase their efficiency and investment opportunities. However, they have conversely little incentive to consider the external effects that their behavior might have on their creditors and the broader financial system.

1.3.2. *Negative Externalities*

Systemic risk is nothing more than a negative externality imposed by financial firms on society, similarly to what smoke is for the environment.[30] Externalities are economic jargon for the beneficial or negative effects on third parties arising from the behavior of agents that are not internalized by those agents. Third parties, therefore, either enjoy the beneficial effects of another party's behavior without paying for it, or they suffer the costs of those behaviors without being able to force the agent to contain them. In the law and economics literature, externalities have usually been associated with the concept of property. An agent is, in principle, free to do whatever he or she wishes to do on his or her property. He can plant a beautiful flower garden that produces a fragrant aroma across the neighborhood. But he can similarly engage in

[29] For a good analysis of the various ways bankers take excessive risks, see Karl S. Okamoto, "After the Bailout: Regulating Systemic Moral Hazard" (2009) 57 *UCLA Law Review* 183, pp. 204–11.

[30] Howard Davies and David Green, *Global Financial Regulation: The Essential Guide* (Cambridge: Polity Press, 2008), p. 16. This definition of systemic risk is further developed by Schwarcz and Anabtawi, who argue that financial firms usually underappreciate the interconnectivities when making business decisions, thereby increasing their level of risk above the socially acceptable. They argue that firms do not take into account the direct externalities of their decisions on other firms with which they are linked. Steven L. Schwarcz and Iman Anabtawi, "Regulating Systemic Risk: Towards an Analytical Framework" (2011) 86 *Notre Dame Law Review* 1349, p. 1355; on the theory of financial regulation, see Armour et al., above note 7, pp. 57–9.

activities that produce unpleasant odors or noises. In both cases, the property holder (the agent) does not fully internalize the benefits and costs of its conduct. Neighbors do not pay for the benefits of having a beautiful garden, and the property holder does not pay the social costs of engaging in unpleasant activities.[31]

In an integrated financial network, the systemic risk inherent in a banking crisis renders the failure of one bank a negative externality for the entire financial system. Since financial systems are structured as networks in which firms are strictly interdependent, the crisis of a single firm inevitably becomes a social problem for the entire financial community. When financial institutions operate, they tend not to take into consideration their participation in a common system, and thus, they often underestimate the real cost of their failure, which is inevitably higher than simple shareholders' losses. Hence, the economic origins of systemic risk always trace back to the individual or collective behavior of firms, which fail to price into their speculative activities the full social costs associated with their risky behaviors.[32]

How, then, to solve those problems? In a perfect market, the self-interested and overly risky attitude of financial institutions will be matched by a decrease in credit. Because the bank is engaging in overly risky activities, few lenders will agree to invest in the bank or deposit their money, or if they do, they will demand a higher interest. However, in reality, it is very difficult for lenders and especially depositors to monitor the activities of the bank. Banks are subject to information asymmetries that prevent lenders having a clear picture of the bank's credit position in the coming months. When they do, it is probably already too late for many of them to withdraw their funds. If some of the depositors do manage to withdraw their funds before the bank collapses, they will eventually condemn the rest of the depositors to lose the entirety of their assets. The inefficiency of the invisible hand in regulating financial markets has been understood since the nineteenth century, when banks started to engage substantially in retail activity.[33] In a free market economy, the only objective of firms is the maximization of profits, rather than the achievement of social objectives. This means that leaving firms free to pursue

[31] The law and economics literature has often analyzed the issue of externalities. For an overview, see Steven Shavell, *Foundations of Economic Analysis of Law* (Cambridge, MA: Harvard University Press, 2004), pp. 77–110.

[32] John Eatwell and Lance Taylor, *Global Finance at Risk: The Case for International Regulations* (New York: The New Press, 2000), pp. 23–4; Kern Alexander, Rahul Dhumale, and John Eatwell, *Global Governance of the Financial System: The International Regulation of Systemic Risk* (Oxford: Oxford University Press, 2006), p. 24.

[33] Barth et al., above note 28, pp. 27–34.

their profit-maximizing objectives will eventually lead to financial instability. In this situation, it is necessary to force or incentivize banks to internalize the externalities of their actions.

1.3.3. *Externalities and the Law*

Given the inability of banks to regulate themselves and address the inefficiencies of the market, someone else had to step in: the State. In a situation of financial integration, the law plays a pivotal role in protecting financial stability, because it can address the externalities of social conduct. The formulation of a norm and threat of punishment associated with its violation incentivizes agents to align their behaviors toward what the legislator consider to be the "socially optimal." In this sense, the law acts as a powerful social incentive or deterrent, no less powerful than that provided by the promise of financial reward or threat of physical harm. How should the law intervene then? And which subjects shall it target? Before addressing externalities, the law must attribute clear rights. In this regard, in their famous *Harvard Law Review* essay, Guido Calabresi and Douglas Melamed stated that the first issue that any legal system faces is to solve what they define as the problem of "entitlement."[34] In a society different groups of people have, invariably, interests or goals that might sometimes collide. The role of the law, in this case, is to solve such conflicts by legitimizing the pursuit of one objective over the other. In the words of the two authors, the law shall decide which of the parties will be "entitled to prevail."[35]

The issue of financial stability fits particularly well within this interpretative framework. From a legal viewpoint, the protection of financial stability in a national financial system could be pictured as a regulatory conflict between the protection of bank insiders' interests and creditors' interests.[36] On the one hand, bank insiders are the group that is interested in the maximization of the firm's profits; it is made by shareholders and managers. Bank managers have an interest in maximizing returns and do not consider long-term risks because they are accountable to shareholders, who will prize them with large bonuses at the end of the year depending on the bank's total profits. There is a large academic literature that demonstrates that profit-based bonuses independent of the long-term return of the investment do increase the risk attitude of managers.

[34] Guido Calabresi and A. Douglas Melamed, "Property Rules, Liability Rules, and Inalienability: One View of the Cathedral" (1971–1972) 85 *Harvard Law Review* 1089–90.

[35] *Ibid.* at p. 1090.

[36] Charles Calomiris and Stephen Haber, *Fragile by Design: The Political Origins of Banking Crises and Scarce Credit* (Princeton, NJ: Princeton University Press, 2014), p. 30.

Sometimes shareholders also have a conflicted interest when it comes to taking extra risks. Although shareholders bear the highest risk of losing their investment, which gives them the power to nominate and control the bank's board of directors, they are often in a weak position when it comes to monitoring the behavior of the top management. Often, executives exert a profound influence over the board of directors, which they select.[37] Moreover, shareholders are sometimes lured by the prospects of increased profits and forget the long-term risks of the bank's strategy.

On the other side of the spectrum are the interests of creditors – depositors, bondholders, short-term lenders, and other investors. Creditors are the ones that will suffer the most in the event of a failure, while not benefitting from any increase in bank profits. This means that, legally speaking, creditors not have any power to control the bank. Their only power is to make the decision to invest in the bank in the first place, but once they do they have limited options at their disposal.

In the conflict between the interests of the bank insiders and the creditors, the law has to choose which one will prevail, and which one will be sacrificed. The choice that most jurisdictions have made is a clear one: the protection of creditors, especially weak creditors such as depositors or retail investors.[38] Hence, in almost all jurisdictions the law has created a legal and policy framework that, without excessively reducing the risk appetite of investors and the natural and healthy desire for profits, explicitly protects the interests of creditors, and thus, financial stability. The rationale behind systemic risk reduction is a simple one: if systemic risk is the result of the failure of financial firms to correctly price their participation in a shared financial system, the prevention of systemic risk must necessarily rely on the adoption of mechanisms that will constrain the behavior of firms toward that which is socially optimal. I name this regulatory mindset the *logic of externality*, as its main objective is to force banks to internalize the social costs of their actions. The main way to do so is through regulation.[39] The power of the law in maintaining financial stability does not rely on a single mechanism, but rather on a set of different strategies, which together reduce the room in which financial institutions can maneuver.[40] Describing in detail 200 years – or more – of financial regulation

[37] Barth et al., above note 28, pp. 58–61.

[38] See, for instance, Mathias Dewatripont and Jean Tirole, *The Prudential Regulation of Banks* (Cambridge, MA: MIT Press, 1993), pp. 31–45.

[39] See. Stephen L. Schwarcz, "Controlling Financial Chaos: The Power and Limits of Law" (2012) 3 *Wisconsin Law Review* 815.

[40] David T. Llewellyn, "Role and Scope of Regulation and Supervision," in Gerard Caprio Jr. (ed.) *Handbook of Safeguarding Global Financial Stability: Political, Social, Cultural, and*

is impossible. However, I will attempt to briefly sketch some of the most significant strategies, which show how the logic of externalities plays out in the battle to contain systemic risk.[41]

1.3.4. *Prudential Regulations*

Undoubtedly the cornerstone of prudential regulations is the Basel Accords (commonly known as Basel I, II, and III) developed by the Basel Committee on Banking Supervision,[42] which require banks to be partially financed through equity capital.[43] As I said above, banks are inherently prone to take socially excessive risks, as they do their business with borrowed money. A high level of debt versus capital will immediately translate into higher profits. Debt acts as a leverage that exponentially increases profits. Crucially, it also exponentially increases losses.[44] In order to force banks to internalize the externalities of their actions, regulators have adopted rules that mandate banks to hold a certain amount of capital as a cushion against external shocks, even though this might entail fewer profits.[45] At present, the amount of regulatory capital that banks must hold is relatively limited in proportion to the liabilities, and it is currently set at 8–12% of the bank's total risk-weighted assets. The logic behind this is that the equity holders who seek to enjoy the bank's profits must also take the biggest commercial risk. Equity holders rank first in the event of insolvency and are obliged to take the first losses. Hence, capital functions as a buffer that protects the first line of creditors against some of the losses. Moreover, capital serves, in theory, also to improve the corporate governance of the bank. As we saw before, since shareholders appoint boards of directors,

---

Economic Theories and Models (London: Elsevier, 2013).

[41] Ewald Nowotny, "The Economics of Financial Regulation," in Andreas Dombret and Otto Lucius (eds.) *Stability of the Financial System: Illusion or Feasible Concept?* (Cheltenham: Edward Elgar, 2013).

[42] However, an 8% mandatory capital buffer cannot by itself reduce all the risk. As Admati and Hellwig have argued, the path toward a safer financial system should be a mandatory capital adequacy ratio of 100%. See Anat Admati and Martin Hellwig, *The Bankers' New Clothes: What's Wrong with Banking and What to Do About It* (Princeton, NJ: Princeton University Press, 2013).

[43] Simon Gleeson, *International Regulation of Banking: Capital and Risk Requirements*, 2nd edn. (Oxford: Oxford University Press, 2012); Hal S. Scott, "Reducing Systemic Risk through the Reform of Capital Regulations" (2010) 13 *Journal of International Economic Law* 763.

[44] Admati and Hellwig, above note 42, pp. 17–31.

[45] David Andrew Singer, *Regulating Capital: Setting Standards for the International Financial System* (Ithaca, NY: Cornell University Press, 2007), p. 19; Pierre-Hugues Verdier, "The Political Economy of International Financial Regulation" (2013) 88 *Indiana Law Journal* 1405, p. 1448.

which are in charge of monitoring the bank top management, they have, in theory, a very strong incentive to make sure that only individuals faithful to the shareholders' interests are appointed in charge of the bank.

Another important regulatory strategy is the adoption of rules that limit the size or the structure of the financial institution. Size is a fundamental problem in the creation of systemic risk. Firstly, the bigger the financial institution is, the higher the systemic impact of its failure will be. For instance, the Financial Stability Board has developed the concept of Systemically Important Financial Institutions (SIFIs) to identify those financial institutions "... whose disorderly failure, because of their size, complexity and systemic interconnectedness, would cause significant disruption to the wider financial system and economic activity."[46] In order to partially offset the problem of size, the Basel Committee has developed an indicator-based approach to SIFIs that has applied from 2011 onwards. This categorizes international banks into various categories and subjects them to additional loss-absorbency requirements varying from 1% to 3.5% depending on their systemic importance.[47]

Secondly, the bigger and more interconnected a financial institution is, the higher the chance that, in the case of failure, Treasuries will be forced to intervene to bail it out, thereby transferring the social costs of the failure to the public sector. This is the so-called "too-big-to-fail doctrine."[48] The availability of bailouts in turn produces a massive moral hazard that only further incentivizes banks to carry on with their growth strategies. The problems arising from the activities of too-big-to-fail institutions were at the core of the 2007–8 financial crisis, and the use of public money to bail out financial firms was met with disapproval everywhere.[49] As a result, regulators changed their views. As former Bank of England's Governor Mervyn King put it, "if a bank

[46] Financial Stability Board, *Reducing the Moral Hazard Posed by Systemically Important Financial Institutions – FSB Recommendations and Time Lines* (Financial Stability Board, 20 October 2010).

[47] The BCBS identified five major indicators: the size of the banks, their interconnectedness, the lack of readily available substitutes for the services they provide, their global (cross-jurisdictional) activity, and their complexity. See Basel Committee on Banking Supervision, "*Global Systemically Important Banks: Assessment Methodology and the Additional Loss Absorbency Requirement*," Basel Committee on Banking Supervision (July 2011).

[48] Edward F. Greene, Knox L. McIlwain, and Jennifer T. Scott, "A Closer Look at 'Too Big to Fail': National and International Approaches to Addressing the Risks of Large, Interconnected Financial Institutions" (2010) 5 *Capital Markets Law Journal* 117; Arthur E. Wilmarth Jr., "Reforming Financial Regulation to Address the Too-Big-To-Fail Problem" (2010) 35 *Brooklyn Journal of International Law* 707; Okamoto, above note 29.

[49] Randall D. Guynn, "Are Bailouts Inevitable?" (2012) 29 *Yale Journal on Regulation* 121.

is too-big-to-fail, it is simply too big to exist."[50] In the United States, the Dodd-Frank Act adopted the so-called Volcker Rule, which prohibits banks from carrying out speculative investments that do not benefit their customers.[51] In essence, it has banned banks from any proprietary trading activity.[52] The same philosophy also formed the basis of the Glass-Steagall Act – repealed in 1999 – which created a separation between commercial banking (including deposit taking and lending) and investment banking (including securities underwriting and investing).

A third strategy is to reduce dangerous interconnectedness by limiting the concentration of investments to one particular asset class or institution. Exposure limits are not new in finance: the Basel Committee on Banking Supervision first issued supervisory guidance on large exposures in 1991 in the framework of Basel I. After the crisis, however, it has revamped its efforts with the revised *Supervisory Framework for Measuring and Controlling Large Exposures*. This standard requires international banks to communicate to their national regulators any large exposure toward counterparties, and set precise concentration limits.[53] The above-mentioned standard is complemented by the 2014 *Capital Requirement for Bank Exposures to Central Counterparties*,[54] which sets various rules regarding the bilateral exposures between a bank and central counterparties or their members. Large exposure limits aim to reduce the potential loss a bank could face in the event of a sudden failure of a counterparty. They also prevent the creation of a financial system in which firms are dangerously exposed to only a few core nodes.

1.4. FINANCIAL STABILITY AND THE STATE

In the previous section, I have argued that one of the fundamental objectives of financial policy is to regulate the behavior of financial institutions to minimize their risk-taking activities. However, not all market failures in

[50] Cited in Avinash Persaud, "The Locus of Financial Regulation: Home versus Host" (2010) 86 *International Affairs* 637, p. 638.

[51] Dodd-Frank Wall Street and Consumer Protection Act, sec. 619, §13.

[52] Charles K. Whitehead, "The Volcker Rule and Evolving Financial Markets" (2011) 1 *Harvard Business Law Review* 39.

[53] Each bank must communicate exposures that are equal to or above 10% of the bank's eligible capital. Moreover, the value of a firm's exposure toward counterparties must not exceed 25% of the Tier 1 capital base at any time. The value is reduced to 15% if the counterparty is a Global Systemically Important Bank. See Basel Committee on Banking Supervision, "Supervisory Framework for Measuring and Controlling Large Exposures" (April 2014).

[54] Basel Committee on Banking Supervision, "Capital Requirements for Bank Exposures to Central Counterparties" (April 2014).

finance can be addressed simply by constraining the behavior of individual financial institutions. Besides minimizing risk there are other fundamental legal problems that any financial system has to address. Among them, the regulation of entry, the enforcement of contracts, and the distribution of losses are particularly important in the context of our analysis. None of these issues can be solved efficiently by the market alone: information asymmetries, different preferences, and enforcement problems would make this impossible. Yet, without addressing them, financial intermediaries will probably not be able to conduct their business or financial stability might be compromised. In this situation, the state exerts again a fundamental function as regulator, monitor, and enforcer. The utility of having an enforcer can be better appreciated when we will contrast the functioning of a national financial system with that of the international financial system.

1.4.1. *Choice of Players*

Every creditor assumes a financial risk at the very moment it enters the financial system either as a customer or operator; frauds, bad investment decisions, or technological disruptions are just some of the dangers of finance that are outside the control of creditors. In an interconnected financial network like the present one, financial contagion adds a further element of vulnerability that highlights just how exposed financial creditors are to external threats. For this reason, before accepting newcomers into the system, it would be sensible to scrutinize very carefully which entities are eligible to operate as banks or offer financial services. This surely comes at a price: a closed market may inhibit innovation or increase price. However, in a purely free market with no barriers to entry, the risks of financial frauds or systemic instability would probably outstrip the benefits in terms of competition. For this reason, one of the mechanisms adopted to contain risk is the careful selection of the entities able to provide financial services.

The purest and strictest form is the charter value system, which was often used from the seventeenth to the early twentieth century to regulate market entry.[55] A charter value is essentially a license to engage in the business of banking in a more favorable market position than would otherwise be available under perfect competition. Under this regulatory arrangement, the financial

[55] Richard S. Grossman, *Unsettled Account: The Evolution of Banking in the Industrialized World since 1800* (Princeton and Oxford: Princeton University Press, 2010), pp. 135–45; Gorton, *Misunderstanding Financial Crises*, above note 22, pp. 125–9; Calomiris and Haber, above note 36, pp. 60–1.

system is organized as an oligopoly in which only a handful of entities are able to operate as banks. In exchange for the absence of competition and the exemption from certain activities – such as paying interest on deposits – governments ask the banks to reduce their business risk to a minimum. The charter value system is a win–win situation, if it can be maintained,[56] because it guarantees a certain amount of profit for the banks, while at the same time reducing the risk of instability. In their recent book, Calomiris and Haber point to the example of Canada, which has adopted a charter value system and has been historically immune from financial crises.[57]

Besides the charter value system, in all jurisdictions, an entity wishing to operate as a bank needs to obtain a banking license from the local supervisory authority.[58] Before granting it, financial supervisors carefully scrutinize the internal corporate and business structure of the individual firm to ensure that it meets the minimum requirements in terms of financial capabilities and corporate structure. Supervisors routinely engage in "fit and proper" tests in which they scrutinize managers to rule out those with a record of reckless or fraudulent behavior who might show a tendency toward excessive risk taking. Furthermore, throughout their lives, banks and investment firms are subject to constant supervision by financial authorities. These can, at any time, intervene to remove managers, or impose changes in the financial or corporate models of the firms, or even to revoke the licenses of the firms.[59]

The careful choice of players performs a fundamental function in the management of systemic risk. However, in recent years the limits of this strategy have become clear. Over the last two decades, financial intermediation has grown outside the regulated banking sector into the shadow banking system, in which non-regulated and non-supervised financial institutions offer bank-like services to other financial institutions or corporations.[60] The systemic risk

[56] Gary Gorton has showed that, although the United States adopted a charter value system, which was in place until the 1980s, the increased competition from outside the regulated banking sector in the provision of credit ultimately forced banks to adopt a riskier attitude. Gorton, *ibid.*, p. 127.

[57] Calomiris and Haber, above note 36, p. 283.

[58] Llewellyn, above note 40.

[59] On supervision, see Armour et al., above note 7, pp. 50–98, 577–96.

[60] There is no common definition of what a shadow bank is. This term of art was coined in 2007 by Paul McCulley to describe the opaque legal structure used by banks in the process of securitization. However, over time it extended to cover the whole non-regulated financial sector. In this book I use the latter definition. See The Economist, "A Non-bank by Any Other Name" (10 May 2014); Stjin Claessens and Lev Ratnovski, "What Is Shadow Banking?" (2014) IMF Working Paper WP/14/25, International Monetary Fund; Gorton and Metrick, above note 10, p. 261; Avgouleas, above note 9, pp. 51–4.

of shadow banking became evident during the 2007–8 crisis, as shadow banks played a major role in the liquidity crunch that paralyzed the US economy.[61]

1.4.2. *Distribution of Losses*

Not all the externalities of banks' activities can be corrected through prudential regulations. Sometimes, it is necessary for the State to step in to prevent an already dangerous situation escalating further into a full-blown financial crisis. This might require the provision or emergency financing to the ailing financial institution, public guarantees, or painful creditors' haircuts. Irrespectively of the form it might take, financial crisis containment necessarily requires a distribution of losses among a wide spectrum of interest groups that, directly or indirectly, have a stake in the fate of the financial system.

In their fundamental book on the political economy of finance, Calomiris and Haber argue that the regulation and structure of every financial system is the result of a series of political bargains between the government, bank shareholders, and bank creditors.[62] Bank resolution policies can be analyzed as a particular political agreement between those actors. The failure of a bank inevitably triggers a series of consequences for all the actors involved: the shareholders, the managers, and the depositors. Shareholders are bound to lose their investment in the bank; creditors are bound to lose some of all the money they have lent in the bank. Moreover, because the bank is part of the financial system, other institutions may find themselves on the receiving end of systemic risk. Because the social and economic consequences of a financial crisis inevitably transcend the simple individual losses – depositors may lose their savings – governments intervene directly in the market. They do so by protecting certain stakeholders from losses, and by transferring on to others the financial costs of the bank's collapse. In essence, governments allocate losses based on a political agreement. If we examine the entire set of crisis containment policies – insolvency law, recovery and resolution, and deposit insurance – these are nothing more than powers attributed by law or statute to the government to distribute losses across the system, depositors, taxpayers, shareholders, and creditors.

Three strategies are particularly important in this regard: deposit insurance, bailouts, and bail-ins. All involve a fundamental reattribution of financial losses from banks to external stakeholders to maintain financial stability. In its simplest form – demand deposit – banking is a risky business. When depositors

[61] Gorton and Metrick, *ibid.*; Avgouleas, *ibid.*, p. 54.
[62] Calomiris and Haber, above note 36.

open an account with a bank, they take the risk that the bank will not experience such losses as would wipe out all the liabilities and hence, their investments. The bank, on the other hand, takes also the risk that only a fraction of the depositors will demand their money back at any given time. Until the creation of deposit insurance schemes, the main response of creditors to the rumors of a banking crisis was to pull out their deposit. Under banking law, demand deposits are contracts that legally oblige banks to make the funds available for withdrawal to their customers without notice. Thus, because depositors have the right to withdraw all of the money when they please, they tend to do so at the first sign of a crisis. This however was inefficient because only the first wave of depositors could succeed, leading the bank to collapse, while the rest had to take the losses. The peculiar treatment of depositors in insolvency law and the use of deposit insurance have now virtually eliminated this risk. In a deposit insurance scheme, the government commits to cover the losses of depositors up to a certain threshold. The goal is to discourage depositors from withdrawing their money from an ailing bank, which may force the bank into declaring insolvency. Deposit insurance entails a political bargain between the government and depositors whereby the state commits to transfer financial resources to depositors to cover their financial losses. Some say that in this political economy bargain banks often win, as they are less encouraged to monitor their solvency and liquidity.

In a bailout, the government directly recapitalizes the bank or offers other forms of financial support to the bank through the purchase of bad assets, or the provision of financial guarantees. In each case, the government supports the bank creditors by transferring the costs of the crises to taxpayers. The political economy logic underlying government support can be motivated with the need to protect a very concentrated interest group (creditors) that, because they stand to lose most of their savings, could create serious political difficulties to the government. Taxpayers, on the other hand, represent a very disaggregated and fragmented interest group that does not have enough incentives to set up a political campaign against the government. Because the losses will be shared among millions of taxpayers, none of them has a direct interest in fighting the government. Moreover, due to the lack of transparency of bailouts, it is also very difficult for taxpayers to understand the true cost of the intervention.[63]

In recent years, bailouts became the epicenter of a public debate on the role of the state during financial crisis. The use of public money to recapitalize a

[63] See Guynn, above note 49.

private enterprise disrupts the incentives of bank managers to behave prudently, thereby increasing moral hazard. From an economic viewpoint, the implicit guarantee offered by bailouts accounts for an implicit subsidy for bank shareholders, as it reduces the bank's borrowing costs. In a banking crisis, the use of taxpayers' money is politically challenging for supervisory authorities, as it entails a transfer of fiscal resources from the public to a private enterprise, which in the general public view should probably had been allowed to fail like any other commercial entity. The European Commission calculated during the recent crisis, nation states spent around 442 billion Euro to bail out their failing banks.[64] As a result, one of the most important outcomes of the financial crisis is a widespread aversion for bank bailouts and a push for private sector-financed support. The response of regulators took two forms: bail-ins and Contingent Convertible Debt Obligations, commonly known as CoCos. The two instruments present various similarities. Both mechanisms involve the compulsory participation of the bank's senior creditors instead of government intervention, when the bank reaches or is near to the point of non-viability. Senior and unsubordinated creditors are forced to convert their debt into equity or to write down part of their debt, to make the bank solvent.[65]

In all circumstances, what is important to understand is that the government occupies a central position in the *game of bank bargains* as the entity with the power to allocate the losses among the local constituencies. This is particularly important when it comes to international bank resolution, as in this case the objective of governments changes drastically.

1.4.3. *Contractual Rights and Legal Protection*

The business of financial institutions is to intermediate money. When they invest their money, financial institutions take the calculated risk that the borrowers will pay the interests on the loan and the principal. In a free market economy with no law, the incentive for a borrower to repay the lender remains

[64] European Commission, "State Aid Scoreboard: Report on state aid granted by the EU Member States –Autumn 2012 Update" (21 December 2012), p. 3.

[65] Jianping Zhou, Virginia Rutledge, Wouter Bossu, Marc Dobler, Nadege Jassaud, and Michael Moore, "From Bail-out to Bail-in: Mandatory Debt Restructuring of Systemic Financial Institutions" (2012) IMF Staff Discussion Note SDN/12/03, International Monetary Fund; John C. Coffee, Jr., "Systemic Risk After Dodd-Frank: Contingent Capital and the Need for Regulatory Strategies Beyond Oversight" (2011) 111 *Columbia Law Review* 795; see also Ceyla Pazarbasioglu, Jianping Zhou, Vanessa Le Leslé, and Michael Moore, "Contingent Capital: Economic Rationale and Design Features" (2011) IMF Staff Discussion Note SDN/11/01, International Monetary Fund.

solely on its desire to maintain a good credit reputation. This will be important if the creditor will need to borrow money in the future or engage in private contracts with other individuals or firms. Indeed, the banks will most probably refuse to lend him money or provide financial services; moreover, nobody will trust him if he has developed a reputation as an untrustworthy individual who does not fulfill his contractual obligations. Thus, the recalcitrant debtor will be forced out of the business community and forced to rely on its own funds. Banks can adopt a few strategies to reduce the credit risk, such as requesting part of the loan to be pledged as a collateral that the bank can retain if the debtor defaults. However, the collateral does not cover the entire risk of the loan and is sometimes very illiquid and difficult to monetize. In this situation, financial institutions are in the weakest position because, for the portion of the loan that exceeds the value of the collateral, they can only rely on the fear of the borrower to develop a bad credit history.

The state, through its coercive powers, addresses this asymmetry of power between creditors and borrowers by forcing the borrower to honor its obligations. It does so by creating legal institutions that recognize the economic value of the promise enshrined in a financial contract and make compliance with contracts a legal obligation punishable by law. It does so by establishing a dispute settlement system that interprets the law of the contract, establishes what were the obligations of each party, and ultimately provides a set of remedies to place the injured party in the position where it would have been had the contract been performed. The state, through the legal system it enforces, helps in understanding when a contract could not possibly have been carried out. Rules of law such as necessity, error, impossibilities and so forth serve to discharge a borrower from its obligations.

The history behind negotiable instruments is particularly revealing in this regard. The rise of long-distance trade confronted medieval merchants with a problem: how to ensure that financial obligations were recognizable and enforceable by the community of merchants rather than single individuals. To do so, they devised a financial instrument called the *bill of exchange* in which the bearer of the instruments who wanted to use it in payment for something – and transfer it to another party – had to sign it on its back. By doing so, the bearer was automatically assuming the responsibility for the full face value of the bill. The person who received it just had to trust the person who transferred it. Clearly, the more a bill was used, the more signatures it had on its back, which ultimately reinforced the financial value of the instrument. This very concept eventually led to the creation of modern money. In the rise of negotiable instruments, the law played a fundamental part. Before the rise of sixteenth-century bills of exchange, debts were personal promises, which required the assistance of public notaries to be recorded, and which could be enforced only bilaterally. In order to have this new financial instrument legally recognized, it was necessary to enact statute and laws that made personal promises transferable.[66]

The role of the law and the government is therefore of fundamental importance for maintaining financial stability. However, as we will see in the next chapters, when it comes to international finance, the absence of a common government able to impose on each party the obligation to respect contracts and international law becomes a critical limit for effective global financial governance.

[66] See Jacob Rabinovits, "The Origin of the Negotiable Promissory Note" (1956) 104 *University of Pennsylvania Law Review* 926.

2

Nationalism and Cooperation in International Finance

The 26th of June 1974 began as a seemingly normal day for Bankhaus Herstatt, a small German bank involved in highly speculative operations in the foreign exchange markets. In the morning, several of its US counterparties had already paid it a large part of their foreign exchange trading in Deutsche Mark, which was settled in Germany as usual. The foreign exchange trading operations would have been fully completed when, later in the afternoon, Herstatt would have paid its part of the deal in US dollars to its counterparties in New York. However, things did not go as usual that day. At 3:30 pm in Frankfurt, the German financial supervisory authorities decided that Herstatt was an insolvent bank that could no longer continue its operations. Thus, they revoked its banking license, shut its trading operations, put it into liquidation, and appointed a receiver. All this, while the US market was still open.

The immediate impact of the German authorities' decision was the freezing of all Herstatt's outstanding payments. The receiver indeed immediately prohibited the bank from completing all the outgoing payments until the insolvency proceedings were completed. This left US counterparties, which had already transferred Deutsche Marks to Germany earlier that day and still waiting to receive their part in US dollars, completely exposed to the full value of their earlier payments to Germany.[1] The consequences were huge losses on the side of US banks. The German authorities' decision was totally legitimate and in line with their statutory mandate – to protect local depositors and prevent an insolvent bank from continuing its business. However, it failed to consider the financial implications that this carried for the US financial system.

1 See Charles Goodhart, *The Basel Committee on Banking Supervision: A History of the Early Years 1974–1997* (Cambridge: Cambridge University Press, 2011), pp. 32–47.

The Herstatt failure did not trigger a systemic crisis of the kind experienced more recently with Lehman Brothers. The German bank was a rather small player in the Eurocurrency market, and it was far less systemically important than modern multinational banking conglomerates. However, for the first time its insolvency shined a powerful light on a fundamental problem of financial integration: how to coordinate national financial policies. In a world where financial markets are interconnected, but in which financial policy is still preserved as a national prerogative, regulatory and policy asymmetries sometimes represent a dangerous risk for the maintenance of financial stability. This is because the main objective of national regulators will inevitably be the maximization of national interests rather than the protection of global stability. I define this regulatory philosophy as the *logic of financial nationalism*. This broad policy and legal approach to the problem of financial instability can be found in every corner of international financial law, from cross-border banking supervision to sovereign debt.

This chapter will set the theoretical background of the book. It will discuss the challenges of international policy coordination, how financial instability develops in an integrated financial system, and it will analyze the role of the law in creating and preventing it.

2.1. FINANCIAL INTEGRATION AND GLOBAL SYSTEMIC RISK

In the decades between the late 1960s until the global financial crises of 2007, the global financial system underwent profound transformations. After the collapse of the Bretton Woods system, financial markets and institutions increasingly started a process of internationalization spurred by technological innovations and by a powerful political movement promoting the reduction of barriers to free capital mobility.[2] These changes were accompanied by a progressive growth of the financial sector in the economy. Financial institutions became more globalized and often too-big-to-fail. Monetary, fiscal, and financial policies became increasingly interdependent to the point that a problem in one area would immediately reverberate in others. This evolution exponentially increased the risk that an event originating in one country could propagate systemic spillovers into another's financial system.

[2] See Dirk Schoenmaker, *Governance of International Banking: The Financial Trilemma* (Oxford: Oxford University Press, 2013), pp. 34–68; Emilios Avgouleas, *Governance of Global Financial Markets: The Law, The Economics, The Politics* (Cambridge: Cambridge University Press, 2012), pp. 35–54; Rawi Abdelal, *Capital Rules: The Construction of Global Finance* (Cambridge, MA: Harvard University Press, 2007).

Global financial integration operates across different levels. At the horizontal level, it connects financial institutions operating in different countries. The period between the 1980s until the European sovereign debt crisis of 2011 witnessed an unprecedented increase in the level of international financial integration.[3] According to Bank for International Settlements (BIS) and International Monetary Fund (IMF) studies, cross-border banking claims increased sharply between the 1990s and the 2008 crisis, reaching more than half of global GDP, although this tendency partially reversed after the crisis.[4] Furthermore, the removal of barriers to capital allowed banks and investment firms to offer their services to foreign consumers without the need to establish local operations.[5] Banks offered loans and financial advice to customers located in another country, and issued securities in foreign stock markets. In most cases, however, banks and financial institutions exploited the opportunities of an extended market by establishing permanent commercial operations in foreign countries in the form of branches or subsidiaries. In certain cases, the size of multinational banks grew to such an extent that their simple failure would trigger a cascade of effects across the entire domestic and foreign structure.[6] Economists define them as Global Systemically Important Banks (G-SIBs).

G-SIBs are multinational financial institutions operating across different countries through a centralized structure relying on a parent bank and a network of foreign affiliates. According to the Financial Stability Forum (FSB), there were thirty G-SIBs around the globe as of November 2015, fifteen of them headquartered in Europe.[7] Citigroup, HSBC, Deutsche Bank, and UBS are just some of the names that appear on the list. By relying on an integrated network between the parent bank and its affiliates, they can collect credit where it is cheaper and offer it where it is more profitable. G-SIBs have two fundamental characteristics that make them particularly prone to transmitting instability across borders. The first is their peculiar structure, which

[3] IMF, "Understanding Financial Interconnectedness" (2010) International Monetary Fund; IMF, "Understanding Financial Interconnectedness – Supplementary Information" (2010) International Monetary Fund.

[4] IMF, Global Financial Stability Report: Navigating Monetary Policy Challenges and Managing Risks (April 2015), pp. 57–63.

[5] Federico Lupo-Pasini, "Movement of Capital and Trade in Services: Distinguishing Myth from Reality Regarding the GATS and the Liberalization of the Capital Account" (2012) 15 *Journal of International Economic Law*, pp. 595–7.

[6] Schoenmaker, above note 2, pp. 34–64; Eugenio Cerutti et al., "How Banks Go Abroad: Branches or Subsidiaries?" (2007) 31 *Journal of Banking and Finance* 1669.

[7] Financial Stability Board, "Update of List of Systemically Important Banks" (3 November 2015).

acts as a bridge between different national financial systems. The second characteristic is the width of their business operations, which typically span all sectors of financial activity, encompassing trades and investments in virtually every financial product.[8] As pointed out by the FSB, given their structure and size, "their distress or failure would cause significant dislocation in the global financial system and adverse economic consequences across a range of countries."[9]

Financial interconnectedness also extended vertically between firms and the public sector, thereby increasing the linkages between macroeconomic policies and financial stability. As soon as the barriers to the movement of capital were removed in the 1970s, investment firms and banks began immediately to exploit the immense potential of dealing with foreign currency. Banks allowed the opening of foreign currency-denominated deposits, while investment firms began trading in foreign exchange.[10] Furthermore, financial liberalization spurred innovations in sovereign debt financing and in the regulatory framework for sovereign debt. Since the 1980s, governments resorted less and less to syndicated loans, and returned to issuing sovereign bonds in international capital markets as a means to finance their budget.[11] Furthermore, over the last ten years, sovereign lending took more sophisticated and complex forms, including Credit Default Swaps, which, according to some authors, might increase the systemic effect of a sovereign default.[12]

At the same time, banks became increasingly interested in holding a large portfolio of sovereign bonds, especially those of OECD countries. Sovereign debt has usually been considered a no-risk or low-risk financial instrument, because of the allegedly unlimited repayment capacity of states. This assumption was underscored by Basel I, which gave sovereign debt from OECD member countries a zero risk profile when calculating required capital.[13] Basel II

[8] See IMF, above note 3, p. 7.

[9] Financial Stability Board, "Reducing the Moral Hazard Posed by Systemically Important Financial Institutions: FSB Recommendations and Time Lines" (20 October 2010).

[10] Abdelal, above note 2, pp. 7–8; Goodhart, above note 1, pp. 25–31.

[11] Philip J. Power, "Sovereign Debt: The Rise of the Secondary Market and Its Implications for Future Restructurings" (1996) 64 *Fordham Law Review* 2701; James Hays II, "The Sovereign Debt Dilemma" (2010) 75 *Brooklyn Law Review* 550.

[12] Steven L. Schwarcz, "Sovereign Debt Restructuring Options: An Analytical Comparison" (2012) 2 *Harvard Business Law Review* 95, 97; Elena Kalotychou, Eli Remolona, and Eliza Wu, "What Makes Systemic Risk Systemic? Contagion and Spillovers in the International Sovereign Debt Market" (2014) HKIMR Working Paper No.07/2014.

[13] See Simon Gleeson, *International Regulation of Banking: Capital and Risk Requirements*, 2nd edn. (Oxford: Oxford University Press, 2012), p. 115.

and Basel III, while removing the explicit preference for OECD country debt, nonetheless achieved the same result, as they allowed national supervisors to decide autonomously the risk profile of their national debt. Governments were therefore incentivized to give a very low-risk profile to their debt in order to encourage banks to buy it.[14]

The use of bond financing further increases the interconnectedness between financial firms and foreign governments. This occurs primarily for two reasons. The first has to do with the direct exposure of banks to foreign debt risk, as reflected in the balance sheet. Second, since debt issued by OECD sovereigns is usually used by the bank as collateral for its financing operations, the declining value of sovereign bonds immediately makes it difficult for banks to carry out their daily financing operations. The combination of those two factors increases by twofold the global systemic risk potential of a sovereign default, because a banking crisis might turn into a sovereign debt crisis and vice- versa. Economists define this situation as the "vicious circle" between banks and sovereigns.[15] This was demonstrated during the recent Spanish and Irish crises, when the bailout of the national financial systems by the national governments led the two countries to the verge of default.[16]

The increased interconnectedness between foreign firms and the parallel reduction in regulatory barriers to finance has exponentially increased the dangers of global financial instability for national financial systems. In a world where financial institutions operate across borders, financial instability does not originate any longer simply from domestic market inefficiencies, but can be easily imported from outside events. Understanding how global instability develops is key to devising appropriate regulations. In this regard, the majority of the literature on international financial crises analyzes the question of global instability based on two main assumptions. The first is that financial instability originates from market failures inherent in any financial systems,

[14] See Daniel Nouy, "Is Sovereign Risk Properly Addressed by Financial Regulation?" in "Public Debt, Monetary Policy and Financial Stability" (2012) 16 *Banque De France Financial Stability Review* 95; Jaime Caruana and Stefan Avdjiev, "Sovereign Creditworthiness and Financial Stability: An International Perspective," in "Public Debt, Monetary Policy and Financial Stability" (2012) 16 *Banque De France Financial Stability Review* 71.

[15] See Silvia Merler and Jean Pisani-Ferry, "Hazardous Tango: Sovereign-Bank Interdependence and Financial Stability in the Euro Area," in "Public Debt, Monetary Policy and Financial Stability" (2012) 16 *Banque De France Financial Stability Review* 201; Lucrezia Reichlin and Luis Garicano, "Squaring the Eurozone's Vicious Circle," Project Syndicate, 27 January 2014.

[16] See Federico Lupo-Pasini, "Economic Stability and Economic Governance in the Euro Area: What the European Crisis Can Teach on the Limits of Economic Integration" (2013) 16 *Journal of International Economic Law* 211–56, p. 239.

no different from the market failures analyzed in the previous chapter. For instance, Kindleberger and Aliber describe international financial crises either as the result of cross-border financial contagion due to the well-known financial cycle of boom and bust,[17] or as the result of the exuberance of international financial investors. The second assumption is that such systemic risk is transmitted through an integrated financial system in which regulatory asymmetries and different policy preferences are nonexistent.

In the global financial system, however, *some* (and by all means, not all) of the problems affecting global finance are very different from those of systemic risk that we examined in the previous chapter. In a global economy where markets are integrated and financial institutions operate across different jurisdictions, domestic policies play an increasingly fundamental economic role. That is because in a world of sovereign states, the ultimate control over the soundness and stability of a multinational bank or the stability of the financial sector lies ultimately in the hands of national financial authorities. They set the rules according to which firms will operate, decide how they will be supervised, and how any troubles will be resolved. Furthermore, in the context of sovereign debt, national governments are the only entities capable of determining the amount of external borrowing, deciding the domestic economic policies on which the prompt servicing of the debt ultimately depends. Undoubtedly, they call the shots with regard to repayment. In general, national governments are the only entities able to influence domestic economic variables – such as fiscal sustainability, credit, and monetary stability – that have a direct impact on the stability of the financial system.

Given the global interconnectedness between firms and markets, global financial stability is a public good whose protection requires the active contribution of all states.[18] Consequently, when we come to the problems of global financial instability, under certain circumstances, market failures represent the mere epiphenomena of very different problems: governance failures. An analysis of global financial instability based only on systemic risk theory would probably fail to understand a fundamental aspect at the core of any global financial crises: the role of international cooperation.

[17] Charles Kindleberger and Robert Z. Aliber, *Manias, Panics and Crashes: A History of Financial Crises* (New York: Palgrave, 2011), pp. 154–91, 229–57.

[18] For an overview of the problem of international contagion, from an economic perspective, see Charles Wyplosz, "International Financial Instability," in Inge Kaul, Isabelle Grunberg, and Marc Stern (eds.) *Global Public Goods: International Cooperation in the 21st Century* (Oxford: Oxford University Press, 1999), pp. 154–91.

2.2. GLOBAL FINANCIAL STABILITY IN A WORLD OF SOVEREIGN STATES

The protection of global financial stability confronts the global financial system with fundamentally different challenges than those faced by national regulators. From a legal perspective, global financial instability can be simply described as a financial threat originating from events *outside* the jurisdiction of national regulators. This situation puts regulators in a difficult position, as the regulatory and supervisory powers they enjoy are no longer sufficient to address the origin of financial instability – at best, regulators can intervene to minimize the impact in their own financial system. To remove the trigger events, international cooperation is necessary.

Yet, the global financial system is built upon a dangerous asymmetry between the global scope of financial markets and the national scope of financial policies. This means that while financial institutions and markets enjoy the freedom to operate across borders, there is no single global regulator able to set common policies and enforce them on the market players irrespective of their location. Instead, each country is in principle competent in regulating its own market and implementing financial, monetary, and fiscal policies within its jurisdiction. How it does so is entirely dependent on domestic policy calculations.

Since the birth of modern nation states in 1648, economic sovereignty is the "default mode" of the international economic system, and policy coordination is the exception. Given the role of finance in the economy and its political sensitivity, it is not surprising that states very rarely and reluctantly relinquish their control on it. Moreover, given the strict link between banks and central banks, reducing the level of control on the financial system could imply a reduction of the policy space of monetary authorities.[19] This will make it impossible for central banks to control inflation and other economic variables like employment, growth, savings, or investments.[20] Whatever the reason behind financial sovereignty might be, the absence of a common global regulator and economic policymaker bears fundamental implications for the maintenance of global financial stability. Understanding what drives and equally prevents international cooperation is essential in this respect.

[19] Emily Gilbert, "Forging A National Currency Money, State-Making and Nation-Building in Canada," in Emily Gilbert and Eric Helleiner (eds.) *Nation States and Money: The Past, Present and Future of National Currencies* (London and New York: Routledge, 1999).

[20] On the legal theory of *lex monetae*, see Rosa Maria Lastra, *Legal Foundations of International Monetary Stability* (Oxford: Oxford University Press, 2007), pp. 14–21.

2.2.1. *The National Interest*

In a world of sovereign states, governments necessarily formulate and implement financial, fiscal, and monetary policies with the only objective of achieving the *national interest*. In economic policy this can be intended in many ways, such as financial stability, economic growth, a correct level of inflation, or an adequate level of government spending. Irrespective of its different connotations, the national interest can be broadly defined as an *increase* in the *aggregate* level of *national* welfare, rather than that of a single individual or group to the detriment of the broader society. In most cases the national interest can result in certain groups achieving more than others. Distributional tradeoffs, however, do not matter as long as the aggregate level of national economic welfare increases.

Nowadays we take for granted that government policies aim at the welfare of citizens. However, throughout history, government policies have targeted other objectives, such as the welfare of the king or powerful elites. It took over a hundred years and various revolutions to incorporate citizens' welfare into policymaking. For many states, regrettably, widespread corruption or the presence of a totalitarian regime make this an objective yet to be achieved. However, to make the analysis simpler I will now generalize and assume that all countries formulate policies that satisfy the national interest, rather than that of a single individual or group.

These changes led to the formation of a particular political alliance between the government and its citizens. The strict bond between regulators and their citizens (both taxpayers and financial institutions) plays an important role in our analysis. Many countries in the world have developed and adopted institutional and legal frameworks that make the government accountable to its citizens. This can be the result of democratic institutions or other forms of political accountability. The protection of the national interest is sometimes stated explicitly in the Constitution or in statutes of central banks and financial supervisory authorities.[21] This means that adopting a policy that violates the law will bear legal consequences for the officials involved in the decision. In a democracy, citizens have the power to vote for their politicians, which in turn will exert their political pressure on the regulators. In certain circumstances, regulators are also liable for gross violations of their duties, which might take them to court. The degree of independence between the principal and the

[21] See Francois Gianviti, "The Objectives of Central Banks," in Mario Giovanoli and Diego Devos (eds.) *International Monetary and Financial Law: The Global Crisis* (Oxford: Oxford University Press, 2010).

agent varies. Monetary authorities enjoy a high degree of independence from political power.[22] Financial authorities, on the contrary, are historically more subject to political control and citizens' support.[23]

We can conceptualize the particular bond between regulators and their citizens as a *principal–agent relationship*. The principal–agent model was developed in institutional economics literature to analyze information problems and transaction costs in industrial organizations.[24] This theory tries to explain the behavior of two or more subjects – a principal and his agent – linked together in a particular relationship but in different positions. In its simplest formulation, an entity (the principal) transfers to another entity (the agent) the performance of a particular task, which the agent cannot execute adequately alone. In this relationship, the principal can therefore make decisions that have a direct impact on the agent. Given the relative simplicity of the model, this theory is used in a wide variety of situations to explain different economic problems, from moral hazard, to information asymmetries, or transaction costs.[25] The political science literature has also developed a consistent body of research adapting the model to the realm of politics and government structures.[26]

When it comes to finance, the principal–agent model is useful to explain the relationship between citizens and financial supervisory or regulatory authorities. Given the impossibility to control financial and monetary stability by themselves – due to obvious coordination and capability problems – citizens need to transfer this task to the state. In this relationship, citizens are therefore the principals, while the state is the agent entrusted with the power

[22] On central bank independence, see Rosa Maria Lastra, *Central Banking and Banking Regulations* (London: London School of Economics and Political Science, 1996); Rosa Maria Lastra" 'The Independence of the European System of Central Banks" (1992) 33 *Harvard International Law Journal* 475.

[23] Stavros Gadinis, "From Independence to Politics in Financial Regulation" (2013) 101 *California Law Review* 327; David Andrew Singer, "Capital Rules: The Domestic Politics of International Regulatory Harmonization" (2004) 58 *International Organization* 531.

[24] Adolf Berle and Gardiner Means, *The Modern Corporation and Private Property* (New York: Macmillan, 1932).

[25] Daniel Lewis, "Incongruent Incentives in Banking Supervision: The Agent's Problem" (1997) 23 *The Journal of Economics* 17; Edward J. Kane, "Changing Incentives Facing Financial-Services Regulators" (1989) 2 *Journal of Financial Services Research* 265; Edward J. Kane, "Principal–Agent Problems in S&L Salvage" (1990) 45 *Journal of Finance* 755.

[26] A good quick overview of the literature is provided in Michelle Egan, "Regulatory Strategies, Delegation and European Market Integration" (1998) 5 *Journal of European Public Policy* 485; for a more extensive analysis, see Timothy Besley, *Principled Agents? The Political Economy of Good Government* (New York: Oxford University Press, 2006).

to safeguard domestic stability on the citizens' behalf.[27] The state becomes in turn a principal itself when it transfers to a specialized agency (the agent) the duty to implement financial stability policies. Such specialized agencies are the central bank and, in those countries where the two tasks are separated, the financial supervisory and resolution authority.[28]

2.2.2. *Principal–Agent Model in an International Setting*

Applied to international relations, the principal–agent model does not focus merely on the simple vertical interactions between citizens and their regulators, but extends instead to the horizontal relations between states. In the realm of international finance, the model is particularly useful in explaining the behavior of different national authorities in the formulation of financial policies and, more generally, the problems of cooperation for the protection of global financial stability.[29]

In a domestic setting, the role of the state as a regulator and economic policymaker is considered as exogenous. It is taken for granted that a centralized authority empowered with regulatory and enforcement powers can impose its policies on citizens, even with coercion. However, the global financial system does not rely on a centralized regulator able to target policy interventions toward the *international interest* and to enforce compliance with the rules. Hence, without a global government, international policymaking inevitably requires the cooperation of states.

The fiduciary duty that binds policymakers to their citizens nonetheless creates a barrier to cooperation as it forces regulators to focus their intervention on the protection of financial institutions and consumers located *within their jurisdiction*.[30] When exercising their delegated powers policymakers must

[27] Martin Schüler, "Incentives Problems in Banking Supervision: The European Case," ZEW Discussion Paper No. 03-62 (2003), available at ftp://ftp.zew.de/pub/zew-docs/dp/dp0362.pdf, p. 11.

[28] For an overview of the different supervisory systems, see Sylvester Eijffinger and Donato Masciandaro (eds.) *Handbook of Central Banking, Financial Regulation and Supervision: After the Financial Crisis* (Cheltenham: Edward Elgar Publishing, 2011).

[29] See Gerard Caprio Jr., Douglass D. Evanoff, and George G. Kauffman (eds.) *Cross Border Banking: Regulatory Challenges* (Singapore: World Scientific Studies in International Economics, 2006).

[30] There is a wide economic literature on the subject, especially in the context of cross-border banking. See David Andrew Singer, *Regulating Capital: Setting Standards for the International Financial System* (Ithaca, NY: Cornell University Press, 2007); Katia D'Ulster, "Cross Border Banking Supervision: Incentive Conflicts in Supervisory Information Sharing between Home and Host Supervisors," World Bank Policy Research Working Paper 5871 (2011).

ignore *external* factors, unless they bear a direct consequence for the domestic market, such as massive capital outflows or disinvestment of foreign-invested enterprises. Therefore, from the point of view of domestic authorities, it is irrelevant whether the protection of the national interest undermines economic integration, or that it produces spillovers to partner countries. As long as the national interest is achieved, national authorities fulfill their legal mandate.

From a policy viewpoint, the ultimate effect of the principal–agent relationship is that policy coordination between two countries can voluntarily occur only when domestic policy interests are aligned. This can occur naturally under certain circumstances; for instance, when countries share similar macroeconomic fundamentals or broader regulatory and policy objectives. However, most of the time, diverging policy preferences and different definitions of the national interest make international policy coordination challenging. In the context of international finance, this in turn increases the risks of global instability. In light of the above, we can therefore define global financial instability as the *negative externality of globally Pareto-inefficient domestic policies*. To draw a parallel with the legal theory of financial instability discussed in the previous chapter: if at the national level, systemic risk results from the difficulty of financial institutions to internalize the social costs of their actions, at the global level, financial instability is similarly the result of the difficulty of nation states to take into account the external effects of their domestic policies.

In the course of the book I will analyze different examples of global financial instability caused by globally Pareto-inefficient domestic policies. As I will explain in Chapter 4, policy coordination is of fundamental importance to solve cross-border banking crises during all phases, from the provision of emergency liquidity, to bailout, to insolvency. In this context, the principal–agent model explains the difficulties of financial authorities to cooperate with foreign counterparts during the bank resolution phase.[31] In the context of sovereign debt, the refusal of the borrowing country to service the debt, while protecting the (short-term) national interest of the debtor country, nonetheless transmits systemic risk to the foreign creditors. When it comes to monetary policy, the principal–agent model explains why central banks ignore the cross-border spillovers from quantitative easing or other macroeconomic policies. Finally, the principal–agent model is useful to explain why soft laws are, in principle, ineffective in addressing distributive problems. In the absence of strong compliance mechanisms, whenever the incentives of national authorities to defect are higher than their incentive to cooperate, national authorities will be bound to the protection of national interests.

[31] D'Ulster, *ibid.*

2.3. COORDINATION PROBLEMS

Before moving on to the role of international law in addressing the problems of regulatory coordination, it is useful to mention that cooperation problems in finance are not all the same. Finance is a *mare magnum* that comprises multiple and very different areas, from insurance to interest rate swaps. Hence, the cooperation problems that states might face in agreeing to common capital adequacy for large insurance companies are very different from those encountered in cross-border issuance of securities. In the next four chapters, I will analyze different situations cutting across different themes, from sovereign debt to cross-border banking.

One of the oldest and most discussed problems of financial cooperation is *regulatory convergence*, which is particularly important when it comes to international financial standards. Financial regulation must be necessarily tailored to the broader macroeconomic environment of the country. Consequently, regulatory and policy asymmetries reflect different underlying policy priorities or different macroeconomic fundamentals. Certain states may prefer to adopt more stringent prudential rules, while others may favor economic growth and a more relaxed regulatory environment. For instance, before Basel I came into play, the United States and the United Kingdom had the prevention of financial instability as their main goal. Therefore, they applied relatively high capital adequacy ratios. Japan, on the contrary, focused more on economic growth. Therefore, it kept the capital adequacy ratio of its banks very low in order to increase the competitiveness of its firms.[32] Yet, regulatory asymmetries can have negative effects as they prevent economies of scale and increase compliance costs for international firms. Above all, lax regulation might create dangerous regulatory loopholes that could eventually increase systemic risks. For these reasons, states often argue whether to harmonize their laws. Regulatory convergence confronts regulators with the challenging initial task of accommodating different regulatory preferences and goals. Sometimes states want to achieve regulatory coordination with other states because they know this will bring greater individual benefits than unilateralism, but they might fight on which alternative is best. Yet, once a common position is reached, states have very few incentives to change.[33]

[32] See Singer, above note 30.

[33] See Pierre-Hugues Verdier, "Transnational Regulatory Networks and Their Limits" (2009) 34 *Yale Journal of International Law* 113; Chris Brummer, "How International Financial Law Works (and How It Doesn't)" (2011) 99 *Georgetown Law Journal* 257; Chris Brummer, "Why Soft Law Dominates International Finance and Not Trade" (2010) 13 *Journal of International Economic Law* 623.

At other times, cooperation presents different problems. Often states can easily agree on a common globally optimal cooperative equilibrium but, later on, face very high incentives to deviate in search for unilateral gains. Without a centralized authority able to coerce states to comply with their obligations, states will inevitably disregard their international commitments whenever the costs of defection will be lower than the costs of compliance.[34] In simple terms: states will gain more by cheating their partners. This problem, commonly known as the *Prisoner's Dilemma*, is particularly important in the context of international bailouts, where the incentives for resolution authorities to adopt a nationalist approach to the resolution of cross-border banks are extremely high. In an international bailout, the home and host authorities should cooperate in resolving the cross-border bank as this will reduce the overall resolution costs, protect financial stability, and minimize creditors' losses. However, because of the sovereignty costs attached to the bailout in terms of increased public financial disbursements, and the increased public pressure faced during the crisis, regulators sometimes opt for a national solution. A similar situation could also occur with regard to international bail-ins, as the host resolution authorities might refuse to recognize and implement the bail-in of creditors located in the host jurisdiction in order to protect their national interest.

Finally, the Prisoner's dilemma is particularly important to understand the question of sovereign defaults and the incentives of sovereigns to renege on their commitments toward their international creditors. Creditors and sovereigns are separated by jurisdictional discontinuities that, legally speaking, shield the sovereigns against the right of creditors. In the absence of an international law of sovereign debt, creditors are therefore unprotected against the decision of a sovereign borrower not to repay its debt. Only the threat of retaliation from capital markets in the form of financial blockades or market access denial can compel sovereigns to comply with its commitments.

Under other circumstances, cooperation problems are the result of asymmetry of information that lead states to engage in *preemptive stability wars* in order to protect their national financial system. Even if states know that cooperation is their best option, they might be incentivized to defect in the fear that the other party might do the same. The problem is due to lack of trust between two parties, which are unsure about the other party's behavior.

[34] On this point, see Eric A. Posner and Alan O. Sykes, "Efficient Breach of International Law: Optimal Remedies, Legalized Noncompliance, and Related Issues" (2011) 110 *Michigan Law Review* 243; Jack L. Goldsmith and Eric A. Posner, *The Limits of International Law* (New York: Oxford University Press, 2005); Andrew T. Guzman, *How International Law Works: A Rational Choice Theory* (New York: Oxford University Press, 2008).

Unlike the prisoner's dilemma situation described above, here states have no unilateral incentives to deviate from cooperation, but they are compelled to do so to minimize their risk of losses that they might incur if the other party decides to defect first. This is what usually happens during cross-border bank insolvencies when the host supervisory authorities decide to ring-fence local subsidiaries or branches in order to minimize the risk that the parent bank repatriates the assets to protect the parent's creditors. Ring-fencing is a form of capital control as it prevents the parent bank from moving the assets across the bank group. Like any control on the movement of capital, it is an inherently globally inefficient solution to an international problem as it eliminates the benefits of financial integration and discourages financial institutions from engaging in further internationalization.

Creditors' coordination is a common theme in the context of sovereign debt. The absence of a sovereign bankruptcy court to adjudicate and manage sovereign debt restructuring under agreed international rules is a long-standing problem of the international financial system. Unlike firms, sovereigns are not subject to a bankruptcy code. This situation creates innumerable problems for both the creditors as well as the borrowing state. On the one hand, creditors are sometimes subject to the vagaries of sovereigns refusing to service their debts on time. This situation – which is the direct result of the international law principle of foreign immunity of states – is nonetheless often addressed by market discipline.

On the other hand, sovereigns are often prevented from achieving a quick restructuring outcome due to the absence of an institutional mechanism able to coordinate different creditors. The problem of holdouts has unfolded in all its complexity in a recent New York court case between a group of hedge funds and the government of Argentina. In the *NML* v. *Argentina* dispute, a group of holdout vulture funds had been able to block the repayment of Argentina's debt toward non-holdouts by obtaining an injunction against Argentina's trust bank – Bank New York Mellon. This created a situation of financial nationalism in reverse, albeit still dangerous. In this dispute, a national court adjudicated a sovereign debt problem based on the application of local law. What's more, by protecting a tiny minority of creditors and by blocking the mechanisms of payment, the court managed to hurt the interest of the large majority of creditors located in third countries – de facto pushing Argentina to the verge of a second default.

2.4. EXTERNALITIES AND THE ROLE OF INTERNATIONAL LAW

In a global financial system, the lack of cooperation can produce detrimental effects such as regulatory barriers and financial instability. Hence, the next step is to understand what role international law could play to solve cooperation problems. In a world in which domestic policies directly influence the level of protection of global public goods, the locus of regulatory intervention must shift from the micro-level – individual firms – to the macro-level – the state. International law is the tool that enables policy coordination. The literature on the economics of international law broadly agrees that one of the main functions of international law is to incentivize states to internalize the externalities of their actions by formulating globally Pareto efficient policies.[35] This also indirectly implies that global public "bads" such as global financial instability are the consequence of poorly calibrated or nonexisting international norms.

Before turning to the role of international law, it is nonetheless important to clarify one point: successful cooperation can arise even without international law. For instance, when the gains of policy coordination outweigh the costs, cooperation can arise naturally between states, without the need of international treaties. This is not different than what would happen between two individuals. If both parties to an agreement decide that cooperating will bring mutual benefits, they will voluntarily behave according to the pact. In this context, law is not necessary. The same occurs with international relations.

Notwithstanding this, under many circumstances relying on voluntary and unregulated cooperation might not work. For instance, a change in circumstances not envisaged during the bargain process might modify the payoffs associated with the agreement for one of the parties, which now prefers noncompliance. Doing so would inevitably cause a problem to the other party, which has invested time and resources in the agreement. This would lead to a standoff between the parties and, sometimes, a war. Without clear rules to explain under what circumstances the agreement can be modified, each party would be essentially free to do what it pleases, thereby disregarding the interest of the other party. In other circumstances, a disagreement might arise as to what the agreement implied or what precise outcomes each party might have expected from the other. Clear and detailed rules, possibly coupled with a system to interpret them, overcome this problem. In certain cases, voluntary

[35] For a quick overview of the concept of externalities applied to international law, see Eric A. Posner and Alan O. Sykes, *Economic Foundations of International Law* (Cambridge, MA, and London: Harvard University Press, 2012), pp. 17–20; see, for instance, Joel P. Trachtman, "Externalities and Extraterritoriality: The Law and Economics of Prescriptive Jurisdiction," in Jagdeep S. Bhandari and Alan O. Sykes (eds.) *Economic Dimensions in International Law: Comparative and Empirical Perspectives* (New York: Cambridge University Press, 1997); Jeffrey L. Dunoff and Joel P. Trachtman, "Economic Analysis of International Law" (1999) 24 *Yale Journal of International Law* 1, 12–28; Joel P. Trachtman, *The Economic Structure of International Law* (Cambridge, MA and London: Harvard University Press, 2008); Eric A. Posner, 'International Law: A Welfarist Approach' (2006) 73 *University of Chicago Law Review* 487, 518–22; Goldsmith and Posner, above note 34, pp. 45–78.

cooperation does not work because states have conflicting policy preferences that prevent them from entering into an agreement in the first place. Even though coordination would be the preferable outcome, each party might be incentivized not to cooperate due to internal reasons such as short-term vision or the resistance of powerful lobbies. Law can address this problem by modifying the long-term payoffs associated with the agreement and by mobilizing different interest groups.

In a world of sovereign states, international law acts as a contract.[36] It solidifies a particular bargain by clarifying the terms of the agreement and, more generally, by setting precise rules of behavior. This gives certainty to all the parties as to what is expected by them and what is prohibited. It allows states to invest time and resources in activities that would otherwise be subject to uncertainty. For instance, in the case of international investment, international investment treaties reduce the risk of irrational and unfair behavior of the host government and give to foreign investors the certainty that if this does happen they have a remedy under international law.

This is not different to what law does in a domestic transaction between two parties. However, the absence of a centralized enforcement mechanism makes compliance with international laws more complicated. To offset this problem, it is necessary to create a legalized system of compliance that reduces the incentive of states to defect. In his seminal book on compliance in international law, Guzman argued that compliance with international norms is due to three factors: reputation, retaliation, and reciprocity.[37] Each of these influences the payoffs associated with compliance with international rules, thereby incentivizing obedience. The role of international law is to institutionalize and embed these three mechanisms into international lawmaking to make their use legitimate. When a state signs a treaty, it does not only give a signal to the other parties of its intention of abiding by the treaty, but it also gives the other parties the rights to punish the state for the violation of the treaty. International law therefore creates the expectation that the violation of the treaty or any other rules of international law will be matched by an equivalent or higher level of retaliation in return carried out by other states. A welfare-maximizing government will thus decide to abide by the treaty whenever the costs of non-compliance will be higher than the returns. The legalization of retaliatory powers is a fundamental element in the analysis set in this book,

[36] On the economics of international law, see, Posner and Sykes, *ibid.*; Trachtman, *ibid.*; Robert E. Scott and Paul B. Stephan, *The Limits of Leviathan: Contract Theory and the Enforcement of International Law* (New York: Cambridge University Press, 2006).

[37] Guzman, above note 34.

as legalization is precisely what the current international law of finance lacks. I will discuss in the last chapter how this can be changed.

Before concluding this overview on the economics of international law, it is worth discussing the role of domestic political coalitions and interest groups.[38] The theory of cooperation discussed above is based on the basic assumption that states are unitary actors in which citizens have homogeneous policy preferences. Conceptualizing the state as a single entity makes it easier to explain when policy coordination works and when it does not. However, this does not reflect the reality of domestic politics. Policy formulation is a process that invariably involves distributional tradeoffs between different interest groups. This occurs also in financial policymaking. We discussed in the previous chapter the presence of diverging policy preferences of managers, shareholders, and depositors in the regulation of banks. Another important tradeoff can be seen in the context of bailouts, when the interests of bondholders often clash with those of taxpayers. In international relations, the bargaining table is necessarily extended to comprise foreign interest groups. Moreover, these groups are not homogeneous within the same state. In the same state you might find lobby groups that favor international cooperation and others that oppose it. For instance, in the context of international trade relations, consumers in country A and export industries in country B might favor the reduction of trade barriers in country A. On the other hand, import-competing industries in country A might oppose them.

International law can play an essential role in creating political coalitions between interest groups located in different countries but with homogeneous policy preferences. By giving to foreign interest groups the right to challenge a foreign state's illegal measures under international law or to pressure for the adoption of friendly regulations, international law gives a voice to lobby groups that would be otherwise be too dispersed or weak to influence policymaking by themselves. International trade law offers again a very clear example of how this works. Consumers are typically dispersed groups with little voice in economic policymaking, and export interests do not have any legal representation in a foreign country's trade policy formulation. Conversely, import-competing industry are typically very powerful and well connected to the government. International trade agreements create a political coalition between those two interest groups that is powerful enough to offset the influence of import-competing industries, thereby leading to a reduction of trade barriers.

[38] Joel P. Trachtman, "International Law and Domestic Political Coalitions: The Grand Theory of Compliance with International Law" (2010) 11 *Chicago Journal of International Law* 127.

2.5. THE LOGIC OF FINANCIAL NATIONALISM

Despite its potential to address coordination problem, the international law of finance often fails to do so. The question of global financial stability in international law can be conceptualized as a tradeoff between two broad and interrelated objectives: (1) the protection of national interests; and (2) the protection of global stability, which we should intend to be a situation that favors Pareto-optimal global cooperation. In the conflict between national interest and global financial stability, international law largely drifts toward the protection of national interests and financial sovereignty. It does so throughout a different set of legal doctrines that invariably favor the protection of national interests over those of the financial community. I define this approach as the *logic of financial nationalism*. The logic of financial nationalism does not always emerge as an explicit policy strategy, but it is a rather broad approach toward the problems of international financial integration that favors the achievement of individual interests over a coordinated solution. Nationalism is not exclusive to economic stability, but it affects many other aspects of public policy, from biodiversity to health issues.[39] However, given the role of finance in modern economies, the problems of financial nationalism are somehow more visible, as they influence negatively many international financial policies – from financial supervision to crisis resolution, to sovereign debt, and monetary policy. In the next four chapters I will analyze those policies in detail. However, certain issues cut across different areas, and it is worth discussing them briefly.

2.5.1. *Financial Nationalism in International Law*

The *Right to Regulate* is the quintessential example of financial nationalism and the purest expression of financial sovereignty. It allows regulators to choose their preferred regulations and, crucially, it grants states the fundamental freedom to choose their policy priorities. More specifically, the right to regulate that states enjoy extends to the freedom *not* to regulate, if a state so chooses. The right to regulate does face some limitations when states voluntarily coordinate their policies, as in the case of financial standards or when they sign Mutual Recognition Agreements. Yet, in principle, states are free to regulate their financial sector, even in the presence of international agreements promoting financial integration, like the WTO General Agreement on Trade in Services. In an

[39] See Eyal Benvenisti, "Sovereigns as Trustees of Humanity: On the Accountability of States to Foreign Stakeholders" (2013) 107 *American Journal of International Law* 295.

interconnected global financial system, the right to regulate is particularly risky because it could create dangerous regulatory discontinuities. States are free to adopt lax financial regulations, pursue unsustainable fiscal or monetary policies, default on their sovereign debts, or allow a too-big-to-fail domestic financial institution to go bankrupt, even if these actions produce global systemic risk.

Economic Necessity is a long-standing principle of international law. It broadly allows states to suspend the application of an international treaty whenever doing so jeopardizes the economic stability of the invoking state. As such, economic necessity operationalizes a choice between the interests of one state against another's. In the context of international economic relations, this principle of law implicitly assumes that the protection of national economic stability must necessarily rank higher than the protection of trading partners' interests. This principle has been used in various situations, from temporary fiscal or monetary unbalances, to more serious financial crises. Economic necessity is a fundamental element of the international finance law as it can be welfare-maximizing under certain circumstances. For instance, when a state has a balance of payment crisis, suspending imports allows the invoking state to restore monetary reserves and regain access. Notwithstanding, in the context of financial relations, the same principle might lend itself to abuses, which inevitably lead to a Pareto-suboptimal outcome.

The first problem is that, in a financial relation between two parties, the failure of one party to repay its debt will lead to a credit loss by the other party. Under certain circumstances – for instance in the context of sovereign debt transactions worth billions of dollars – debt repudiation could transmit global systemic risk on to the financial system where creditors are located. Moreover, in the context of cross-border supervisory cooperation, the failure of the home supervisory authority to provide liquidity assistance to the host country could leave the host country's banks or depositors exposed to a liquidity crisis. As I will discuss in the next chapter, this is what happened when, in the midst of a banking crisis, Iceland refused to protect the depositors of Icelandic banks' foreign branches, as originally mandated by EU law.

Second, if interpreted as a blank check that allows states to escape international obligations, economic necessity could create monstrous moral hazards. States would recklessly borrow on international markets or indulge in risky and unsustainable domestic policies. By doing so, they would transfer on to their partners the economic costs of their policies. This does not mean that economic necessity should never be invoked. Often, suspending financial obligations is the only way for a state to regain its feet in financial markets. Nevertheless, the application of this principle should be subject to specific criteria that guarantee a globally Pareto-efficient outcome.

Soft Law presents very similar problems. The absence of legalization – defined as binding laws, detailed rules, and a compliance mechanism – is the preferred mode of cooperation in many areas of international finance. It allows quick regulatory convergence without the hassle of treaty negotiation and implementation. Regulators have used it successfully to establish prudential standards for banks, such as Basel I, II, and III. Still, soft legalization carries its own risks. Soft laws indeed allow nation states to refrain from complying with their (soft) obligation whenever they deem compliance detrimental to their own interests. This is particularly dangerous when the incentives to comply with a regulatory standard or agreement are not naturally present. For instance, in the context of cross-border banking supervision and resolution, states have often refused to comply with bilateral Memorandum of Understandings whenever this involved a net welfare or financial loss.

The problem is particularly acute with regard to cross-border bank bailouts, as they require the transfer of fiscal resources from one state to another. This in turn creates a problem for the state's partner, which relied on the implementation of the agreement by the other party. Market discipline and peer pressure can sometimes obviate the fallacies of soft law, but not always. Bilateral agreements between regulators do not always bear a direct impact on private investors. If markets are indifferent to the successful implementation of an agreement, they will not have an incentive to punish the violating state. In this situation, only binding rules and a compliance mechanism can minimize frictions.

The *Right to Isolate* gives states the power and freedom to suspend the process of financial integration and limit capital mobility. Although states are free to decide whether to open their financial system and the degree of liberalization they want to achieve, they nevertheless usually retain the option to isolate their financial system in order to preserve domestic stability or protect a domestic interest. They do so through the adoption of capital controls,[40] trade restrictions, revocation of licenses of financial intermediaries, ring-fencing techniques during a banking crisis, and other macroeconomic measures that limit the degree of financial integration.

If not properly controlled, the right to isolate could give rise to *Stability Wars*. This term denotes regulatory wars between different national financial authorities in the context of a banking crisis that arise from the inability of financial authorities to coordinate on a common Pareto optimal equilibrium.

[40] For a good overview of capital controls to control capital inflows, see IMF, "Recent Experiences in Managing Capital Inflows – Cross-Cutting Themes and Possible Policy Framework," International Monetary Fund (14 February 2011).

The classical example, which I will discuss in detail in Chapter 4, is a cross-border insolvency. When a cross-border bank reaches the point of non-viability, it must be recapitalized or left insolvent. Irrespectively of the choice, a cross-border bank crisis requires the cooperation between the home authorities where the bank is headquartered and the host authorities where it has subsidiaries or branches.

In a perfect world, the home and the host would agree on a common intervention that minimizes disruption and preserves the economic value of the failing bank. However, more often than not, cooperation is prevented by the logic of financial nationalism. Both the home and the host authorities have incentives to minimize the costs associated with the resolution or the insolvency borne by the local financial system. To do so they engage in tactics – such as the refusal to share information or provide liquidity support, or the repatriation or blocking of the bank's assets – which ultimately lead to a race-to-the-bottom and a costly resolution. For instance, one of the worst fears of a host supervisor is that the home regulator might order the bank to repatriate all its assets held abroad in light of an insolvency. This would leave the host operations illiquid and local creditors empty. To prevent this, host supervisors sometimes ring-fence the assets of the bank or sell an otherwise healthy subsidiary at a below market price.

This situation is not dissimilar to what is known in international relations as pre-emptive wars. Even though war is a sub-optimal scenario compared to cooperation, a state might nonetheless decide to strike first, believing that the other is about to attack. International law can potentially play a fundamental role in addressing this problem. By setting precise rules that reduce uncertainty on the other player's move, and by punishing deviations, international law can change the payoffs associated with non-cooperation and create a system of trust. However, none of this occurs in finance. States have until now refused to agree on common rules on cross-border bank insolvency, and only rarely have they have engaged in successful cooperation with other partners in a bank resolution.

The *absence of rules on states' responsibility for the creation of global instability* is a major hole in the regulatory apparatus for international finance. In an integrated financial system in which states are interconnected, and in which domestic policies can generate negative externalities, international law should prevent states from creating cross-border financial spillovers or global systemic risks. Yet, the current international law of finance largely ignores the responsibility that comes from the participation in an integrated market. The concept of global financial instability is a very recent concept of international law that still lacks a proper theoretical understanding. The only norms that explicitly protect it are contained in the IMF Articles with reference to the concept of *Systemic Stability*. The IMF developed this idea in its 2007 Bilateral Surveillance Decision, which formulated the concept of *external stability* to define the situation where a country's balance of payment position does not and is not likely to give rise to disruptive exchange rate movements.[41] The same concept was eventually reformulated and replaced in the new IMF 2012 Integrated Surveillance Decision to broaden the scope of the domestic policies under surveillance.[42] The new Decision defines *systemic stability* as the situation in which both the balance of payment positions of the member as well as its domestic policies are stable.[43] According to IMF law, whenever one or both conditions are not present the member's policies are likely to endanger the stability of other members and, more generally, of the monetary system.

This new concept acknowledges that both sustainable and unsustainable domestic macroeconomic and financial policies have a direct effect on the stability of the international monetary system and might produce global spillovers. However, even in this case the level of protection accorded by IMF law is extremely limited. Indeed, when instability arises because of unstable domestic policies or an unstable balance of payment position, the Fund has, in principle, the possibility to intervene under its bilateral surveillance mandate and to request the member to modify its policies.[44] The reference to a stable system of exchange rate, contained in the chapeau of Article IV:1, however, narrows down the scope of protection to only those policies that indeed create *exchange rate* instability, rather than financial instability. Secondly, the level of protection to systemic stability accorded by Article IV:1 is different, depending on whether instability originates from balance of payment and

[41] Decision No. 13919-(07/51), preamble (15 June 2007) [hereinafter 2007 Surveillance Decision], in 34 *Selected Decisions and Selected Documents of The International Monetary Fund* 37 (2009); for a legal commentary on the 2007 Surveillance Decision, see Sean Hagan, "Enhancing the IMF's Regulatory Authority" (2010) 13 *Journal of International Economic Law* 955, 959–63; Claus D. Zimmermann, "Exchange Rate Misalignments and International Law" (2011) 105 *American Journal of International Law* 423, 430–7; Ross Leckow, "The IMF and Crisis Prevention – The Legal Framework for Surveillance" (2008) 17 *Kansas Journal of Law and Public Policy* 285.

[42] According to the Fund, "The concept of external stability is now being replaced with 'balance of payments stability'. . . to refer to an individual member's external accounts – not the stability of the overall system (the latter concept being covered by the term 'systemic stability'." See Executive Board Decision, Bilateral and Multilateral Surveillance (18 July 2012) [hereinafter, Integrated Surveillance Decision], p. 7.

[43] Integrated Surveillance Decision, paras 5–9.

[44] The central provision in this regard is Article IV, section I, of the IMF Articles, which disciplines the obligations of the members with regard to exchange rate policies.

exchange rate misalignments, or whether it originates from domestic policies. While the obligations dealing with exchange rate misalignment and balance of payment stability (contained in sub-sections iii and iv of Article IV:1) are, in principle, hard obligations,[45] those dealing with domestic policies (subsections i and ii), were formulated specifically as "soft" obligations. Hence, they only require members to make their best efforts to achieve certain results, and they do not provide any centralized legal mechanism able to enforce compliance.

Finally, the current formulation of external stability does not tackle those spillovers that arise from *stable* domestic policies – i.e. policies that are in principle beneficial to the domestic economy but nevertheless produce negative external spillovers. In this last situation, the 2012 Decision relegates the discussion of problems to multilateral surveillance. Consequently, the Fund will only be able to discuss the matter with the members, but without the right to advise on the appropriate policy actions and without any obligation on the member to modify its policies.[46]

In the context of sovereign debt, another problem is the excessive *power of national courts*. In sovereign debt, creditors can sue the sovereign in the court that has jurisdiction over the contract, and they can request the recognition and enforcement of the award in the jurisdiction where the sovereign holds some assets. Without a common international standard on the interpretation of sovereign debt contract – for instance the interpretation of *pari passu* clauses – national courts have the total freedom to decide how a sovereign debt contract should be interpreted based on national law. Creditors will naturally seek to locate the dispute in the jurisdiction that is more favorable to them. The issue is very similar to forum shopping in international arbitration where claimants sue the respondent in what they perceive to be the most favorable jurisdiction. The economics of forum shopping suggests that forum shopping is inefficient as it prevents claimants from internalizing the full costs of the litigation. Moreover, in the context of sovereign debt, the freedom to choose the court has the very important function to protect creditors. Yet, leaving the power to adjudicate sovereign debt disputes to national courts nonetheless creates particular problems. National courts are required to adjudicate a dispute based on their interpretation of the contract pursuant to national law, which does not offer any guidance on the peculiarities of sovereign debt. Judges might therefore offer an interpretation of the dispute that, albeit correct for a corporate dispute, does not reflect the underlying macroeconomic

[45] Whether they are hard obligations is, however, highly disputed. For an overview of the issue, see Zimmermann, above note 41, pp. 427–37.

[46] Integrated Surveillance Decision, above note, 42, p. 8.

and international implication of a sovereign debt restructuring. Moreover, when they interpret the contract, national courts are not bound to consider the external effects of sovereign debt restructuring outside to what it implies for the parties of the contract.

2.5.2. *Financial Nationalism as a Negative Externality*

Financial nationalism is a legitimate policy from a legal viewpoint. However, in an integrated financial system, this approach to financial regulation is highly inefficient. To better understand my argument, it is necessary to compare the role of domestic law in national financial systems, and the role of international law in the global financial system.

As I demonstrated in the previous chapter, in a national financial system, firms would naturally pursue only their own interests, without taking into account the implication of their actions on other banks, investors, and depositors. The achievement of financial stability is the result of the power of law. More specifically, financial stability results from a legal and institutional framework that forces financial firms to internalize the externalities of their actions and enable the state to intervene in the market. If the maintenance of financial stability requires the internalization of externalities, it logically follows that, even at the international level, the protection of global financial stability should be based on the same principle. Thus, states participating in an interconnected global financial system should be required to internalize the externalities of their actions. However, in the realm of global finance, the logic of externality has been substituted by the logic of financial nationalism.

Hence, in the current financial system, there is no international law forcing states to internalize the externalities of their actions or take into account the interests of their neighbors. Financial nationalism allows states to borrow too much, and become too-big-to-fail, thereby transferring the problems of sovereign defaults from nation states to the global community. It insulates them from any possible external influence, thus exacerbating the already careless attitude of politicians to indulge in fiscal profligacy. By protecting regulatory freedom, financial nationalism creates dangerous regulatory asymmetries. Finally, in the presence of international agreements, it allows national authorities to disregard their commitments, thereby putting the stability of their partner countries in jeopardy.

In sum, states are free to promote their own interests by framing their own domestic policies or by refusing to implement their international commitments. However, by doing so, they also transfer the social costs of their actions to the international community. The protection of financial sovereignty that was meant to guarantee a stable global financial system in the pre-crisis period exacerbated the risks of global instability. Financial regulators failed to understand that in a globalized financial system where states have the full control over their jurisdictions, self-interested domestic policies constitute an externality to partner countries, no different from what the excessive leverage of financial institutions is to domestic financial systems. In both cases, those who create instability – banks at the domestic level, or governments at the international level – fail to price correctly their participation in a common financial system. In this situation, partner countries are those who suffer most of the negative consequences of financial nationalism. Indeed, they bear the burden of protecting themselves against the external instability caused by other states, while being impotent in preventing it. The logic of financial nationalism therefore transfers the burden of dealing with global instability to the party that is in the worst position to control or prevent it. Therefore, it achieves an inefficient control of the risk. All that being said, the question now is how to address more efficiently financial instability in a situation of economic interdependence.

2.6. WHEN INTERNATIONAL LAW WORKS

Before entering into the details of financial nationalism in the next four chapters, it is necessary to keep in mind a few caveats. Financial nationalism is only one side of the coin. Since the Herstatt crisis, much progress has been made in reducing the cooperation problems in international finance. These are even more evident since the regulatory upheaval that took place after the global financial crisis. For instance, in the area of money laundering and terrorism-financing OECD members and some emerging economies have achieved substantial regulatory cooperation. The *Financial Action Task Force on Money Laundering* founded in 1989, through the issuance of Recommendations and the use of black-lists of non-cooperative countries, has managed to level the regulatory playing field on dirty money and force a number of recalcitrant jurisdictions to comply with their standards.

Moreover, since 1975, financial regulators have been increasingly engaging in regulatory cooperation efforts through so-called Transnational Regulatory Networks (TRNs). TRNs are fora where regulators periodically meet to discuss common policy problems, analyze best regulatory practices, and coordinate their supervisory efforts.[47] Among the most representative are the Basel

[47] Verdier, above note 33.

Committee on Banking Supervision (hereinafter, the Basel Committee),[48] the FSB, the International Association of Insurance Supervisors (IAIS) or the International Organization of Securities Commission (IOSCO). In less than two decades, those institutions have produced a large set of non-binding regulatory instruments, ranging from statements of principles or guidelines to more precise standards. The objective of those instruments is to encourage members to adopt what are considered the best regulatory techniques to tackle a particular regulatory problem. By doing so, best practices level the regulatory playing field for finance across the different jurisdiction members of the TRN, which are encouraged to transpose them into national legislation. How diligently regulators do so depends largely on the level of precision of those guidelines, and on the willingness of regulators to accept the standard as adequate for the national financial system. In this regard, the use of soft laws greatly enhanced the likelihood of regulatory convergence, as regulators did not feel constrained to comply with those standards if they did not feel they were suitable for their system. Moreover, the often very general nature of the standards allowed regulators to target them to the peculiarities of their financial system. Hence, over the years those instruments have permitted substantial regulatory convergence in critical areas of financial policymaking. For instance, the Basel Accords (commonly referred to as Basel I, II, and III), which since 1988 discipline the thorny issue of capital adequacy for banks as well as liquidity and market risk in the new version, are unanimously considered a pillar of any prudential regulatory system throughout the world.[49]

Finally, states' financial stability and financial regulatory frameworks are now regularly monitored by the TRNs and international financial institutions like the International Monetary Fund. Many of those TRNs have devised informal and non-adjudicatory systems to monitor the progress of their members in the adoption of the standards. For instance, the Financial Stability Board periodically issues different types of reports such as the *Report to the G20*, the *Monitoring of Priority Areas*, and the *Monitoring of Other Areas* that check the compliance of members with the standards and the problems that prevent their correct implementation. In addition, the FSB issues annual peer-reviews of each member which analyzes and discusses the regulatory situation in each country with regard to the standards issued by the FSB. Probably, the most important peer-review reports are the IMF–World Bank *Financial Sector Assessment Programme*, and the *Report on the Observance of Standards and Codes*, which provide a comprehensive review of the regulatory framework of

48 See Goodhart, above note 1.

49 Gleeson, above note 13.

each IMF–WB member. Moreover, the IMF has recently increased its work on the supervision of members with regard to cross-border instability through the bi-annual IMF Financial Stability Report.

Yet, TRNs and soft laws do not address all the problems of finance. Despite the efforts toward increased convergence, too many loopholes still ultimately reduce the benefits of a global financial market. Many critical areas of finance are not subject to international standardization, thus leaving states separated by substantial and costly regulatory asymmetries. Besides, soft laws do not address the distributive problems that are at the core of cross-border banking resolution. Moreover, the soft monitoring mechanisms of TRNs and international financial organization cannot guarantee compliance with the standard or cooperation during a crisis. Furthermore, the public international law of finance is still unable to address cooperation problems when it comes to sovereign debt.

The goal of this book is to analyze what is still missing in the quest for a better and more stable global financial system.

3

The Perils of Home-Country Control

One of the biggest barriers to global financial integration is the presence of different national regulatory and supervisory requirements. Legal and supervisory discontinuities can hinder market access as they force financial institutions wishing to operate in a foreign jurisdiction to abide by different – sometimes more complex – regulatory requirements. To overcome these difficulties, regulators have devised particular arrangements which I group under the heading of "home-country models," by virtue of which the national authority of the parent bank (the home authority) takes the leading role in regulating or supervising the financial institution in its consolidated global structure, while the foreign authorities where the bank operates through branches or subsidiaries (the host authority) takes a more subordinated role. In essence, these arrangements expand extraterritorially the supervisory or regulatory powers of the home authorities over the operations of their financial institutions in a foreign country.

Home-country models take many forms, from home-host agreements for the supervision of cross-border banks, to more complex Single Passport programs, or even Mutual Recognition Agreements (MRAs). Over the years, those international arrangements played a fundamental role in streamlining regulatory cooperation in financial services, especially when it came to banking policy. For instance, home-country control was used by European authorities in the build-up of the single market for financial services, and still remains for certain countries one of the fundamental tools of financial integration.[1]

[1] On the EU law of financial supervision and regulation, see Larisa Dragomir, *European Prudential Banking Regulation and Supervision: The Legal Dimension* (New York: Routledge, 2010); Eddy Wymeersch, Klaus J. Hopt, and Guido Ferrarini (eds.) *Financial Regulation and Supervision: A Post-Crisis Analysis* (Oxford: Oxford University Press, 2012).

The same concept also applies in the field of securities where regulators sometimes use MRAs to govern cross-border listings.[2]

The rise of home-country control in banking was not an accident. When supervisory coordination for cross-border banks started to become an issue in the late 1970s, host authorities retained most of their supervisory and regulatory powers over foreign banks operating in their jurisdiction.[3] However, while the host-country control model was safe from a stability viewpoint, it nonetheless had the weakness of inhibiting financial integration. Since the 1980s and 1990s, international financial law has switched progressively to home-country control.[4] By transferring the burden to exercise consolidated supervision only on the home country, this model streamlines supervisory operations and, more importantly, prevents the balkanization of the banking group into separate entities.[5]

In spite of its benefit for financial integration, home-country control increases the global systemic risk associated with supervisory or regulatory failures.[6] In a home-country model, the host country does not fully supervise and regulate the foreign banks in its territory, and it is partially dependent on the home country's intervention. This asymmetry of power can potentially leave the host country fully exposed to the dangers of global instability. For instance, home supervisory authorities might face internal pressures not to disclose relevant information to the host or to implement extraterritorially their supervisory mandate. Sometimes, home regulators might simply choose a regulatory framework for their banks that is not fit for the peculiarities of the host's financial system. Or they might simply be unwilling to consider the broader macroeconomic effects that their banks' international operations produce in the host's financial system. In this chapter, I will show how the logic of financial nationalism plays out in the international law of home–host relationships.

2 Pierre-Hugues Verdier, "Mutual Recognition in International Finance" (2008) 52 *Harvard International Law Journal* 55.

3 Katharina Pistor, "Host's Dilemma: Rethinking EU Banking Regulation in Light of the Global Crisis" (2010) ECGI Working Paper Series in Finance No 286/2010, available at http://papers.ssrn.com/sol3/papers.cfm?abstract_id=1631940; Avinash Persaud, "The Locus of Financial Regulation: Home versus Host" (2010) 86 *International Affairs* 637.

4 Jean Dermine, "Banking Integration and the Societas Europaea: From Host Country to Home Country Control," in Gerard Caprio Jr., Douglass D. Evanoff, and George G. Kauffman (eds.) *Cross Border Banking: Regulatory Challenges* (Singapore: World Scientific, 2006).

5 Eugenio Cerutti, Giovanni Dell'Ariccia, and Maria Soledad Martınez Peria, "How Banks Go Abroad: Branches or Subsidiaries?" (2007) 31 *Journal of Banking & Finance* 1669.

6 Robert A. Eisenbeis, "Home Country Versus Cross Border: Negative Externalities in Large Banking Organizations Failures and How to Avoid Them," in Douglas D. Evanoff, George G. Kaufman, and John R. LaBrosse (eds.) *International Financial Instability: Global Banking and National Regulations* (Singapore, World Scientific, 2007).

3.1. HOME–HOST SUPERVISORY COOPERATION IN INTERNATIONAL LAW

The Herstatt crisis in the early 1970s coincides with the beginning of the era of international banking conglomerates. Given the highly interconnected structure of a cross-border financial institution, the first problem that international financial law had to face was how to distribute and allocate regulatory and supervisory powers between the various jurisdictions where the bank operates through its affiliates.

In this regard, the operational structure of a multinational bank classically relies on a parent company located in the home country, and on the establishment of a "commercial presence" abroad in the host country. Such commercial presence usually takes one of two forms: a branch or a subsidiary. In a few words, subsidiaries are foreign banks legally incorporated in the host country. This means that subsidiaries are treated as domestic banks in terms of licensing and regulatory compliance.[7] For instance, subsidiaries must conform to local prudential requirements. Subsidiaries are, in principle, less integrated with the parent bank in terms of inter-bank capital flows and exposures, as they need to rely on local capital to perform their services. On the contrary, branches are nothing more than offices of the parent bank in a foreign territory, which are not locally incorporated and, from a financial viewpoint, rely on the parent. [8] The different legal stance does not prevent branches from conducting all of the important functions of a bank: they can lend money, receive deposits, or borrow.

In 1974 the central bank governors of the Group of Ten [hereinafter, G-10] countries decided to create the Basel Committee on Banking Supervision [hereinafter, Basel Committee]. Their plan was to enhance regulatory cooperation on critical aspects of banking policy and reduce those regulatory loopholes that were increasing the risks of crises.[9] The very first regulatory instrument issued by the Basel Committee in 1975 was the *Report on the Supervision of Bank's Foreign Establishments* [hereinafter, the 1975 Concordat],[10] setting

[7] Hal S. Scott, "Supervision of International Banking Post-BCCI" (1992) 8 *Georgia State University Law Review* 487.

[8] Scott, *ibid.*

[9] Charles Goodhart, *The Basel Committee on Banking Supervision: A History of the Early Years 1974–1997* (Cambridge: Cambridge University Press, 2011), pp. 11–39.

[10] Committee on Banking Regulations and Supervisory Practices, "Report to the Governors on the Supervision of Bank's Foreign Establishments – Concordat" BS/75/44e, Basel Committee on Banking Supervision (26 September 1975) [hereinafter, the 1975 Basel Concordat].

the foundations for the 1983 Basel Concordat.[11] The 1975 Concordat can be considered one of the most influential regulatory instruments on cross-border banking issues. The goal of this agreement was to decide under which conditions the responsibility to supervise the foreign operations of a multinational bank had to remain with the home (parent) or host authorities, and to determine how national authorities should cooperate in the supervision of a cross-border bank.

At the outset, it is important to note that the 1975 Concordat and its subsequent evolutions present two main limitations. First, they deal with the supervision of banks, which excludes from its scope other types of financial institutions such as hedge funds, broker-dealer firms, and insurance companies. Second, they only regulate supervision and information sharing. This means that banking regulation and, more importantly, crisis management and crisis resolution – which I will discuss in the next chapter – are excluded from the purview of the Basel Committee's supervisory arrangements.[12]

3.1.1. *The Beginnings: The 1975 Concordat and Host Country Dominance*

The 1975 Concordat operationalized a functional division of jurisdiction between national supervisory authorities based on the unique business structure of a multinational bank, and the regulatory issues that supervisors had to deal with. More precisely, the foreign operations of multinational banks were divided into: (1) branches, (2) subsidiaries, (3) and joint ventures. This last business form, which is somewhat closer to a subsidiary, is no longer common. Hence, the matrix is now simply divided between branches and subsidiaries. The "regulatory issues" on which supervision was coordinated were: (1) liquidity requirements, (2) solvency requirements, (3) and foreign exchange risk and position.

The 1975 Concordat did not envisage a strong role for home countries, as it does now. On the contrary, it put more emphasis on host-country control. According to the 1975 Concordat, *home* authorities had a primary supervisory role only with regard to the solvency requirements of their banks' foreign branches. Since branches rely for their operations on the capital of the parent bank, the solvency of a branch is almost indistinguishable from that of its parent. The supervision of home authorities on the *solvency* of branches

[11] The name "Concordat" was adopted only from the late 1979 onwards to indicate the various documents that were disciplining cross-border banking supervision. To avoid confusion, I will refer to the 1975 report as the 1975 Basel Concordat. See Goodhart, above note 9, p. 102.

[12] See Revised Concordat (1983), p. 1.

was therefore fundamental, as only home supervisors could access the data of the parent bank upon which the stability of the foreign branch depended. Conversely, since subsidiaries rely on local capital, they are considered more independent from the parent bank. This means that, in theory, host authorities are in the best position to monitor the subsidiaries. This does not mean, however, that subsidiaries are completely independent from the parent bank. Subsidiaries are still part of a broader banking group. For instance, most supervisory authorities believe that the parent bank has a "moral commitment" to them.[13] For this reason, in the 1975 Concordat, the solvency requirements of subsidiaries were considered to be a matter of joint supervision, with the host as the lead supervisor.

Host authorities were in control of the bulk of foreign banks' operations in their territories. Besides being the primary supervisors of foreign subsidiaries, host authorities remained in control of the liquidity requirements, foreign exchange risk, and all other requirements of branches. Since both branches and subsidiaries needed to conform to local prudential requirements concerning liquidity management, and because the level of liquidity of a bank is highly connected to domestic monetary policy practices, it was believed that it was safer to leave the supervision of these aspects to the host authorities.[14] Crucially, the division of supervision over liquidity did not – and still does not – comprise lender of last resort operations, which were left outside the scope of the Concordat. Similarly, it was considered safer to leave foreign exchange risk under the control of the host supervisors, due to the fact that such operations were highly connected to balance of payments policies (currency controls), and subject to local prudential requirements.[15]

The reason for the heavy role of the host authorities was to rebalance the burden of supervision between the home and the host authorities and to reduce the free rider problem suffered by home authorities.[16] During the negotiation of the 1975 Concordat, national representatives believed that, since branches and subsidiaries relied heavily on the parent bank and the home authorities during times of crisis, the burden to guarantee the stability of the banks' foreign operations would have been borne largely by the home central bank or

[13] As originally stated in the Concordat. See Committee on Banking Regulations and Supervisory Practices, above note 10, p. 3.

[14] Goodhart, above note 9, pp. 116–18.

[15] However, in practice the division was not so neat. Indeed, it was mostly subject to the general principle of joint cooperation between home and host authorities. See Committee on Banking Regulations and Supervisory Practices, above note 10, p. 3.

[16] Richard Dale, *The Regulation of International Banking* (Cambridge: Woodhead-Faulkner, 1984), p. 77.

by the home supervisors. This would have increased the moral hazard of host authorities, which could have free-ridden on the home's intervention.

The host-country model is extremely careful in its management of international stability. In essence, the higher the level of host-country control, the higher is the power that each country retains over its domestic stability. Indeed, it not only controls its own domestic banks, but it also controls the stability of the foreign banks operating in its territory. However, host-country control suffered from one fundamental problem: it increased the regulatory and supervisory barriers for foreign banks and, therefore, it inhibited financial integration. Indeed, in a host-country model, multinational banks needed to comply with a different set of legal requirements, which in turn reduced the incentives of global banks to enter into foreign markets.[17] Furthermore, economists argued that host-country control reduced the level of capital flows, as each foreign or domestic operation of a multinational bank was subject to local rules or policies before transferring assets from one part of the banking group to the other.[18]

3.1.2. *The Rise of Home-Country Control in Banking Supervision*

From the late 1970s and during the 1980s the landscape of global finance changed drastically. Banks established non-branch affiliates in foreign countries to take advantage of lower solvency requirements. These affiliates were *de facto* shadow banks set up to avoid the supervisory and prudential requirements of host authorities, which ignored the existence of these parts of bank groups. This situation created major problems for home supervisors, which were unable to gain information on the consolidated solvency and liquidity situations of their national banks. Furthermore, multinational banks began to avoid the ceilings on the size of loans to individual customers by granting two different loans to the same customer from the parent bank and the subsidiary.

To respond to the practice of multinational banks, G-10 supervisors began to exercise consolidated supervision over the solvency and capital adequacy requirements of their multinational banks. At the beginning, consolidated supervision by home authorities was simply the voluntary practice of each

17 See Piotr Bednarski and Grzegorz Bielicki, "Home and Host Supervisors' Relations from a Host Supervisor's Perspective," in Gerard Caprio Jr., Douglass D. Evanoff, and George G. Kauffman (eds.) *Cross Border Banking: Regulatory Challenges* (Singapore: World Scientific, 2006).

18 Stijn Claessens, "Competitive Implications of Cross-Border Banking," in Gerard Caprio Jr., Douglass D. Evanoff, and George G. Kauffman (eds.) *Cross Border Banking: Regulatory Challenges* (Singapore: World Scientific, 2006).

individual supervisor, and was not subject to any coordination. Two events, however, questioned more than anything else the wisdom of host-country control and contributed to the shift of supervisory power over cross-border banks back to the home authorities.

The first event was the Banco Ambrosiano crisis in June 1982, which led to the collapse of the Italian bank and well-publicized scandals. The crisis originated from the failure of the home supervisor – the Banca D'Italia – and the host supervisors to oversee the stability of Banco Ambrosiano's foreign establishments in Luxembourg, Nicaragua, and Peru. The core problem of Banco Ambrosiano arose from the holding company in Luxembourg, which conducted much of the shadow banking business. Its peculiar legal structure created a supervisory loophole that enabled the establishment of other foreign operations hidden from Banca D'Italia's control.

The problems evidenced by the Banco Ambrosiano crisis led the Basel Committee to formally revise its position on the proper role of home authorities and to restructure the supervisory architecture on the principle of consolidated supervision of home authorities. The changes in the international supervisory architecture on cross-border banks were enshrined in a new revised version of the 1975 Concordat issued by the Basel Committee in 1983.[19] This new version is commonly known as the 1983 Basel Concordat.[20] According to the revised document, "where a bank is the parent company of a group that contains intermediate holding companies, the *parent authority* should make sure that such holding companies and their subsidiaries are covered by adequate supervision. Alternatively, the parent authority should not allow the parent bank to operate such intermediate holding companies."[21]

The 1983 Basel Concordat provides a set of broad principles that guide banking supervisors, based on two main pillars. The first is that no foreign banking establishment shall be allowed to escape supervision, and home and host authorities share a joint responsibility over the supervision of foreign banking establishments. In order to do so, each supervisor (both the home and the host authorities) must ensure that the foreign banking establishment is adequately supervised from its perspective. The second is that each supervisor must cooperate with its foreign counterparts by sharing data and information, by allowing in-country inspections and, more generally, by removing any legal

[19] Basel Committee on Banking Supervision, "Principles for the Supervision of Bank's Foreign Establishments" (May 1983).

[20] In the original document, the BCBS explicitly states that the document is known as the Basle Concordat, using the English name. To avoid confusion, in this book I will use the French name Basel – which has been adopted in the large majority of BCBS documents.

[21] Revised Concordat (1983), para. 13–14.

restraints (especially with regard to national secrecy) that might hinder such cooperation.

The 1983 Basel Concordat stressed the need for cooperation between authorities, especially with regard to information and data sharing. In this context, the revised Concordat states that when the home authority is of the opinion that the host's supervision is not adequate, the home authority must either extend its supervisory role extraterritorially, or otherwise discourage the parent bank from operating in the host market. Similarly, whenever the host authorities fear that the supervision of the home authorities is not adequate, they shall deter the bank from operating in the host's jurisdiction. According to the principle of consolidated supervision stated in the 1983 Basel Concordat, parent banks and home supervisory authorities should monitor the risk exposure and the capital adequacy of the cross-border bank in their jurisdiction based on the totality of the bank's business, irrespective of the location and the legal form adopted. Yet, the original version of this principle did not substantially diminish the role of the host authorities, but simply required host authorities to enable home supervisors to access relevant information on the parent bank's foreign operations.[22]

The second event was the 1991 crisis of Bank of Credit and Commerce International (BCCI), at that time one of the largest banks in the world. As in Banco Ambrosiano, the BCCI crisis originated from supervisory loopholes due to the use of shadow banking operations across two continents.[23] As Charles Goodhart succinctly put it, BCCI managers used "both loopholes and weaknesses in the Concordat principle of consolidated supervision to prevent any single effective G-10 supervisor from obtaining a consolidated view of the totality of BCCI's balance sheet."[24] BCCI did so by breaking the supervisory control chain through its shadow banking operations in Luxembourg and Grand Cayman. The BCCI crisis showed the problem faced by home authorities in exercising supervision over the consolidated banking group. This was evident whenever the use of holding companies or lack of cooperation from host authorities prevented the home authorities from accessing the necessary information concerning the bank's health.[25] During the 1980s, most "host-country problems" emerged from operations in non-BCBS members, such as developing and emerging markets, which put more emphasis on

[22] George Alexander Walker, *International Banking Regulation: Law, Policy, and Practice* (London: Kluwer Law International, 2001), p. 104.

[23] See, Goodhart, above note 9, p. 107.

[24] *Ibid.*, p. 107.

[25] Pistor, above note 3.

attracting foreign capital than establishing themselves as cooperative jurisdictions These two facts increased the proclivity of banks to evade supervision by creating operations abroad.

Even in the presence of cooperation, regulators nonetheless recognized that giving too much power to host authorities would have probably exposed the bank to supervisory gaps. These could arise from asymmetries in the definition of a bank, whereby a bank was recognized by the home supervisor but not by the host. Furthermore, they could arise from asymmetries in supervisory standards, whereby home authorities would have looked at the global impact of the bank's operations, while the host would have focused more on the impact in their jurisdiction.[26] Hence, regulators became increasingly convinced of the fundamental role of home-consolidated supervision in maintaining the stability of cross-border banks. To address the regulatory problems that arose over time, in 1992 the Basel Committee issued a document stating the minimum standards that each supervisory authority had to respect when supervising multinational banks.[27]

Under the Minimum Standards, the host country essentially acted as the last line of defense against cross-border banking failure. Its role was essentially to verify that the bank's foreign operations in its territory were subject to consolidated supervision by the parent authorities, which were willing and capable of exercising adequate supervision over the banking group and implementing the minimum standards of supervision, as identified in the 1992 document. More specifically, the host country had to verify whether the home authorities consented to the parent bank's expansion and whether the parent bank was chartered in a jurisdiction that gave enough guarantees of adequate supervision and cooperation in information-sharing.[28] Whenever the host country deemed that the parent's authorities did not give enough guarantee of consolidated supervision, the host country had the discretion to prevent the bank from establishing a business in its territory or impose more stringent prudential and supervisory requirements.[29] As argued by Walker, the immediate effect triggered by these regulatory innovations was that the bulk of the responsibility of cross-border banking supervision switched to home authorities.[30]

[26] Walker, above note 22, p. 90.

[27] See Basel Committee on Banking Supervision, "Minimum Standards for the Supervision of International Banking Groups and Their Cross-Border Establishments" (July 1992) [hereinafter, Minimum Standards].

[28] *Ibid.*

[29] *Ibid.*

[30] Walker, above note 22, p. 120.

However, during the early 1990s, in spite of the Minimum Standards, home authorities experienced various problems in the exercise of their consolidated supervision.[31] Most of the problems were again the result of the unwillingness or incapability of host-country supervisors to cooperate with home authorities. For instance, home authorities had trouble obtaining the necessary information and data on the cross-border operation of the banks subject to their consolidated supervision due to bank secrecy standards in host countries. They also experienced difficulty in getting permission for on-site inspections. Furthermore, asymmetries in the criteria used by the home and the host authorities in evaluating what constituted "good supervision" further aggravated the problems of coordination between the home and the host authorities.[32]

To overcome those difficulties and the regulatory asymmetries between supervisors the Basel Committee published in 1997 the Core Principles for Effective Banking Supervision (hereinafter, the Core Principles).[33] The 1997 Core Principles contained a set of 25 principles that would clarify the most important practical aspects of supervisory coordination and cooperation. The Core Principles further strengthened and clarified the concept of home consolidated supervision, which was defined as

> . . . a group-wide approach to supervision whereby all the risks run by a banking group are taken into account, wherever they are booked. In other words, it is a process whereby a supervisor can satisfy himself about the totality of a banking group's activities, which may include non-bank companies and financial affiliates, as well as direct branches and subsidiaries.[34]

This means that the home as well as the host supervisor should explicitly approve the establishment abroad. Meanwhile, home-country authorities are entrusted with the explicit oversight of the entire consolidated balance sheet of the parent bank, including foreign branches and controlled subsidiaries. Like all other BCBS instruments, the 1997 Core Principles also underwent various revisions and amendments. Following the 2012 review, the Core Principles

[31] Goodhart, above note 9, pp. 107–9.

[32] Walker, above note 22, pp. 128–9.

[33] Basel Committee on Banking Supervision, "Core Principles for Effective Banking Supervision" (September 1997) [hereinafter, the Original Core Principles]. The Original Core Principles were revised in 2006 and 2012.

[34] This principle is now enshrined in Principle 12 of the Core Principles of Cross-Border Banking Supervision (September 2012) and states that: "An essential element of banking supervision is that the supervisor supervises the banking group on a consolidated basis, adequately monitoring and, as appropriate, applying prudential standards to all aspects of the business conducted by the banking group worldwide."

increased in number from 25 to 29. Home authorities continue to be well in command of their national banks.[35]

3.2. THE EVOLUTION OF THE HOME-COUNTRY MODEL IN EUROPE

The power of home authorities, however, was not solely concentrated in the Basel Committee's home–host supervisory arrangements. Home-country control also became a fundamental principle of financial regulation in the context of the European Single Market in financial services, where the powers of home authorities extended well beyond the simple issue of supervision.[36]

Home-country control has a long history in EU law. Indeed, the first Banking Directive of 1977 entrusted home supervisors with the responsibility for the supervision of credit institutions operating within branches in other European countries. The home-country control principle in the European Union, however, was more developed than in the context of the BCBS supervisory arrangements. Indeed, in the context of the complex EU legislation on financial services, home-country control encompassed the classical home–host supervisory responsibilities, the provision of deposit insurance to the bank's foreign customers, as well as the principle of mutual recognition of domestic financial regulations.

While international supervisors in Basel worked on international supervisory coordination, European policymakers in Brussels were confronted with the thorny problem of regulatory asymmetries, which were preventing the establishment of a truly integrated financial market. In order to reduce regulatory barriers in finance, European bureaucrats developed a new regulatory mechanism that managed to solve most of the political and regulatory problems to date: mutual recognition.[37]

From the late 1970s, the European Court of Justice started an innovative interpretation of the freedom of movement, culminating in the famous *Cassis De Dijon* judgment, whereby all restrictions imposed by the host state on

[35] The new 2012 version of the Core Principles unifies in one document the Core Principles and the Core Principle Methodology. See Basel Committee on Banking Supervision, "Core Principles for Effective Banking Supervision" (September 2012), available at http://www.bis.org/publ/bcbs230.pdf.

[36] The home-country and mutual recognition principles have an exception in NAFTA. Indeed, in NAFTA, market access is subordinated to host-country approval. See Kern Alexander, Rahul Dhumale, and John Eatwell, *Global Governance of the Financial System: The International Regulation of Systemic Risk* (Oxford: Oxford University Press, 2006).

[37] Kalypso Nicolaidis and Gregory Shaffer, "Transnational Mutual Recognition Regimes: Governance without Global Government" (2005) 68 *Law and Contemporary Problems* 263.

cross-border trade were considered unlawful.[38] In order to enhance economic integration, European regulators had to find a legal mechanism that would have ensured the highest level of liberalization with the minimal amount of political effort. When capital movements were liberalized in the 1980s, the European Commission adopted a series of Directives – including the second Banking Directive, the Investment Services Directive, the Public Offers Directive, and amendments to the Listing Particulars Directive – that explicitly imposed the obligation to recognize and accept other members' national laws as sufficient.

Mutual recognition had an immediate appeal for European bureaucrats because it offered a way to achieve meaningful economic integration without the need to remove regulatory barriers or to change national legislation. In its simplest formulation, an MRA between two countries – the home (exporting) country and the host (importing) country – enables the home country's firms to access the host territory and to offer their products or services without the need to comply with the host country's laws. The host country recognizes the home country's regulations as adequate, and it allows foreign firms to access its market based only on the home country's regulation. Thus, banks operating in a foreign jurisdiction were subject only to the rules and the supervision of their parent's financial authorities. In the words of Shaffer and Nicolaidis, mutual recognition regimes operationalized a mutualized extraterritoriality of home-country laws.[39] Host countries, on the contrary, gave up their regulatory sovereignty over the foreign firms hosted in their territory.

The role of home countries was further enhanced in the early 1990s. At that time, the achievement of financial integration became the top priority of EU policy. In 1992 the Commission launched the *Single Passport* program, which enabled banks and other financial institutions to provide services across Europe without any limitations. According to the Single European Passport, all financial firms located in one European country were able to access and provide services in other European countries without duplicative supervisory or regulatory requirements. The home supervisors were the consolidated supervisors, and home regulations were considered as equivalent to host-country regulations. To reduce the risk of regulatory races to the bottom the European Commission imposed only a minimum level of harmonization

[38] Joseph H. H. Weiler, "Mutual Recognition, Functional Equivalence and Harmonization in the Evolution of the European Common Market and the WTO," in Fiorella Kostoris and Padoa Schioppa (eds.) *The Principle of Mutual Recognition in the European Integration Process* (London: Palgrave Macmillan, 2005).

[39] Nicolaidis and Shaffer, above note 37, p. 268.

for essential financial regulations, while the host-country authorities retained the right to impose further requirements on the foreign financial institutions.[40]

The Single Passport program was extremely successful in promoting banking integration across Europe. Indeed, the simple registration of a credit institution in one member country automatically allowed it to provide services in other member states through branches without the need for prior approval from the host state.[41] One fundamental aspect of the machinery for financial governance in the EU was the extension of the home-country's control to deposit insurance. According to the Deposit Guarantee Schemes Directive of 1994,[42] which partially harmonized deposit insurance schemes throughout Europe, in the event of a bank failure the home state is obliged to guarantee depositor compensation to the customers of the bank it has authorized, including to its branches' customers. The host country is however free to top up the coverage of the insurance if the one provided by the home country is less generous than that applied in its jurisdiction. The question of home-country control in deposit insurance is particularly important for the question of global systemic risk, and it gave rise to an international dispute between the EFTA Surveillance Authority and Iceland that I will examine in the next section.

The principle of home-country control remained largely operative until the European sovereign debt crisis, especially in the context of supervision and deposit insurance, after which the Single Supervisory Mechanism superseded it – at least for Eurozone countries. The use of mutual recognition in financial regulation, on the other hand, softened over the years.[43] Indeed, regulators considered mutual recognition inadequate for enhancing the integration of capital and insurance markets, in which national host requirements were still widely used.[44] For this reason, in 1999 the European Commission launched an ambitious program, the Financial Services Action Plan – supplemented two years later by the guidelines of the Lamfalussy Committee – that replaced

[40] Verdier, above note 2, p. 72.

[41] Dragomir, above note 1, pp. 165–81.

[42] Directive 94/19/EC of the European Parliament and of the Council of 30 May 1994 on deposit-guarantee schemes. Published in Official Journal L 135, 31/05/1994 P. 0005 – 0014 [hereinafter, Deposit Guarantee Schemes Directive 94/19/EC].

[43] For a good historical overview, see Matteo Ortino, "The Role and Functioning of Mutual Recognition in the European Market of Financial Services" (2007) 56 *The International and Comparative Law Quarterly* 309.

[44] See Niamh Moloney, "New Frontiers in EC Capital Markets Law: From Market Construction to Market Regulation" (2003) 40 *Common Market Law Review* 809–11; Andrea M. Corcoran and Terry L. Hart, "The Regulation of Cross-Border Financial Services in the EU Internal Market" (2002) 8 *Columbia Journal of European Law* 221, pp. 242–43, 264–5.

mutual recognition with a more centralized and harmonized regulatory framework.[45]

3.3. HOME-COUNTRY MODEL AND FINANCIAL INTEGRATION

With the only exception of the North American Free Trade Agreement, home-country control went on to dominate a great part of the supervisory system for cross-border banking.[46] It also influenced financial regulation albeit to a limited extent, as the large majority of regulatory cooperation took place through regulatory harmonization. At present, its influence has somehow diminished. Among Eurozone countries, home-country control was replaced in 2014 by the Single Supervisory Mechanism, and remains valid only for deposit insurance.[47] At the international level, Supervisory Colleges now complement home–host agreements in the supervision of cross-border banks. Supervisory Colleges ensure that, where the bank operates, all supervisors meet at least once per year to discuss the problems faced by the bank and its vulnerabilities.[48] Having said that, Supervisory Colleges are far from replacing home-country control and challenging the position of prominence of home authorities. Indeed, outside the European Union (where colleges among EU banks have important decision-making roles subject to the European Banking Authority's mandatory guidelines), Supervisory Colleges do not entail a binding cooperative decision-making mechanism. This means that home authorities still retain the highest degree of control over the consolidated bank's balance sheet and are not legally required to receive the approval of the host supervisors before making a decision. In practical terms, as I will discuss in the next chapter, it is unlikely that during a crisis supervisory colleges would be able to resolve the information asymmetry problems and conflict of interests between national authorities.

A question therefore arises as to why home-country models acquired this prominent position in cross-border bank relations. The answer can be found

[45] The Committee of Wise Men, "Final Report of the Committee of Wise Men on the Regulation of European Securities Markets" (15 February 2001), available at http://ec.europa.eu/internal_market/securities/docs/lamfalussy/wisemen/final-report-wise-men_en.pdf, p. 10.

[46] See Alexander, Dhumale, and Eatwell, above note 36, pp. 126–7.

[47] Veilis Ferran and Valia S.G. Babis, "The European Single Supervisory Mechanism" (2013) 13 *Journal of Corporate Law Studies* 255; Christos Gortsos, "Competence Sharing Between the ECB and the National Competent Supervisory Authorities within the Single Supervisory Mechanism (SSM)" (2015) 16 *European Business Organization Law Review* 401.

[48] Basel Committee on Banking Supervision, Principles for Effective Supervisory Colleges (June 2014); Duncan Alford, "Supervisory Colleges: The Global Financial Crisis and Improving International Supervisory Coordination" (2010) 24 *Emory International Law Review* 57.

in the powerful role of those regulatory strategies in promoting easy market integration. In spite of their differences, both home–host supervisory arrangements and MRAs are based on a very similar template, which envisages a predominant role for home authorities. In the classical home–host supervisory arrangement the state, where the multinational financial institution is headquartered, becomes the dominant authority that is in charge of monitoring the stability of the bank in all of its foreign operations, except for its subsidiaries. In the context of mutual recognition, the country where the financial institution is licensed applies its rules extraterritorially in all countries where the institution operates. The ultimate result is that, in both models, banks or investors can operate internationally without lengthy regulatory approvals from the host country and without costly duplicative regulatory or supervisory requirements.

In the area of cross-border banking supervision, financial authorities wishing to open their jurisdiction to foreign financial institutions have two choices. On the one hand, they can opt for a light level of financial integration in which market entry for foreign financial firms is permitted only through subsidiaries. This technique is called "subsidiarization," and has been adopted in a few jurisdictions, such as New Zealand and Mexico.[49] Since the BCBS rules grant the host authority primary control over the foreign subsidiaries in its jurisdiction, the host country retains full control over its domestic financial stability. However, by doing so, the host country also reduces the level of penetration of foreign banks in its territory. As explained before, subsidiaries are usually considered more expensive as they generally rely more on the host market's credit. In light of these findings, the economic literature sometimes associates subsidiarization with financial protectionism and a low level of financial development,[50] because multinational banks cannot raise the capital where it is cheaper and offer it where it is most profitable.

On the other hand, a state can opt for a more open approach by allowing market penetration through branches. Various economists have argued that home-country control provides many benefits to the host economy in terms of financial integration and financial stability. First of all, unlike subsidiaries, the capital and liquidity of the branch is a function of the bank's

[49] Kathia D'Ulster, "Cross Border Banking Supervision Incentive Conflicts in Supervisory Information Sharing between Home and Host Supervisors" (2011) World Bank Policy Research Working Paper 5871, The World Bank, available at http://elibrary.worldbank.org/doi/pdf/10.1596/1813-9450-5871, pp. 24–5.

[50] Claessens, above note 18; Cerutti, et al., above note 5.

worldwide capital.[51] Hence, the loan capacity of branches is much higher, which ultimately renders them more competitive than subsidiaries. Secondly, since branches are primarily subject to home-country supervisory control, the home-country model does not create jurisdictional discontinuities, and therefore does not inhibit financial integration. As long as they choose to enter a market through branches, multinational banks do not need to comply with different national regulatory and supervisory standards. Furthermore, since the home-country model grants to the home state the power to look after the stability of the whole bank, it transfers the burden of controlling and monitoring financial stability to the party that is in the best position to do so. Indeed, the home-country supervisor is in the best position to gather the data about the bank in its consolidated structure and, in the case of trouble, is in the best position to intervene with regard to the management of the bank. The home authorities' supervision of the parent bank's foreign branches reduces substantially the funding costs of banks and, therefore, explains why for a long time this was the preferred model of internationalization of bank groups. It also explains why the European Commission embedded this strategy into the Single Passport to spur financial integration across Europe.

Furthermore, from a purely political economy viewpoint, mutual recognition regimes help mobilize export interests that usually do not have a loud voice in financial policymaking, thereby increasing the proclivity of national authorities to support financial integration.[52] As I will explain in detail in the last part of the book, in the absence of international agreements on financial liberalization, national regulators are likely to be subject to high levels of pressure exerted by domestic financial firms, which will try to reduce the level of penetration of foreign firms in order to prevent competition. In this context, domestic exporting firms do not have a loud voice because they cannot rely on their parent authorities to convince foreign authorities to reduce their regulatory barriers. However, as soon as financial liberalization agreements – of which mutual recognition is an example – are put in place, multinational firms will finally have an institutional channel to promote their business expansion. National financial authorities will be more incentivized to sign MRAs with foreign regulators to enhance the export competitiveness of their domestic firms, which in turn will require a corresponding reduction in domestic regulatory barriers.

51 For a good overview of the pros and cons of branches and subsidiaries, see Jonathan Fiechter, İnci Ötker-Robe, Anna Ilyina, Michael Hsu, André Santos, and Jay Surti, "Subsidiaries or Branches: Does One Size Fit All?" IMF Staff Discussion Note SDN/11/04, International Monetary Fund (2011).

52 Verdier, above note 2.

3.4. THE LOGIC OF FINANCIAL NATIONALISM IN HOME-COUNTRY FAILURES

The rise of home-country control was, in part, a reaction to the threat of regulatory and supervisory failures in the host country as well as the result of a specific strategy to promote the expansion of global financial conglomerates. However, with the benefit of financial integration came also the risks of financial instability arising from the regulatory failures of home authorities.[53]

In the home-country model, host authorities retain only a peripheral role as guardians of their domestic stability. This role is essentially limited to the regulation and supervision of subsidiaries. For the rest, home authorities are essentially dependent on the stability of their multinational banks. They decide the regulatory framework to which their parent bank and its branches will be subject. They monitor compliance with the rules, and they decide when the financial institution is illiquid or insolvent. Moreover, they are in control of all the micro- and macro-prudential variables that indirectly influence the level of liquidity and solvency of the bank in its consolidated structure. Finally, in the context of EU law, home-country control also envisages the critical aspect of deposit insurance, which subjects the depositors of home banks' foreign branches to the depositor protection schemes of the home country. Since the home-country model transfers the whole management of financial stability to one country only, the inability or unwillingness of the home-country authorities to carry out their supervisory mandates, or their failure to consider the impact of domestic macro-financial policies on the level of liquidity in the host country, can easily endanger the host country's stability.[54] In the event of a crisis, host regulators are virtually powerless, and they will regain full control over their banking system only when it is too late.

The problems of home-country control are not the result of economic inefficiencies, but rather the result of the inefficiency of the law in understanding the dynamics of the home-country model and taking into account the principal–agent relationship at the core of supervisors' behavior. Given the pivotal role of home states in protecting financial stability, one would have expected the creation of legal mechanisms to force home states to abide by their obligations. However, the allocation of power to home states was often not accompanied by any mechanisms of compliance, especially in home–host

[53] On the dangers of home-country control, see Pistor, above note 3; Persaud, above note 3; Guillermo Ortiz, "Cross-Border Banking and the Challenges Faced by Host Country Authorities," in Gerard Caprio Jr., Douglass D. Evanoff, and George G. Kauffman (eds.) *Cross Border Banking: Regulatory Challenges* (Singapore: World Scientific, 2006).

[54] Pistor, *ibid.*

supervisory agreements. Moreover, both mutual recognition and home–host arrangements do not adequately take into account the possibility of regulatory failures in home states. In essence, they give the home country a blank check to manage the stability of its international banks, while asking the host country to simply have faith in its success.

3.4.1. *Principal–Agent Problems*

The principal–agent model can shed some light on the problems of cooperation in home–host relationships. One of the biggest problems of home-country control is the lack of incentives for home authorities to consider the macro-prudential implications of cross-border banking in the host countries. Macro-prudential policies are one of the core competences of bank supervisors; they look at the macroeconomic impact of banking practices, such as increasing inflation, surging house prices, or excessive indebtedness, which are not normally considered in prudential regulation frameworks. Examples of macro-prudential tools include loan-to-value ratios, debt-to-income ratios, or countercyclical capital buffers.[55] In a classical cross-border bank establishment in which the parent operates abroad through branches, all the loans originated by the foreign branches rely on the capital raised by the parent bank, which is then channeled to the branches abroad. If the economic conditions in the host country are positive, local customers will naturally tend to invest in real estate and business projects. If the market is particularly good, as during boom times, banks will naturally tend to go along with their customers and increase their lending. History tells that it is precisely the cyclical nature of lending that might lead to an investment bubble. Since branches do the lending, host authorities have only limited control on the operation of the bank and cannot control this excessive credit creation. If the bank operates abroad through subsidiaries, the host authorities might use their powers and intervene on the foreign bank by limiting lending. However, experience suggests that the parent bank would easily circumvent the requirements by lending across borders directly from the parent bank.

Given the difficulty for host supervisors to tackle the macro-prudential effects of cross-border lending, the burden would naturally shift to the home supervisors. In a domestic environment, supervisory authorities would naturally intervene by imposing measures to reduce the lending boom, such as

[55] See Stijn Claessens, Douglass D. Evanoff, George G. Kaufman, and Laura E. Krodes (eds.) *Macroprudential Regulatory Policies: The New Road to Financial Stability?* (Singapore: World Scientific, 2012).

countercyclical capital buffers. However, since the effects of the lending are not felt in the home country, there is no interest for the home authority to limit the investment opportunities of their banks by imposing a *de facto* tax on their foreign business. Problems for the host country would also continue if the macroeconomic conditions in the home countries deteriorate. In this case, the parent bank will contract its cross-border lending and concentrate it in the home country. This sudden stop will cause serious economic contraction in the host country, as it will reduce the overall level of liquidity in the market. In this situation, the host authorities will again be impotent, as they do not have a direct control on the parent bank's decisions. The problem is particularly acute in those countries where foreign banks occupy a large share of the market.

The experience with the Eastern European states upon their accession to the European Union in the early 2000s is particularly revealing in this regard. When the former Soviet bloc republics entered the European Union, they were literally "invaded" by western banks, which went to occupy a very large share of the local financial markets, from 36% in Slovenia up to 98% in Estonia. According to studies, the pace of credit growth almost tripled in many of those states, going from 17% to 64%, with an annual growth rate of 30%.[56] When the host regulators tried to slow the pace of credit growth by imposing caps on the lending of foreign subsidiaries, banks started lending directly from the parent banks abroad. As soon as the global financial crisis arrived in Europe, those banks retrenched their lending operation back home, leaving the host markets exposed to sudden stops and massive capital outflows, which eventually required the intervention of the International Monetary Fund (IMF).[57]

Another classical principal–agent problem in home–host relations is the unwillingness of supervisors to actually comply with their soft obligations enshrined in home–host agreements. According to the regulatory framework set by the Basel Concordat and sometimes also by bilateral Memoranda of Understanding [hereinafter, MoU] on supervisory cooperation,[58] home and

[56] Charles Enoch, "Credit Growth in Central and Eastern Europe," in Charles Enoch and Inci Ötker-Robe (eds.) *The Causes and Nature of the Rapid Growth of Bank Credit in the Central, Eastern and South-Eastern European Countries* (Austria: Österreichische Nationalbank, 2007); Peter Backe et al., "Credit Growth in Central and Eastern Europe Revisited," in Charles Enoch and Inci Ötker-Robe (eds.) *The Causes and Nature of the Rapid Growth of Bank Credit in the Central, Eastern and South-Eastern European Countries* (Austria: Österreichische Nationalbank, 2007).

[57] Katharina Pistor, "Governing Interdependent Financial Systems: Lessons from the Vienna Initiative" (2011) 2 *Journal of Globalization and Development* 4.

[58] In Europe, the weaknesses of home-country control model with regard to the absence of coordination mechanism on crisis resolution were reduced by the signing of three non-binding Memoranda of Understanding (MoUs) in 2002, 2005, and 2008, respectively, which disciplined

host supervisory authorities must share information on the stability of the cross-border bank and, sometimes, coordinate their interventions. As I will discuss later in the book, those agreements are not actually binding, but nonetheless give a very serious expectation that they will be actually implemented. However, experiences in cross-border supervision have showed that, in various circumstances, states do not abide by their commitments.[59] In the economic literature, there are various demonstrations of the asymmetry of incentives that regulators suffer in the context of home–host supervisory arrangements, and their consequent negative impacts on global stability.[60] The ultimate reason is, again, the protection of domestic interests.[61]

The **home supervisor** is likely to be reluctant to share bad news with other supervisory authorities when it fears that the leakage of bad news could precipitate a liquidity crisis. For instance, when the health of the parent bank deteriorates, the home supervisors will have no incentive to communicate to the host supervisors the real condition of the parent bank. Hence, the home supervisor will forbear or minimize the problems. A good example in this regard is the behavior of Icelandic supervisory authorities during the recent financial crisis. Since the late 1990s the Icelandic national banks had opened branches in England, the Netherlands, and northern Europe, where they collected most of their deposits. When the Icelandic economy was on the verge of collapse, in spite of the serious problems faced by the Icelandic financial system, national supervisors did not communicate the status of their banking sector to the host authorities until it was too late, thus leaving the host authorities powerless in

---

cooperation between the treasuries and financial authorities of European countries. See Federico Lupo-Pasini, "Economic Stability and Economic Governance in The Euro Area: What the European Crisis Can Teach on the Limits of Economic Integration" (2013) 16 *Journal of International Economic Law* 211.

59 Similar events happened in other countries before, such as in Argentina, during the South East Asian crisis, as well as in various developing countries. Rosengren argues that during the Argentine crisis of 2000, well-capitalized parents decided to abandon branches and subsidiaries when the financial difficulties became acute. Eric Rosengren, "An Overview of Cross-Border Bank Policy Issues," in Gerard Caprio Jr., Douglass D. Evanoff, and George G. Kauffman (eds.) *Cross Border Banking: Regulatory Challenges* (Singapore: World Scientific, 2006), p. 468.

60 D'Ulster, above note 49; Martin Schüler, "Incentives Problems in Banking Supervision: The European Case" ZEW Discussion Paper No. 03-62 (2003), available at ftp://ftp.zew.de/pub/zew-docs/dp/dp0362.pdf, p. 11.

61 Stijn Claessens, Richard Herring, Dirk Schoenmaker, and Kimberly Summe, "A Safer World Financial System: Improving the Resolution of Systemic Institutions" Geneva Reports on the World Economy 12, International Center for Monetary and Banking Studies and Centre for Economic Policy Research (2011), available at http://personal.vu.nl/d.schoenmaker/Geneva12.pdf, pp. 27–41.

dealing with the crisis.[62] Similarly, the home supervisor is unlikely to cooperate with the host when it feels that the other supervisory authority might act unilaterally to constrain the home supervisor's discretion in dealing with the problem. Thus, the home supervisor will use its discretion to forbear so long as there is a possibility that the bank's condition may be self-correcting, particularly if the alternative is closure. Richard Herring reports an example of the reluctance of supervisory authorities to share bad news with their counterparts. A trader in the New York office of Daiwa Bank – a Japanese conglomerate – had lost around US$ 1.2 billion over a series of unauthorized transactions from 1985 to 1996. When the Japanese home authorities learnt of the massive loss, they avoided sharing the information with the US authorities for over two months, presumably for the fear that the American would have imposed more stringent requirements on the Japanese bank.[63] Sometimes, supervisors will forbear information until losses are so large that there can be no reasonable doubt that the institution is insolvent. Meanwhile the home supervisors will try to convince the parent bank to repatriate most of the available assets that are in foreign jurisdictions.[64] This was the case with the Lehman Brothers' collapse, which we will discuss in the next chapter. Conversely, **the host regulators** will be reluctant to share data with the home regulators on the worsening conditions of the host subsidiary, in the fear that this might incite the parent company to withdraw funds.

3.4.2. *The Lack of Accountability*

As pointed out by Nicolaidis and Shaffer, in an efficient home-country control regime "the home state must consider the 'consumption' of its rules by consumers and citizens outside its borders."[65] However, this does not happen in reality. In the absence of effective compliance mechanisms, the home country does not have any incentive to internalize the externalities that its domestic policies produce on partner countries. The unwillingness of national

[62] Franklin Allen, Thorsten Beck, Elena Carletti, Philip R. Lane, Dirk Schoenmaker, and Wolf Wagner, *Cross-Border Banking in Europe: Implications for Financial Stability and Macroeconomic Policies* (London: Center for Economic Policy Research, 2011), p. 43.

[63] Richard Herring, "Conflicts between Home & Host Country Prudential Supervisors" (2007) Financial Institution Center, Wharton School, University of Pennsylvania Working Paper, p. 10.

[64] The Vicker Report explicitly proposed to return to the ring-fencing of capital and assets, or mechanisms to achieve this, such as requiring international branches to become nationally regulated subsidiaries. The Independent Commission on Banking, "Final Report Recommendations" September 2011 (commonly referred to as the *Vickers Report*), available at www.parliament.uk/briefing-papers/sn06171.pdf; see also, Persaud, above note 3.

[65] Nicolaidis and Shaffer, above note 37, p. 299.

supervisors to collaborate with their counterparts is certainly due to the principal–agent problem. However, beneath the principal–agent relationship there is an even more fundamental problem of accountability that international law has failed to address.

Home-country models imply a horizontal transfer of sovereignty from the host to the home state, in which the home country takes it all, and the host is essentially passive. Host regulators lose control over parts of their financial system, and they cannot control the global systemic risk brought by foreign financial institutions, as those firms are regulated and supervised by foreign authorities. In essence, home-country control can act as a potential Trojan horse for the host country, which is left at the mercy of the home-country authorities' decisions. Since home-country models do not aim at legal or policy convergence, they are unable to create a level playing field between national financial authorities.[66] On the contrary, home-country control promotes a lawful asymmetry of powers that, if not properly controlled, could extend the dangerous effects of regulatory or supervisory laxity in one country toward its partners. For instance, a strong centralized institution or the host country could verify that the home country maintains in place a strong and stable regulatory framework. The host state might conduct a regulatory impact assessment of the home state's laws or its policy goals before entering into the agreements. However, it would be impossible for the host state to insure itself from the risk of regulatory failures in the home country, especially with regard to cross-border activities.[67]

The dangers of home-country control are compounded by the lack of accountability of home authorities. Home-country models promote an asymmetry of monitoring power between the home country's citizens and the host country's citizens. The home-country's citizens can directly influence home regulators and push them to only protect their own interests. The host-country's citizens, on the contrary, do not have any oversight power over home regulators, even though they are affected by home-authorities' rules and supervision.[68] Indeed, they cannot vote and they cannot lobby to have their interests protected. Since host country's constituents lose part of their democratic power, the role of accountability as a mechanism to diminish systemic risk is clearly reduced. As Schmidt succinctly summarized, "(in a home-country model) the previous unity of territory, legitimation and the setting of rules is

[66] Chris Brummer, *Soft Law and the Global Financial System: Rule Making in the 21st Century* (New York: Cambridge University Press, 2012), p. 56.

[67] Verdier, above note 2.

[68] On the question of accountability, see Nicolaidis and Shaffer, above note 37, pp. 299–300.

broken up. Governments have to trust other member states to regulate and control their companies sufficiently."[69] However, as the principal–agent model of finance clearly explains, home authorities will not do so.

The absence of principals' oversight increases the moral hazard of home authorities, especially in the context of home–host arrangements. The discrepancies between the home and host countries' responsibilities create a double risk. On the one hand, since the home-country consolidated supervisor is not democratically accountable to the host country's taxpayers, the home supervisor does not have any incentive to use the home taxpayers' money or to release important information to ensure the stability of the foreign branches of its parent bank. On the other hand, the host country's supervisors are either in a position where it is impossible for them to supervise the foreign branches, or in the case of a subsidiary, they might not be in the perfect position to assess the stability of the consolidated entity, as a result of not having access to important information.[70]

3.5. THE *Icesave* DISPUTE[71]

A recent case – commonly referred to as the *Icesave* dispute – brought against Iceland by the European Free Trade Association Surveillance Authority (EFTA Surveillance Authority) undoubtedly represents a case in point when it comes to the dangers of home-country control.

The *Icesave* dispute concerned the refusal of the Icelandic government to cover foreign depositors under the deposit insurance scheme of the Icelandic bank Landsbanki in the Netherlands and United Kingdom.[72] Iceland is not part of the European Union. However, being an EFTA member,[73] Iceland

[69] Susanne K. Schmidt, "Mutual Recognition as a New Mode of Governance" (2007) 14 *Journal of European Public Policy* 667, p. 673.

[70] Gillian G.H. Garcia and Maria Nieto, "Banking Crisis Management in the European Union: Multiple Regulators and Resolution Authorities" (2006) 6 *Journal of Banking Regulation* 206, p. 218.

[71] Case E-16/11, *EFTA Surveillance Authority* v. *Iceland*, 2011, EFTA Court, 28 January 2013.

[72] For a good analysis of the case, see M. Elvira Méndez-Pinedo, "The Icesave Saga: Iceland Wins Battle before the EFTA Court" (2013) 1 *Michigan Journal of International Law Emerging Scholarship Project* 101, available at http://www.mjilonline.org/wordpress/wp-content/uploads/2013/07/MendezPinedo.pdf; M. Elvira Mendez-Pinedo, "Iceland and the EU: Bitter Lessons after the Bank Collapse and the Icesave Dispute" (2011) 3 *Contemporary Legal and Economic Issues* 9.

[73] The European Free Trade Association is an international organization formed by four states – Iceland, Switzerland, Norway, and Liechtenstein – to promote free trade among its members. Three EFTA countries – Iceland, Norway and Liechtenstein – formalized their participation with the European Single Market in 1994 by the signing of the European Economic Area

is also part of the European Economic Area – an economic market between EU and EFTA members that entitles EFTA countries to participate in the EU Single Market. One of the conditions for such participation is the adoption of almost all EU legislation related to the Single Market. As mentioned before, one of the peculiarities of the home-country control model in the EU is its extension to deposit insurance schemes. Thus, according to EU law, home states have the primary responsibility to supervise home banks' foreign branches and to protect local depositors, even if located in another country.[74] In the context of EU law, this responsibility entails, among others, the duty of each member state to set up a national deposit insurance fund able to cover national and foreign depositors of their national banks.

In 2007, the economy of Iceland experienced one of the worst and most abrupt economic crises in recent history. In the previous decade the local financial sector had experienced a period of boom. The national financial system grew in size to ten times the GDP of the country, while local banks began to expand their operations across borders. Based on the EU Passport Directive, local banks could automatically enter other EU markets without the need for prior approval from the local authorities. Various Icelandic banks therefore established branches abroad where they offered saving accounts to local customers. The most active among the local banks was undoubtedly Landsbanki, which operated various types of deposit accounts in England and the Netherlands. At the height of its operations, the bank had around 425,000 foreign depositors, with total deposits of 6.7 billion Euro.[75] *Icesave* was the brand name used by Landsbanki to promote their saving account. When the bubble burst, however, in a matter of days the entire financial system was completely wiped out, thereby bringing the economy of Iceland to its knees. When the three systemically important Icelandic banks went bankrupt at the outset of the 2007 crisis their operations abroad filed suit, thereby leaving the local foreign depositors fully exposed.

According to EU law, the home state – Iceland – would be in this circumstance expected to use the deposit insurance fund to cover the depositors of its home banks' national operations and foreign branches. Since the Icelandic supervisor was the consolidated supervisor for the consolidated cross-border

Agreement. Switzerland achieved the same result by signing a set of bilateral agreements with the EU.

[74] Directive 94/19/EC of the European Parliament and of the Council of 30 May 1994 on deposit-guarantee schemes, OJ 1994 L 135.

[75] "Iceland Reaches Accord Depositors with UK and Netherland," Bloomberg online, available at: www.bloomberg.com/apps/news?pid=newsarchive&sid=aijgJy15_hJI (accessed on 30 May 2014).

bank, it was the only entity able to monitor and supervise the stability of the bank in all of its operations. Furthermore, since Landsbanki's foreign operations were in the form of branches, the host supervisors in the United Kingdom and the Netherlands had serious difficulties in accessing the consolidated data of the foreign bank. However, just one day before declaring the insolvency of Landsbanki on 6 October 2008, the Icelandic government passed a law in which it guaranteed that in the event of a bank insolvency the deposit insurance fund would have covered only local Icelandic depositors but not foreign ones. Landsbanki was then split up into a bad bank – with around 10 billion Euros in liabilities – that owned the foreign operations in the UK and the Netherlands, and a fully solvent bank owned by the government to which all the remaining assets and the local deposits were transferred. Despite the requests by the UK and Dutch governments, Iceland refused to back up the national deposit insurance fund, thereby forcing host country authorities in the UK and the Netherlands to intervene at the last minute to protect their local customers and, more generally, to maintain stability in their territories.

The behavior of the Icelandic authorities is fully in line with the principal–agent model discussed before; home authorities are always reluctant to use national funds to cover foreign depositors.[76] Domestic regulators are primarily responsible to their own depositors, and are concerned about financial stability only when a problem in the host country might negatively affect the home country's economy. Since deposit insurance relies on the fiscal backstop of the treasury, home authorities will face tremendous criticism for not intervening when they are expected to do so.[77] The refusal to cover foreign depositors seems to contravene the EU legislation on deposit insurance protection. For this reason, both the UK and the Netherlands – immediately followed by the EFTA Surveillance Authority and the EU Commission – launched a dispute against Iceland based on the applicable EU law.

The major point of contention for the Court was whether Iceland had to step in to protect the totality of its home banks' customers, by backing up the national deposit insurance fund. This was the claim of the EFTA Surveillance Authority and the EU Commission. Iceland, on the contrary, argued that the home-country principle worked only during normal times. Since Iceland was experiencing a systemic crisis, the EU regulations on deposit insurance would

[76] See Michael Krimminger, "Banking in a Changing World: Issues and Questions in the Resolution of Cross-Border Banks," in Gerard Caprio Jr., Douglass D. Evanoff, and George G. Kauffman (eds.) *Cross Border Banking: Regulatory Challenges* (Singapore: World Scientific, 2006), p. 273.

[77] *Ibid.*, pp. 201–22.

not apply, and Iceland considered itself free to discriminate between national and foreign depositors in order to safeguard its domestic stability. To sustain its position, Iceland argued that its national deposit insurance fund did not have enough capacity to cover all of the deposits of the home banks abroad. To protect its foreign depositors Iceland would have been forced to use its fiscal resources, thereby risking a Spain-like sovereign default. Truth be told, both the UK and Dutch governments offered a total of 4 billion Euro repayment loans to Iceland to cover the costs of the deposits, but these offers were refused by Iceland.

In light of the systemic risk implications of sovereign–bank linkages highlighted by Iceland's behavior, the real legal question of the dispute was to what extent the protection of national interests would excuse the creation of instability in host countries. The Court took Iceland's view. The economic logic of the decision was inescapable if analyzed from Iceland's perspective. The Spanish and Irish quasi-default due to the bailout of their financial sectors during the European crisis demonstrates that the extensive use of fiscal backstops to maintain the stability of the banking sector might easily expose states to sovereign defaults. However, from a global stability perspective, the decision has left a lot to be desired. A few questions in particular deserve an answer.

The first is whether a state should have the duty to take into account the external effects of its policies when it participates in an integrated financial area. Iceland was sharing a common financial market with other EEA countries. By virtue of the Single Passport program, which provides mutual recognition of financial laws across the EEA,[78] Icelandic banks were automatically allowed to invest and offer services in other jurisdictions. Given the interconnectedness between its economy and partner countries due to the full removal of regulatory barriers for finance, Iceland should have taken into account the external effects that its domestic stability policies would have produced in partner countries. However, it did not do so. It promoted over the years a process of financial deregulation and it adopted risky macroeconomic policies. When the crisis erupted the entire Icelandic banking sector became insolvent – including the deposit insurance fund and the Icelandic banks' foreign operation abroad. Iceland transmitted global instability but it refused to intervene or even to accept the loans from the United Kingdom

[78] Paulina Dejmek, "The EU Internal Market for Financial Services: A Look at the First Regulatory Responses to the Financial Crisis and a View to the Future" (2009) 15 *Columbia Journal of European Law* 455, p. 460; Gerard Hertig, "Imperfect Mutual Recognition for EC Financial Services" (1994) 14 *International Review of Law and Economics* 177, at 180; Verdier, above note 2, pp. 71–82.

and the Netherlands, which would have enabled Iceland to implement its obligations under EU law. The right of market access – represented here by the Single Passport program – necessarily implies the obligation upon the exporting countries to internalize the costs of their domestic policies. Without this obligation, the law inevitably encourages moral hazard. The obligation contained in EU law to cover foreign depositors is a necessary element of the broader governance of European finance. Consequently, the refusal of Iceland to implement its obligations is not only unlawful, but it also represents a clear example of free-riding on European integration.

The second question is to what extent the protection of an essential interest of one country can entail the sacrifice of another. This problem is at the core of the concept of necessity in international law. The answer to this question is not simple. In choosing between two evils, it seems reasonable that the party that is experiencing the emergency should be in principle allowed to deviate from the law. When the EFTA Court accepted Iceland's view that backing up the Icelandic Deposit Insurance Fund would have turned a banking crisis into a sovereign debt crisis[79], the court implicitly adopted this point. Thus, according to the Court, the protection of domestic interests ranks above global stability. Consequently, partner countries are those that bear the burden to cope with instability.

This reasoning is particularly revealing of the general attitude of international law toward global stability. However, it is filled with a fundamentally erroneous logic. First of all, it is important to stress here that the party that invoked the condition of necessity is also the one that created the conditions that led to the crisis. Hence, if we ask the host country to bear the costs of an emergency, we transfer the cost of the crisis to the wrong side. Indeed, partner countries (the host regulator) are in the worst position to maintain stability, as they do not have enough capacity to supervise and regulate home-country banks. By transferring the burden to cope with the instability to the host authorities, the law transfers the risk to the party that is in the worst position to reduce it, and therefore is highly inefficient in protecting financial stability. Secondly, by excusing home countries from complying with their supervisory duties whenever they are experiencing a crisis, the law drastically increases the moral hazard of home authorities in adopting unsustainable or inefficient financial policies or, more generally, in externalizing the social costs of their reckless behavior. I will develop this analysis further in Chapter 5 where I will discuss the economics of financial necessity in international law.

[79] Case E-16/11, *EFTA Surveillance Authority* v. *Iceland*, [2011], EFTA Court, 28 January 2013, paras 124–80.

Finally, a question naturally arises as to how does the *Icesave* dispute fit with the problem of soft-law in home–host relations briefly discussed before. The entire legal machinery of home-country control in EU financial governance – and indirectly in the EFTA – is subject to a binding and extremely detailed legal framework and to a very sophisticated compliance mechanism, and not on soft laws. The judgments of the EFTA court can rely on a stringent compliance mechanism in which the violating state is subject to heavy fines or other penalties. Thus, the presence of a binding legal framework and a compliance mechanism should in theory address the weakness of the home-country model caused by principal–agent problem. This may suggest that the problems of financial nationalism in home–host relationships go well beyond the mere use of soft laws. Rather, they originate from a fundamental misunderstanding of the role of international law in controlling financial instability and allocating the costs of financial crises.

3.6. CONCLUDING REMARKS

This chapter shows how the logic of financial nationalism applies in the context of supervisory coordination. The home-country control model produces a dangerous asymmetry between the power of home authorities, which are in control of the stability of their multinational banks even outside their territory, and the power of host authorities, which on the contrary, are extremely limited with regard to their ability to manage the stability of the foreign banks in their jurisdiction. Under certain circumstances, home authorities boycott their commitments to maintain the stability of the foreign banks in the host country, thereby leaving the host country fully exposed to global instability. In the context of the European Union's financial market a recent dispute showed that the protection of individual state interests is so entrenched in the very foundations of international law that it can also apply in the presence of hard laws. The *Icesave* dispute demonstrates that even in the context of a binding and highly sophisticated legal framework for home-country control, the protection of global stability still lacks a proper conceptual understanding in terms of legal principles.

4

Cross-Border Banking

The previous chapter discussed the problems of international cooperation in cross-border banking relationships within a framework governed by international law. Yet, not all banking policies are subject to regulatory cooperation. Until very recently, bank resolution remained firmly excluded from global financial rulemaking. Unlike international commercial enterprises, whose bankruptcy is regulated by the UNCITRAL Model Law on Cross-Border Insolvency, cross-border bank insolvency does not rely on any international agreement.[1] Similarly, bank resolution tools such as bailouts, bridge-banks, or good/bad banks were left largely outside the purview of international law. The absence of guidelines on how to deal with an ailing multinational financial institution created an asymmetry in the international financial system whereby banks were allowed to operate across borders but resolved nationally. In the words of Mervyn King, the former Governor of the Bank of England, "global banks are global in life but national in death."[2]

Regulatory freedom is a fundamental aspect of financial sovereignty. It insulates financial authorities from external constraints, and it permits a more targeted and quick regulatory intervention, thus increasing regulatory efficiency. Yet, in an interconnected financial network regulatory asymmetries and different policy preferences can sometimes jeopardize the achievement of global financial stability. Nothing could show it better than the resolution of a cross-border bank.

The reason behind the regulators' reluctance to cooperate is found primarily in the potentially destabilizing fiscal and financial costs associated with bank insolvencies and recapitalizations. The failure of a financial institution is the

[1] For a good overview of the legal problems affecting cross-border bank resolution, see Rosa Maria Lastra (ed.) *Cross Border Bank Insolvency* (Oxford: Oxford University Press, 2011).

[2] Originally quoted in "The Turner Review: A Regulatory Response to the Global Banking Crisis," UK Financial Services Authority (March 2009), p. 36.

quintessential threat to financial stability, as the social costs of a banking crisis inevitably transcends the destiny of the individual bank to impact depositors, counterparties, and the entire financial system. Resolution tools, likewise, involve fundamental distributional tradeoffs, as they require painful haircuts for the bank's creditors and, sometimes, the use of taxpayers' money. In an international context, these distributional problems become nightmares. Multinational financial institutions with operations across the globe often rely on complex corporate structures in which assets are always highly mobile within the group.

This bears two fundamental consequences. First, the more centralized a bank group is, the more likely that a problem in one part of the bank group will be immediately transmitted to all the other parts. Second, in a large majority of cases, the failure of a cross-border bank will be dealt with under myriad different regulatory and policy regimes. In the absence of international law, cross-border bank resolution remains prone to financial nationalisms, in which the main goal of national authorities will inevitably be the protection of national interests. However, to maximize national welfare national regulators must ignite a cold war in which the gains of one are inevitably the losses of another. The ultimate outcome of this perverse situation is a disorderly resolution that increases creditors' losses and often leads to instability.

This chapter analyzes the problems of coordination and financial nationalism in cross-border bank insolvencies and resolutions. In particular, it will discuss three important crisis-resolution tools – insolvency, bailout, and bail-in – and it will highlight the challenges in achieving international regulatory and policy cooperation in each of them. This chapter is structured as follows: first, I introduce cross-border banking resolution law and policies, and discuss coordination problems in the context of a cross-border banking crisis. In the second, third, and fourth sections, I analyze in detail the problems of financial nationalism in international bankruptcies, bailouts, and bail-ins, respectively, and show the inefficiency of national approaches. The last section discusses recent reforms and the remaining challenges in creating a truly efficient international legal regime for resolving cross-border banks.

4.1. CRISIS RESOLUTION POLICIES IN INTERNATIONAL LAW

In the last 40 years, global banking conglomerates have emerged as distinctive features of international finance.[3] Business expansion is by no mean a

[3] A good analysis of Global Systemically Important Banks (G-SIBs) is provided in Dirk Schoenmaker, *Governance of International Banking: The Financial Trilemma* (Oxford: Oxford University Press, 2013), pp. 34–67.

peculiarity of financial firms. However, what differentiates multinational banks from other multinational enterprises is their high level of capitalization, which often reaches trillions of US dollars, and sometimes is far larger than the GDP of the country hosting them.[4] Given their systemically important status across different jurisdictions, those Global Systemically Important Banks (G-SIBs) enjoyed an implicit guarantee that in case of trouble, the government would have intervened financially to keep the financial institution afloat.[5] Yet, their systemic importance is not the only element that makes their resolution complex. The real problem derives from their peculiar business structure. Indeed, while G-SIBs operate across the globe, they rely on an integrated network in which capital is highly mobile within the group.[6] The tight financial interconnectedness is not a peculiarity of branches, but it extends also to subsidiaries, which despite their independence are often largely subsidized by the parent, which invests in them in various forms. This means that a solvency or liquidity problem in the parent bank or in one of its foreign operations is immediately felt across the entire banking structure. Thus, any problem of the branch or the subsidiary would likely be transmitted to the parent bank. At the same time, the life and stability of branches and subsidiaries are also strictly linked to the particular conditions of the host's economy. This means that financial instability can be easily transmitted either from the parent bank to the host financial system, or vice versa. The combination of these three factors – (1) an integrated network, (2) multiple operations across the globe, and (3) systemic importance – renders the resolution of G-SIBs a regulatory nightmare.

4.1.1. *The Policy of Financial Crises*

When a banking crisis strikes, national authorities have in their arsenal a large variety of measures to reduce systemic risk, depending on the stage of the crisis and the gravity.[7] For instance, Lender of Last Resort (LOLR) operations serve to sustain a bank that is primarily solvent, but is experiencing

[4] For instance, Avinash Persaud argues that the assets of Barclay's Bank – which is not even the largest British bank – are around 200% of the UK's annual tax revenue. Avinash Persaud, "The Locus of Financial Regulation: Home versus Host" (2010) 86 *International Affairs* 637, p. 639.

[5] Rosa Maria Lastra, "Systemic Risk, SIFIs, and Financial Stability" (2011) 6 *Capital Markets Law Journal* 197, p. 209.

[6] See Schoenmaker, above note 3, Chapter 3.

[7] For a good overview of those policies, see John Raymond Labrosse, Rodrigo Olivares-Carminal, and Dalvinder Singh (eds.) *Financial Crisis Management and Bank Resolution* (London: Informa Law, 2009).

some temporary liquidity problems. When a bank is insolvent, authorities usually rely on three major types of legal and policy mechanism: insolvency, government-funded recapitalizations (the so-called bailouts), and private sector-funded recapitalizations.

On the one hand, there are free-market solutions, which are usually implemented when there is no systemic risk associated with the bank's failure. As the name suggests, free-market solutions do not entail direct government intervention. The quintessential example is a **insolvency** procedure.[8] As for any other firm in a free-market economy, a financial institution that is no longer able to conduct its business profitably should be allowed to die. Insolvency laws provide the legal framework in which dying banks are assisted in their winding-up. They determine when a financial institution is no longer viable; they decide who should manage the insolvency procedure; and crucially, they determine how to distribute the remaining assets. When supervisory authorities decide in favor of insolvency, the main goal is to extract from the firm all of the possible remaining economic value in order to cover creditors. Since the insolvency of a financial institution is the result of its inability to meet its financial obligations, not all creditors will be satisfied. Some – the privileged or senior creditors – will be able to recover all or some of their credits, while others – the subordinate or ordinary creditors – will simply share the remaining spoils. The role of a insolvency regime is therefore to decide in advance the distributional tradeoffs, and to maximize the amount of recoverable assets in a way that does not endanger financial stability.

On the other hand, there are government-driven solutions. Under various circumstances, insolvency is not an option. When a bank is too-big-to-fail (TBTF) – which is the case for all G-SIBs – it is imperative to keep that bank afloat. Responsible authorities do so through different techniques, which, invariably, involve a fundamental disruption of the logic of the free market. In a nutshell, when a bank is approaching the point of non-viability, it does not have any more capital to sustain losses. In this situation, there are only three options available, if the bank is to remain as a going concern: a recapitalization funded by outside investors, a forced recapitalization by existing creditors, or a government-funded recapitalization.

Among the three tools, the latter is, undoubtedly, the best known among the public. **Bailouts** came to prominence during the recent financial crisis of 2007 and during the European sovereign debt crisis, when various firms

[8] Thomas H. Jackson and David A. Skeel, Jr., "Dynamic Resolution of Large Financial Institutions" (2012) 2 *Harvard Business Law Review* 435.

were saved by last-minute government intervention.[9] In a bailout, the state becomes a shareholder of the bank by purchasing shares and (sometimes) other forms of debt. From a policy viewpoint, what makes bailouts particularly contentious is the fact that they are executed with the use of taxpayers' money. In various situations, the costs of bailing out a failing financial institution can be extremely high.[10] As Reinhart and Rogoff have documented, governments have spent an average of 10% of their national GDP on interventions to restore financial stability.[11] Furthermore, Jonathan Kats has argued that, if we consider the whole arsenal of measures deployed by the US authorities to maintain financial stability at the outset of the global financial crisis, the amount would reach the astronomical number of US$ 3.7 trillion.[12]

This means that, even in the context of a bailout, there is a fundamental tradeoff between the protection of financial stability (via the protection of banks' creditors) and the use of taxpayers' money. Arguably, a bailout would be necessary only when the social costs of the bank's failure would outweigh the costs in terms of public money.[13] Supervisors need, therefore, to strike a delicate balance between competing interests, which often entails a choice between two evils that necessarily sacrifices competition and taxpayers' money for the sake of domestic financial stability. However, under certain circumstances, the level of capital injection required is such that a bailout would transform a banking problem into a fiscal problem. Indeed, the recent sovereign debt crises of Ireland and Spain caused by the costs of bailing out the national financial sector showed that in certain cases the costs of maintaining

9 Randall D. Guynn, "Are Bailouts Inevitable?" (2012) 29 *Yale Journal on Regulation* 121; Adam Levitin, "In Defense of Bailouts" (2011) 99 *The Georgetown Law Journal* 435; Jonathan G. Kats, "Who Benefited from the Bailout?" (2011) 95 *Minnesota Law Review* 1567; Matthew R. Shahabian, "The Government as Shareholder and Political Risk: Procedural Protections in the Bailout" (2011) 86 *New York University Law Review* 35; Anna Gelpern, "Financial Crisis Containment" (2009) 41 *Connecticut Law Review* 1051.

10 Guynn, *ibid.*

11 Carmen M. Reinhart and Kenneth S. Rogoff, *This Time Is Different: Eight Centuries of Financial Folly* (Princeton, NJ: Princeton University Press, 2009), pp. 141–71. See also Luc Laeven and Fabian Valencia, "Resolution of Banking Crises: The Good, the Bad, and the Ugly" (2010) IMF Working Paper WP/10/146, International Monetary Fund, available at www.imf.org/external/pubs/ft/wp/2010/wp10146.pdf.

12 Furthermore, he argued, quoting the TARP report, that if we take into account all non-banking expenditures – such as FED asset purchase and Federal Deposit Insurance Corporation expansion of the coverage – the total government risk exposure would reach the astonishing figure of US$ 13.9 trillion, more than 1.5 times US GDP. See Kats, above note 9, at 1585; Office of the Special Inspector General for the Troubled Asset Relief Program, "SIG-QR-10-03, Quarterly Report to Congress 135" (July 2010), p. 5.

13 Schoenmaker, above note 3, p. 25.

financial stability can be extremely high.[14] Moreover, bailouts are economically inefficient as they encourage moral hazard of banks and protect excessively senior bondholders (mostly large financial institutions).[15]

Given the problems associated with government interventions, a private-sector solution is usually considered the best option to resolve an ailing bank. As I said before, when a bank has depleted its capital, there are various possible solutions to maintain it as a going concern. The first is to rely on the voluntary intervention of investors, usually through mergers, good/bad bank splits, or bridge-banks. This option, however, is very difficult as few investors would take on the burden of becoming shareholders of a failing bank, especially during a systemic crisis. Sometimes the central bank will try to coordinate private sector interventions – the so-called "lifeboats" – in which the bank's creditors are pushed to agree on a common recapitalization of the bank.[16] This technique, however, suffers from the same problem seen before, as it relies on creditors' consent.

Bail-ins are the latest solution to the creditors' coordination problem.[17] One of the legacies of the recent financial crises is the progressive drop of political support for bailouts. In its July 2011 document, the Financial Stability Board requested members "to ensure that the costs of resolution are borne by the firm's owners (shareholders) and other unsecured and uninsured creditors, rather than by taxpayers."[18] In response, regulators in Europe and in the United States devised new regulatory frameworks for bank resolution that explicitly banned or minimized the use of public money to recapitalize a TBTF bank, thus transferring the costs of recapitalizing a failing bank to the financial sector.[19] A bail-in is the forced conversion of subordinated debt

[14] See Federico Lupo-Pasini, "Economic Stability and Economic Governance in The Euro Area: What the European Crisis Can Teach on the Limits of Economic Integration" (2013) 16 *Journal of International Economic Law* 211.

[15] PriceWaterhouseCoopers, "Basel III and beyond – The Trillion Dollar Question: Can Bail-in Capital Bail-out the Banking Industry?," PriceWaterhouseCoopers (November 2011).

[16] Rosa Maria Lastra reports that English authorities used this technique during the secondary bank crisis of 1974. See Rosa Maria Lastra, "Cross-Border Bank Insolvency: Legal Implications in the Case of Banks Operating in Different Jurisdictions in Latin America" (2003) 6 *Journal of International Economic Law* 79, pp. 85–6; similarly, in 1998 the US bank Long Term Capital Management (LTCM) was rescued by a lifeboat operation involving the biggest New York banks.

[17] See Simon Gleeson, "Legal Aspects of Bank Bail-Ins," London School of Economics Financial Market Group, Special Paper 205 (January 2012), pp. 5–6.

[18] Financial Stability Board, "Effective Resolution of Systemically Important Financial Institutions; Recommendations and Timelines" (19 July 2011).

[19] For instance, § 214 of the Dodd-Frank Act states that "No taxpayer funds shall be used to prevent the liquidation of any financial company . . .".

into equity or the write-down of debt activated by the competent resolution authority based on a predetermined statutory power. By reducing the level of debt, the bail-in restores the debt–equity level of the bank to the regulatory minimum. The ultimate effect of bail-ins is no different from that achieved by loss-absorbing financial instruments, such as Contingent Convertible Bonds. However, the procedures required to reach that outcome are fundamentally different. In a bail-in the conversion of the debt into equity takes place at the supervisor's discretion rather than at a predefined trigger point identified in the contract. For instance, in a bail-in the regulator will decide the moment when the bail-in will be activated, the class of creditors subject to bail-in, and the quantum of write-down or the conversion rate.

4.1.2. *The Challenges of an International Legal Regime*

From a legal viewpoint, given the highly interconnected structure of a cross-border bank and the global systemic risks associated with its failure, one would expect crisis-resolution policies and supervisory interventions to be coordinated across the entire banking group. If that were the case, in the event of a crisis the failing institution would be subject to a single crisis-resolution regime, which assigns to each authority precise powers and obligations. The economic logic of a single authority with extraterritorial jurisdiction has always been evident. In an 1888 *Harvard Law Review* essay on cross-border bankruptcy, John Lowell wrote: "It is obvious that . . . it would be better in nine cases out of ten that all settlements of insolvent debtors with their creditors should be made in a single proceeding, and generally at a single place."[20] By assigning the jurisdiction over the cross-border bank to a single authority, the asymmetry between the scope of the market and the scope of financial policies could be avoided, economies of scale could be achieved, and dangerous coordination problems could be prevented.[21] However, this would come with substantial sovereignty costs that affect both the country in control of the resolution procedure and the country that hosts the bank's foreign operations.

The tension between the efficiency of a universal approach to the resolution and the sovereignty costs that come with it is at the foundation of cross-border bank resolution policymaking and, arguably, at the origin of most coordination failures in cross-border banking crises. The diffidence toward

[20] John Lowell, "Conflict of Laws as Applied to Assignments of Creditors" (1888) 1 *Harvard Law Review* 259, p. 264.

[21] Frederick Tung, "Is International Bankruptcy Possible?" (2002) 23 *Michigan Journal of International Law* 31, p. 41.

universalism is motivated by the need to protect national interests, which may arise from the need to protect local financial stability against the forbearance of foreign authorities, by the reluctance to assign regulatory power to a foreign entity, or by the desire to defend the social and policy values implicit in local laws. This is most visible in the context of insolvency, where different regimes reflect the complex policy tradeoffs between the protection of creditors' interests, economic efficiency, fair competition, and financial stability.

For these reasons, multilateral international coordination on crisis resolution is, historically, difficult in international financial law. As said earlier, the 1983 Basel Concordat explicitly leaves lender of last resort measures, recapitalization, and deposit insurance policies outside the ambit of application of the agreement,[22] leaving the matter to voluntary bilateral cooperation. National regulators, however, have only rarely engaged in meaningful bilateral coordination of crisis resolution policies – and often, secretly, to reduce moral hazard.[23] Moreover, when they have, the level of cooperation has remained quite limited. First, and foremost, memoranda of understanding (MoUs) on crisis resolution are non-binding. Second, only rarely do MoUs tackle the critical issues in a cross-border banking crisis, such as recapitalization or LOLR measures. For the most part, these agreements set up a framework for coordination between responsible national agencies that disciplines the procedures to be followed by each authority in the event of a crisis. For instance, the 2008 Memorandum of Understanding on Cross-Border Financial Stability[24] – which disciplined the issue among EU financial authorities – did not touch on burden-sharing arrangements or on the precise responsibilities of national authorities during a bailout. In sum, unlike prudential regulations, most of the financial policies that deal with crisis resolution and crisis management have historically been subject to national control, and have been regulated independently by each national financial authority.

Before explaining in detail how financial nationalism creates global instability, it is necessary to briefly explain the distributional tradeoffs of crisis-resolution policies in a cross-border banking crisis. In the next sections, I will

[22] See Basel Committee on Banking Supervision, "Principles for the Supervision of Banks' Foreign Establishments – Concordat" (May 1983) [hereinafter, the Revised Concordat], p. 1.

[23] There are indeed few examples of coordination on crisis resolution. The few examples are only between European countries, such as the Nordic countries, or Benelux.

[24] Memorandum of Understanding on Cooperation between the Financial Supervisory Authorities, Central Banks and Finance Ministries of the European Union on Cross-Border Financial Stability (1 June 2008), ECFIN/CEFCPE(2008)REP/53106 REV REV [hereinafter, the 2008 Memorandum of Understanding on Cross-Border Financial Stability], available at www.ecb.europa.eu/pub/pdf/other/mou-financialstability2008en.pdf.

examine three different crisis-resolution policies – insolvency, bailout, and bail-in – and I will demonstrate that in all cases, the protection of national interests ultimately produces global instability.

4.2. REGULATORY ASYMMETRIES IN BANK INSOLVENCY REGIMES

In a normal situation in which the bank is not systemically important, insolvency would be regulators' first option. However, even when the bank is systemically important, financial authorities may permit a bank to go bankrupt whenever the costs of a bailout outweigh the benefits in terms of domestic stability. This was the case with Lehman Brothers, for example. Even in the context of a insolvency procedure, however, national financial authorities face contrasting objectives that ultimately reduce the chances of cooperation.

4.2.1. *Regulatory Asymmetries in Bank Insolvency Regimes*

Different regulatory regimes and the absence of a truly harmonized international legal framework for cross-border bank insolvency play fundamental roles in increasing the likelihood of a disorderly resolution. Regulatory asymmetries in cross-border bank insolvency and bankruptcy laws have been recognized for some time as one of the most serious problems threatening global financial stability.[25]

The first asymmetry concerns the place of financial institutions in a bankruptcy procedure. Commentators have often debated that the specificities of finance require an ad hoc procedure that is able to address the systemic implications of a bank collapse.[26] However, not all countries provide for a *lex specialis* dealing specifically with the bankruptcy of financial institutions.[27] Secondly, even when they do, the law might determine different thresholds for public intervention or for the declaration of insolvency. For instance, in some countries, the law mandates public intervention when the bank becomes illiquid or

[25] Rosa Maria Lastra, above note 16; Rosa Maria Lastra and Henry N. Schiffman (eds.) *Bank Failures and Bank Insolvency Law in Economies in Transition* (The Hague: Kluwer Law International, 1999); IMF, "Resolution of Cross-Border Banks – A Proposed Framework for Enhanced Coordination," International Monetary Fund (11 June 2010), available at www.imf.org/external/np/pp/eng/2010/061110.pdf; IMF, "The Key Attributes of Effective Resolution Regimes for Financial Institutions – Progress to Date and Next Steps," International Monetary Fund (27 August 2012), available at www.imf.org/external/np/pp/eng/2012/082712.pdf.

[26] Rosa Maria Lastra, "Cross Border Resolution of Banking Crises," in Douglas D. Evanoff, George G. Kaufman, and John R. LaBrosse (eds.) *International Financial Instability: Global Banking and National Regulations* (Singapore: World Scientific, 2007), pp. 312–15.

[27] *Ibid.*, pp. 311–30.

when its net worth declines to zero. However, in other countries authorities have the power to intervene at an earlier point. The United States, for instance, adopts the so-called "Prompt Corrective Action" policy, which specifies that corrective actions must be taken before the bank's net worth reaches zero.

Furthermore, even when authorities are in principle legally authorized to intervene, they might decide to forbear or to postpone the liquidation for a variety of reasons – from conflicts of interests to agency costs. Delays or excessive forbearance, however, might increase liquidity costs and augment credit losses. When a cross-border bank is involved, losses might be quite high, especially if the bank is systemically important. Let us consider, for instance, the case of a large cross-border bank that is systemically important in the host country, but not in the home country. Home authorities will not feel the pressure to intervene promptly as there is no immediate impact on local depositors and creditors. However, delaying liquidation will severely affect customers in the host country, as they will not have access to their funds.[28]

Yet, the most pressing problem is perhaps the asymmetry of bankruptcy laws between those countries that adopt a universal approach to insolvency (like EU states), and those that adopt a territorial approach (like the United States). The regulatory asymmetry is by no means limited to cross-border banking issues, as it applies to all types of businesses. Indeed, there is vast legal literature examining the problems of international bankruptcy laws that dates back even to the nineteenth century.[29] The difference between the two regimes can be quickly sketched.

In the territorial approach, different national courts adjudicate on the insolvency of the cross-border bank, with each court's competency limited to the part of the bank that is located in its jurisdiction.[30] The law where the assets are found controls their distribution and the claims. During insolvency proceedings, each national court adjudicates the claims only against the assets present in its territory. In doing so, they favor local creditors over foreign ones. Assets present in one jurisdiction are transferred to another jurisdiction only if

[28] Robert A. Eisenbeis, "Home Country versus Cross Border Negative Externalities in Large Banking Organizations Failures and How to Avoid Them" in Douglas D. Evanoff, George G. Kaufman, and John R. LaBrosse (eds.) *International Financial Instability: Global Banking and National Regulations* (Singapore: World Scientific, 2007), p. 189.

[29] As Prof Tung reports, "in the very first volume of the *Harvard Law Review* . . . Professor John Lowell of the Harvard Law School made the case for 'a single proceeding . . . at a single place.'" See Lowell, above note 20, cited in Tung, above note 21, p. 34.

[30] See Lynn M. LoPucki, "The Case for Cooperative Territoriality in International Bankruptcy" (2000) 98 *Michigan Law Review* 2216; Lynn M. LoPucki, "Cooperation in International Bankruptcy: A Post-Universalist Approach" (1999) 84 *Cornell Law Review* 697.

all local claims are satisfied. Those countries that adopt a universal approach, on the contrary, allow a single court to adjudicate the totality of the assets and claims, irrespective of the location of the assets. The cross-border bank is therefore liquidated in its totality according to the law where the insolvency takes place. The competent court conducts the main insolvency proceedings and distributes the assets, while the other jurisdictions simply collect the assets that are present in their territories to be distributed in the main proceeding. Crucially, in a universal approach, there is no discrimination between national and foreign creditors. This approach shares the same underlying logic of the home-country control principle discussed in the previous chapter: to concentrate regulatory and policy control over a multinational bank to a single jurisdiction to eliminate dangerous regulatory discontinuities. The difference between the two is that, while in the home-country control principle, only the home country is responsible for extraterritorial control over the stability of the bank's foreign operations, in the universal approach the power to control the resolution is accorded based on a range of predetermined criteria.[31]

Even in the context of a insolvency procedure, states will try to maximize their own interests by trying to locate the insolvency in their own jurisdictions. Indeed, each country has an interest in moving the majority of the assets to its own jurisdiction in order to control the whole procedure from a legal and administrative perspective. National regulators will therefore engage in a preemptive war in which true information about the solvability of the bank is not disclosed to partner authorities until it cannot be hidden any more – which is just before the bank is declared insolvent. By refusing to disclose the stability problems to their foreign counterparts, national authorities essentially try to buy time in the hope of bringing back to their jurisdiction as much of the assets as possible. In this regard, powerful financial centers like the United States benefit most from this situation, as international banks might have many assets in their territories.[32]

This could also explain why US authorities have always refused to align their bankruptcy laws with those of the European Union. For instance, in the days before the Lehman Brothers' insolvency, American regulators tried to convince the company to repatriate most of its assets back to New York. When the bank was declared insolvent, the US authorities provided an orderly resolution for the

[31] For a general discussion on the international law of cross-border bank insolvency, see Rosa Maria Lastra, "International Law Principles Applicable to Cross-Border Bank Insolvency," in Rosa M. Lastra (ed.) *Cross-Border Bank Insolvency* (Oxford: Oxford University Press, 2011). For an overview of universality in bankruptcy, see Andrew T. Guzman, "International Bankruptcy: In Defense of Universalism" (2000) 98 *Michigan Law Review* 2177.

[32] Pierre-Hugues Verdier, "The Political Economy of International Financial Regulation" (2013) 88 *Indiana Law Journal* 1405, p. 1456.

US operations, while most of its European operations were left without cash and were therefore forced to declare insolvency themselves. Ultimately, the Lehman Brothers group was subject to 50 different national proceedings with limited international coordination, which resulted in a suboptimal resolution and, more importantly, in the transmission of global systemic risk across the European banking system.[33] Most commentators singled out the Lehman Brothers insolvency as an example of the inefficiencies of the territorial approach.[34]

However, even in the presence of uniformity in insolvency procedures, investors will engage in forum shopping by playing with the interpretation of the rules, while national courts will try to situate the insolvency within their jurisdiction.[35]

4.2.2. *Ring-Fencing and "Stability Wars"*

When a financial institution is experiencing problems, either on a consolidated basis or in one of its local operations, each national regulator will face tremendous pressure to protect its own domestic interests. Ultimately, the safeguarding of domestic interests boils down to the protection of creditors and depositors, and gives rise to a situation that logically requires having enough disposable assets to cover their losses. As stated by former supervisors, "When times are rough, [supervisors] will think like administrative officials, rather than judges. They will grab whatever they can."[36]

From a home supervisor's viewpoint, the most immediate concern before declaring the insolvency of the cross-border bank is to ensure that domestic creditors (especially local banks) are satisfied. To do so, home supervisors will try to repatriate the assets held in the bank's foreign branches or even subsidiaries. Expecting this outcome, host supervisors will try to anticipate their moves by seizing the host bank's assets. This strategy is called "ring-fencing."[37] From a legal viewpoint, ring-fencing entails a legal prohibition against moving the

[33] Schoenmaker, above note 3, p. 76.

[34] Schoenmaker, *ibid.*, pp. 72–6; Stijn Claessens, Richard Herring, Dirk Schoenmaker, and Kimberly Summme, "A Safer World Financial System: Improving the Resolution of Systemic Institutions," Geneva Reports on the World Economy 12, International Center for Monetary and Banking Studies and Centre for Economic Policy Research (2011).

[35] Tung, above note 21, pp. 91–3.

[36] See Thomas C. Baxter, Jr., Joyce M. Hansen, and Joseph H. Sommer, "Two Cheers for Territoriality: An Essay on International Bank Insolvency Law" (2004) 78 *American Bankruptcy Law Journal* 57, 88.

[37] On ring-fencing and cross-border financial crises, see The Independent Commission on Banking, "Final Report Recommendations," September 2011 (commonly referred to as the *Vickers Report*), available at www.parliament.uk/briefing-papers/sn06171.pdf.

failing bank's assets until all domestic creditors of the bank have been satisfied.[38] Ring-fencing is one of the most widely used strategies to protect domestic interests in the context of a cross-border banking crisis.

The principal–agent model is particularly useful to explain the political economy of ring-fencing. Domestic depositors will likely not understand how the sharing of responsibility between different supervisors works. At the same time, national supervisors will face a tremendous amount of pressure to cover creditors' losses on time, as the prolongation of the insolvency procedure will have a significant political impact domestically. Furthermore, host authorities will also be concerned with preventing a banking crisis from evolving into a full-blown financial crisis. Thus, in the event of a parent bank failure, host authorities will have to adopt drastic measures through a territorial ring-fencing approach.[39] Hence, when the bank is on the verge of collapse national regulators will try to locate the insolvency in their territory, or to amass all of the bank's available assets to satisfy local creditors. According to US law,[40] when US authorities decide to ring-fence the assets of a foreign multinational bank, they do not limit themselves to seizing the assets of the branch, but rather they extend their grabbing to the assets of the parent bank in the territory.

Take the case of two states. State A (the Home country) and State B (the Host country) share a common bank QUB headquartered in State A but with substantial local operations in State B. The bank is systemically important in State B, and its insolvency would trigger systemic effects in the wider economy. QUB's collapse must be avoided at all costs. The bank suddenly finds itself in trouble and is on the verge of collapse. State A has various incentives to control the whole procedure and to push the parent bank to collect and repatriate all of its foreign-held assets, including those pertaining to the operations in State B. The decision to repatriate some funds can be made because of problems in the parent bank (as in the Lehman Brothers case), or because of problems in the host country's operations. The repatriation of assets minimizes the costs of failure in the home jurisdiction. Conversely, the consequences in the host country would be disastrous, as the host bank would

[38] Eugenio Cerutti, Anna Ilyina, Yulia Makarova, and Christian Schmieder, "Bankers without Borders? Implications of Ring-Fencing for European Cross-Border Banks" (2010) IMF Working Paper WP/10/247, International Monetary Fund, available at www.imf.org/external/pubs/cat/longres.cfm?sk=24335.0.

[39] Michael Krimminger, "Banking in a Changing World: Issues and Questions in the Resolution of Cross-Border Bank," in Gerard Caprio Jr., Douglass D. Evanoff, and George G. Kauffman (eds.) *Cross Border Banking: Regulatory Challenges* (Singapore: World Scientific, 2006), pp. 201–22.

[40] 12 U.S.C. § 3102(j) (2006) (Establishment of Federal branches and agencies by foreign bank).

find itself without liquidity to finance local operations. Furthermore, as the bank is systemically important in State B, its collapse would trigger a reaction chain in other local banks leading to a downward spiral of instability.

Likewise, State B authorities' only goal is to protect their own depositors and creditors. State B will therefore have high incentives to anticipate the parent bank's move and block the assets of the branch or subsidiary by ring-fencing them. Host authorities will not have all of the information on the health of the parent bank at their disposal. Ring-fencing the assets is therefore the easiest option for host regulators. It allows them to buy time, to localize the insolvency process, and define the terms of the insolvency, thereby protecting local depositors and controlling the exposure. Such a move protects economic stability in the host country, but it consequently produces externalities in State A. Ring-fencing is, by all means, a control on the movement of capital (on the outflow), and it clearly reduces financial integration. Furthermore, the seizing of assets prevents a quick and safe insolvency procedure in State A, as it prolongs the shortage of liquidity for the bank, thereby creating instability.[41]

The likelihood of ring-fencing will also influence the home authorities' and parent bank's decisions. Ring-fencing makes the overall process extremely difficult for home authorities as well. Therefore, home authorities will try to reduce communication with host supervisors and to anticipate their moves. Each party in the insolvency process will be likely to avoid cooperation with the other in fear that their cooperation would increase their exposure and negatively affect domestic interests, thereby creating negative externalities for the other regulators.[42] Hence, the chess game between home and host authorities will likely result in a collapse or reduction of communication, thereby leading to a suboptimal liquidation.[43]

4.3. THE BAILOUT GAME

No bailout is alike. However, despite the different circumstances that may lead to a crisis and the level of intervention required, three elements are featured constantly in every government-funded recapitalization. First, governments intervene with taxpayers' money. Therefore, regulators face a tremendous amount of pressure from citizens, other financial institutions, as well

[41] Krimminger, above note 39, pp. 201–22.

[42] See Richard Herring, "Conflicts between Home and Host Country Prudential Supervisors," in Douglas D. Evanoff, George G. Kaufman, and John R. LaBrosse (eds.) *International Financial Instability: Global Banking and National Regulations* (Singapore: World Scientific, 2007), pp. 213–15.

[43] Krimminger, above note 39, pp. 201–22.

as politicians to address the sources of instability with the minimum amount of fiscal intervention in public finances and without distorting competition. Second, bailouts are always the last option considered by financial authorities, after all others prove unfeasible. This means that the systemic risk of the bank's collapse is so high that keeping the bank as a going concern is mandatory. Third, when financial authorities finally decide that it is necessary to proceed with the bailout, they only have a matter of days at their disposal to assess the level of intervention and to coordinate the entire procedure. Usually, the stabilization phase of a banking resolution takes place during the weekend, when financial markets do not operate.[44] Indeed, while an ordinary commercial company would be able to conduct its business activity even during the insolvency process, a bank would not, because no other financial firm would agree to do business with it.[45] As Simon Gleeson succinctly put it, "the essence of a bank is solvency, and an insolvent bank is by definition not a going concern."[46]

The combination of these three factors – the use of taxpayers' money, the need to prevent a dangerous escalation of the crisis, and the short time-frame of a weekend – makes a bailout an extremely challenging policy intervention. When a cross-border bank fails, the same problems that face national regulators in a domestic crisis become exponentially more complicated. Crisis resolution policies are all about how losses are distributed between different stakeholders.[47] Given the time and political pressures to which supervisors are subject during a banking crisis, each national authority will naturally be inclined to safeguard its national interests first.

The core problem of a cross-border bank resolution lies in the different systemic importance of the bank's various foreign operations. While a multinational bank in its consolidated structure is always systemically important, its individual national operations – branches or subsidiaries – are not necessarily equivalently important. For instance, while a cross-border bank headquartered in a large developed country might be of medium systemic importance for that economy, its operations in a developing country with an underdeveloped and highly connected financial sector might be of high systemic importance. In this situation, home and host supervisory authorities might suffer from an asymmetry of incentives or powers when coordinating the resolution of the

[44] Thomas F. Huertas, "Safe to Fail," LSE Financial Markets Group Paper Series Special Paper 221 (May 2013), p. 3.

[45] Gleeson, above note 17, p. 3.

[46] *Ibid.*, p. 3.

[47] Levitin, above note 9, p. 480.

multinational bank.[48] This means that each country will try to minimize its fiscal outlays to those that are strictly necessary in order to guarantee its own domestic stability, or it will try to free-ride on other countries' intervention. The unwillingness of national authorities to extend enough capital to protect the stability of a global bank in its consolidated structure, however, results in a suboptimal level of global stability and, ultimately, may lead to the bank's collapse or a more expensive bailout.

4.3.1. *The Economics of International Bailouts*

The coordination problems faced by financial supervisors in the context of a cross-border bank bailout can be represented in game theory as "prisoner's dilemma" situations.[49] In the context of a cross-border banking crisis, each national authority has the goal to protect its domestic stability. However, owing to the three factors discussed earlier, in the absence of a strong legal framework, cooperation is extremely challenging.

Let us assume that a country will agree to recapitalize a bank only to the extent that the gains of recapitalization in terms of domestic stability are equal to or higher than the costs in terms of fiscal resources utilized. Hence, each country will simply factor in its domestic gains and losses the decision to recapitalize a bank. Let us now assume that by providing £500 million to bail out a bank, the country has a return of £800 million in terms of stability. In a bi-country model in which the cross-border bank is systemically important in both jurisdictions, the cooperative solution would envisage that each country contributes £250 million for a net return in terms of stability of £300 million, which means a net gain of £150 million each (upper-left quadrant in Table 4.1). If neither country decides to cooperate, each authority saves £250 million from the cost of the bailout, but the banking crisis would materialize, which would cost £400 million (£800 million for both jurisdictions), which means that each country would lose £150 million (lower-right quadrant in Table 4.1).

As in the traditional prisoner's dilemma, where the two prisoners do not know what the other will do, in a real bailout situation, without a clear and binding legal framework the two states do not know precisely how the foreign authority will respond. Indeed, they have only limited hours at their disposal

[48] Schoenmaker, above note 3.

[49] Various authors have recently resorted to game theory to explain policy options in a cross-border bank bailout. This part draws on these authors' analyses. See Schoenmaker, above note 3, pp. 27–33; and Zdenek Kudrna, "Cross-Border Resolution of Failed Banks in the European Union after the Crisis: Business as Usual" (2012) 50 *Journal of Common Market Studies* 283.

TABLE 4.1. *Prisoner's dilemma and bank bailouts*

	Cooperate	Do not cooperate
Cooperate	+£150; +£150	+£400; –£100
Do not cooperate	–£100; +£400	–£150; –£150

to stabilize the bank before markets open, and assess their gains and losses. In this situation, each state has an incentive to free-ride on the other. State A provides full coverage of the bailout for £500 million, while State B does not participate. In this situation State A has a net loss of £100 million, while State B enjoys a net gain of £400 million. In essence, State B free-rides on the bailout of State A. The same would occur if State B decided to cooperate, while State A refused. We can see both situations in the upper-right and lower-left quadrants. If both countries decide not to cooperate, the cross-border bank will be subject to a disorderly resolution, which increases systemic risk in both countries. Thus, both State A and State B incur a net loss of £150 million (lower-right quadrant in Table 4.1).

The prisoner's dilemma shows that the local national authority has considerable incentives for not cooperating with its foreign counterpart. In this situation, either the bank would fail, or it would be subject to a disorderly resolution. Furthermore, it is important to take into account that prisoner's dilemma games for banking resolution cannot be modeled as repeated games, as banking crises seldom occur.[50] This means that in the absence of a strong mechanism of coordination, each country will adopt measures that lead to a non-cooperative outcome in which global stability will be sacrificed. I show this game in Table 4.1.

The situation in which a failing bank is systemically important in both countries is nevertheless rare. Most of the time, only one of the countries where the bank operates will have a real interest in keeping the bank afloat. This is usually the country where the bank is systemically important. The nightmare scenario is when the foreign entity is systemically important for the host country, while it is considered small relative to the parent group and not systemically important for the home authorities. In this case, the home country lacks the incentive to exercise the strong consolidated supervision necessary to ensure systemic stability in the host country.[51] When the costs of bailout are too big compared to the returns in terms of financial stability for

[50] Schoenmaker, above note 3, p. 29.

[51] These kinds of situations are increasingly prevalent in Central Europe, Latin America, and Africa. See Herring, above note 42.

the home country, the home authority will have no incentive to bail out the foreign operation of the parent bank. For instance, during the Argentine crisis, well-capitalized parent banks decided to abandon their branches and subsidiaries as their financial difficulties became acute.[52] In this situation, the host country suffers instability, as the stability of the bank's operations in its territory depend on the willingness of the parent authorities to keep the bank afloat.[53] This last situation demonstrates that as the internationalization of the bank increases, the domestic fraction of the total benefits of the bank's recapitalization decreases. This situation in turn further discourages national authorities from contributing beyond what is necessary to maintain domestic stability.[54]

Some authors[55] have recently tried to explain cooperation problems in banking crises by using the economic theory of alliances, originally developed by Olson in 1966.[56] In a multicountry setting, financial stability is considered a pure public good that provides benefits to the global society. However, maintaining stability comes at a high cost. Each country decides to devote a certain number of resources to maintaining global stability, thereby also benefitting other states. Assuming that all other countries do the same, each country would choose to contribute at a level that is proportionate to its GDP. In this model, the outcome would be a non-cooperative Nash equilibrium. The reason is that each country will choose an optimal allocation of resources that maximizes its own domestic stability, without taking into account the interests of other members. More specifically, each state will choose an allocation of resources in which its marginal benefit will be equal to its marginal cost. In this situation, the level of resources devoted to global stability would be Pareto suboptimal compared to that which is necessary to maintain global stability (rather than each individual country's welfare), because no country considers the costs and benefits that flow to other countries within its resource-allocation decisions in producing a pure public good.

[52] Eric Rosengren, "An Overview of Cross-Border Bank Policy Issues" in Gerard Caprio Jr., Douglass D. Evanoff, and George G. Kauffman (eds.) *Cross Border Banking: Regulatory Challenges* (Singapore: World Scientific, 2006), p. 468.

[53] Krimminger, above note 39, pp. 201–22.

[54] Schoenmaker, above note 3, p. 29.

[55] Vitor Gaspar and Garry J. Schinasi, "Financial Stability and Policy Cooperation," Banco du Portugal Occasional Paper 01-2010 (2010), available at http://papers.ssrn.com/sol3/papers.cfm?abstract_id=1645801; Maria J. Nieto and Garry J. Schinasi, "EU Framework for Safeguarding Financial Stability: Towards an Analytical Benchmark for Assessing its Effectiveness" (2007) IMF Working Paper WP/07/260, International Monetary Fund, available at www.imf.org/external/pubs/ft/wp/2007/wp07260.pdf.

[56] Mancur Olson and Richard Zeckhauser, 'An Economic Theory of Alliances' (1966) 48 *Review of Economics and Statistics* 266; Mancur Olson, *The Logic of Collective Action: Public Groups and the Theory of Groups* (Cambridge, MA: Harvard University Press, 1965).

The decentralized approach that characterizes financial stability as a public good – in which there is no centralized global provider of bailouts – has another consequence. If states try to overcome the negotiation hurdles and decide to provide a level of resources that maximizes global stability, big countries will likely be the ones to bear the higher costs, as they will be able to provide a level of contribution that is higher than their GDP. On the contrary, small countries will be likely to free-ride on the big ones (this implies that there is a perfect substitutability of the public good). This situation has, in turn, a third implication. More specifically, in a Nash equilibrium, countries' propensities to provide the public good (that is, their policy reactions to a threat to their financial stability) will depend on four factors: country-specific income, the relative cost of producing financial stability, the aggregate amount of resources devoted to financial stability by other countries, and the commonly perceived level of threat of financial instability.[57] The ultimate outcome of this model is that, only by centralizing global stability functions is it possible to overcome the coordination constraints and maintain an optimal level of global stability.

4.3.2. *The Resolution of Fortis Bank*

The Fortis case is the clearest example of the problems faced by national authorities in the context of a cross-border bank bailout. Fortis Bank was a cross-border bank headquartered in Belgium, but with substantial operations in Luxembourg and the Netherlands. At the outset of the Lehman Brothers' collapse in 2008, Fortis experienced a run by institutional investors. Despite the LOLR assistance provided by the European Central Bank, Fortis remained in a precarious position and required further capital injections to survive. The three national authorities initially intervened according to the rules set out in the MoU. However, when the coordinated recapitalization failed to calm the markets, each national government decided to proceed individually to protect its own stability by focusing on the part of Fortis that was systemic for its own market.[58] Jonathan Edwards explains that the refusal to cooperate was due to the principal–agent problem. In his words,

> After the agreement to sell most of the Belgian bank to BNP Paribas, Belgian shareholders challenged the sale – delaying resolution for six months.

[57] Nieto and Schinasi, above note 55, p. 15.

[58] Emilios Avgouleas, *Governance of Global Financial Markets: The Law, The Economics, The Politics* (Cambridge: Cambridge University Press, 2012), pp. 250–1; Schoenmaker, above note 3, pp. 79–81.

> The court granted shareholders the right to vote on the sale, which they initially rejected but subsequently accepted after modifications. The delays caused by shareholder disputes were allowed because Belgian law (as well as Dutch law) does not provide national authorities with the power to take actions that override shareholders' rights in order to maintain financial stability during a crisis.[59]

To a different extent all three governments intervened heavily to purchase shares of the local operations of Fortis in their territory, de facto nationalizing a great part of the Bank. This ultimately resulted in a loss of the franchise value of Fortis. The failure of cooperation between the three regulators illustrates the problems associated with coordinating the protection of local depositors, equity holders, and national taxpayers in a cross-border banking resolution. More importantly, it also shows the value of a timely and swift intervention, in absence of which states will be more likely to proceed on their own.[60]

4.4. CHALLENGES IN INTERNATIONAL BAIL-INS

Bail-in undoubtedly represents the most important evolution in the international regulatory landscape for bank resolution. Given the impracticability of a global financial authority responsible for resolving and funding cross-border banks, national authorities remained trapped in the same old problem of how to deal with a TBTF bank. Experience demonstrates that it is precisely in these situations that coordination becomes particularly troublesome. Bail-in provides a possible response to the political problems of cross-border bank bailouts, making coordination more likely in times of crisis.[61]

Creditors' recapitalizations were not designed specifically for the problems of cross-border resolution. Indeed, they were meant to be applied to both domestic and international banks. However, the particular dynamics underlining these new tools offered a potential solution to the problems of international bailouts. By relying on the financial sector itself to recapitalize a failing bank, supervisory authorities are free from the political and economic pressure that comes with the use of taxpayers' money. This means that

[59] Jonathan M. Edwards, 'A Model Law Framework for the Resolution of G-SIFIs' (2012) 7 *Capital Markets Law Journal* 122, p. 132.

[60] Franklin Allen, Thorsten Beck, Elena Carletti, Philip R. Lane, Dirk Schoenmaker, and Wolf Wagner, *Cross-Border Banking in Europe: Implications for Financial Stability and Macroeconomic Policies* (London: Center for Economic Policy Research, 2011), p. 43.

[61] For a general discussion on problems of coordination in international bail-ins, see Federico Lupo-Pasini and Ross P. Buckley, "International Coordination in Cross-Border Bank Bail-ins: Problems and Prospects" (2015) 16 *European Business Organization Law Review* 203.

coordination problems present in international bailout are eliminated. In a bail-in, authorities have much less incentive to boycott an international recapitalization, being that they will transfer the burden of dealing with the failing bank to big financial institutions. By doing so, they will avoid the political costs associated with the use of taxpayers' money (especially when diverted to sustain the bank's foreign operations), and eliminate the fiscal sustainability problems highlighted by the bank–sovereign vicious link.

In spite of their apparent benefits, bail-ins are not the definitive solution to cross-border bank resolution. First of all, they tackle only TBTF firms that must necessarily be kept alive. Hence, bail-ins do not solve the coordination problems associated with smaller cross-border bank insolvencies, which apply to banks whose insolvency can be dealt with under insolvency law. This means that the historical cross-border insolvency problems between home and host countries, separated between the universal and territorial approaches to these insolvencies, remain unsolved. Moreover, by transferring the burden of recapitalization on to creditors, bail-ins add a new player in the coordination game of bank resolution: financial investors in junior and senior bank debt. By shifting the focus away from the state to private investors, bail-in triggers two major evolutions in the policy framework for bank resolution.

The first is shifting the terrain of the dispute from fiscal burden-sharing to regulatory cooperation. From a legal viewpoint, bail-ins entail the sacrifice of creditors' rights. In a bail-in, as in a insolvency, the stability of the bank can only be achieved by overriding the normal legal relationships between the bank, its creditors, and other counterparties. This requires rewriting debt contracts, bypassing normal property rights and, above all, allocating the financial costs of the recapitalization between the different classes of creditors. However, countries have historically had different approaches to insolvency that might lead to different levels of creditors' protection.[62] These regulatory asymmetries can affect creditors' rights and bail-in procedures in various ways, from the declaration of insolvency, to the constitutional protection of fundamental property rights. In certain countries, the fact that a bail-in is recognized as an insolvency might authorize trade creditors to require the authority to undo certain transactions that occurred before the bail-in procedure, or to close out their agreement based on the fact that there is a debt restructuring.[63] In the context of a bank-resolution procedure, which must take place over a weekend, the possibility that a court might suspend the bail-in until the claims

[62] Jianping Zhou et al., "From Bail-out to Bail-in: Mandatory Debt Restructuring of Systemic Financial Institutions" (2012) IMF Staff Discussion Note SDN/12/03, p. 11.

[63] *Ibid.*, p. 14.

are settled would destroy the very purpose of the procedure, which is to make the bank a going concern able to operate during restructuring.[64]

The second evolution concerns the potential involvement in the resolution of a third jurisdiction different from the home and the host. Indeed, when raising capital, international banks often issue their debt in capital markets where the cost of credit is cheaper and where the legislation is considered more favorable. Typically, large banking conglomerates issue their debt in London under English law or in New York under US law. The law governing the contract becomes a fundamental element at play in the resolution game: only when the *lex contractus* allows overriding creditors' rights can the bail-in safely take place. This, however, requires the cooperation of the jurisdiction that governs the contract. This means that the bail-in of a multinational bank would potentially involve three jurisdictions: (1) the home country where the bank is headquartered; (2) the host countries where it has subsidiaries or branches; and (3) the country where the parent bank or its subsidiaries have issued the liabilities subject to the bail-in.

The addition of a third country complicates the coordination. Investors will push banks to issue debts in creditor-friendly jurisdictions where they will be more protected. Furthermore, bank investors are very likely to be hedge funds or pension funds with extensive experience in litigation. Recent sovereign debt restructurings have shown that investors are very likely to oppose any attempt to reduce their credits and, to the extent possible, they will use all remedies available under the law governing the contract.[65] The recent resolution of Portugal's Banco Espirito Santo highlights precisely this problem. Following forced losses on their credits in Banco Espirito Santo, a group of hedge funds had filed a number of disputes in various courts in Portugal and England against the Portuguese Central Bank to recover the funds lost as a result of the bank's restructuring.[66]

4.5. THE FSB'S STANDARDS ON INTERNATIONAL COOPERATION

Cooperation failures in cross-border bank resolution are not a novelty: the failures of Bankhaus Herstatt in 1974, BCCI in 1991, Barings in 1996, and Long Term Capital Management (LTCM) in 1998 all led to disorderly resolutions.

[64] In this regard, the IMF recognizes that for a quick and effective resolution procedure, it would be advisable to limit the role of the courts. *Ibid.*, p. 12.

[65] See Lupo-Pasini and Buckley, above note 61.

[66] Martin Arnold, "Investors File Legal Challenge over Portugal's BES Rescue," *Financial Times* (1 November 2014).

Eurozone countries have bypassed the problems of cooperation by creating in 2014 and 2015 two common supervisory and resolution systems: the Single Supervisory Mechanism and the Single Resolution Mechanism. Given the problems with creating an international authority responsible for resolving cross-border banks, the rest of the world has had to rely on other solutions. Some authors have proposed the adoption of burden-sharing agreements in which home and host supervisors agree in advance on the allocation of losses and the fiscal contribution provided by each authority to keep the bank afloat.[67] However, this option was disregarded by the policy community in view of the reluctance of regulators to commit to future fiscal disbursements.

Bank resolution plans (commonly referred to as "living wills") have provided some useful guidance to regulators on how the different parts of a cross-border bank could be dealt with during a crisis.[68] Living wills are documents provided by banks to supervisory authorities (which approve them), laying out the contingency plan adopted by the bank in the eventuality of a crisis. Among the issues addressed are: the location of assets and liabilities; the regulatory framework applicable for each part of the bank group in a insolvency scenario; and the bank's plans with regard to liquidity support and the selling of toxic assets. However, these living wills are not binding on regulators, and are based on assumptions regarding future market and regulatory conditions that might turn out to be wrong.[69] As such, they are unable to solve the myriad legal, jurisdictional, and economic problems faced by home and host authorities when resolving a failing bank.[70]

From an international law perspective, the Financial Stability Forum (FSB) has taken centrestage in coordinating the work on an international regulatory framework for bank resolution. Since its creation, the FSB has played a pivotal role in promoting regulatory convergence, and in proposing solutions to global financial instability. It has done so by issuing guidelines and financial standards to be implemented in national jurisdictions, and by subjecting its members to peer-review mechanisms. One of its most influential proposals,

[67] Charles Goodhart and Dirk Schoenmaker, "Fiscal Burden Sharing in Cross-Border Banking Crises" (2009) 5 *International Journal of Central Banking* 141; Dirk Schoenmaker, "Burden Sharing for Cross-Border Banks" (2011) 18 *Estabilidad Financiera* 31.

[68] See Emilios Avgouleas, Charles Goodhart, and Dirk Schoenmaker, "Bank Resolution Plans as Catalyst for Financial Reforms" (2013) 9 *Journal of Financial Stability* 2010.

[69] Mehrsa Baradaran, "Regulation by Hypothetical" (2014) 67 *Vanderbilt Law Review* 1247.

[70] For a critique, see Nizan Geslevich Packin, "The Case against the Dodd-Frank Act's Living Wills: Contingency Planning Following the Financial Crisis" (2012) 9 *Berkeley Business Law Journal* 29.

the use of creditor-funded recapitalization, has proved to be a cornerstone of the current regulatory landscape for bank resolution across the Atlantic.

Successful reform of the bank resolution regime is one of the FSB's core policy objectives.[71] Over the years, it has issued numerous policy papers and international standards to assist national authorities in resolving failing banks in an orderly manner. The 2011 *Key Attributes of Effective Resolution Regimes for Financial Institutions* [hereinafter, the Key Attributes] represent undoubtedly the most important piece of international law in this regard. This soft-law instrument sets out a list of twelve core elements that any domestic resolution regime should feature, ranging from the power of resolution authorities during a resolution to resolvability assessments. Like other classic international financial law instruments, the Key Attributes aim at harmonizing domestic resolution laws, by proposing the adoption of a common core regulatory and policy framework across the members' jurisdictions. By doing so, they eliminate potentially dangerous regulatory loopholes, thereby reducing the likelihood of disorderly resolutions.

International coordination is a fundamental aspect of the Key Attributes, albeit not the only one. Among the most important recommendations are the creation of Crisis Management Groups to prepare and facilitate the resolution of cross-border banks,[72] the use of MoUs between home and host authorities of systemically important banks,[73] and some guidelines for the legal framework for cross-border cooperation,[74] which I will deal with partially in the next section of this chapter. Crisis Management Groups, in particular, are the equivalent of Supervisory Colleges for resolution authorities, and serve to solve some of the most troublesome issues in the context of resolution, such as identifying and removing obstacles to resolvability, sharing information on the stability of the bank group, and discussing the group's resolution plans. The Attributes play a fundamental role in laying the groundwork for successful cooperation between national authorities. However, alone they do not suffice in ensuring meaningful cooperation, especially during a crisis, and they do not bind regulators to a particular coordination mechanism during a crisis.

In the European Union, however, the degree of cooperation has become much higher than that proposed by the FSB's standards. Under the 2014 EU Bank Recovery and Resolution Directive further complemented by the

[71] See www.financialstabilityboard.org/what-we-do/policy-development/effective-resolution-regimes-and-policies/.

[72] Key Attribute 8.

[73] Key Attribute 9.

[74] Key Attribute 7.

European Banking Authority's binding guidelines,[75] European banks that do not operate solely in the Banking Union must establish Resolution Colleges among the national and supranational authorities competent for resolving the bank.[76] Under the EU legislation, Resolution Colleges must adopt binding decisions on a range of issues such as the valuation of solvency, obstacles to an effective resolution, the approval to the bank's resolution plans, and the determination of the total-loss-absorbing-capacity. On top of it, in case of disagreement among the resolution authorities in the Resolution Colleges, the issues can be decided by a mandatory conciliation under the auspices of the European Banking Authority' or directly by the European Banking Authority.[77]

4.5.1. *The FSB Principles for Cross-Border Effectiveness of Resolution Actions*

Predictably, it became immediately clear that unless national authorities coordinate their resolution rules and recognize each other's powers in the resolution, it would be impossible to implement cross-border bank resolutions. Without a common framework, each authority would be able to refuse to implement the bail-in in its jurisdiction or recognize the primacy of foreign resolution powers over domestic laws. The problem is particularly acute in bail-ins, as they rely on the bank issuing debt in third countries. For this reason in November 2015 the FSB released the *Principles for Cross-Border Effectiveness of Resolution Actions* [hereinafter, the Principles], which spells out a few proposals on legal mechanisms to achieve international coordination in banking resolution.[78] In the Principles, the FSB recommends a mixed private and public approach relying on (1) binding resolution clauses contained in debt contracts that force investors to recognize the power of the resolution authorities in conducting the resolution actions (the contractual approach); and (2) mutual recognition

[75] Directive 2014/59/EU of the European Parliament and of the Council of 15 May 2014 establishing a framework for the recovery and resolution of credit institutions and investment firms.

[76] This means that Resolution Colleges will be established among EU banks operating in non-banking union countries but still in the EU (for instance, a bank established in the Czech Republic with subsidiaries in Poland and Hungary), and banks operating in both Banking Union countries and non-banking union EU countries (for instance, a bank established in Italy with subsidiaries in Poland). Banks operating exclusively among Banking Union countries will be subject to the centralized resolution procedures under the Single Resolution Mechanism.

[77] Anna Gardella, "La Risoluzione dei Gruppi Finanziari Cross-Border nell'Unione Europea," in Raffaele D'Ambrosio (ed.) *Scritti Sull'Unione Bancaria* (Rome: Banca D'Italia, 2016), pp. 164–6.

[78] Financial Stability Board, "Principles for Cross-Border Effectiveness of Resolution Action" (3 November 2015).

of resolution action that automatically allows the extraterritorial application of the resolution in host and third countries (the statutory approach).

The **contractual approach** seems, from a *prima facie* analysis, a very easy solution to the problem of investors' opposition to the resolution and, therefore, to the entire cross-border resolution conundrum. By inserting into the debt contract a clause that essentially obliges investors to renounce their normal creditors' rights, investors will not have any legal claim against the resolution authority that will convert their debt into shares or imposes a forced haircut. This would allow the competent authority to recapitalize the failing bank irrespective of the location of the debt and without relying on difficult burden-sharing negotiations with foreign counterparts.

However, contractual approaches are unanimously recognized to be of limited use without explicit statutory backing. The same FSB document recognizes that they can only be considered a temporary measure.[79] What the contractual approach aims to achieve is, essentially, to import the power of one resolution authority into another jurisdiction by the explicit contractual waiver of the rights normally enjoyed under the local law. However, even the voluntary waiver of creditors' rights will not be effective – and will not be recognized by the local courts – when it derogates fundamental principles of public law, or it is in violation of essential elements of domestic property, bankruptcy, or company laws. In this situation, there is a high risk that the jurisdiction where the debt is issued will not recognize the mandate of the resolution authority or will refuse to implement the supportive measures required to conduct the resolution in the local jurisdiction.

For this reason, the **statutory approach** is the most credible mechanism to ensure effective cross-border coordination in the event of a resolution. The FSB's Principles solves the dilemma between the territorial and universal approaches by recommending a modified universal approach. This approach was already clearly spelled out in the *Key Attributes*. Key Attribute 7.5 states that "Jurisdictions should provide for transparent and expedited processes to give effect to foreign resolution measures, either by way of a mutual recognition process or by taking measures under the domestic resolution regime that support and are consistent with the resolution measures taken by the foreign home resolution authority."[80]

The rationale of statutory recognition is essentially similar to that of universality of insolvency: to prevent duplication of resolution actions and reduce the spillovers of a disorderly resolution. The goal is to extend the scope of resolution

[79] *Ibid.*, p. 11.
[80] *Ibid.*, Key Attribute 7.5.

powers enjoyed by the authority in charge of the resolution on to the foreign jurisdictions; essentially, to achieve extraterritorial effect for the resolution. In a single-point-of-entry approach – in which the resolution is implemented at the parent bank level – the home authority needs to gain rapid control over the bank's foreign operations and the firm's assets located in host jurisdictions. Without the guarantee of support from host authorities, the bail-in of the debt in the foreign branches or subsidiaries would simply be impossible.[81] In a multiple-point-of-entry approach – in which resolution is implemented separately in each jurisdiction – coordination is similarly fundamental. Although under this approach national authorities implement the resolution separately, they do not do it independently. Indeed, they still need to coordinate their interventions to prevent fire-sale externalities, enforce stays on early termination rights, and provide liquidity assistance. Above all, supervisory authorities must resist the temptation to ring-fence the local banks to protect national interests.[82]

In particular, cooperation in resolution needs to address three aspects. First, host authorities need to cooperate with home authorities in resolving the foreign *branch* of a bank resolved by home authorities. Second, whenever the failing bank has a subsidiary in a foreign jurisdiction, the direct involvement and cooperation of the host authority is crucial. In particular, "host jurisdictions may need to provide a process to allow the transfer of shares in the subsidiary to another institution or to require local subsidiaries to continue to provide essential services to the parent company or other group entities."[83] The FSB's Principles sets out two coordination mechanisms to achieve the aforementioned objectives: Recognition and Direct Support.

Recognition of foreign resolution action is, essentially, a commitment to cooperate with a foreign authority in resolving the part of the foreign bank situated in the national territory, based on the decision of a foreign resolution authority. Recognition of resolution actions is already a well-known principle in commercial cross-border insolvency. The UNCITRAL Model Law on Cross-Border Insolvency provides various legal mechanisms for the recognition of foreign insolvency proceedings and for assisting courts in coordinating their work in the insolvency of a cross-border group. Under the Model Law, national courts are forced to grant stays upon the recognition of the foreign proceeding as the main proceeding, thereby enabling the universality of the bankruptcy.[84] Unfortunately, however, the Model Law does not cover banks.

[81] See above note 44, p. 20.
[82] *Ibid.*, p. 28.
[83] See above note 78, pp. 4–5.
[84] See above note 78, p. 7.

As the FSB states, recognition implies that "at the request of a foreign party, a jurisdiction would accept the commencement of a foreign resolution proceeding domestically and thereby empower the relevant domestic authority (either a court or an administrative agency) to enforce the foreign resolution measure or grant other forms of domestic relief, such as for example a stay on domestic creditor proceedings."[85] In granting recognition, it is irrelevant whether the jurisdiction of the recognizing authority has in place a resolution framework that sets similar conditions for resolution, such as similar thresholds for insolvency etc. What matters is that the two jurisdictions have agreed ex-ante to recognize the proceeding taken in the foreign jurisdiction.

Direct support, on the other hand, entails the direct implementation of resolution measures in the part of the banking group located in the recognizing authority jurisdiction, at the request and upon the decision of the foreign initiating authority. In doing so, it is essential that the recognizing authority act within its own resolution proceedings. Direct support is particularly important when the debt subject to bail-in is located in the foreign operations, and therefore it is necessary to use the local resolution powers to convert it.

4.5.2. *Challenges Ahead*

The statutory approach advocated by the FSB would guarantee uniformity of intervention mechanisms, certainty in the procedures to be followed, and a high degree of coordination. If properly implemented, the statutory recognition of foreign resolution action would discipline the rights and obligations between the various authorities involved in the resolution, and allocate the burden of intervention between the parties, thereby reducing the dangerous regulatory asymmetries that usually plague cross-border resolution. Nevertheless, it would be naïve to consider the FSB standards as the definitive solution to cross-border resolutions.

First of all, the statutory approach will work only if all states harmonize their regulatory environments by inserting in their domestic resolution laws the recognition and mutual support clause, and by requiring banks to have at their disposal a minimum level of loss-absorbing capacity.[86] However, cross-border resolution will not be coordinated through a binding treaty, but only through voluntary compliance with the FSB standards. More importantly, while the FSB rules provide a very sound regulatory mechanism for cooperation, they

85 *Ibid.*, p. 5.

86 See Financial Stability Board, "Adequacy of Loss-absorbing Capacity of Global Systemically Important Banks in Resolution," Consultative Document (10 November 2014).

nonetheless fail to provide the necessary institutional infrastructure to guarantee cooperation. In particular, the FSB rules do not tackle the misalignment of incentives between authorities and the principal–agent problem that are at the core of disorderly resolution. The experience with MoUs and the impossibility of achieving meaningful coordination in cross-border bankruptcies have demonstrated that the sovereign costs associated with home-country control often prevent countries from abiding by the rules set in agreements. Without addressing those underlying issues, it is uncertain whether resolution authorities would conform to the agreement, especially in the context of a crisis.

Cross-border bail-ins have very similar characteristics to insolvencies. In both cases, the restructuring of the bank requires the rewriting of every legal relationship between the bank and its creditors, often by overriding the contractual and property rights enjoyed by creditors during normal times. To do so, the authorities competent to deal with the distressed bank need to be empowered with particular statutory rights that allow them to place the stability of the financial system (however perceived in the context of the resolution) over the respect of contractual and property rights. To achieve this objective, it is necessary to have a very clear picture of the legal relationships between the parties and to evaluate the tradeoffs between the social costs of the insolvency and the return in terms of financial stability.

However, it is precisely the difficulty in achieving a harmonized view over myriad corporate, commercial, and banking law that makes it very difficult for foreign authorities to have the same view over resolution. As Tung excellently put it:

> the recognition of a foreign proceeding effects the wholesale import of another state's regime for deciding sensitive policy issues. Political judgments about local asset disposition and allocation of local losses from the foreign firm's demise are left in the hands of a foreign court. Universalism effectively requires a state's precommitment to wholesale deferral to other states' various prescriptions for financial distress. This is no small request.[87]

In the context of a resolution, the law might determine different thresholds for the authorities' intervention, which might give rise to time-inconsistency problems. For instance, in some countries, the law mandates public intervention when the bank becomes illiquid or when its net worth declines to zero. However, in other countries authorities have the power to intervene at an earlier point.[88] Furthermore, different jurisdictions might have different approaches to identifying critical economic functions.

87 Tung, above note 21, p. 52.

88 This policy has been recently adopted in the UK, Japan, South Korea, and Taiwan.

5

Nationalism in Sovereign Debt

Lending is the core feature of finance. The law plays a fundamental role to support this function, as it gives much-needed support whenever one party of the transaction incurs difficulty. In a pure free-market situation where creditor and debtor are private parties subject to law enforcement, the decision of a borrower to borrow a certain amount of money would depend only on its ability to repay. The law has, in this context, a fundamental function. In the case of non-repayment, the lender can rely on an efficient legal mechanism that forces the borrower to pay back the initial sum, either by selling other assets or by obliging him or her to progressively repay the debt.[1] This reduces the willingness of the debtor to default strategically. Secondly, the existence of a binding legal framework and a credible compliance mechanism reduce the debtor's willingness to borrow, thus leading to an optimal level of debt.[2] If the debtor is unable to service its debt and bankruptcy or reorganization is required, the law plays a similarly fundamental role. Bankruptcy law reduces coordination problems between creditors by transferring to a centralized legal mechanism the organization of the bankruptcy process that guarantees a socially efficient division of assets, and a fresh start for the defaulting company.

The process of sovereign borrowing is, from a business viewpoint, not very different from that of a domestic transaction. In both instances, a lender (a financial institution) offers credit to a borrower (a state) upon the promise of the former to repay the principal and the interest. However, sovereign debt is different from any other credit transaction due to the legal, institutional, and

[1] On the various remedies available and relative damages, see Robert Cooter and Melvin Aron Eisenberg, "Damages for Breach of Contract" (1985) 73 *California Law Review* 1432; Victor Goldberg, *Framing Contract Law: An Economic Perspective* (Cambridge, MA: Harvard University Press, 2006).

[2] On the role of the law as a deterrence mechanism, see Robert E. Scott and George G. Triantis, "Anticipating Litigation in Contract Design" (2006) 115 *Yale Law Journal* 814.

economic underpinnings behind the entire debt process. These differences make international coordination in sovereign debt policy extremely challenging and often subject to the logic of financial nationalism.

More than any other topic, sovereign debt exemplifies the difficulties for financial sovereignty and financial integration to coexist peacefully. Bankers and sovereigns have had a long history of cooperation dating back centuries.[3] The emergence of banking business in Florence in the fourteenth century was spurred by the constant financing needs of sovereigns to wage wars. Until modern times, bankers have thrived on the political or economic ambitions of states, thereby making sovereign lending a very profitable business.[4] Yet, sovereign lending has often proved to be a highly risky endeavor. At the foundation of the sovereign debt process lies an asymmetry of power between debtors and their creditors, which puts the two legs of the sovereign debt transaction on an uneven playing field. On the one hand, debtors are sovereign entities enjoying the utmost control over their economic policies and their ability to repay. On the other hand, creditors are private enterprises, which enjoy relatively limited legal protection under international law.

For centuries, the inability of a sovereign to service its debt did not carry systemic economic implications outside the solvency of its creditor. And while sovereign defaults undoubtedly gave rise to political standoffs that were sometimes solved through power politics, the broader financial and economic effects associated with those defaults were not such to transmit a systemic shock. In the current global financial system, on the contrary, sovereign defaults can easily become a global concern. As I explained in Chapter 2, the increased proclivity of sovereigns to rely on capital markets to finance their public budget and banks' increased appetites to hold sovereign debt in their portfolios[5] creates a direct link between the macroeconomic stability of the sovereign and the stability of the financial system. Thus, in a highly integrated economic system, domestic macroeconomic problems in one country can easily transmit shocks to the broader financial system and, from there, negatively affect other

[3] Charles Tilly, *Coercion, Capital, and European States AD 990–1990* (Malden, MA and Oxford: Blackwell, 1990).

[4] Niall Ferguson, *The Ascent of Money: A Financial History of the World* (New York: Penguin Books, 2009).

[5] Basel III, like its predecessors, assigns a zero-risk weight to OECD countries' bond in calculating capital requirements. For instance, according to ECB reports, Eurozone banks held an average of 14% exposure in sovereign bonds, while in certain countries the exposure toward domestic sovereign bonds account for 10% of the overall portfolio. See European Banking Authority, "EU-wide Transparency Exercise 2013 Summary Report," European Banking Authority (December 2013).

countries.[6] The experience of the 2010 Greek quasi-default and the propagation of financial contagion across the periphery of the Eurozone, albeit strictly connected to the peculiar institutional loopholes in the Eurozone economic architecture, reveals that in a situation of financial integration, even a small country can trigger a powerful wave of financial shock.

Moreover, when the debt burden of a sovereign proves to be unsustainable and restructuring is the only feasible option, sovereigns and foreign creditors are often stuck in prolonged and tense negotiations for the control of the restructuring process. Without mechanisms that guarantee coordination between the different parties, restructurings are sometimes frustrated by the uncooperative behavior of some creditors, which hold out from the process in order to extract a higher payout. This can lead to disastrous restructuring outcomes that will eventually force the sovereign into a full default and impose huge losses on other creditors. Furthermore, recent creditors' disputes show that, in the absence of an international legal framework for debt restructuring, the benefits of cooperation can give way to a logic of financial nationalism in which the creditors' forum-shopping in strategic jurisdictions coupled with the extraterritorial reach of domestic law could paralyze the entire restructuring process.

Thus, at present the international law of sovereign debt is unable to address the limits of international coordination in sovereign debt. To highlight the question of financial nationalism in this field and the shortcomings of international law, I will discuss three different issues: (1) the dangers of overborrowing; (2) the law of sovereign defaults; (3) and the role of national courts in adjudicating sovereign debt restructuring disputes. I will then look at the role and limits of private mechanisms to address those inefficiencies, and conclude by suggesting the potential role of international law.

5.1. THE POLITICAL ECONOMY OF SOVEREIGN BORROWING AND DEFAULTS

Sovereign debt is probably the area of finance that is most linked to public policy. Unlike private finance, sovereign borrowing serves to achieve an essential

[6] The literature on sovereign defaults is vast. For a good overview, see Carmen M. Reinhart and Kenneth S. Rogoff, *This Time Is Different: Eight Centuries of Financial Folly* (Princeton, NJ: Princeton University Press, 2009); Robert W. Kolb (ed.) *Sovereign Debt: From Safety to Default* (Hoboken, NJ: Wiley, 2011); Lorenzo Bini-Smaghi, "Sovereign Risk," in Andreas Dombret and Otto Lucius (eds.) *Stability of the Financial System: Illusion or Feasible Concept?* (Cheltenham: Edward Elgar, 2013); Mark L. J. Wright, "Theory of Sovereign Debt and Default," in Gerard Caprio Jr. (ed.) *Handbook of Safeguarding Global Financial Stability: Political, Social, Cultural, and Economic Theories and Models* (London: Elsevier, 2013).

common objective: to finance government spending. The decision of a government to default from its international financial obligations is also strictly connected to the broader economic and societal implications that the debt repayment process entails for the local community. To understand the global implications of sovereign debt, it is therefore first necessary to understand the political economy of sovereign borrowing and defaults. The literature on sovereign debt is enormous, and it would be impossible to summarize it in a few sentences. Here I will focus on a recent stream of literature that analyzes the incentives faced by those who make the actual borrowing and payment decisions.

5.1.1. *Overborrowing*

In modern democracies government spending is financed by the use of a common government fund in which the collection of internal taxes as well as external government financing are pulled together.[7] The money is then invested by the state in all those activities that a modern government engages in, such as welfare state policies and pensions, building of roads, public administration, and maintenance of universities. One of the fundamental economic problems of fiscal policy is that those who bear the costs of contributing to this common fund are not those who enjoy its benefits. Economists define it as a "common pool" problem. Common pool problems are the equivalent of environmental pollution but for fiscal policy.[8] They exist at different levels.[9] For instance, they can operate horizontally between different social groups or between different areas of the country. Or they can operate vertically between generations. Given the time lapse typical of sovereign debt contracts, the practice of external borrowing entails the latter.

Sovereign borrowing is, at its essence, a redistributive policy within generations, because the costs of borrowing are paid after many years. Sovereign debt contracts are long-term agreements in which the performance of the debtor will take place a long time after the signing of the contract, between 5 to even 30 years. During the period of time that separates the borrowing decision from the actual servicing of the debt, many things can change in the debtor's

[7] Barry Eichengreen, Robert Feldman, Jeff Liebman, Jürgen von Hagen, and Charles Wyplosz, "Public Debts: Nuts, Bolts and Worries," Geneva Reports on the World Economy 13, International Center for Monetary and Banking Studies (2011), available at http://dev3.cepr.org/pubs/books/CEPR/Geneva13.pdf, p. 15.

[8] Mark Hallerberg and Jurgen Von Hagen, "Electoral Institutions, Cabinet Negotiations, and Budget Deficits in the EU," in James Poterba and Jurgen Von Hagen (eds.) *Fiscal Institutions and Fiscal Performance* (Chicago, IL: University of Chicago Press, 1999).

[9] Eichengreen, Feldman, Liebman, von Hagen, and Wyplosz, above note 7, pp. 15–18.

country. The ruling party might have gone to the opposition, or a new state might have formed. In both circumstances, the desire of the predecessors to borrow to satisfy short-term interests might not be matched by an equal willingness of the successors to repay.

The time-consistency problem typical of sovereign debt creates an externality. If those who bear the costs of sovereign financing were the same as those who enjoy the benefits of an increased level of credit, they would probably have chosen a level of sovereign indebtedness that would equate with their social or political marginal benefits. However, since the two groups are separated by a generational gap, those who benefit from a policy tend to seek higher levels of spending without taking into account the costs of repayment borne by future generations.[10] As recent research has succinctly put it, the real risk now is that sovereigns might borrow "beyond the point at which the social cost of one additional unit of debt equals the social benefit of an additional unit of debt-financed government expenditure."[11] Surprisingly, with only few exceptions, developed countries have a higher level of sovereign indebtedness, and a higher risk of default. For instance, as of September 2016, Italy has a debt–GDP ratio of 132%, Greece of 177%, the United States of 104%, and France of 96%, compared to 66% of Brazil, 43% of Mexico, or 17% of Chile.[12] Indeed, developing and emerging economies face a much lower risk of over-indebtedness, as their precarious legal institutions, weaker macroeconomic conditions, and generally higher proclivity for default reduce the willingness of capital markets to lend to them.[13]

The problem of overborrowing is, paradoxically, more acute in countries that adopt a democratic political system. The high political turnover and the need to conquer the vote of citizens are an explosive combination that incites sovereign borrowing. The ruling government always faces strong incentives to overborrow. Besides the difficulties of precisely calculating and factoring in the long-term growth prospects of a country in its decision to borrow, democratic governments need to please their electorates for reelections. Thus, they face a high political incentive to adopt more expensive welfare or social

[10] *Ibid.*, p. 16.

[11] Committee on Economic Policies and Reform, "Revisiting Sovereign Bankruptcy," The Brookings Institution (October 2013), p. 8.

[12] See www.tradingeconomics.com.

[13] Barry Eichengreen, Ricardo Hausmann, and Ugo Panizza, "The Pain of Original Sin," in Barry Eichengreen and Ricardo Hausmann (eds.) *Other People's Money* (Chicago, IL: University of Chicago Press, 2005); Carmen M. Reinhart, Kenneth S. Rogoff, and Miguel A. Savastano, "Debt Intolerance" (2003) 34 *Brookings Papers on Economic Activity* 1; Committee on Economic Policies and Reform, above note 11, pp. 9–10.

policies that favor short-term interests rather than long-term fiscal sustainability goals. Borrowing is, ultimately, the easiest option. Unlike taxing, it does not anger the population. On the contrary, it allows the government to finance social projects.[14] Thus, without constitutional checks limiting the amount of spending and borrowing, every political constituency will have a natural proclivity for borrowing beyond the socially optimal level.[15] The problem is not dissimilar to that encountered by governments in monetary policies. In this last case, however, the principle of central bank independence was created exactly to counter the natural impulse of sovereigns to manipulate their monetary policies to serve short-term interests.

5.1.2. *The Logic of Sovereign Defaults*

It is not necessary to be a finance specialist to grasp the concept of a sovereign default. Newspapers report almost on a weekly basis the news of a state failing to service its debt or fighting with creditors over the restructuring of its debt obligations. Defaults represent the quintessential problem in the policy of sovereign debt. Unlike other financial concepts, sovereign default underscores fundamental legal implications; it could be easily said that default is, primarily, a legal concept. It denotes the failure of the borrower to service the debt it owes to its creditors under the conditions set in the debt contract. As such, a default does not necessarily mean that the sovereign repudiates its debt in its entirety by simply refusing to pay. This is a possibility, although very rare, due to the broader political and financial consequences that this would entail. Default could simply mean that the sovereign suffers a temporary liquidity problem that makes it unable to pay the interest or the principal on time. In this situation the sovereign will try to negotiate with the creditors a restructuring of the debt that might entail a deferral of the payment owed to the creditors, or its reduction – a "haircut" – or a combination of both.[16]

Hundreds of years of history on sovereign debt teaches that there is no single reason for why countries sometimes fail to pay their debts on time. Depending on the perspective from which sovereign debt problems are analyzed, there

[14] Other authors point out that overborrowing could also result from other factors, such as herding behavior that leads governments to take up too much debt during a phase of economic growth, or moral hazard resulting from bailout packages and other forms of official sector support. See Olivier Jeanne and Jeromin Zettelmeyer, "International Bailouts, Moral Hazard and Conditionality" (2001) 16 *Economic Policy* 409.

[15] Eichengreen, Feldman, Liebman, von Hagen, and Wyplosz, above note 7.

[16] Molly Ryan, "Sovereign Bankruptcy: Why Now and Why Not in the IMF" (2014) 82 *Fordham Law Review* 2473, p. 2479.

are different theories that could explain why states default. The literature has for a long time focused on the economics of sovereign debt problems, linking sovereign defaults to a mix of unsustainable fiscal positions and adverse capital market circumstances, such as sudden capital outflows. For instance, in the presence of tighter international financial conditions – such as a run on debt or reduced appetites of investors – states will find sovereign borrowing more expensive. If investors sense an imminent default, they will increase the interest rates charged to the sovereign, which could put the state in a position where it would be impossible for it to roll over its short-term debt and would have to issue new debt. Consequently, if investors believe that other investors will refuse to buy the new debt, they will refuse to purchase the debt, thereby forcing the sovereign to default. In this situation, states will have difficulty in obtaining new credit, thereby becoming insolvent.[17] In most developing or least-developed countries, which often rely on the export of few commodities, sovereign defaults are often the result of adverse market prices or natural disasters.

More recently, a new stream of scholarship has focused on the unwillingness of politicians to bear the political costs of debt crises that would eventually lead to a too-late restructuring. In the previous section, I discussed how the time-consistency problem of sovereign debt encourages policymakers to overborrow. The same problem also occurs at the moment of repaying the debt. While democratic governments are, in principle, reliable in taking up their predecessors' obligations, they nonetheless have little incentive in assuming the political costs attached to those obligations.

One common pool problem comes from the difficulty in transferring the social costs of reduced budget spending from one sector of the economy to another.[18] In this regard, Alesina and Drazer provide a model that explains how budget cuts and the subsequent fiscal solidarity between different groups reduce the political incentives of debtor countries to enforce the debt.[19] When a state is on the verge of default, it can simply agree with its creditors to reschedule the debt, especially if the problem is only of a temporary nature, like a liquidity crisis. However, more often than not, reduced interest on the principal or a deferral on the payment do not suffice. When a country suffers a solvency problem it needs to request emergency liquidity assistance from the International Monetary Fund (IMF) or some other official mechanism, in addition to a reduction in the level of debt owed to the private creditors.

[17] Mark J. Wright, "Sovereign Debt Restructuring: Problems and Prospects" (2012) 2 *Harvard Business Law Review* 153.

[18] *Ibid.*, pp. 175–6.

[19] *Ibid.*, p. 175.

With liquidity assistance comes also the request to implement substantial economic and structural reforms: the so-called IMF conditionality.[20] Examples are the liberalization of strategic sectors, privatization of public companies, pension and labor market reforms, and debt reduction. In spite of their necessary adoption, the local population always meets austerity measures with a high level of distress. The economic literature has often highlighted that, given the political costs of debt repayment, governments often procrastinate on the decision to request a debt restructuring, thus exacerbating the already weak macroeconomic conditions. Recently, a group of high-level experts on sovereign debt argued that "because policymakers are often replaced after a debt default late restructurings may be caused by self-interested agents that have incentives to gamble for redemption, even when delays entail economic costs for society as a whole."[21] In certain cases, given the effect of a declaration of default on foreign investors, governments might decide to delay the declaration of default in order to keep a small credit line with international capital markets. However, by doing so they only further increase the level of indebtedness without solving the underlying solvency problems.[22] Finally, in certain circumstances, policymakers might request the assistance of the private financial sector, thereby exacerbating the already dangerous credit loop between the official and the private financial sector.[23]

5.2. FISCAL SOVEREIGNTY AND MORAL HAZARD

After explaining the political economy of sovereign debt, the next step is to understand what are the implications of sovereign defaults for the international community and what are the potential barriers to international cooperation in order to minimize the global systemic risk. The protection of fiscal and financial sovereignty under international law is at the center of this debate.

5.2.1. *Fiscal Sovereignty*

Overborrowing is not always a dangerous policy, at least from an international perspective. For instance, if the borrowing state finances its expenditures by

[20] For an overview on conditionality, see IMF, "GRA Lending Toolkit and Conditionality: Reform Proposals" (13 March 2009).

[21] Samuel Malone, "Sovereign Indebtedness, Default, and Gambling for Redemption" (2011) 63 *Oxford Economic Papers* 331.

[22] *Ibid.*, p. 18.

[23] Viral V. Acharya and Raghuram R. Rajan, "Sovereign Debt, Government Myopia and the Financial Sector" (2013) 26 *Review of Financial Studies* 1526.

relying only on domestic debt, the question of repayment carries only internal implications. Indeed, the borrowing country always has the option to print extra money to service the debt. Japan is, probably, the quintessential example in this regard. Although Japan probably carries the worst debt-to-GDP ratio (around 229% of the GDP), most of its debt is held domestically by local investors.[24] The fact that local banks, trusts, and retail investors took the risk of lending to the government arguably acts as an extra incentive for policymakers to adopt sustainable economic policies that will, in the long term, permit the government to service the debt and reduce systemic risk. Moreover, subjecting the debt transaction to local law protects creditors from the risk of arbitrariness on the side of the state. In sum, domestic sovereign borrowing guarantees the harmony of incentives between the lenders and the borrower that make the debt transaction successful.

However, if a government decides to finance its expenditures by relying on external financing, the situation changes drastically. In this case, the implicit political and legal partnership between lenders and domestic borrowers is broken. From a policy and legal viewpoint, borrowing from external investors frees the sovereign from the systemic and political consequences of a default that it would have faced had it borrowed from local creditors. More importantly, when sovereign bonds are issued in foreign jurisdictions and subject to foreign law, the borrower and the lender are separated by jurisdictional discontinuities that render the legal process of repayment more complex. In this situation, the borrowing country has, arguably, very different incentives when it comes to formulating domestic policies and repaying the debt.

The power of a state to design and implement fiscal policy according to its own interests has always been treated as a strictly national matter, excluded from any international coordination.[25] With the only exception of European Union members, which must respect fiscal balance rules and undergo periodical monitoring by EU institutions, all other states have retained the highest discretion in fiscal matters.[26] They can decide the levels and modalities of

[24] Luigi Buttiglione, Philip R. Lane, Lucrezia Reichlin, and Vincent Reinhart, "Deleveraging? What Deleveraging?," Geneva Reports on the World Economy 16 (2014).

[25] Eric A. Posner and Alan O. Sykes, "International Law and the Limits of Macroeconomic Cooperation" (2012) Institute for Law and Economics Working Paper No. 609, University of Chicago Law School.

[26] On the problems and evolutions of the EU framework on fiscal and economic policies, see Benoît Coeuré and Jean Pisani-Ferry, "Fiscal Policy in EMU: Towards a Sustainability and Growth Pact?" (2005) 21 *Oxford Review of Economic Policy* 598; Sebastian Barnes, David Davidsson, and Lucasz Rawdanowicz, "Europe's New Fiscal Rules," OECD Economics Department Working Papers No. 972, OECD Publishing, Organization for Economic Co-operation and Development (2012); Anna Kocharov (ed.) "Another Legal Monster?

taxation for their own citizens and the enterprises located in their territories, and how much to borrow from international financial markets – with potentially no real limits. Furthermore, they retain the right to decide how to spend their tax revenues. In a closed economy, fiscal policy problems largely remain a matter of national concern. However, in an open economy in which sovereigns are able to borrow from international markets, the sovereign control that states exert on their fiscal and economic policies can potentially become troublesome.[27] Indeed, in the absence of constraints that international law normally exerts on the domestic policy space, governments are free to indulge in fiscal profligacy and adopt unsustainable macroeconomic policies that may eventually lead to a default, with disastrous consequences for the sovereign, its creditors, and its neighbors.

The problem of excessive sovereign debt exposure in an interconnected country is quite similar to that faced by private financial institutions. The higher the level of debt of a bank, the more likely it is that, in the event of an external or internal shock, the bank will go bankrupt. This would trigger a systemic reaction that would transmit instability to all those banks that are exposed to the failing bank. To reduce systemic risk, regulators require banks to limit their leverage or their concentration of exposures. Yet, the same regulatory rationale does not apply to sovereigns. Like banks, states may also be too-interconnected-to-fail, especially when they participate in free trade areas or common markets, but they are very rarely constrained in their ability to borrow.

Given the political difficulties of constraining national policymakers' desires to borrow or repay, the protection of fiscal sovereignty is inefficient in addressing the sovereign debt problem. In a situation of financial integration, the protection accorded by fiscal sovereignty simply increases the moral hazard of sovereigns in taking up too much debt. Indeed, it shields them from the political, legal, and economic pressures that would normally be exerted by local creditors and stakeholders. With the full freedom to borrow, governments are naturally inclined to take up socially excessive levels of debt. However, without internal mechanisms that force policymakers to reduce the level of indebtedness, and without external monitoring mechanisms to guide sovereigns in adopting sustainable economic policies, there is a high risk that such excessive levels of indebtedness might eventually turn into a sovereign default.

An EUI Debate on the Fiscal Compact Treaty," EUI Working Papers LAW 2012/09, European University Institute (2012).

[27] On the economics of fiscal policy in an open economy, see Guido Tabellini, "Domestic Politics and the International Coordination of Fiscal Policies" (1990) 28 *Journal of International Economics* 245; Vito Tanzi, "International Coordination of Fiscal Policies" (1988) 8 *Journal of Public Policy* 111.

In this situation, the freedom of external borrowing might endanger not only the debtor country's future generations, but also the global financial system.

5.2.2. *Sovereign Immunity*

The situation becomes more critical when it comes to actually repaying the debt. The protection accorded by international law to sovereigns plays a fundamental role in the debt repayment process. To understand the economics of international law it is useful to draw a brief parallel with the domestic law of finance. In a commercial lending transaction, the debtor has the obligation of repaying to the creditor the principal plus the accrued interest. Only under limited circumstances is a debtor legally excused from the obligation of repaying its debt. Outside those scenarios, if the debtor nonetheless chooses to default, the creditor can legitimately rely on a legal system that forcibly compels the debtor to perform the contract by attacking its assets. The power of the law and the threat of the legal consequences attached to a strategic nonperformance of the contract play essential roles in guaranteeing the level of certainty that is necessary to conduct business. By forcing the debtor to perform the contract, the law increases the incentives of the parties to cooperate in the interests of a successful transaction.

International law has, on the contrary, developed a normative framework that, with a few exceptions,[28] shields sovereigns from their debt obligations. More specifically, under international law, the external debt of a sovereign is excused, not only when a sovereign is experiencing macroeconomic instability or economic depression, but also whenever the sovereign deems that repaying the debt is not worth it. The rationale for this high level of legal protection is entrenched in the very concepts of sovereignty and statehood, and it is grounded on the old idea that private commercial interests cannot bind sovereigns. It relies on a set of legal doctrines that, on different grounds, privilege the interest of the sovereign and its citizens, over those of foreign investors.

Sovereign immunity is a legal doctrine that can be traced back to the roots of international law, and it is based on the idea that those who make the laws

[28] Under international investment law, sovereign debt is protected as an international investment, and as such falls under the scope of protection of international investment treaties. Hence, sovereigns are bound to a specific legal framework that prevents, among others, discrimination, unfair and inequitable treatment, and the unlawful expropriation of the investment. See Giorgio Sacerdoti, "BIT Protections and Economic Crises: Limits to Their Coverage, the Impact of Multilateral Financial Regulation and the Defence of Necessity" (2013) 28 *ICSID Review* 351.

cannot be bound by them.[29] The first immediate implication of such a doctrine is that, under international law, sovereigns cannot be sued in a foreign court. This sovereign privilege did not cover only the international relations between states, but it extended to all the acts of a sovereign, even those with private subjects. Under the theory of absolute immunity, which lasted until the middle of the twentieth century, foreign creditors were at the mercy of the debtor state. Unless the sovereign specifically renounced its immunity, creditors could not sue sovereign debtors either in their own courts or in the debtor's courts.

However, things began to change after the Second World War, when the United States' courts started adopting a more restrictive interpretation of the doctrine that excluded foreign states' commercial activities that were carried on within the United States' territory, or were having effects within it.[30] This restrictive version was subsequently enshrined in US legislation,[31] and was taken on by the United Kingdom and other countries.[32] Hence, according to the current doctrine of sovereign immunity, a creditor can always sue a sovereign in domestic courts for any commercial transaction that has been carried out in the creditor's jurisdiction, or whenever the sovereign expressly waives its immunity.

Immunity waivers are now common in many bond contracts, as they are considered by both sovereigns and investors as a sign of the debtor's commitment to honor its debt.[33] The change in the doctrine of sovereign immunity exposed, for the first time, sovereigns to the power of law, and led to a surge in sovereign debt litigation, especially in New York courts.[34] More recently, the power of this doctrine has been further reduced by the use of International Investment

[29] Thomas Hobbes was the first to enunciate it in the *Leviathan*. See Thomas Hobbes, *Leviathan* (Cambridge: Cambridge University Press, 2002, originally published in 1651).

[30] Ugo Panizza, Federico Sturzenegger, and Jeromin Zettelmeyer, "The Economics and Law of Sovereign Debt and Default" (2009) 47 *Journal of Economic Literature* 651, 653.

[31] Specifically, in the Foreign Sovereign Immunities Act 1976. See Foreign Sovereign Immunity Act, 28 U.S.C. § 1605(a) (2006).

[32] Panizza, Sturzenegger, and Zettelmeyer, above note 30, at 653; Lee C. Buchheit, "Sovereign Immunity" (1986) 7 *Business Law Review* 63; Holger Schier, *Towards A Reorganisation System for Sovereign Debt: An International Law Perspective* (Leiden: Martinus Nijhoff, 2007).

[33] See Stephen J. Choi, Mitu Gulati, and Eric A. Posner, "Political Risk and Sovereign Debt Contracts," John M. Olin Law & Economics Working Paper No. 583, University of Chicago Law School (2011); see also, Stephen J. Choi, Mitu Gulati, and Eric A. Posner, "The Evolution of Contractual Terms in Sovereign Bonds" (2012) 4 *The Journal of Legal Analysis* 131.

[34] See Jonathan I. Blackman and Rahul Mukhi, "The Evolution of Modern Sovereign Debt Litigation: Vultures, Alter Egos, and Other Legal Fauna" (2010) 73 *Law and Contemporary Problems* 47, 53; Anna Gelpern, "Sovereign Damage Control," Peterson Institute for International Economics Policy Brief 13-12 (2013).

Agreements (IIAs) covering portfolio investments[35]. Over the years, international investment law has developed a body of bilateral investment treaties that protect foreign investors against the sovereign power of nation states, and that subject a party that violates an investment treaty to an impartial arbitration tribunal, such as the International Centre for the Settlement of Investment Disputes (ICSID) Tribunal in Washington. According to international investment law, the host government is prohibited from adopting behaviors that are considered to negatively impact on the life of the foreign investment.

In spite of the increased availability of remedial mechanisms for creditors, the business of sovereign debt is still subject to a strong asymmetry of power between the state and the foreign investors. Even when the creditors win their battles in national courts – with the sovereign ordered to repay the debt – they have not won the war. The real problem for creditors is to execute the award. The **execution of the award** is probably the single most important problem faced by creditors now, because there is no legal remedy available to coerce the sovereign to execute the courts' orders. Creditors can request the execution of a court's order in all jurisdictions that recognize the validity of the award. Thus, they can seize the sovereign's financial assets held in foreign bank accounts, or they can seize movable and immovable property, such as houses, planes, boats or fine art exhibitions.[36] However, typically, these are peanuts compared to the amount of outstanding debt that should be recovered. The bulk of the sovereign debtor's assets is always located in the debtor's jurisdiction, and without its consent to execute the court's order, the award is essentially useless.

Furthermore, even if the debtor holds substantial assets abroad, certain categories of assets are subject to a special legal regime that shields them from any creditor's attack. For instance, under certain foreign immunity laws, including the US Foreign Sovereign Immunities Act, central bank assets, such as gold reserves, are subject to full protection. The reason for this has to do with the independence of the central bank, which is not liable for the acts of the government.[37] However, even if the sovereign debt contract was issued by the central bank itself – where usually the issuer is the Treasury – sovereign gold reserves held in the Bank for International Settlements in Basel are excluded from any possible attack.

35 See Jessica Beess und Chrostin, "Sovereign Debt Restructuring and Mass Claims Arbitration before the ICSID, The Abaclat Case" (2012) 53 *Harvard International Law Journal* 506; Ellie Norton, "International Investment Arbitration and the European Debt Crisis" (2012) 13 *Chicago Journal of International Law* 291; Michael Waibel, "Opening Pandora's Box: Sovereign Bonds in International Arbitration" (2007) 101 *American Journal of International Law* 711.

36 Wright, above note 17, p. 158.

37 Panizza, Sturzenegger, and Zettelmeyer, above note 30, p. 654.

5.3. THE ECONOMICS OF FINANCIAL NECESSITY

One of thorniest issue in the law of sovereign debt and, more generally, in international financial relations concerns the right of states to suspend their financial obligations toward their creditors and partners due to a situation of economic emergency. The various legal principles governing this situation can be generally grouped under the heading of "financial necessity." The question of financial necessity has a long and troubled history that traces back to the nineteenth century with the *Russian Indemnity* case.[38] More recently, this issue was at the center of various international financial disputes, from the *EFTA* v. *Iceland* discussed in Chapter 3 to the various rulings following the 2001 Argentine sovereign debt crisis.[39]

5.3.1. *Financial Necessity in International Law*

Sovereign debts covenants, like home–host supervisory agreements or international economic treaties are, essentially, international contracts between two or more parties.[40] As in private contracts, parties to an international agreement sometimes find it difficult to perform the duties they have originally agreed to. This might occur owing to an unforeseeable emergency or a pressing necessity to protect a public interest. When a state is confronted with the necessity to violate an international agreement, it faces a dilemma; on the one hand, if the state does not violate the agreement, it might aggravate an already precarious domestic situation. On the other hand, if it does violate the agreement, it will most certainly cause harm to its treaty partner. For instance, in sovereign debt matters, the borrowing state declares default when it is already impossible for it to pay back the loans, or because doing so would further aggravate its already unstable macroeconomic situation. As a result of the impossibility of or unwillingness to pay the debt on time the sovereign therefore finds itself

[38] A good overview of the application of necessity in sovereign debt is provided in Michael Waibel, "Two Worlds of Necessity in ICSID Arbitration: CMS and LG&E" (2007) 20 *Leiden Journal of International Law* 637, pp. 88–102.

[39] See Ross Buckley and Douglas Arner, *From Crisis to Crisis: The Global Financial System and Regulatory Failures* (The Hague: Kluwer Law International, 2011), Chapter 6.

[40] In the law and economics of international law, international treaties have often been assimilated to contracts in domestic law. See Posner and Sykes, above note 25, pp. 24–6; Jeffrey L. Dunoff and Joel P. Trachtman, "Economic Analysis of International Law" (1999) 24 *Yale Journal of International Law* 1, at 28–36; Joel P. Trachtman, *The Economic Structure of International Law* (Cambridge, MA and London: Harvard University Press, 2008), pp. 119–50; Robert E. Scott and Paul B. Stephan, *The Limits of Leviathan: Contract Theory and the Enforcement of International Law* (New York: Cambridge University Press, 2006).

in a dilemma. If it services its debt, it might prolong and aggravate an already painful economic situation, thus enhancing the likelihood of social and political turmoil. But if it does not pay, it might be sued in international courts and cut off from emergency lending from international financial institutions.

To obviate this problem, states can rely on customary international law principles or specific treaty clauses that allow suspension of the treaty application when an unforeseen circumstance prevents the invoking state from performing its treaty obligations. These norms can take many forms, from Balance of Payments exceptions,[41] to State of Necessity or Force Majeure.[42] Despite their widespread use, there is hardly any uniformity in the formulation, ambit of application, and interpretation of those norms.[43] Certain clauses, like Balance of Payment, are very specific on the conditions upon which they can be triggered. Others are generic provisions that simply refer to the presence of a situation of grave and imminent peril or harm.[44] In certain circumstances, the clause is self-judging, which means that the invoking state does not need to demonstrate the presence of a peril, while in other circumstances the requirements are more stringent.[45]

Despite their differences, all necessity clauses achieve the same effect. By excusing non-compliance, they give prevalence to the protection of the pressing interests of the invoking party over the right of the other to receive the performance agreed in the treaty. The law therefore produces a zero sum game in which the protection of a state's essential interest (for instance, its domestic stability) deprives partner states from their incompatible interests enshrined in the treaty. The economic logic of necessity posits that, in the long term, the failure to abide by the treaty by the invoking party produces an aggregate welfare gain that outweighs the cost for the other parties. Hence, the society

41 For an overview, see Annamaria Viterbo, *International Economic Law and Monetary Measures* (London: Edward Elgar, 2012), pp. 220–5, 346–53.

42 William J. Moon, "Essential Security Interests in International Investment Agreements" (2012) 15 *Journal of International Economic Law* 481; Jurgen Kurtz, "Adjudging the Exceptional at International Investment Law: Security, Public Order and Financial Crisis" (2010) 59 *International and Comparative Law Quarterly* 325; William W. Burke-White, "The Argentine Financial Crisis: State Liability under BITs and the Legitimacy of the ICSID System" (2008) 3 *Asian Journal of WTO and International Health Law and Policy* 199; Federica Paddeu, "A Genealogy of Force Majeure in International Law" (2012) 1 *British Yearbook of International Law* 1.

43 Robert D. Sloane, "On the Use and Abuse of Necessity in the Law of State Responsibility" (2012) 106 *American Journal of International Law* 447.

44 Katia Yannaca-Small, "Essential Security Interests under International Investment Law," in *International Investment Perspectives: Freedom of Investment in a Changing World* (Paris: OECD, 2007).

45 On this, see Kurtz, above note 42.

is, overall, better off by allowing a state to suspend the treaty, even though this causes harm to its partners. The question, then, is whether this logic is efficient in the context of international finance.

In finance, the use of necessity to excuse compliance with an agreement usually occurs during financial or economic crises when suddenly deteriorated economic conditions require the adoption of extraordinary measures. In the context of international financial agreements, non-compliance can entail the failure of the sovereign borrower to service its debt obligations, or the refusal of the home supervisor to adequately supervise the foreign operations of its national bank – including providing financial assistance. Inevitably, as for any treaty violation, the decision of a government not to comply causes harm to the other treaty party. What is unique about finance, however, is that the consequence of non-compliance for the receiving party can go beyond the simple legitimate expectations arising out of the treaty but entail global financial instability. Given the interconnected nature of financial markets, a financial loss can be transmitted across the entire financial system through intra-banks links or systemic chains. As a consequence, this creates an avalanche of financial losses where disruptive effects will be much larger than the initial loss.

In this situation, the issue that the jurisprudence has to decide is whether it is better – or more efficient – to protect the legitimate interest of the non-violating parties or to safeguard the stability of the host country.[46] The answer offered by international law to the above question is by no means consistent between tribunals. In some cases, tribunals have favored the debtor, while in others they have protected creditors. While in certain arbitrations the tribunal clearly dismissed the use of the principle, in others, on the contrary, it found it applicable to the peculiar macroeconomic situations of the country, thereby excusing the debtor from its obligations.[47]

In general, it is safe to assume that to achieve an efficient outcome, necessity clauses need to discourage inefficient deviations and permit efficient non-compliance. However, in the context of finance, a sometimes very "liberal" interpretation of necessity fails to punish the adoption of those inefficient domestic policies that eventually leads to a situation of impossibility. In essence, the law fails to promote the internalization of the negative externalities of inefficient domestic policies. This ultimately leads to situations in which the invoking

[46] See Waibel, above note 38; William W. Burke-White and Andreas von Staden, "Investment Protection in Extraordinary Times: The Interpretation and Application of Non-precluded Measures Provisions in Bilateral Investment Treaties" (2008) 48 *Virginia Journal of International Law* 307; Kurtz, above note 42.

[47] Sacerdoti, above note 28; Burke-White, above note 42; Waibel, *ibid.*

state's partners end up paying the costs of Pareto-inefficient domestic policies. To understand better this argument, it is necessary to draw a parallel with the domestic law of contracts.

5.3.2. *The Economics of Necessity*[48]

In the common law of contracts a party must either perform the contract or pay compensations.[49] The choice between them is a matter of efficiency. Economic theory holds that whenever the breaching party's gains from non-performance are higher than its gains from performance minus the compensation to the other party, breaching the treaty produces a more efficient outcome, which the law shall promote.[50] A rational actor would decide to exercise its "efficient breach" only when such conditions arise. Even when a party chooses under these conditions to breach, the achievement of global welfare efficiency requires that the non-breaching party must at least have its losses compensated. Hence, an efficient law allows efficient breach but imposes mandatory compensations.

The only occasion in which a party is excused from performing the contract without paying compensations (thus, producing a loss to the non-breaching party) is when it faces a situation of impossibility to perform the contract on which it has no control.[51] Such situation is usually called impossibility or *force majeure*. Like efficient breaches, impossibility clauses allow parties to breach the contract. However, unlike efficient breaches, impossibility clauses cannot be invoked when the breaching party is facing a better option than

[48] On the economics of necessity in international law, see Alan O. Sykes, "Economic 'Necessity' in International Law" (2015) 109 *American Journal of International Law* 296.

[49] Charles J. Goetz and Robert E. Scott, "Liquidated Damages, Penalties and the Just Compensation Principle: Some Notes on an Enforcement Model and a Theory of Efficient Breach" (1977) 77 *Columbia Law Review* 554, 558.

[50] See Clark Remington, "Intentional Interference with Contract and the Doctrine of Efficient Breach: Fine Tuning the Notion of the Contract Breacher as Wrongdoer" (1999) 47 *Buffalo Law Review* 645; Melvin A. Eisenberg, "Actual and Virtual Specific Performance: The Theory of Efficient Breach, and the Indifference Principle in Contract Law" (2005) 93 *California Law Review* 975. The theory of efficient breach originates in the American common law tradition, and it is largely neglected in civil law countries. See Ronald J. Scalise Jr., "Why No 'Efficient Breach' in the Civil Law? A Comparative Assessment of the Doctrine of Efficient Breach of Contract" (2007) 55 *The American Journal of Comparative Law* 721.

[51] James Gordley, "Impossibility and Changed and Unforeseen Circumstances" (2004) 52 *American Journal of Comparative Law* 513; Victor P. Goldberg, "Impossibility and Related Excuses" (1988) 144 *Journal of Institutional and Theoretical Economics* 100; Keith N. Hylton, "The Economics of Necessity" (2012) 41 *The Journal of Legal Studies* 269; Omri Ben-Shahar and Eric A. Posner, "The Right to Withdraw in Contract Law" (2011) 40 *The Journal of Legal Studies* 115.

compliance. On the contrary, as the name suggests, impossibility clauses can be invoked only when one party is forced to breach the contract because it has no alternative. By not performing the contract, both the breaching party and the non-breaching party suffer a loss.

The rationale of impossibility clauses satisfies a basic demand for fairness and equity. It is unfair that the cost of an unplanned and unexpected event, on which none of the parties had control, is assumed only by one of the parties. By not imposing the costs of impossibility only on one party, the clause distributes the losses deriving from the impossibility equally between the parties. Had the breaching party been forced to pay compensation to the non-breaching party, the costs of the unexpected event would fall disproportionately on one side, with no gains for the society as a whole. Thus, the use of impossibility clauses requires the presence of two fundamental elements: the absence of any possibility to control the risk, and, of course, the absence of the contribution in creating the event. The event is neutral, as it does not enter into the sphere of action of either of the parties.

In the context of public international law, Article 25(2)(b) of the Articles on the Responsibility of States for Wrongful Act, developed by the International Law Commission, achieves precisely such an objective. The provision states:

> Necessity may not be invoked by a State as a ground for precluding the wrongfulness of an act not in conformity with an international obligation of that State if . . . The State has contributed to the situation of necessity.[52]

Furthermore, by denying the benefits of the impossibility when the state contributed to it, the law encourages also the efficient protection of the treaty. Indeed, if the law excused the breaching party from paying damages or compensations even when it contributed to the event that causes the impossibility or had the possibility to act in time to reduce its effects, the law would have the ultimate effect of discouraging parties from exerting the proper control on their actions. It would transfer equally to both parties the losses of the breach while, in reality, only one of the parties was in the position of practical impossibility. The other simply did not control it or may have even contributed to it.

Yet, the current international law of finance sometimes treats necessity as a pure impossibility to perform the treaty. Through the different legal mechanisms that excuse compliance, the law permits the transmission of global instability to partner countries. An efficient use of these clauses would demand the event that brought instability to be completely outside the sphere of control of

[52] International Law Commission, Articles on the Responsibility of States for Wrongful Act, Article 25(2)(b).

the parties, as suggested by Article 25(2)(b) in the context of the application of state of necessity. However, only rarely are the necessary elements for the use of impossibility clauses present in the context of financial crises or sovereign defaults. A legitimate situation of impossibility would arise when an agriculture-intensive economy (such as most least-developed countries) experiences a bad harvest or an earthquake that reduces its export potential, thereby leading to a bad balance of payments position. In such case the deferral of certain debt obligations would be tolerated. The social costs of the default would be placed on both the breaching and the non-breaching countries, as none of them had the possibility to control the natural event. Most of the time, however, necessity situations are impossibilities to perform the treaty caused by negligence in controlling the risk. The Argentine and Greek crises were essentially the result of unsustainable domestic policies. Another example is the Icelandic banking and monetary crisis, which originated from the wrong and risky financial deregulatory process adopted by national financial authorities.

The principle of necessity therefore focuses on enabling countries to protect their stability, rather than controlling or minimizing the externalities of such policies. However, in doing so it is inefficient. The current law does not satisfy the minimum requirement for an efficient use of impossibility clauses. It treats all stability policies as if they were impossibilities outside the control of the parties, while most of the times they actually are the result of negligence or carefully calculated decisions of non-compliance. The use of necessity acts as a shield that encourages states to abuse their right. Knowing that whatever event might happen the state would be free to opt out from the treaty, the law discourages them from taking into account the externalities on partner countries from domestic policies. In the words of Prof Sloan, the law forgot that "one state's safeguarded essential interest will often be another's seriously impaired essential interest."[53]

In this context, the law shall prohibit the application of the clause whenever there is such discretion, as in the case of necessity or non-precluded measures clauses. A good example is the non-application of state of necessity in the context of the *CMS* v. *Argentina* case.[54] The ICSID tribunal considered that the state of crisis that forced Argentina to adopt emergency measure was the result of a negligent management of domestic policies by the Argentine government. Thus, it placed the burden of the crisis entirely on Argentina by demanding the payment of damages to the foreign investors. However, this interpretative outcome is not always adopted.

[53] Sloane, above note 43.

[54] *CMS Gas Transmission Co.* v. *Argentina*, ICSID Case No. ARB/01/8, Award (12 May 2005).

5.4. FINANCIAL NATIONALISM IN SOVEREIGN DEBT RESTRUCTURINGS

Debt repudiation is rarely an option for defaulting sovereigns. In economic terms, a default would easily transmit a systemic shock to the domestic financial system and turn a sovereign debt crisis into a banking or economic crisis. Furthermore, domestic exporters may suffer adverse terms of trade with their foreign partners because of the economic sanctions imposed on the defaulting country or because of the reduced access to trade finance.[55] Moreover, the stigma attached to a default, and the political and legal consequences it would carry with it, prevents sovereigns from choosing this hard stance against their creditors. Hence, a large majority of the time, the solution to a debt problem is the restructuring of the debt.

This term of art denotes a contractual arrangement between the debtor and the creditors whereby the original contractual debt obligations are amended in order to take into account the needs of the debtor. In this regard, depending on the underlying debt problems, a debt restructuring may involve two distinct elements. First, the sovereign and the creditors may agree to a debt rescheduling. In this circumstance, the principal payments due on the maturing debt are deferred, often with a parallel decrease in the contractual interest rates. In essence, the sovereign is granted a debt relief that postpones the payment to a later date. Second, the two parties may agree to a "haircut," which reduces the face value of the outstanding principal payment. Essentially, creditors agree to take a loss on their projected initial investment.[56] In certain circumstances, when getting liquidity from capital markets is not possible, a restructuring needs to be complemented by official liquidity assistance from international institutions. For instance, the International Monetary Fund, through its policy of "lending into arrears," rescues sovereigns with a temporary liquidity problem that cannot access financial markets.

The logic of restructuring is relatively simple. When it is clear that it is impossible for a sovereign to service its debt, creditors have two options. On the one hand, they can accept the default of the sovereign and be content with recovering only a minimal part of their investment. On the other hand, they can agree to extend the maturity of the debt or take a haircut, thereby giving precious oxygen to the sovereign's economy. In this last case, the hope is that, over time, the economic situation in the debtor country will improve, thereby allowing the sovereign to service its debt, albeit not in full. In sum, faced

[55] Wright, above note 17, p. 159.

[56] Ryan, above note 16, p. 2479.

between the choice of recovering nothing or recovering less than originally agreed, creditors choose the latter option: the debt restructuring.

5.4.1. *Creditors' Coordination and Creditors' Battles*

Debt restructuring requires a very high level of coordination between the debtor and its creditors. Until the 1980s, when sovereign debt was mostly constituted by syndicated loans, achieving a successful agreement required only the approval of a relatively limited number of financial institutions. Institutions such as the Paris Club had been set up precisely to coordinate creditors during a restructuring negotiation. However, over time, syndicated loans have been replaced by securitized debt as the primary form of sovereign debt financing. This innovation has ultimately spread the scope of creditors across very dispersed and non-homogeneous groups, such as hedge funds, retail investors, or banks, often separated geographically. In this situation, achieving an agreement has become more complex, from a legal and negotiation viewpoint.[57]

Since agreeing to a restructuring outcome is, in principle, voluntary, creditors' incentives have to be somehow harmonized. However, in various circumstances, this proves to be quite difficult. From an economic viewpoint, sovereign debt restructuring gives rise to a classical collective action problem. In the hope of extracting the highest payment from the restructuring, creditors have an incentive to hold out from the negotiations and free-ride on the other creditors who have previously agreed to the restructuring. By threatening to block a restructuring, holdout creditors can secure better financing conditions at the expense of the other creditors. As in a domestic bankruptcy proceeding, without common rules to set an order of priority between creditors and prevent uncooperative behaviors, there is the risk that each creditor will act only in its best interests, thereby disregarding the collective benefit of an organized restructuring proceeding. In this situation, the inability to achieve a quick and successful restructuring outcome also negatively influences the debtor countries. Indeed, if the debt restructuring process takes too long or restructures too little, the debtor country may eventually be forced to declare full default on its debt.

Furthermore, debt securitization has created a secondary market for distressed sovereign debt prompted by the need of banks to get it off their balance

[57] Ronald J. Silverman and Mark W. Deveno, "Distressed Sovereign Debt: A Creditor's Perspective" (2003) *American Bankruptcy Institute Law Review* 179, p. 185; see also Lee C. Buchheit, "The Capitalization of Sovereign Debt: An Introduction" (1988) *University of Illinois Law Review* 401–2.

sheets. This has ultimately given rise to vulture funds specializing in buying distressed debt sold at a fraction of its face value. The strategy of vulture funds essentially consists of buying distressed bonds on the secondary market and investing time and money on litigation with the hope of being repaid in full. With extensive funds at their disposal, vultures bet that the huge investment in litigation fees will bring a financial return that will outstrip the cost of the bonds and the litigation. To do so, vultures adopt very aggressive litigation tactics that rely on holding out from the debt-restructuring process and going after the debtor's assets throughout the world. The most cited example in this regard is the lawsuit brought by Elliot Associates, a vulture fund, against the government of Peru, which at that time was trying to restructure its debt. The fund purchased the distressed debt in the secondary market for a value of US$ 11 million. Through an aggressive litigation strategy, the fund managed a repayment of US$ 55 million.[58]

The question of coordination in debt restructuring has been primarily an internal problem between creditors, in which domestic politics has played a limited role. However, in recent years it has become apparent that jurisdictional control of sovereign debt by national courts could increase the international coordination problems in debt restructuring and sometimes subject them to a logic of financial nationalism.

5.4.2. *Forum-Shopping in Sovereign Debt*

In the previous section, I argued that the current public international law of sovereign debt is sometimes set on a socially inefficient level of protection for defaulting debtors. However, recent events seem to point out that, under certain circumstances, creditors might overpower defaulting sovereigns and similarly lead to a suboptimal debt-restructuring outcome. The power holdout creditors enjoy does not rely on an established set of international legal entitlements, but rather on legal tactics that are based on a strategic application of domestic laws in jurisdictions that occupy a critical position in the context of the debt transaction. More specifically, holdout creditors forum-shop in jurisdictions where their legal claims against the sovereign have more chance to be won due to a more favorable legal framework and judicial attitude toward creditors.

Under the right conditions, an injunctive order from a national court against the sovereign could paralyze the entire sovereign debt-restructuring process and create international spillovers. This would occur because the court can exert its jurisdictional powers over local banks or financial infrastructures such

[58] Elliott Assocs., *L.P.* v. *Banco de la Nación*, 194 F.3d 363 (2d Cir. 1999).

as clearing and settlement firms that occupy a pivotal role in the mechanics of the debt transaction, thereby extending its effect to all the other entities that are financially connected to them. In other words, the application of national law to an international dispute could have extraterritorial effects in the debtor country and in third countries where the non-holdout creditors are located. The recent legal dispute between the vulture fund NML against Argentina litigated in New York courts best illustrates these dangers.[59]

The *NML Capital Ltd. et al.* v. *Republic of Argentina* case originates from the ashes of the Argentine sovereign default of 2001. After years of negotiations, in 2005 the Argentine government struck a deal with the majority of its creditors whereby Argentina exchanged its original bonds for US$ 100 billion new bonds issued in two tranches in 2005 and 2010. Unlike the majority of the creditors, NML Capital refused to accept the offer and instead chose to pursue a very aggressive litigation strategy claiming the full repayment of the original bonds purchased on the secondary market for a very low price. To do so, NML chased Argentina's properties all over the world, mostly without much success. However, in 2011 it successfully brought action in a New York federal district court, obtaining an injunction that blocked Argentina's payments to the exchange bondholders unless Argentina agreed to pay the holdout creditors ratably. The only other option for Argentina was to default on all of the outstanding debts. Moreover, the court's injunction forbade market infrastructures located in third countries to process payments linked to the Argentine bonds, threatening them with sanctions.[60]

Argentina immediately challenged the order in higher US courts, which nevertheless confirmed it. The legal basis of the court's order lies in a particular interpretation of the *pari passu* clause contained in the original Argentine debt contracts. *Pari passu* clauses have been a feature of debt contract documentation for hundreds of years,[61] although their meaning has never been clear. They impose an obligation to grant equal treatment to different classes of creditors. The question is whether the obligation applies to debts of the same issuance, or whether it binds a sovereign with regard to all of its outstanding debt. The difference is fundamental, because in the latter case, such a

[59] There is a huge legal literature on this dispute. For an overview, see Natalie Wong, "*NML Capital, Ltd. v. Republic of Argentina* and the Changing Roles of the Pari Passu and Collective Action Clauses in Sovereign Debt Agreements" (2014–2015) 53 *Columbia Journal of Transnational Law* 396; Gelpern, above note 34.

[60] W. Mark C. Weidemaier and Anna Gelpern, "Injunctions in Sovereign Debt Litigation" (2014) 31 *Yale Journal on Regulation* 189.

[61] Mark Weidemaier, Robert Scott, and Mitu Gulati, "Origin Myths, Contracts, and the Hunt for Pari Passu" (2013) *Law and Social Inquiry* 38, pp. 72–105.

clause could in principle give to the creditors of a particular debt offer, a right of equal treatment that extends its power to all the subsequent debt issuances. Without entering into the question of the correct interpretation of the clause, which has given rise to extensive commentary, in the context of the *NML* v. *Argentina* dispute, the court interpreted this clause as referring to the entire outstanding debt, which included the exchange offer. In practice, by applying the *pari passu* clause to the entire existing debt, the court's order had put Argentina's entire external debt policy on a standstill.

The question, then, is: how can a New York court prevent a sovereign state from paying the debt owed to foreign creditors, even when the sovereign does not suffer from a liquidity or solvency problem? In theory, Argentina could have simply ignored the court's order, by shielding itself behind its immunity as it did before. From a purely practical perspective, however, the power of the New York court lies in the fact that all the payments that Argentina owed to its exchange bondholders had to be made through the designated trust bank (Bank New York Mellon), located in New York and under the jurisdiction of New York law. Subjecting bond contracts to foreign law, usually the law of England and Wales or New York, is one of the first strategies adopted by creditors to offset the asymmetry of power they suffer against the sovereign. By attaching the contract to the law of a third country that is considered as having a transparent and sophisticated legal system, creditors have the guarantee that the sovereign will not unilaterally change the law applicable to the debt contract. In essence, foreign law is insurance for creditors against the time-consistency problem discussed before.

Thus, by virtue of its jurisdiction over the payment infrastructures through which the debt was serviced, the New York Court had the control over the performance of the entire debt transaction. In practice, the Court enforced a financial blockade against Argentina by directing its effects on to the creditors and the payment channels. Bearing in mind that the Argentine bonds were issued under New York law, we could judge the court's order as a simple matter of economic retaliation following Argentina's refusal to pay. As I will explain in the next section, it is not unusual for creditors to seek a court injunction preventing local banks from lending to a recalcitrant debtor. This behavior would not be different from the imposition of a trade barrier in response to a prior violation of the law by a non-complying country. In sum, due to the impossibility of forcing Argentina to comply, the judge decided to use a financial blockade as a form of blackmail.[62]

[62] Mark, Weidemaier and Gelpern, above note 60.

However, what it is strikingly different in the NML case is the fact that most of the direct and immediate impact of the crisis has not been on Argentina but on third countries. From the perspective of the exchange bondholders, the US court order threatened to create a potential systemic risk across the globe just to protect a tiny minority of litigants. Argentina has managed to rely on domestic financing for more than 15 years, thus a credit embargo would not have changed its disposition to pay. On the contrary, third country investors and market infrastructures – which had legitimately agreed to a restructuring with Argentina – risked suffering the worst consequences. In sum, the US court strategy, which was supposed to force Argentina to comply, ultimately overshot by directing its effects on the wrong parties. Furthermore, it is striking that in this case the retaliation is grossly disproportionate when compared to the damage. In the case of Argentina, the payment of around US$ 1.4 billion to foreign investors has been threatened because of the willingness of the court to protect the interests of investors worth only US$ 50 million. The dispute standoff between Argentina and the holdouts was eventually solved in April 2016 when the newly elected Argentinian government agreed to a settlement with the creditors.

If we look at the dispute from the perspective of international regulatory coordination, it is evident that the logic of financial nationalism underpins the court's decision. In order to protect the national interest – in this case represented by the interests of a few creditors – a national court exerts its judicial power extraterritorially, thereby negatively influencing the interests of other countries. By doing so, the court de facto bypassed the long-standing principle of "comity," which prevents the adoption of acts that might endanger the political relations between two states and undermine financial governance. This situation is, ultimately, the result of an international sovereign debt system in which creditors are forced to rely on creditor-friendly domestic laws to offset the absence of a binding international legal regime able to organize creditors and tame sovereigns. This in turn results in a sovereign debt system in which national courts are de facto acting as international sovereign debt judges, extending the effects of their national laws across the international financial system.

Despite the uncontestable jurisdiction of the New York Court over local financial claims, it is questionable whether international law should continue to tolerate the outsourcing of sovereign debt litigation to national courts. National judges are clearly bound to interpret and apply local laws, and do not have the competence and the experience necessary to oversee international financial disputes with clear economic and political ramifications. Judging a sovereign debt dispute through the lenses of domestic law prevents the adoption of an interpretative solution that is globally socially optimal. This leads to a form of judicial nationalism that looks only at domestic interests without taking into account the global effects of the decision. This interpretation of the law could have disastrous effects on future debt restructurings. Indeed, by transferring the direct costs of the blockade on the restructuring creditors, such an interpretation would discourage future creditors from participating to achieve socially optimal restructurings. Furthermore, by incentivizing litigation strategies as a means to extract the recovery, it would increase the use of holdouts.[63]

5.5. WHICH SOLUTIONS? PRIVATE MECHANISMS V. INTERNATIONAL LAW

Political constraints within debtor countries are at the origin of most sovereign defaults. At the moment of borrowing or when it is time to repay, policymakers suffer from distorted incentives that ultimately enhance the likelihood of a default. Sovereign defaults, however, do not affect only the economy and the society of debtor countries. In a tightly integrated financial system in which lenders and borrowers often operate on a cross-border basis and in which financial institutions are highly exposed to sovereign debts, the failure of a state may well translate into a failure of the entire market. As Professor Schwarcz has argued, it is now time to recognize that the problem of too-big-too-fail does not exist only in banking. In a highly interconnected global financial system, the collapse of a highly interconnected economy must be avoided at all costs.[64] In a world where sovereign defaults have become global public bads, debtor countries must also share some responsibilities. In this situation, the logic of financial nationalism is unfit to address the problems of sovereign debt. Indeed, it legitimizes the transmission of global instability to neighboring countries and increases the moral hazard of sovereigns with the adoption of bad and unsustainable economic policies. Furthermore, in the absence of a centralized restructuring mechanism, sovereign debt restructurings are subject to coordination problems that, if left to national judicial interventions, can only increase the systemic impact of the debt problem. In this section I will discuss two different approaches to financial nationalism in sovereign debt: private mechanism and international law.

63 IMF, "The Fund's Lending Framework and Sovereign Debt – Preliminary Considerations" (June 2014), pp. 30–31.

64 Steven L. Schwarcz, "Sovereign Debt Restructuring Options: An Analytical Comparison" (2012) 2 *Harvard Business Law Review* 95, p. 97.

5.5.1. *Private Mechanisms*

In the previous section, I have argued that the fallacies of the current international legal framework for sovereign debt and fiscal policy play a fundamental role in creating financial instability. Implicit in this argument is the assumption that only a proper international legal framework can address those shortcomings. Before explaining in detail what would be the role of the law in this regard, it is necessary to discuss first the role and the limits of the market as a source of discipline, as well as private solutions to coordination problems in debt workouts.

Denial of market access is one of the most powerful tools to force a reluctant debtor to pay its debts. In a world where the debtor and the creditors are separated by an asymmetry of power, the doctrine of sovereign immunity certainly poses a fundamental problem in constraining the behavior of debtor countries. Thus, creditors have had to rely on other mechanisms to reduce the desire of states to repudiate their obligations. In this situation, power politics and market mechanisms have often replaced the law as the main regulatory tool of sovereign lending. In the early days, the natural response of creditors was to ask their states to wage war against the debtors.[65] Over time, however, financial markets have acquired a very powerful role in inducing compliance.

A sovereign with a bad credit history will have difficulties in accessing financial markets, as no bank or investor will be willing to lend. Thus, unless it can rely on its sole domestic tax base, or on other bilateral financing options with other countries, the state often chooses to repay the debt. Anna Gelpern reports that "litigation was a factor in only 29 out of 180 sovereign debt restructuring episodes involving private creditors between 1976 and 2010."[66] Therefore, the financial risks that arise from the absence of a central enforcer were often mitigated by the constant need of the sovereign to access financial markets. Thus, the desire of sovereigns to maintain a good reputation as trustworthy borrowers often sufficed to guarantee repayment.

Sometimes, market access is prevented by a forced financial blockade. More clearly, since most of the sovereign debt contracts are set in either London or New York, where the major investment banks are headquartered, the court can order seizure of all the loans made by local financial intermediaries directed toward the debtor. Without a formal bankruptcy procedure, contracts last forever. Thus, if they can afford it, creditors can pursue sovereigns for decades in

[65] Michael Waibel, *Sovereign Defaults in International Courts and Tribunals* (Cambridge: Cambridge University Press, 2011), p. 8.

[66] Mark, Weidemaier and Gelpern, above note 60, p. 3.

search of any possible dollars available. Hence, most of the time, sovereigns agree with creditors on a rescheduling of the debt or a haircut, leading to the well-known problem of holdouts.[67] However, in spite of the effectiveness of unofficial remedies, if a sovereign chooses not to pay and is able to stand on its feet financially, creditors are essentially powerless.

Contractual solutions have been often proposed to reduce coordination problems in sovereign debt restructuring. When it comes to allowing efficient debt restructurings, solving the collective action problem that gives rise to holdouts is the most pressing issue. In recent years, new solutions have been implemented that seem to eliminate or sensibly reduce the dangers of blocking minorities. The most important of those is the use of Collective Action Clauses (CACs) contained in debt contracts. These clauses enable a supermajority of creditors (usually around 75%) of a particular bond issuance to bind the remaining dissenting minority of creditors to the terms of the restructuring. By doing so, CACs prevent litigious minorities from holding out and blocking the restructuring. According to the IMF, as of 2013, 75% of the US$ 1.2 trillion foreign law bonds outstanding already included CACs.[68]

One important limitation of those clauses is that they usually operate on bonds of the same issuance. This means that minorities slightly above 25% could still block the restructuring. For instance, if a state has issued three different bond offers of roughly the same value, it would be enough that only one of these agreements fails to reach a supermajority voting in favor of the restructuring to make the blocking minority hold out against the other creditors.[69] In this regard, some countries have started to insert in their debt contracts provisions that allow the aggregation of bond series subject to a double voting threshold in order to avoid the risk of blocking minorities.[70]

Supermajority voting is a contractual solution to a coordination problem that fills a regulatory gap. In the absence of an international bankruptcy regime for sovereigns, that imposes precise rankings to creditors and coordinates differing incentives during resolution, private voluntary solutions can replace a statutory option. However, private solutions suffer from one fundamental flaw: they are voluntary fixes whose adoption ultimately depends on the unanimous favorable response of the market. Only if investors agree to buy debt subject

67 Since this book is focused on systemic risk, I will leave the problem of holdouts outside the scope of the chapter. For an overview, see Schwarcz, above note 64; Committee on Economic Policies and Reform, above note 11, Chapter 3; Wright, above note 17, p. 160.

68 IMF, above note 53, pp. 30–31.

69 Schwarcz, above note 64, pp. 106–7.

70 Anna Gelpern, "Contract Hope and Sovereign Redemption" (2013) 8 *Capital Markets Law Journal* 132, p. 143.

to CACs can the holdout problem can be eliminated. In theory, funds could still buy individual debt not subject to CACs and use the *pari passu* clause to hold out and block a restructuring. Moreover, investors could demand a higher return for a bond with a CAC, thereby increasing the cost of financing for sovereigns. This could perhaps explain why, after an initial period in which sovereigns inserted CACs in all of their bond issues, a few countries have recently started to quietly remove them from their bond offers.[71]

5.5.2. *International Law*

Private mechanisms undoubtedly help to minimize the risks of financial nationalism in sovereign debt. This is especially so when it comes to reducing the risks of strategic defaults by sovereigns. Yet, a question arises as to whether private solutions can address all the inefficiencies of sovereign debt. Irrespective of the power of market access denial, it is undeniable that this solution only works for those countries that need external financing. The 15 years battle waged by Argentina against its creditors, albeit unique, shows that a few sovereigns do consider sovereign immunity to be a weapon against creditors. This inevitably leads to a situation in which borrowing states are naturally discriminated against based on their economic power, thereby creating an international financial system where, paraphrasing Orwell, "some countries are more equal than others." On the one side, we will have countries that can afford to bully creditors because they can rely on their own domestic tax base to finance their budget. On the other hand, we will have those countries that, given their particular economic conditions, need to rely on capital markets, and thus will be obliged to respect their sovereign debt contracts. Contractual solutions too provide useful but still limited assistance in addressing the problem of holdouts as they are not able to eliminate entirely the risk of blocking minorities.

Finally, private contracting alone cannot guarantee quick and efficient debt restructurings. First, an ideal debt contract would try to set a perfect tradeoff between the reduced costs of credit for the sovereign, on the one hand, and a viable restructuring mechanism that would guarantee a socially optimal restructuring outcome that takes into account the interests of the debtor and the creditors, on the other. When a sovereign borrows, its main interest is to reduce the cost of credit. To do so, it would negotiate with the creditors contractual conditions that would make more burdensome for the sovereign the

[71] Elaine Moore, "Missing Sovereign Bond Clauses Keep Door Open to Holdouts," *Financial Times* (20 April 2015).

cost of a restructuring. A very tight contractual solution would also reduce the incentive of the sovereign to default, thus promoting good fiscal governance. However, if later on, the sovereign finds it necessary to request a restructuring of the debt, it would have the opposite incentive: to acquire the widest policy space to reschedule or reduce its debt obligations. This can be pictured as a classical time-inconsistency problem. Since it is impossible at the moment of the issuance of debt to picture all possible scenarios, the outcome of the restructuring decision would depend on the clauses of the contract. However, since it is impossible to negotiate in advance a debt contract that foresees all possible scenarios, it is necessary to rely on an established mechanism that could determine the outcome of restructuring in advance. This could be a multilateral debt-restructuring mechanism.

Hence, in the absence of internal political controls, international law has a pivotal role to play. First, international law could promote good fiscal governance and reduce the risk of overborrowing. In a global financial system made up of sovereign states, it is impossible to legally coerce national governments to adopt particular economic policies. However, with the adoption of the right legal mechanisms, and by attributing rights to the correct stakeholders, binding international law can increase the pressure on policymakers for the adoption of sustainable and globally Pareto-efficient fiscal and economic policies. As I will explain in detail in the third part of the book, international law can create regional or multilateral institutional mechanisms to monitor periodically the macroeconomic and fiscal policies of states and punish them for the violation, similar to the European Union's Stability and Growth Pact.

Second, international law could eliminate the moral hazard that sovereigns now enjoy when it comes to repaying their debts. A binding international law regime that reduces the level of protection accorded to sovereigns and attributes precise international legal responsibilities in the case of a default would reduce the incentives of sovereigns in taking up excessive debt and defaulting strategically. The role of the law in domestic financial transactions is exemplary in this regard. By attaching precise responsibilities to a violation of the contract, the law reduces the incentives of borrowers to take on excessive levels of debt. Thus, in a free market in which sovereign debt contracts could be subject to a binding international legal regime, a country would probably borrow only to the extent that it could repay.[72] Furthermore, by attaching precise responsibilities to a violation of the debt contract, sovereigns would have more incentives to adopt better economic governance.

[72] In this situation, the main risk of sovereigns is to underborrow, thus limiting drastically their access to credit and their economic growth prospects.

Finally, international law could eliminate the risks of forum-shopping and allow an efficient restructuring that would put the sovereign back on its feet. The adoption of a multilateral sovereign debt-restructuring mechanism with a sovereign bankruptcy court could address the organization problems currently faced by creditors during a restructuring, and also replace national courts as the only avenues for creditors' litigation. As discussed before, CACs suffer from various limits, which would make them work only if backed by a binding regulatory framework imposing aggregation by law. Hence, the only solution to the debt-restructuring problem is to adopt a bankruptcy-like mechanism for sovereigns that would organize creditors and facilitate a quick and painless restructuring for the sovereign, with the end goal of maximizing the return for the creditors. This could be achieved only by the adoption of an international convention along the lines of the former Sovereign Debt Restructuring Mechanism proposed by the IMF in 2003.

Alternatively, national legislation could set provisions preventing vulture funds and holdouts from attacking payment and settlement systems.[73] By carving out market infrastructures from the political and legal battles of debt restructuring, holdouts would have fewer options at their disposal.[74] Some European countries have already done that, most notably during the *Elliot Associates* v. *Peru* dispute, when Belgium enacted a law that granted immunity to Euroclear – the Brussels-based payment and settlement firm – against creditors' injunctions. However, to be effective, this would require regulatory convergence in national legislation. This could be similarly done through an international bankruptcy regime, which could require signatories to grant immunity to payment infrastructures in national legislation.

[73] Committee on Economic Policies and Reform, above note 11, Chapter 3; Wright, above note 17, pp. 31–2.

[74] See Gelpern, above note 70, p. 148.

6

Coordination Battles in OTC Derivatives Regulation

Regulatory cooperation is one of the oldest and most discussed topics in the international financial law and policy literature.[1] It defines both the actual process of cooperation in which national financial regulators work together in various fora to address common regulatory issues, as well as the outcome of this joint activity. At the outset, it is important to highlight that regulatory cooperation can entail different forms and lead to various results. At the most basic level, cooperation can result in broad statements of principles to guide national regulators in the establishment of a particular regulatory regime, such as the International Organization for Securities Commission (IOSCO) Principles of Securities Regulation. A more advanced form of cooperation is the recognition of equivalence of host-country laws. This defines the process whereby national regulators partially waive the application of national laws to institutions that are licensed and supervised in a foreign country whose regime is considered similar to their own. As we will see in this chapter, mutual recognition is particularly common in the field of securities regulation. The most advanced form of cooperation is undoubtedly regulatory harmonization, which broadly defines the total or substantial identity of national regulatory regimes.[2] A mild form of harmonization is the Basel III framework, which is broadly consistent in its national formulation across the BCBS members, although it leaves each jurisdiction with the freedom to tailor certain rules to

[1] See Andrew Singer, *Regulating Capital: Setting Standards for the Financial System* (Ithaca, NY: Cornell University Press, 2007); Kern Alexander, Rahul Dhumale, and John Eatwell, *Global Governance of Financial Systems: The International Regulation of Systemic Risk* (Oxford: Oxford University Press, 2007); Andreas Busch, *Banking Regulation and Globalization* (Oxford: Oxford University Press, 2008); Chris Brummer, *Soft Law and the Global Financial System*, 2nd edn. (Cambridge: Cambridge University Press, 2015).

[2] A good basic overview of harmonization in finance is provided in Junji Nakagawa, *International Harmonization of Economic Regulation* (Oxford: Oxford University Press, 2012), pp. 215–77.

the specificities of the local financial system. The European Union's Single Rulebook is, conversely, the most stringent example of harmonization as it obliges each EU member state to adopt the same set of prudential rules for local firms with very little flexibility.

Since the start of the debate about harmonized capital regulation regimes in the 1980s and the increased efforts of national regulators to agree on common international financial standards, commentators have debated in length the pros and cons of a common regulatory regime, especially with regard to harmonization. On the one hand, scholars like Roberta Romano argue that harmonization is an inefficient and sometimes counterproductive way to regulate finance as it discourages innovation and prevents a healthy competitive environment. According to these theories, regulatory competition allows the market to decide the best regulatory framework, thereby forcing states to provide optimal rules for firms.[3] On the other hand, regulatory race theories argue that harmonization is the only way to prevent dangerous races-to-the-bottom in the regulatory architecture for international finance.[4] Finally, from an economic standpoint, regulatory cooperation produces various benefits. According to international economic theory, regulatory coordination reduces the incentives for protectionism and allows firms to exploit economies of scale, thereby eliminating regulatory discontinuities that reduce the benefit of free trade.[5]

When it comes to reducing global systemic risk and promoting financial stability, the main issue is how to prevent regulatory freedom from leading to dangerous loopholes. By allowing a country to decide whether or not to adopt stringent prudential standards, others in the rest of the financial community that opt for harder regulations not only risk competitive disadvantage but, more importantly, that a domestic crisis in the non-complying country might

[3] Roberta Romano, "Empowering Investors: A Market Approach to Securities Regulation" (1998) 107 *Yale Law Journal* 2359; Roberta Romano, "For Diversity in the International Regulation of Financial Institutions: Critiquing and Recalibrating the Basel Architecture" (2014) 31 *Yale Journal of Regulation* 1.

[4] Beth A. Simmons, "The International Politics of Harmonization: The Case of Capital Market Regulation" (2001) 55 *International Organization* 589; Daniel W. Drezner, "Globalization, Harmonization, and Competition: The Different Pathways to Policy Convergence" (2005) 12 *Journal of European Public Policy* 841.

[5] See Khalid Nadvi, "Global Standards, Global Governance and the Organization of Global Value Chains" (2008) 8 *Journal of Economic Geography* 323; Jagdish Bhagwati and Robert Hudec, *Fair Trade and Harmonization, Vol. 1: Economic Analysis* (Cambridge, MA: MIT Press, 1996); Joel P. Trachtman, "Unilateralism, Bilateralism, Regionalism, Multilateralism, and Functionalism: A Comparison with Reference to Securities Regulation" (1994) 4 *Transnational Law and Contemporary Problems* 69.

spread systemic risk across borders. This is especially so with regard to lax regulatory and supervisory standards for securities and financial investment, and also with low capital adequacy ratios for banks, as they reduce drastically the resilience of financial institutions to external shocks.[6] Regulatory coordination would force authorities to commit to a given standard, thus enabling weak domestic authorities to resist domestic lobbying pressure for deleveraging.[7] Furthermore, given the beneficial effect of harmonization in extending economies of scale, a wide enough group of countries adopting the same rules could indirectly push other countries to do the same, if they want to participate in this extended market. The rationale is not different from the policy of free trade agreements, where the wider the market is, the greater is the appeal for external states to join in. For instance, in their studies on the politics of harmonization in financial regulations, Simmons and Drezner demonstrated how dominant centers, such as the United States or the EU, pushed weaker actors to accept their standards.[8]

The regulation of derivatives is a particularly interesting topic in the debate on regulatory coordination. Over-the-counter (OTC) derivatives had been poorly regulated before the financial crisis and were considered one of the origins of systemic risks at national and international levels. For these reasons, as one of the very first measures taken at the outset of the global financial crisis, the G20 recommended the adoption of a set of reforms aimed at reducing the systemic risks of global derivatives trading.[9] Yet, the US and the EU regulators proceeded in their regulatory reforms independent of each other, thereby leaving the global derivatives market without a clear direction. The battle for derivatives regulation was fought for many years, and it almost led to a global turf war between the two most important financial markets. Only in February 2016, after various attempts and heavy lobbying by the financial industry, did the two regulators finally agree to mutually recognize their regulation.

A question therefore arises as to why national regulators resisted for a long time against a common regime for securities regulation. The question bears particular importance if we think that both regulators openly praised the benefits of a coordinated regulatory framework to address the risks of derivatives trading. The tale of the struggle for Atlantic regulatory convergence in global derivatives regulation is particularly revealing of the underlying logics of

[6] See Alexander, Dhumale, and Eatwell, above note 1, p. 26.

[7] Andrew T. Guzman, "International Regulatory Harmonization" (2002) 3 *Chicago Journal of International Law* 271, 278.

[8] Simmons, above note 4; Drezner, above note 4.

[9] G20 Leaders' Statement: The Pittsburgh Summit (Pittsburgh: 24–25 September 2009).

nationalism and cooperation in financial regulation, which pushes regulators toward national solutions irrespective of suboptimal global impact of local policies.

6.1. DERIVATIVES AND SYSTEMIC RISK

Derivatives are financial instruments that allow traders to allocate the risks of fluctuations in the price of an underlying reference asset, which could be anything from the interest rates on a bundle of loans to the future price of a commodity. Essentially, derivatives act as an insurance that protects individuals, governments, or companies – including financial institutions – against financial risks.[10] A derivative transaction is performed by two parties: the seller of the derivative, which offers the protection, and the buyer, which pays the seller a premium for the protection against the risks insured by the derivative. Among all types of derivatives, SWAPS are probably the instruments that concerned regulators the most as they were used heavily by the financial industry to protect against financial risks, such as interest-rate fluctuations as well as counterparty defaults. For instance, in a Credit Default Swap (CDS), the protection-seller commits to reimburse any losses incurred by the protection-buyer in the event of a default of a counterparty (the reference entity) with which the protection-buyer has entered into a financial contract, or any other credit event that the parties agreed to cover. CDSs were used by financial institutions, for instance, to protect against losses related to bonds, loans, or complex financial instruments.

Like any financial instrument, derivatives entail some risks, chiefly the risk of counterparty default. Yet the riskiness of CDSs was somehow higher owing to the fact that virtually all financial institutions used them to protect against other financial institutions' risk of default. In a swap transaction, the protection-seller faces the contractual risk inherent to the transaction itself, which will oblige him to offset the loss incurred by the protection-buyer in the event of a credit event. This risk clearly is part of the game and the reason why the derivative-seller is paid a premium.[11] The protection-buyer too, however, faces the risk that the protection-seller might be unable to honor the derivative contract, thereby leaving the protection-buyer exposed to the financial losses for which it had originally insured itself. If market conditions

[10] Norman Menachem Feder, "Deconstructing Over-the-Counter Derivatives" (2002) *Columbia Business Law Review* 677.

[11] Timothy E. Lynch, "Derivatives: A Twenty-First Century Understanding" (2011) 43 *Loyola University of Chicago Law Journal* 1, p. 19.

are favorable – for instance, if the reference entity whose default costs the buyer wants to avoid is not actually defaulting – the protection-buyer can try to negotiate another derivative with a different protection-seller. Yet, in a period of widespread financial distress, this could be extremely difficult. If various institutions default at the same time – including the reference entity – the protection-buyer will be unable to find another protection-seller. Hence, the protection-buyer will be exposed to the risk that it wanted to transfer, and it will lose both the value of the derivative contract that it had purchased as well as that of the underlying asset. Thus, we can imagine that the failure of a large financial institution that had a very high concentration of derivatives could create systemic risks across the market.[12] Moreover, without the protection offered by derivatives, financial institutions might reduce their lending, thus leading to a sudden liquidity problem in the market.[13]

Counterparty risk is an inherent feature of finance. Yet, firms have developed over time various strategies to contain it, from the imposition of disclosure requirements, to the use of intermediaries able to absorb counterparty credit and settlement risks. In the context of standardized derivatives trading, specialized exchanges such as the Chicago Board of Trade oblige their members to a precise set of rules concerning membership, orders execution, approval of new products, or clearing that aimed precisely at containing those risks.[14] In addition, derivatives exchanges served a fundamental monitoring function, as their unique position gave them a "bird's eye view" over the financial interconnectedness between their members. This allowed them to spot anomalies and problems among their members.

Yet not all derivatives were traded through exchanges. A great part of the derivatives market operated privately between firms; in financial jargon, "over-the-counter." The OTC derivatives market achieved the staggering volume of US$683.7 trillion before the crisis, spurred by the need of firms to bypass the constraints of structured derivatives products.[15] OTC derivatives added an additional layer of complexity to the correct functioning of the derivatives market as firms that traded without the disclosure and operating rules mandated

[12] Manmohan Singh and James Aitken, "Counterparty Risk, Impact on Collateral Flows, and Role for Central Counterparties" (2009) International Monetary Fund Working Paper No. 09/173.

[13] Charles K. Whitehead, "The Volcker Rule and Evolving Financial Markets" (2011) 1 *Harvard Business Law Review* 39, pp. 65–7.

[14] Dan Awrey, "The Dynamics of OTC Derivatives Regulation: Bridging the Public–Private Divide" (2010) 11 *European Business Organization Law Review* 155.

[15] Bank for International Settlements, "OTC Derivatives Market Activity in the First Half of 2008" (November 2008).

by derivatives exchanges were allowed to take very large and opaque positions. The systemic risk in OTC derivatives market arises from information asymmetries between the parties, which force the market to operate in the dark.[16] Since each party of the OTC transaction knows only the extent of the exposure that its counterparty holds, it cannot measure its overall risk position. This also prevents the regulator and the market from having an idea of the global derivatives exposure. During a crisis, the opacity of the market increases the risk aversion of market intermediaries, which are not able to assess the true position and financial strengths of their counterparties, thereby forcing them to ask for higher margins or even withdraw their liquidity.[17] The problem with OTC derivatives was augmented by the fact that trading was highly concentrated in twenty systemically important institutions with very large exposures, and with limited knowledge of the true extent of their counterparties' positions.

The collapses of American International Group (AIG), Lehman Brothers, and Bear Sterns at the onset of the 2007–8 global financial crisis epitomize the dangers posed by OTC derivatives to financial markets. AIG underwrote CDSs for around US$410 billion for various institutions. When the value of subprime mortgage CDOs went down, AIG found itself without enough liquidity to face its contractual obligations toward its customers, a situation that ultimately forced the US Treasury to intervene with a US$180 billion bailout to keep AIG afloat.[18] Bear Stearns and Lehman Brothers shared a very similar story with regard to their derivatives trading. Both had very large trading exposures – Lehman Brothers, for instance, was counterparty to around 930,000 derivatives transactions – which they were using as collateral for their borrowed funds. Their declined value of their exposures led to immense losses in their trading portfolio. When market confidence turned into panic, their counterparties started to demand more collateral, thereby triggering a liquidity problem.[19]

6.2. THE ATLANTIC REGULATORY DIVIDE ON OTC DERIVATIVES

For most of their history, the global market for derivatives operated in a legal vacuum.[20] Public regulation was instead replaced by voluntary codes of

[16] Rene M. Stulz, "Credit Default Swaps and the Credit Crisis," National Bureau of Economic Research Working Paper 15384/2009.

[17] Colleen M. Baker, "Regulating the Invisible: The Case of Over-the-Counter Derivatives" (2010) 85 *Notre Dame Law Review* 1287.

[18] William K. Sjostram Jr., "The AIG Bailout" (2009) 66 *Washington and Lee Law Review* 943.

[19] Levon Garslian, "Towards a Universal Regulatory Framework for Derivatives" (2016) 37 *University of Pennsylvania Journal of International Law* 941, pp. 976–7.

[20] Awrey, above note 14, p. 162.

conduct promoted by private associations, such as the International Swaps and Derivatives Association (ISDA).[21] However, it was clear at the outset that increased regulation and oversight was necessary in the global market for derivatives. OTC derivatives in particular, given their role in the crisis and the externalities they posed on the financial system, were the primary target of regulatory intervention. At the 2009 Pittsburgh summit, G20 leaders agreed to tackle the question of OTC derivatives and proposed that:

> All standardized OTC derivative contracts should be traded on exchanges or electronic trading platforms, where appropriate, and cleared through central counterparties by end-2012 at the latest. OTC derivative contracts should be reported to trade repositories. Non-centrally cleared contracts should be subject to higher capital requirements.[22]

6.2.1. *The EU and US Responses*

The recommendations of the G20 were immediately welcomed by regulators on both sides of the Atlantic. In the United States, the regulation was concentrated in Title VII of Dodd-Frank Act, the Wall Street Transparency and Accountability Act of 2010, which focuses on swaps. According to US law, the responsibility over derivatives is shared between the Securities Exchange Commission (SEC), which has authority over securities-based swaps, and the Commodities Futures Trade Commission (CFTC), which deals with swap market participants and market infrastructures.[23] In the European Union, on the other hand, the regulatory framework for derivatives was scattered across different pieces of regulation, the most important of which is undoubtedly the European Market Infrastructure Regulation (EMIR).[24] This Regulation sets out the general regulatory framework for OTC derivatives, which is then implemented through the technical standards on clearing and reporting developed by European Securities Market Authority (ESMA). This agency is also entrusted with the authorization and monitoring of trade repositories and clearinghouses, including mutual recognition. The regulation of electronic trading platforms, the

[21] Gabriel V. Rauterberg and Andrew Verstein, "Assessing Transnational Private Regulation of the OTC Derivatives Market: ISDA, the BBA, and the Future of Financial Reform" (2013) 54 *Virginia Journal of International Law* 9; Baker, above note 17.

[22] G20 Leaders' Statement, above note 9.

[23] Dodd-Frank Wall Street Reform and Consumer Protection Act § 712(a).

[24] Regulation 648/2012/EU of the European Parliament and of the Council of 4 July 2012 on OTC Derivatives, Central Counterparties and Trade Repositories, 2012 O.J. (L 201/1) [hereinafter EMIR].

list of exemptions, and some guidance on market structure were embedded in the general legislation on securities trading, the second Market in Financial Instruments Directive (MiFID II)[25] and the Market in Financial Instruments Regulation (MiFIR).[26]

The EU and US regulation of derivatives was based on common principles, but it eventually diverged into various areas.

6.2.1.1. Scope

The European and US regimes diverge with regard to the instruments covered. The EU framework focuses on OTC derivatives in general, while the United States deals with particular categories of swaps. For instance, in the United States, foreign exchange swaps and security forwards are excluded and, therefore, are exempted from the burdensome clearing and reporting requirements. Commentators argued that, while the large majority of OTC derivatives are covered by both regimes, difference in terminology could give rise to regulatory arbitrage, thereby allowing companies to modify their operations or rename their products in a way that allowed them to bypass regulation. For instance, studies show that traders were restructuring their swaps contracts into futures contracts in order to bypass the EU regime.[27] On the other hand, the EU regime exempts from clearing obligations those "non-financial entities" that trade below certain thresholds with regard to specific derivatives products. On top of it, the EU regime exempts what it defines as "hedging activities" from the calculation of the thresholds, but without a uniform definition of "hedging" it is very difficult for regulatory partners to assess equivalency.[28]

6.2.1.2. Reporting

Both the United States and the EU consider reporting a fundamental pillar of the derivatives regulatory regime. Yet, the two regulators diverge substantially

[25] Directive 2014/65/EU of the European Parliament and of the Council of 15 May 2014 on Markets in Financial Instruments and Amending Directive 2002/92/EC and Directive 2011/61/EU, 2014 O.J. (L 173/349) [hereinafter MiFIDII].

[26] Regulation 600/2014/EU of the European Parliament and of the Council of 15 May 2014 on Markets in Financial Instruments and Amending Regulation 648/2012/EU, 2014 O.J. (L 173/84) [hereinafter MiFIR].

[27] Gabriel Rosenberg and Jai Massari, "Regulation Through Substitution as Policy Tool: Swap Futurization Under Dodd-Frank" (2013) *Columbia Business Law Review* 667.

[28] Atlantic Council, *The Danger of Divergence: Transatlantic Financial Reform & the G20 Agenda* (2013), p. 33.

as to the precise reporting requirements. As a start, while the United States requires only one party to report their trade to the recognized trade repository, the EU puts the obligation on both parties. Second, the two regulators diverge on the data that must be provided and the timing of the reporting. For instance, the EU requires traders to report the collaterals and to differentiate among sensitive and non-sensitive information. On the other hand, the US regime is stricter when it comes to the timing for the deposit of the data, which is to be provided in real time or immediately after receipt. Most importantly, the two regulators allow traders to report their data only to trade repositories registered in their jurisdiction, thus forcing traders to choose between a particular regime. One of the main reasons behind the difficulty for Europeans to agree on a data-sharing mechanism with their American counterparts was the strict data-privacy law in Europe. Moreover, as in cross-border banking supervision, regulators are very protective of their information, which they are reluctant to divulge to their partners in order to keep them ahead.[29] Yet, it was undoubted that these regulatory discontinuities create substantial hurdles for cross-border firms as they face burdensome and duplicative requirements that might increase uncertainty over when and where to report. Firms that are forced to operate across border might eventually drop products on which reporting requirements are uncertain or too costly in favor of products that are subject to a similar regime.

6.2.1.3. Clearing

Clearinghouses are the bedrock of the regulatory regimes for OTC derivatives in both the EU and the United States. One of the biggest problems of the pre-crisis regime was the opacity of the OTC derivatives market, which increased manifold counterparty risks and, consequently, systemic risk. Clearinghouses are private institutions financed and managed by financial traders that have as their main role to mutualize – and therefore reduce – the individual risks of their members. The function of a clearinghouse is to eliminate individual counterparty risk in derivatives transactions by acting as an intermediary in the transaction between two parties. Through the use of novation, the clearinghouse interposes in the original bilateral contract between the parties and acts as a counterparty to both, thus creating two different contracts: one as a purchaser of the financial instrument and one as the seller.[30] Since

[29] *Ibid.*, p. 35.
[30] Yesha Yadav and Dermot Turing, "The Extraterritorial Regulation of Clearinghouses" (2016) 2 *Journal of Financial Regulation* 21, p. 28.

the clearinghouse assumes the financial risk for all the bilateral contracts of its members, it must adopt strategies to minimize the risk of default. Among those strategies are the requirements for all traders to post collateral, to contribute to a default fund, the use of netting in calculating margins, the adoption of sophisticated risks management protocols, and the use of particular insolvency procedures to distribute losses between the members in the event of the clearinghouse's default.

The economics of clearinghouses is such that, the more members choose to trade through the clearinghouse, the less expensive it is for the organization to run its business. Thus, clearinghouses have an incentive to increase in size and acquire a pivotal place in the derivatives market. Yet, clearinghouses represent critical nodes in the system as they concentrate systemic risk in one single institution with substantial market interconnectedness.[31] Hence, it is no surprise that regulators want to maintain a grip on them. Probably, this is why regulatory convergence between the EU and the United States was so difficult to achieve. One of the first differences was in margin requirements, which were at the core of the harmonization debate between the two regulators, as they weigh heavily on the profitability of traders and, hence, on the efficiency of the market. The issue was the convergence of holding periods and gross versus net settlement. The holding period is the time that regulators require to terminate, value, and close-out a position. While the United States opted for a 1-day holding period, the EU regime opted for a 2-days period, which would have resulted in a higher liquidation time and higher margins required. On the other hand, while the EU required members to post the net amount of margins with the clearinghouse (which results from the mutual offset of position among members), the US regime mandated the full gross amount that excluded the netting from the calculation and, therefore, resulted in higher margin requirement. Second, regulators differed with regard to the institutional financial backstops from which clearinghouses can benefit. Third, EU and US clearinghouses are subject to different default rules. Finally, clearinghouses are subject to different recognition and supervision regimes.[32]

6.2.2. *Regulatory Battles*

Both the EU and the US regimes meet the G20 and Financial Stability Forum (FSB)'s guidance and standards on derivatives regulation. The two approaches,

[31] Julia Lees-Allen, "Derivatives Clearinghouses and Systemic Risk: A Bankruptcy and Dodd-Frank Analysis" (2012) 64 *Stanford Law Review* 1079.

[32] Yadav and Turing, above note 30, pp. 34–45.

while different on some technical aspects, are indeed designed to achieve a broadly similar regulatory outcome.[33] As commentators have pointed out, the two regimes do not deviate substantially in quality. Both aim at achieving a tradeoff between stability and market efficiency.[34] Asking total harmonization of derivatives rules would have been too much as it would have reduced the necessary margin of flexibility that financial regulation needs to guarantee to let the market run its course. Yet, the technical differences between the two regimes nonetheless mattered substantially for traders and clearinghouses, as they increased uncertainty, duplicated compliance costs and, in some cases, forced market operators to choose between one of the two regimes.

A question arises as to why the EU and US regulators decided to regulate unilaterally such a truly global market as derivatives without any coordination attempt. The decision is quite striking if we think that both the EU and the United States were adamant in their pledges toward more international regulatory cooperation. Yet, from a purely strategic perspective, unilateralism is the logical (initial) choice for each regulator. Unlike other cooperation problems discussed in this book, regulatory coordination does not involve substantial distributional tradeoffs and large asymmetrical gains that increase the fear of defection. Similarly, it does not involve a single Pareto-superior efficient equilibrium. On the contrary, in cooperation games states can choose multiple Pareto efficient equilibria. The classical example of coordination problems is to decide which side of the road to drive on. Both options – left and right – are equal as long as everybody cooperates. The question is simply to decide which one is preferable.[35]

The standard account of regulatory cooperation in international finance posits that states will find it somehow easier to converge on a common approach once they decide which approach they should choose. The classic example in this regard is the regulation of capital adequacy under Basel I, II, and III. In game theoretical terms, this is usually associated with the Assurance (or stag-hunt) game, in which two parties need to coordinate their action to achieve a similar objective.[36] Both know that if they cooperate they will get a much bigger payoff than if they try to achieve the same objective alone. In the context of capital regulation, the gain for states coming from a

[33] Financial Markets Law Committee, "Resolving Issues of Legal Uncertainty Relating to the Recognition and Supervision of Central Counterparties," Comment Paper (September 2015), pp. 7–10.

[34] See Yadav and Turing, above note 30, pp. 45–46; Financial Markets Law Committee, *ibid.*

[35] See Andrew H. Kydd, *International Relations Theory: The Game-Theoretic Approach* (Cambridge: Cambridge University Press, 2015), pp. 46–7.

[36] Pierre-Hugues Verdier, "Transnational Regulatory Networks and Their Limits" (2009) 34 *Yale Journal of International Law* 113, p. 123.

shared approach of capital adequacy regulation (irrespectively of the precise ratio chosen) is much higher if all states adopt the same capital ratio, as regulatory competition will be avoided. Yet, this does not tell the whole story.

The starting point for our analysis is a simple fact: states do not adopt regulatory standards over the same topic at the same time. This was, for instance, the case with the US regime (adopted in 2010) and the EU regime (adopted between 2012 and 2014). The lag between the time when the first piece of national regulation is released and the time the other national regulatory standards are promulgated changes the incentives for cooperation. When it comes to regulating a new and complex field, such as derivatives, the chances that the first-mover state will change its newly adopted regulatory regime in favor of a more convergent regime that accommodates the needs of its follower partners are minimal. Regulation entails substantial transaction costs: listening to requests from different national lobby groups, conducting regulatory impact-assessments, designing and drafting the regulation to make it compliant with national and international norms, and winning parliamentary approval. All these passages are necessary steps in any new legislation and yet, they are extremely costly both financially and politically as well as time-consuming. From a negotiating perspective, a state that promulgates the legislation first will be in a position of command because it will have already made its policy choices and without any external constraints. Follower foreign regulators will be, conversely, in a more difficult position as they will be the one with the actual burden to decide for regulatory convergence or divergence. Indeed, they will have to decide whether to opt for a regime that is in line with the existing foreign regulatory regime or else ignore the pleas for convergence and go ahead with a national approach that accommodates local interests.

The decision will be based on a multitude of considerations, but most of it will depend on the structure and composition of the local market. Presumably, globally active institutions will prefer a harmonized approach, as it will reduce their costs of compliance and increase their market. For instance, important lobby groups from the financial sector such as the Financial Markets Law Committee made it immediately clear that they favored a common position.[37] On the other hand, we can presume that legislators and regulators will find it hard to bend over the foreign regulatory regime, especially when the local market is not made solely by globally active firms. Moreover, if the follower jurisdiction aims at becoming or is a dominant financial market, such as the

[37] Financial Markets Law Committee, above note 33; Financial Markets Law Committee, "Discussion Paper on Coordination in the Reform of International Financial Regulation," Interim Feedback Statement (September 2015).

EU, United States, or Japan, it might be unwise to importing foreign rules, especially from a competitor financial system. Legislators will want to preserve their independence and individuality when drafting legislation, and will not like being told what to do. More importantly, legislators will have to consider the needs of the local market and its peculiarities. While financial institutions and clearinghouses might prefer harmonization over anything else, consumers or locally active firms might prefer an approach that preserves their existing right or is not overly cumbersome.[38] In sum, the more the two markets are in competition to attract global capital, or the more is the share of locally active firms in the follower jurisdiction, the higher is the chance that the initial approach will be regulatory divergence.

We can see how this regulation game plays out in Table 6.1. The First-Mover has the total freedom to tailor the regulation to its market with no international constraints. By doing so, it receives a payoff of seven. Yet, the First-Mover will receive the highest payoff – ten – only if the Follower will adopt a regulatory regime that is identical or very similar to its regime. The problems for the First-Mover are that it does not know which regime the Follower will adopt and that it has no influence over the Follower. The Follower, on the other hand, will not have very high incentives to coordinate its policy with the First-Mover as it will imply a loss of political legitimacy. Hence, for the Follower, the decision to forgo its national interests – i.e., to avoid tailoring the regime to the specificities of its local market or broader regulatory regime – in order to coordinate its policies will imply a gain of only five. Here we have to bear in mind that coordination is not a total loss for the Follower as its financial institutions that are globally active will gain substantially from a common global regime. The best option for the Follower is still the adoption of a national approach to regulation, as it preserves its political legitimacy and it will accommodate the needs of the local market. Moreover, since a unilateral approach by the Follower (which gains eight) will force local financial institutions to comply with the local regime and choose between operating in only one of the two regimes, the Follower's decision will reduce the market share of the First-Mover. Hence, for the Follower the best decision is still not to coordinate.

This incentive structure suggests that without a global regulatory authority to oversee the development of national regulations, states with substantially similar market power – such as the EU, United States, and Japan – will have problems in striking a regulatory compromise. The First-Mover – in the case of derivatives regulation in the United States – will probably get the bigger payoff

[38] On this, see Stavros Gadinis, "The Politics of Competition in International Financial Regulation" (2008) 49 *Harvard International Law Journal* 447.

TABLE 6.1. *Initial incentives to regulatory cooperation*

	First-Mover	Follower
Coordination	10	5
Unilateralism	7	8

if the rest of the world adapts to its regime. However, since coordination is a suboptimal option for the Follower states – in this case, the EU – they will try to compete with the First-Mover. They will therefore devise a local regulatory regime that – while still guaranteeing a well-regulated and FSB-compliant market – incentivizes globally active firms to move their operations locally in order to win market share from the First-Mover. In the case of the US–EU battle for derivatives regulation, the choice of the EU to provide substantially lower capital requirements for firms trading with EU-approved clearinghouses can be regarded as a move to win market share from the United States. The ultimate outcome of this battle is that the globally Pareto-optimal solution – cooperation – is not achieved. This means that globally active firms will be forced to choose between two substantially similar regimes, resulting in fundamental costs.

6.3. REGULATORY ARBITRAGE AND EXTRATERRITORIALITY

From a purely regulatory perspective, the lack of cooperation makes the implementation of local regulations more challenging for national authorities. Unlike exchange-trade derivatives, which are bound to geographical and jurisdictional constraints, OTC derivatives can rely on a truly global market. For instance, when it comes to CDSs, around 80% of the transactions involve counterparties located in different countries.[39] This means that derivative traders can choose where to transact, where to report their trading, and the clearinghouse they want to use. Their choice of jurisdiction and clearinghouse in particular will be influenced greatly by the trading and compliance costs, such as margin or reporting requirements. Clearinghouses will also have a choice as to where to operate or under which jurisdiction. Again, their choice will be motivated largely by costs. It is safe to assume that a clearinghouse would prefer to operate in a jurisdiction where supervisory and compliance costs (such as risk management or business continuity strategies) are low, and where trading costs (such as the minimum amount of collateral or margin requirement) can attract enough traders.

[39] Yadav and Turing, above note 30, p. 22.

Let us now imagine a situation in which regulators have no control over the decision of their firms. Absent any response from regulators, the global market for OTC derivatives would probably trigger a race-to-the-bottom in regulation to attract the highest amount of clearinghouses and, subsequently, traders.[40] As I argued in Chapter 1, a regulator would probably choose the regulatory framework that forces traders and marker operators to internalize the social costs of their trading, even though this might increase operation costs. In a world with free capital mobility, this would nonetheless trigger the migration of traders to more favorable jurisdictions. Lured by the prospect of regulatory arbitrage, traders and clearinghouses will move from the jurisdiction that has the most efficient (albeit more costly) regulatory framework, to the jurisdiction that has the cheapest (albeit more inefficient) regulatory framework. In order to compete, jurisdictions would be forced over time to reduce progressively their regulatory requirements.[41] The ultimate outcome is that the global regulatory playing field would move from a socially optimal level to a suboptimal level.

Regulatory arbitrage is always a risk in finance. Before the G20 issued its reforms proposals in 2009, the US Treasury Secretary Timothy Geithner urged the United States and other nations to strengthen their financial system and "protect against cross-border gamesmanship" in derivatives regulation.[42] Regulatory arbitrage can be offset by two ways. The first option is to agree to a common standard. Regulatory harmonization ensures that regulatory loopholes are avoided and races to the bottom are prevented. However, as explained before, harmonization is difficult to achieve and, sometimes, inefficient. In the absence of a harmonized regime, both the EU and the United States had to grapple with the question as to how contain the systemic risks originating from activities outside their jurisdiction, which nonetheless caused or threatened to cause substantial harm. Their answer was the extraterritorial reach of national regulation.

Both the EU and US laws rely substantially on the extraterritorial application of local laws on market actors to ensure that they do not circumvent their regulatory commitments. For instance, the Dodd-Frank Act authorizes the Securities and Exchange Commission to prohibit foreign entities engaging in securities swaps in the United States if the jurisdiction where the firm is licensed does not offer enough guarantees of stability.[43] In the words of Dodd-Frank: the reach of

40 Sean J. Griffith, "Substituted Compliance and Systemic Risk: How to Make a Global Market in Derivatives Regulation" (2014) 98 *Minnesota Law Review* 1291, pp. 1324–9; Victor Fleischer, "Regulatory Arbitrage" (2010) 89 *Texas Law Review* 227.

41 Griffith, *ibid.*, pp. 1324–9.

42 Treasury Secretary Timothy F. Geithner, "Time Is the Enemy of Reform," Written Testimony, House Financial Services Committee on Financial Regulatory Reform (23 September 2009).

43 Dodd-Frank Wall Street Reform and Consumer Protection Act §715. For an overview

US law can stretch to the activities that "have a direct and significant connection with activities in, or effect on, commerce in the United States."[44] The level of extraterritoriality of US law is such that swap dealers or swap market participants that trade beyond US$3 billion over a 1-year period are subject to US law either as an entity or because of a single transaction that touches on the United States. Once they pass that threshold, entities must register with the CFTC irrespective of their location. This reach imposes a burdensome requirement on all firms that have a business with the United States as they are obliged to aggregate data on US derivatives to verify whether they pass the threshold. In order to fall under the reach of US law, financial entities must (1) have transacted with a US counterparty, or (2) enjoyed a financial guarantee provided by a US entity, or (3) have entered into a derivative transaction with a counterparty that was guaranteed by a US entity. Once an entity enters into the reach of US law, it could be subject to two sets of requirements: one focused on the stability and risk-management of the entity, and one focused on the individual transactions, which covers issues such as margin requirements, segregation etc.[45] The SEC can also exercise its jurisdiction to prevent the evasion of the abovementioned rules. Furthermore, Dodd-Frank gives CFTC the extraterritorial jurisdiction over financial activities outside the United States that have a "direct and significant connection with activities in, or effect on, commerce of the US."[46]

Similarly, the EU relies substantially on extraterritoriality to ensure compliance with its rules. For instance, a contract between two or more third parties not located in the EU that has a direct, substantial and foreseeable effect within the EU is automatically subject to the EMIR.[47] This is intended as a contract with which the foreign entities enter into a contract through their EU branches, or if one of the foreign counterparties of the contract is guaranteed by a EU financial institution. Moreover, a financial institution can use a foreign clearinghouse only if this is recognized by ESMA.

Extraterritoriality is not the optimal solution to global regulatory cooperation as it simply ensures the protection of national interests without tacking the problems faced by globally active firms. The US approach, for instance,

of Substituted Compliance in US securities law, see Alexey Artamonov, "Cross-Border Application of OTC Derivatives Rules: Revisiting the Substituted Compliance Approach" (2016) 1 *Journal of Financial Regulation* 206.

44 Dodd-Frank Wall Street Reform and Consumer Protection Act §722(d).

45 Securities Exchange Commission, "Re-Proposal of Regulation SBSR and Certain Rules and Forms Relating to the Registration of Security-Based Swap Dealers and Major Security-Based Swap Participants" (1 May 2013).

46 Dodd-Frank Wall Street Reform and Consumer Protection Act §722.

47 EMIR, Art. 4(1)(a)(v).

was highly controversial due to the extensive extraterritorial reach of US law and the stiff fines of US authorities. In 2013, the Ministries of Finance of nine jurisdictions sent a letter to US Secretary of Treasury Jack Lew to express their disappointment and concerns over the CFTC extraterritorial reach. They wrote:

> Without clear direction from global policymakers and regulators, derivatives markets will recede into localised and less efficient structures, impairing the ability of business across the globe to manage risk. This will in turn dampen liquidity, investment and growth. . . . An approach in which jurisdictions require that their own domestic regulatory rules be applied to their firms' derivatives transactions taking place in broadly equivalent regulatory regimes abroad is not sustainable. Market places where firms from all our respective jurisdictions can come together and do business will not be able to function under such burdensome regulatory conditions.[48]

6.4. THE BATTLE FOR MUTUAL RECOGNITION

Extraterritoriality does not solve the coordination battles in financial regulation. Given the lack of incentives for each national regulator to modify their regulatory approach and rewrite the regulation to accommodate its partners, the question remains as to how to move from a unilateral inefficient equilibrium to a globally Pareto-efficient outcome. Mutual recognition is a possible solution to this problem.[49]

6.4.1. *Mutual Recognition in Securities Regulation*

In Chapter 3, we noted mutual recognition in the context of international banking. In the field of securities regulation, a mutual recognition agreement allows firms authorized and supervised in a foreign country to operate or transact in the host-country jurisdiction without the need of the host country's approval, provided that the host country does the same with the home country's firms. US authorities have a troubled history with mutual recognition, which goes through phases of acceptance and rejection.[50] Until very

[48] Joint Letter to US Treasury Secretary Lew on cross-border OTC derivatives reform (18 April 2013).

[49] Pierre-Hugues Verdier, "Mutual Recognition in International Finance" (2008) 52 *Harvard International Law Journal* 55.

[50] See Howell E. Jackson, "Substituted Compliance: The Emergence, Challenges, and Evolution of a New Regulatory Paradigm" (2015) 1 *Journal of Financial Regulation* 169.

recently, the preferred strategy of US authorities was to act within the existing Transnational Regulatory Networks or to increase the extraterritorial effect of US laws.[51] The first mutual recognition agreement negotiated by the United States was with Canada on matters of securities offerings: the Multijurisdictional Disclosure System (MJDS). This agreement was supposed to operate according to the classic template of mutual recognition. Canadian or US private issuers that met the eligibility criteria according to their national laws were automatically allowed to issue their offers in the partner's jurisdiction.[52] The MJDS did not relinquish too much host-country sovereignty. US authorities indeed demanded that Canadian regulators improve their regulatory framework to a level similar to the United States in order to prevent regulatory free-riding. The agreement was nonetheless perceived as favoring mostly Canadian issuers, and therefore certain parts of the US regulatory establishment opposed to it.[53] Later on, in 2008 the United States and Australia signed a Mutual Recognition Arrangement whereby each country undertakes to exempt foreign stock exchanges and broker dealers from the application of domestic laws.[54] This agreement, however, is more restrictive than the previous one as it envisages a high level of cooperation between the two authorities in order to minimize any regulatory risks.[55]

In Europe, regulators were in principle more open to use mutual recognition due to its past use within Europe itself. Mutual Recognition was one of the driving forces behind the creation of the European Single Financial Market in the 1980s/1990s through its ability to promote financial integration without intruding on states' regulatory sovereignty. This quality explains why recognition is usually considered a very good approach to solve regulatory cooperation problems. In a world where policy coordination can only be achieved through lengthy multilateral negotiations, assigning the whole burden of regulating a financial institution or individual transaction to a single authority is the easiest way to promote efficient financial integration.[56] The

[51] See Detlev Vagts, "Extraterritoriality and the Corporate Governance Law" (2013) 97 *The American Journal of International Law* 289; on territoriality, see Chris Brummer, "'Territoriality as a Regulatory Technique: Notes from the Financial Crisis" (2010) 79 *University of Cincinnati Law Review* 499; Verdier, above note 36.

[52] Ruth O. Kuras, "Harmonization of Securities Regulation Standards between Canada and the United States" (2004) 81 *University of Detroit Mercy Law Review* 465.

[53] Brummer, above note 1, p. 54.

[54] Marguerite Bateman and Cynthia Beyea, "Mutual Recognition: A Step toward Greater Access to Global Market" (2008) 15 *The Investment Lawyer* 67.

[55] Verdier, above note 49, at 55; Brummer, above note 1, pp. 55–6.

[56] The same logic applies to all other sectors, especially in the context of trade in services. See Nicolaidis and Shaffer, above note 46.

simple fact that countries do not need to engage in lengthy negotiations in order to agree on a common regulatory regime, as is the case with harmonization, speeds up negotiations and arguably favors the signing of new agreements. As Brummer argues, "in this dynamic, one would expect either greater concessions from both countries or a greater interest in a purer form of mutual recognition where one another's regimes are recognized and fewer reforms are required."[57]

Yet, mutual recognition might entail substantial risks if the host regime is not up to the standards of the home country. This is why Transnational Regulatory Networks (TRNs) such as the FSB or the BCBS exert a very important role in setting minimum regulatory standards. Having said that, recognition of securities regulations does not present the same problems found in home–host supervisory arrangements or Single Passports for cross-border banking, although sometimes regulators find it difficult to access information from foreign authorities. In securities regulation, regulators are often more wary of the risks of giving access to firms authorized under a weak regulatory regime. In a mutual recognition agreement, regulators give recognition to a foreign regime only after having conducted a compatibility test that ensures the similarity of regulations. Thus, in cross-border securities regulation, recognition usually levels up the regulatory playing field and operates only between partners with fairly similar regimes. This ensures that no "firm can escape regulation" and no "dangerous" transactions can take place in a shared market.

6.4.2. *The Logic of Cooperation in Mutual Recognition*

In a mutual recognition regime the payoffs are clearly changed as they do not entail the loss of regulatory sovereignty. Hence, both the First-Mover and the Follower can safely coordinate their policies without the fear of losing political legitimacy. Thus, mutual recognition makes the time-difference problem connected to the asynchrony in the release of national regulation irrelevant, as each regulator can keep its own regulatory standards. On top of it, mutual recognition can reduce the regulatory barriers that prevent the home's globally active firms operating in the host market, while at the same time it maintains the local regulatory standards for locally active firms and consumers. We can see the payoffs in Table 6.2. Mutual recognition entails ten gains for both the First-Mover and the Follower. Unilateralism, on the other hand, brings the same reduced payoff that we have seen before.

[57] Chris Brummer, "Post-American Securities Regulation" (2010) 98 *California Law Review* 327, p. 371.

TABLE 6.2. *Payoffs in a mutual recognition agreement*

	First-Mover	Follower
Mutual recognition	10	10
Unilateralism	7	8

Yet, despite the various pleas for a mutual recognition regime, the EU and United States took quite some time to agree to it. The two regulators adopt different recognition systems. While the EU adopts the recognition of equivalence of foreign laws, the United States adopts the so-called Substituted Compliance that is more akin to national treatment than real recognition.[58] The battle for recognition was mostly fought over the issue of clearinghouses.

The key provision in the European approach to equivalence recognition for derivatives clearinghouses is Article 25 of the EMIR, which permits European firms to use clearinghouses located outside Europe as long as the ESMA and the Commission recognize them as equivalent. EMIR Article 25(6) requires that foreign clearinghouses authorized in a third country "comply with legally binding requirements which are equivalent to the requirements laid down in Title IV of this Regulation, that those central counterparties (CCPs) are subject to effective supervision and enforcement in that third country on an ongoing basis."[59] The EU approach to regulatory convergence is based on the "equivalence" of the substantive laws and supervisory framework applied in the jurisdiction where the CCP is headquartered. The EU approach therefore gives recognition jurisdiction-by-jurisdiction. Once a CCP proves that it is licensed and properly supervised in that jurisdiction it can automatically operate in the EU without the need of further authorization or registration. In granting the equivalence status, the ESMA – the agency in charge – will conduct comparative studies on myriad laws, regulations, and supervisory practices in the host country to ensure that the level is broadly similar. Once the host clearinghouse regime is approved, the EU regulators will not supervise the foreign clearinghouses. The most important element in the equivalence system of Article 25 is the mutual recognition clause, which subordinates the EU equivalence decision to the fact that "the legal framework of that third country provides for an effective equivalent system for the recognition of

[58] Ethiopis Tafara and Robert J. Peterson, "A Blueprint for Cross-Border Access to U.S. Investors: A New International Framework" (2007) 48 *Harvard International Law Journal* 31; Jackson, above note 50.

[59] EMIR, Article 25(6).

CCPs authorized under third-country legal regimes."[60] The EU approach is a pure mutual-recognition regime, which operates based on full reciprocal treatment. As of September 2015, the EU had recognized 12 jurisdictions, from South Africa to Singapore. However, it had refused to recognize US CCPs, stating that the US regime would have not reciprocated the same treatment to EU CCPs.

The US regime, on the other hand, does not envisage mutual recognition but it is rather based on authorization. Hence, it does not differentiate between US and foreign CCPs insofar as it authorizes foreign CCPs to provide clearing services in the United States so long as they comply with the US regime. The US regime is not based on mutual recognition but on non-discrimination as it puts all firms that are subject to US law on equal footing. This means that it is up to the foreign clearinghouse that wants to operate legally in the United States to comply with the US requirements, even though it is already subject to its home regulator's requirements. If the home regulatory framework is similar or more stringent this would not cause any problems. However, if it is not, the firms might have to face some higher compliance costs or even the choice between its home market and the US market. The US regulator does not give an inch of sovereignty over foreign clearinghouses and, once they operate under US law or in US soil, they are subject to the supervision of the CFTC (in addition to that of its home supervisor).

Behind the different regulatory discipline for cross-border derivatives, there was a subtle financial war to incentivize traders to move to each other's market. As an incentive to use local and foreign-recognized clearinghouses, the European regulator devised a more favorable capital framework for firms dealing with EU-recognized counterparties. The EU Regulation No 575/2013 on prudential requirements for credit institutions and investment firms mandated that firms' exposures would be subject to only 2% risk-weighted capital charge. On the contrary, this would rise to 50% if they use a non-recognized clearinghouse. US clearing firms complained that this rule would have meant an additional capital charge up to thirty times the value of the transaction for non-complying firms, which would have entailed an undue financial burden in excess to the one they already have in terms of required collateral.[61] This would have meant the migration of the deals toward Europe. Paradoxically, the problem was particularly pernicious for European firms that were edging

[60] *Ibid.*

[61] Philip Stafford, "Quick View: Clearing Up Differences: Accord between the EU and the US Is Being Severely Tested," *Financial Times Online* (16 June 2014), at https://next.ft.com/content/3ccba18a-f52d-11e3-91a8-00144feabdc0.

dollar interest rate swaps with Eurodollars in the United States, as they had to clear their trades in Chicago via CME Clearing, the main venue for Eurodollar futures clearing. One could argue that European regulators might have had in mind a strategy to challenge the world dominance of Eurodollar futures clearing and create a European counterpart. As argued by Yadav and Turing, the unwillingness of EU regulators to recognize the equivalence of US clearinghouses might have pushed more trades toward EU clearinghouses.[62] The EU's original deadline for the expiration of the transitional period after which the rule would enter into force – set for 14 July 2014 – was postponed a number of times, thereby creating substantial uncertainty in the market.[63]

The US concern over the recognition of EU CCPs was that US clients that clear swaps with a foreign CCP will not be subject to – and benefit from – the protection accorded by US bankruptcy law. The legal point of contention was the interpretation of the word "customer of a clearing member" in the US bankruptcy code, which allows for a ratable distribution of property in the event of the insolvency of the CCP and is not meant to encompass clients of a clearing member whose derivatives are cleared through a non-US CCP.[64] Moreover, the United States was concerned about the EU rules applying to the segregation of swaps and futures and to the protection of collateral. In particular, the US authorities were not convinced over the level of protection offered by EU rules on the so-called "omnibus segregated client account," which is one of the three types of CCP client accounts under EU law. The EU regime for those accounts provides weaker protection insofar as these accounts involve cross-netting and implies higher mutualization risks among CCP customers.[65] Substituted compliance in the United States is more stringent than the EU as it does not encompass transaction-level requirements, including central counterparty clearing.

We can represent the battle for mutual recognition as a cooperation game (Table 6.3), with the United States in bold type and the EU in standard type. Mutual recognition is the globally Pareto-optimal option as it allows the two countries to increase market access for their firms while retaining regulatory freedom (upper-left quadrant). The status quo option – the refusal of both countries to recognize each other – leaves the payoff unchanged (lower-right quadrant). The upper-right and the lower-left quadrants represent asymmetrically the two

[62] Yadav and Turing, above note 30, p. 47.

[63] See Commission Implementing Regulations 591/2014, 1317/2014, and 2015/880.

[64] Financial Markets Law Committee, "Resolving Issues of Legal Uncertainty Relating to the Recognition and Supervision of Central Counterparties – ADDENDUM" Comment Paper (February 2016), p. 5.

[65] Financial Markets Law Committee, above note 33, p. 12.

TABLE 6.3. *Cooperation game in mutual recognition*

	Recognition	Unilateralism
Recognition	10; 10	5; 10
Unilateralism	10; 5	7; 8

situations in which the home country recognizes the host's regime, while the host refuses to reciprocate. We can see that the country that is recognized but refuses to reciprocate gets the best deal (ten gains) as its firms can access the foreign market with no additional compliance costs while it insulates its market from foreign competition. Conversely, the recognizing country gets the worse deal (five gains) as it does not gain market access abroad, while it forces its own firms to compete with foreign entrants. We can now understand why the EU approach to equivalence required the mutual recognition from the third country in order for the EU to grant equivalence.

The EU and US failure to strike a deal created substantial problems for firms. As various commentators suggest, the asymmetry in the treatment of foreign clearinghouse had the ultimate effect of breaking up the global clearinghouse and derivatives market.[66] On the one hand, once a foreign clearinghouse had been authorized in a foreign jurisdiction that was deemed equivalent by EU law, it could operate in the EU without the hassle of constant supervision. This of course presumed that the foreign clearinghouse had made the effort to comply with the very high standards set by the EU regime. On the other hand, if a clearinghouse had decided to seek only the authorization to operate under US law, it had no possibility to enter the EU market, as the EU authorities deemed the US regime as non-equivalent. The only option for a clearinghouse willing to operate in both markets was to comply with both regimes. However, this was extremely complicated due to the technical requirements of the regimes that eventually translated into higher fees for members.

6.5. THE DEAL

On 10 February 2016, the US CFTC and the ESMA finally announced the deal on the equivalence of CCP regimes, the so-called "common approach."[67] After some months of preparatory work, which included the US substituted

[66] Yadav and Turing, above note 30; Financial Markets Law Committee, above note 33.

[67] European Commission Press Release, "European Commission and the United States Commodity Futures Commission: Common approach for transatlantic CCPs" (Brussels, 10 February 2016).

compliance decision over ESMA rules and the EU's equivalence determination of CFTC requirements, the deal was then crystallized in a Memorandum of Understanding signed by the two authorities on 2 June 2016. The EU's equivalence determination will allow US-authorized CCPs to clear trades for EU customers and operate in the EU while being subject to US law. Moreover, banks that trade with US CCPs will not be subject to the higher regulatory capital requirements that apply to non-equivalent third country CCPs. On the US side, CCPs that are authorized in the EU and registered with the CFTC as derivatives clearing organizations will be able to operate and offer services in the United States without the need of authorization by the CFTC and without the need to comply with CFTC rules. However, the EU's equivalence decision is based on the condition that CFTC-registered US CCPs seeking recognition in the EU confirm that they have adopted internal rules and procedures that ensure enough margins to cover 2 days' liquidation period, margin models that include measures to mitigate the risk of procyclicality, and the maintenance of "cover 2" default resources.[68]

The successful conclusion of the regulatory turf between the two financial superpowers suggests that international coordination on regulatory matters is relatively easier compared to other areas of financial policy. This indicates that in the absence of distributional problems, states that share a common financial market do have an incentive in finding a compromise on regulatory matters; it just takes time. In this chapter, I have expanded the analysis on international regulatory cooperation, which mostly deals with regulatory harmonization, by instead focusing on mutual recognition and extraterritoriality. I have argued that, without full reciprocity, countries have very little incentive to recognize a foreign regime as this would entail the extra burden of accepting and accommodating foreign firms without any market access benefit in the foreign country for the local firms. This explains the EU's reluctance to grant equivalence status to US CCPs. Although the analysis is focused only on the specificities of transatlantic OTC derivatives regulation and the role of CCPs, in particular, it might nonetheless shed a useful light for future analyses in other areas of financial regulation that rely on mutual-recognition agreements.

[68] European Commission and United States Commodity Futures Trading Commission, "The United States Commodity Futures Trading Commission and the European Commission: Common Approach for Transatlantic CCPs" (10 February 2016).

7

Centralization and Its Limits

The allocation of regulatory, executive, adjudicatory, or enforcement functions into a single supranational authority is one of the most commonly proposed solutions to the problems of policy coordination. This tendency can be found in virtually any aspect of government action, from tax to environmental policy, and even human rights.[1] Examples include the creation of international tribunals to persecute war crimes, the establishment of a common customs regime among neighboring countries, or the foundation of an international agency to tackle cross-border pollution. We see the same happening also in finance. Many commentators have argued over the years – usually following a disastrous financial crisis – that the solution of the problems of global finance could rest in the creation of a global supervisory or regulatory authority.

In an interconnected global financial system, delegating the responsibility for financial stability to a single agency often seems a very logical and plausible response to financial turmoil – a response that is, sometimes, endorsed even by the official government statements. For instance, in the G20 Summit in Washington in 2008, the French President Nicholas Sarkozy and the UK Prime Minister Gordon Brown encouraged the creation of a new financial architecture, and suggested the International Monetary Fund (IMF) and the then Financial Stability Board to take a more central role. Eventually, some of these proposals were turned into real policy changes, albeit on a much smaller scale than what originally envisaged. For instance, since the global financial crisis, the IMF has taken a more preponderant role on global financial stability by monitoring actively the financial policies of its members through

[1] On the virtues of global governance, see, for instance, Joel P. Trachtman, *The Economic Structure of International Law* (Cambridge, MA, and London: Harvard University Press, 2008), pp. 150–95.

its different surveillance mechanisms.[2] In 2009, the Financial Stability Board was resurrected from the ashes of its defunct predecessor – the Financial Stability Forum – to become the main think tank for financial policies.[3] In the European financial system, centralization took its purest form with the creation of the European Banking Union among Eurozone countries.

Yet, despite the appeal of a single global rulebook or a global supervisory agency, centralizing government functions into a supranational or international authority entails fundamental political, administrative, and economic costs that cannot be ignored. For this reason, it is an option rarely pursued. This chapter will discuss the logic of centralization in finance, and will analyze when it can work. In doing so, I will discuss, in particular, the establishment of the European Banking Union among Eurozone countries in the aftermath of the European sovereign debt crisis.

7.1. THE ARGUMENTS FOR CENTRALIZATION

In international relations, *centralization* defines the process by which government functions are transferred from the state to a supranational or international organization. Centralization therefore defines the permanent transfer of power from the state level to the international level through the creation of international institutions with delegated authority over a particular policy area and/or function. This in turn implies the corresponding loss of sovereignty at the national level. Because centralization deals with the allocation of government functions and authority, it has to be distinguished from the actual outcome of regulatory or policy convergence in a particular field – such as

[2] IMF, "Financial Sector Surveillance and the Mandate of the Fund," International Monetary Fund (19 March 2010), available at www.imf.org/external/np/pp/eng/2010/031910.pdf; IMF, "Integrating Stability Assessments under The Financial Sector Assessment Program into Article IV Surveillance," International Monetary Fund (27 August 2010), available at www.imf.org/external/np/pp/eng/2010/082710.pdf.

[3] Stavros Gadinis, "The Financial Stability Board: The New Politics of International Financial Regulation" (2013) 48 *Texas International Law Journal* 157; Enrique R. Carrasco, "The Global Financial Crisis and the Financial Stability Forum: The Awakening and Transformation of an International Body" (2010) 19 *Transnational Law and Contemporary Problems* 203; Douglas W. Arner and Michael W. Taylor, "The Global Financial Crisis and the Financial Stability Board: Hardening the Soft Law of International Financial Regulation?," Asian Institute of International Financial Law, Working Paper No. 6, University of Hong Kong (2009); Stephany Griffith-Jones, Eric Helleiner, and Ngaire Woods (eds.) "The Financial Stability Board: An Effective Fourth Pillar of Global Economic Governance?," Special Report, Center for International Governance Innovation (June 2010), available at www.cigionline.org/sites/default/files/fsb_special_report_2.pdf.

the harmonization of capital adequacy laws – which is instead only the actual result of the decision of national authorities to harmonize a particular law.

Centralization takes many shapes and forms. The process can be embedded in a broader project of political and economic integration, like the European Union, in which case the transfer of powers takes different forms in multiple policy and functional areas. Most commonly, centralization is used to solve a specific problem like environmental degradation or development assistance, in which case it can entail the creation of an international organization or agency. When centralization refers to the creation of an international organization, some scholars define it as "international delegation," to highlight the principal–agent relationship that links those who cede the authority to the organization to the newly formed institution.[4] Because centralization defines the final outcome of a political and administrative process, it can be used to describe any vertical redistribution of public functions, from border defense to adjudication and dispute resolution. Furthermore, centralization does not necessarily imply a complete transfer of competence in a particular area, but could be partial and limited to only a few tasks such as regulation or enforcement. For instance, when states agree to create a customs union, they agree to centralize the power to set customs duties and rules of origin at the supranational level and to adopt a common external trade policy. However, this does not necessarily mean that the administration of the customs or the collection of duties is also transferred to a supranational police force. Indeed, in most cases this function is exerted by national authorities.

In the context of economic relations, monetary unions represent perhaps the quintessential example of centralization. The European Monetary Union is, in this regard, probably the most complex and sophisticated monetary arrangement ever negotiated, even though it does not qualify as a complete currency area.[5] In the area of finance, centralization is much less common, although the recent establishment of the European Banking Union among Eurozone countries might start a trend toward centralization also in other regions of the world. In finance, centralization can occur in all classic pillars of financial policy such as regulation, supervision, crisis management, and resolution, or in other areas such as consumer protection, competition, or

[4] Curtis A. Bradley and Judith G. Kelley, "The Concept of International Delegation" (2008) 71 *Law & Contemporary Problems* 1; David Epstein and Sharyn O'Halloran, "Sovereignty and Delegation in International Organizations" (2008) 71 *Law & Contemporary Problems* 77; Kenneth W. Abbott and Duncan Snidal, "Why States Act through Formal International Organizations" (1998) 42 *Journal of Conflict Resolution* 3.

[5] See Paul De Grauwe, *Economics of Monetary Union* (Oxford: Oxford University Press, 2013).

dispute settlement. Finally, centralization can, in principle, encompass also the vertical redistribution of fiscal authority to the supranational level. This might involve the power to formulate the fiscal policy, or the right to collect and administer the public budget, and/or fiscal solidarity among member states, in which case the process of centralization would lead to a fiscal union.[6] As I will discuss later, the centralization of fiscal policy is virtually non existent among international or regional organizations, as it necessarily implies some sort of political union to be found only in federal states.

Centralization entails a fundamental redistribution of public authority. This implies a loss of national sovereignty, on the one hand, and a parallel increase of power at the supranational level, on the other hand. Given the fundamental sovereignty costs that this process entails, a question therefore arises as to why states decide to transfer part of their sovereign powers and rights to a regional or international organization. The answer to this question is not simple as the reasons vary depending on the policy area considered and the specific functions transferred. The standard economics explanation of centralization posits that states decide to centralize those policies or functions that can be performed more efficiently at the supranational rather than the national level. This rationale underpins the principle of subsidiarity in EU law by virtue of which the European Union shall act only when the political objectives cannot be sufficiently achieved by members at the local, regional, or national level.[7]

To understand this logic it is useful to first explain why states decide to keep certain functions at the local level. The seminal argument for decentralization was formulated by Charles Tiebout who argued that the provision of public goods is more efficient when it is delivered closer to those who benefit from it. Local authorities have a better sense of the needs and capabilities of the population and are thus able to target their intervention.[8] Decentralization, in turn, creates regulatory competition between different administrative districts

[6] C. Randall Henning and Martin Kessler, *Fiscal Federalism: US History for Architects of Europe's Fiscal Union* (Brussels: Bruegel, 2012); Carlo Cottarelli and Martine Guerguil (eds.) *Designing a European Fiscal Union: Lessons from the Experience of Fiscal Federations* (London: Routledge, 2014).

[7] The present formulation of the principle of subsidiarity is contained in Article 5(3) of the Treaty on European Union, and it reads: "Under the principle of subsidiarity, in areas which do not fall within its exclusive competence, the Union shall act only if and in so far as the objectives of the proposed action cannot be sufficiently achieved by the Member States, either at central level or at regional and local level, but can rather, by reason of the scale or effects of the proposed action, be better achieved at Union level."

[8] M. Tiebout, "A Pure Theory of Local Expenditures" (1956) 64 *Journal of Political Economy* 416.

as citizens will move to those districts that offer the best cost–benefit scenario in terms of regulatory framework and public service, on the one hand, and level of taxation, on the other. This incentivizes healthier and better regulation. Hence, decentralization should be the default option until there is clear evidence that centralization is more efficient. However, because the case for decentralization rests on a few assumptions (complete knowledge, full mobility, and regulatory power) that may not be realistic at all times, then it is more efficient to delegate a few functions to the upper level of government.

In institutional economics, the case for centralization is usually motivated by the need to address global problems. When a state cannot address global public bads alone, then it is better to create an international institution that groups and coordinates the efforts of many states through the use of a permanent bureaucracy that acts on behalf of, but independently from, the states that have created it. In most cases this new international organization does not exert any legislative or executive powers, but rather limits itself to administering a treaty. For instance, the World Trade Organization is endowed with a permanent secretariat that is responsible for managing the various functions given to the organization by the WTO Agreements, including technical assistance, trade negotiations, and dispute settlement. Some organizations can have more intrusive powers. For instance, the United Nations was originally created to maintain peace and prosperity among its members by offering an institutional avenue where states could discuss their problems and act together to address a common concern. Known to most international affairs experts, the UN has (in theory) powerful muscles when it comes to maintaining security. For instance, it can issue binding Resolutions, authorize the use of force, and dispatch UN security forces in the battleground.

In other circumstances, however, centralization can be the logical step in a broader process of economic integration; a necessary piece in absence of which the entire architecture of integration would collapse. This rationale is particularly important when it comes to centralization in monetary and financial affairs. Unlike other areas, finance cannot be construed as the combination of separate policy silos independent of each other. If some of the policies are transferred to the supranational level while others remain a national competence, regulatory loopholes or broader macroeconomic imbalances might ensue. For instance, the creation of the EMU was considered necessary to maintain the sustainability of the single market in financial services. According to one of the fundamental theories of monetary economics, the so-called Impossible Trinity of monetary policy, a state that opens its capital account must necessarily choose between giving up its monetary autonomy (while maintaining a fixed exchange rate regime), or take the risks of a floating exchange rate (while keeping monetary sovereignty).[9] This view was later made explicit in the 1989 Delors Report that prepared the ground for the creation of the EMU.[10] For this reason, many authors attribute the decision of Eurozone members to enter the European Monetary Union to financial stability problems that could have arisen by having a common financial market and national monetary sovereignty.[11]

7.2. THE FINANCIAL TRILEMMA

In the context of finance, most of the debates on policy convergence have focused on the question of regulatory harmonization[12] and on the rise of Transnational Regulatory Networks.[13] However, none of these debates actually deal with the actual permanent transfer of regulatory and supervisory authority to an international agency. On the one hand, the debate on harmonization deals with the efficiency of a common rulebook for finance rather than the allocation of regulatory power. On the other hand, as the name suggests, Transnational Regulatory Networks are nothing more than regulatory clubs where national regulators discuss regulatory developments or share

[9] This theory was first proposed by the Canadian economist Robert Mundell in his seminal "A Theory of Optimum Currency Areas" (1961) 51(4) *The American Economic Review*, 657–65. A non-reserve currency country cannot have full capital mobility, a flexible exchange rate, and independent monetary policy all at the same time. In the case of a surge of capital inflow that causes inflation, monetary authorities would try to raise interest rates. This would lead to even more capital inflow, as investors move capital where interest rates are higher, and it would also increase inflation. Similarly, in case of economic problems, investors would leave the country. In doing so, they would convert domestic assets into foreign assets, thereby causing a depreciation of the currency. In order to prevent this, monetary authorities would increase the interest rate to maintain an economy that is attractive to foreign investors. At the same time, a high interest rate would prevent authorities from adopting domestic policies that promote domestic investment.

[10] *Report on Economic and Monetary Union in the European Community* (Delors Report), 17 April 1989, p. 11.

[11] Rosa Maria Lastra, *Legal Foundations of International Monetary Stability* (Oxford: Oxford University Press, 2005).

[12] Roberta Romano, "Empowering Investors: A Market Approach to Securities Regulation" (1998) 107 *Yale Law Journal* 2359; Roberta Romano, "For Diversity in the International Regulation of Financial Institutions: Critiquing and Recalibrating the Basel Architecture" (2014) 31 *Yale Journal of Regulation* 1; Beth A. Simmons, "The International Politics of Harmonization: The Case of Capital Market Regulation" (2001) 55 *International Organization* 589; Andrew T. Guzman, "International Regulatory Harmonization" (2002) 3 *Chicago Journal of International Law* 271.

[13] Pierre-Hugues Verdier, "Transnational Regulatory Networks and Their Limits" (2009) 34 *Yale Journal of International Law* 113.

best practices. Hence, they are far from being international institutions with delegated regulatory or enforcement powers over their members.

Yet, during and in the aftermath of the recent financial crises, we have witnessed sporadic calls for the creation of international financial authorities. For instance, at the outset of the destructive East Asian, Russian, and Argentine crises, John Eatwell and Lance Taylor proposed the creation of a World Financial Authority located in Basel that would set binding international financial standards and replace national supervisory authorities around the world.[14] Eric Pan argued on the necessity to centralize supervision in one single international supervisory agency.[15] In 2008, in the midst of the global financial crisis, Barry Eichengreen proposed an enhanced role for the International Monetary Fund on matters of financial stability.[16] Emilios Avgouleas also proposed the transfer of some of the most pressing tasks of global finance such as micro and macroprudential surveillance, crisis resolution, and regulation to specialized global administrative agencies.[17] The arguments put forward in support of centralization might vary from the need to tackle macroprudential concerns to the need to converge on cross-border bank supervision. Nonetheless, underneath those arguments lies the question of financial nationalism and the lack of incentives for national regulators to consider the external implications of their policies. Under this light, the logic of centralization in finance can be simply intended as a redistribution of power to the authority that would use it more efficiently. Since national regulators are unwilling to compromise their national interests, which in turn leads to regulatory inefficiencies or crises, then the only choice is to take their regulatory power away from them and give it to an international authority which will guarantee the pursuit of international goals.

These arguments, however, ignore the fact that states have another option at their disposal: retrench to a situation of financial autarchy. The tradeoffs between stability, integration, and sovereignty can be best understood by referring to the so-called "financial trilemma." Earlier I argued that global stability is the result of two interrelated factors: (1) an integrated global

[14] John Eatwell and Lance Taylor, *Global Finance at Risk: The Case for International Regulations* (New York: The New Press, 2000).

[15] Eric J. Pan, "Challenge of International Cooperation and Institutional Design in Financial Supervision: Beyond Transgovernmental Networks" (2010) 11 *Chicago Journal of International Law* 243.

[16] Barry Eichengreen, "A Blueprint for IMF Reform: More Than Just a Lender" (2007) 10 *International Finance* 153; Barry Eichengreen, "Out of the Box Thoughts about the International Financial Architecture," IMF Working Paper WP\09\116, International Monetary Fund (2009), available at www.imf.org/external/pubs/cat/longres.aspx?sk=22958.0.

[17] Emilios Avgouleas, *Governance of Global Financial Markets: The Law, the Economics, the Politics* (Cambridge: Cambridge University Press, 2012), pp. 429–59.

financial system that channels and transmits instability and (2) unsustainable or welfare-decreasing domestic policies. Thus, the solution to the problem of global instability should accordingly focus on one of these two factors. Dirk Schoenmaker succinctly expressed this view, albeit only with reference to cross-border banking resolution, in his "financial trilemma."[18] He argued that it is impossible to achieve at the same time: (1) national sovereignty over financial stability policies, (2) an optimum level of global financial stability (which means absence of cross-border externalities), and (3) meaningful financial integration. States have to give up one of them.[19]

According to Schoenmaker's theory, if countries choose to maintain financial integration (by not imposing capital controls or ring-fencing assets) and national control over stability policies, they will inevitably suffer instability. Alternatively, if they want to achieve a globally stable financial system, they have two options. One option is to give up entirely national control over financial policies and transfer it to a supranational entity – essentially, to *centralize* financial stability policy. Centralization in finance can take many forms. At the most basic level, it envisages common prudential rules for banks and financial institutions. This would reduce regulatory loopholes and prevent dangerous races to the bottom. Regulatory harmonization would necessarily mean binding rules and, hence, the transfer of regulatory power to a supranational authority with exclusive competence over the formulation of those rules and the establishment of adjudicatory system to interpret them. However, in a situation of tight financial integration, it would be necessary to centralize also the supervisory and crisis-resolution mechanisms. Supervision is the implementation of policies and rules that make a financial system work; hence, an incorrect or inefficient supervision can potentially lead to instability. The centralization of supervision can correct those national biases and supervisory inefficiencies that endanger the long-term stability of a cross-border bank or discourage financial internationalization. Finally, as I showed in Chapter 4, the centralization of the resolution function can break the principal–agent

[18] The trilemma was never presented as a fully-fledged theoretical model, as it is impossible to define and give a numerical value to financial stability. However, the simplicity of its theory did not prevent it from being widely used and cited. Dirk Schoenmaker, "The Financial Trilemma" (2011) 111 *Economic Letters* 57; Dirk Schoenmaker, *Governance of International Banking: The Financial Trilemma* (Oxford: Oxford University Press, 2013).

[19] The financial trilemma looks at the efficiency of financial stability policies, and it does not provide for clear-cut options. However, it gives a sense of the underlying policy problems. Although Schoenmaker's trilemma is principally focused on crisis-resolution policies for finance, it can be easily used to explain other issues. For instance, it can be used to explain the thorny problem of sovereign defaults and investors' rights, or the use of capital controls.

relationship between resolution authorities and their citizens, and relieve national authorities from the political and economic burdens of saving their banks and protecting their creditors.

The opposite option is the reduction of financial integration. This alternative can take many shapes and forms. The most drastic option is a return to a Bretton Woods-like financial system in which there is no capital mobility and financial systems operate only within national lines. Dani Rodrik is probably the most vocal supporter for the return of finance to nation states. Indeed, in his political economy trilemma, he argues that financial internationalization deprives nation states of the power to exert democratic control over financial policies.[20] India and China are probably the most visible examples of this model as both of them retain full control over their domestic financial system with extremely limited room for financial internationalization.[21] China especially has, until very recently, operated a completely closed financial system with no currency convertibility and no capital mobility.[22] The situation is, however, going to change progressively in the near future as the Chinese government has expressed its desire to open the country to financial internationalization.[23]

In the context of cross-border banking policy, a mild form of financial disintegration can be achieved by returning to a host-country control model in which host countries are the main regulators and supervisors of all the banks operating in their jurisdiction. This option is sometimes called *subsidiarization*, as the penetration of foreign banks will take place only through subsidiaries.[24] As discussed in the Chapter 4, subsidiaries are by all means equivalent

[20] Dani Rodrik, *The Globalization Paradox: Democracy and the Future of the World Economy* (New York: Norton, 2010).

[21] Ajay Shah and Ila Patnaik, "Managing Capital Flows: The Case of India," in Masahiro Kaway and Mario B. Lamberte (eds.) *Managing Capital Flows: The Search for a Framework* (Cheltenham and Tokyo: Edward Elgar Publishing and Asian Development Bank Institute, 2010).

[22] Yonding Yu, "Managing Capital Flows: The Case of the People's Republic of China," in Masahiro Kaway and Mario B. Lamberte (eds.) *Managing Capital Flows: The Search for A Framework* (Cheltenham and Tokyo: Edward Elgar Publishing and Asian Development Bank Institute, 2010); see also, Markus Rodlauer and Papa N'Diaye (eds.) "IMF and PBC Joint Conference on Capital Flows Management – Lessons from International Experience," International Monetary Fund and People's Bank of China (2013), available at www.imf.org/external/np/seminars/eng/2013/capitalflows/pdf/032013.pdf.

[23] On the internationalization of the Renminbi, see Arvind Subramanian, *Eclipse: Living in the Shadow of China's Economic Dominance* (Washington, DC: Peterson Institute for International Economics, 2012).

[24] On subsidiarization, see Committee on International Economic Policy and Reform, "Banks and Cross-Border Capital Flows: Policy Challenges and Regulatory Responses," The Brookings Institution (September 2012), pp. 37–43; Kathia D'Ulster, Cross Border Banking Supervision Incentive Conflicts in Supervisory Information Sharing between Home and Host Supervisors,

to domestic banks. Indeed, they are licensed in the host country, they rely on local capital, and are subject to the regulation and supervision of host authorities.[25] Furthermore, in the host-country model, ring-fencing and territorial bankruptcy policy would feature as core elements of supervision. Since the foreign bank will be treated as a local bank, all the remaining assets will be distributed to maximize local creditors' satisfaction.

A few commentators have advocated a return to a host-country model for financial supervision, as national control provides some clear benefits in terms of regulatory coordination.[26] First of all, it would solve regulatory and policy asymmetries in the context of a cross-border banking crisis. Secondly, it would reduce the risks of spillovers from home-country macroprudential regulation currently present with branches. Indeed, under the host-country model, subsidiaries will be required to satisfy local prudential and macroprudential regulations tailored for the financial and macroeconomic cycle of the host country.[27] Yet, in spite of these benefits, the host-country model has never been fully accepted by the mainstream financial literature, owing to its costs in terms of reduced capital mobility.[28] Since banks are regulated, licensed, and supervised by the local authority where the bank operates, banking conglomerates would suffer serious constraints in raising capital where it is cheaper and lend it where is more profitable. After the global financial crisis, however, the use of host-country control has resurged to the top of the agenda of financial regulators.[29] Ring-fencing was indeed one of the main suggestions

World Bank Policy Research Working Paper 5871, The World Bank (2011), available at http://elibrary.worldbank.org/doi/pdf/10.1596/1813-9450-5871, pp. 23–6; Eugenio Cerutti, Anna Ilyina, Yulia Makarova, and Christian Schmieder, "Bankers without Borders? Implications of Ring-Fencing for European Cross-Border Banks," IMF Working Paper WP/10/247, International Monetary Fund (2010), available at www.imf.org/external/pubs/cat/longres.cfm?sk=24335.0.

25 See Chapter 3.

26 Katharina Pistor, "Host's Dilemma: Rethinking EU Banking Regulation in Light of the Global Crisis," ECGI Working Paper Series in Finance No 286/2010 (2010), available at http://papers.ssrn.com/sol3/papers.cfm?abstract_id=1631940; Avinash Persaud, "The Locus of Financial Regulation: Home versus Host" (2010) 86 *International Affairs* 637.

27 This already occurs with regard to the countercyclical capital buffer requirements for multinational banks disciplined by Basel III. The level of the countercyclical capital buffer on the foreign banks is decided by the host authority, and therefore it is a deviation from the standard home-country control approach.

28 See, for instance, the discussion provided by Persaud, above note 26.

29 The Economist, "Balkanized Banking: The Great Unraveling," 20 April 2013; Susan Lund, Toos Daruvala, Richard Dobbs, Philipp Härle, Ju-Hon Kwek, and Ricardo Falcón, "Financial Globalization: Retreat or Reset?," McKinsey Global Institute (2013), available at www.mckinsey.com/insights/global_capital.../financial_globalization; see also, Julian T.S. Chow and Jay Surti, "Making Banks Safer: Can Volcker and Vickers Do It?," IMF Working Paper WP/11/236, International Monetary Fund (2011), available at www.imf.org/external/pubs/ft/wp/2011/

contained in the 2011 Vickers Report on the future of financial regulation,[30] More recently, in the United States the Federal Reserve has recently revised its policy on foreign banks, which from 2015 are required to comply with US capital and liquidity regulations.[31]

7.3. THE EUROPEAN BANKING UNION

The creation of a Banking Union among Eurozone countries was the solution to European Single Financial Market's trilemma, which became explicit during and after the 2010–12 European sovereign debt crisis. After the completion of the Single Market in financial services, European banks started a process of progressive Europeanization. Bank opened branches and subsidiaries in other European countries and increasingly offered financial services on a cross-border basis. Despite the high level of financial integration across Europe, EU members still retained, until very recently, full sovereignty over important financial stability policies, such as financial supervision and financial crisis management.[32] In the event of a pan-European banking crisis, national governments were essentially left to their own in rescuing home country banks. The European Central Bank (ECB) – the institution best placed to effectively monitor cross-border risks and endowed with enough firepower to prevent the escalation of any crisis – had limited and contested powers with regard to financial stability. These remained for the most part in the hand of national authorities.[33] Thus, in the event of a national liquidity or solvency crisis (whether national or cross-border in nature), the EU's crisis-resolution

wp11236.pdf; José Viñals, Ceyla Pazarbasioglu, Jay Surti, Aditya Narain, Michaela Erbenova, and Julian Chow, "Creating a Safer Financial System: Will the Volcker, Vickers, and Liikanen Structural Measures Help?," IMF Staff Discussion Note SDN/13/4, International Monetary Fund (2013), available at www.imf.org/external/pubs/ft/sdn/2013/sdn1304.pdf.

[30] The Independent Commission on Banking, "Interim Report: Consultation on Reform Options" (April 2011), available at http://s3-eu-west-1.amazonaws.com/htcdn/Interim-Report-110411.pdf.

[31] Gina Chon, Tom Braithwaite, and Camilla Hall, "FED Pushes on with New Rules For Overseas Banks," *Financial Times Online*, 19 February 2014 (accessed on 15 February 2017).

[32] On the other hand, prudential regulations are centralized at the European level and largely harmonized across Europe.

[33] See Lastra, above note 11, at p. 306; for an overview of the role of the ECB in financial supervision, see Rene Smits, "The Role of the ECB in Banking Supervision," in Liber Amicorum Paolo Zamboni Garavelli, *Legal Aspects of the European System of Central Banks* (Frankfurt: European Central Bank, 2005), pp. 199–212. Smits argues that the ECB's powers related to supervision are not limited to giving advice to the European Council, but also entail the power to conduct various market operation to maintain financial stability.

regimes were completely national in design.[34] In the event of a solvency crisis, irrespective of its national or cross-border character, the ability to intervene to rescue failing banks or provide financial support was completely in the hands of the national treasuries,[35] with limited coordination among European national authorities.[36] This led to supervisory and resolution wars similar to those discussed in Chapters 3 and 4 in which national authorities failed to cooperate.

Being cut off from the European market, national banks relied on their own governments for support. This created a perverse situation whereby the lives of banks and sovereigns became closely intertwined in a downward spiral. Banks resorted to heavy purchases of national sovereign bonds, incentivized by the low risk of government bonds.[37] When a country's risk was downgraded the perverse relationship between banks and sovereigns came to light. The declining value of government bonds reduced the capitalization of banks, which thus needed to be recapitalized and, so, turned to their governments to protect their depositors and creditors. Governments, in turn, had to guarantee holdings and bail out the banks, which added extra debt to the governments and further decreased their solvability, thus hurting the banks even more. Banks needed to be recapitalized, while States were proportionally losing the

[34] Rosa Maria Lastra understands that since the responsibility on LOLR policies was not explicitly transferred to the ECB, it should remain at the national level. See Lastra, above note 11, p. 306; Rosa Maria Lastra, "The Division of Responsibilities between the European Central Bank and the National Central Banks Within the European System of Central Banks" (2000) 6 *Columbia Journal of European Law* 167, p. 175.

[35] Charles Goodhart, "Some New Directions for Financial Stability?," Per Jacobsson lecture, held in Zurich on 27 June 2004, available at www.bis.org/events/agm2004/sp040627.htm (accessed on 15 January 2013); Charles Goodhart and Dirk Schoenmaker, "Burden Sharing in a Banking Crisis in Europe" (2006) 2 *Sveriges Riksbank Economic Review* 34; Maria Nieto and Garry Schinasi, "EU Framework for Safeguarding Financial Stability: Towards an Analytical Benchmark for Assessing its Effectiveness," IMF Working Paper WP/07/260, (IMF, 2007).

[36] Deposit guarantee schemes are regulated and implemented nationally according to the place where the bank is headquartered, although European Commission Directive 94/19/EC set a minimum regulatory standard and a minimum level of depositor protection of 100,000 Euro. EC Directive 94/19/EC was subsequently amended in 2005 by EC Directive 2005/1/EC, and in 2010 by EC Directive 2009/14/EC. Indeed, the only regulatory tools available to coordinate cross-border bank rescues were three non-binding Memoranda of Understanding (MoUs) signed in 2002, 2005, and 2008, respectively, and which disciplined cooperation between the treasuries and financial authorities of European countries.

[37] The Capital Requirements Directive encouraged financial institutions to buy sovereign debt by assigning a risk weight of 0% to "exposures to Member States' central governments and central banks denominated and funded in the domestic currency of that central government and central bank." See Adamski, above note 25, at p. 1328; see also Gerlach Schulz and Guntram Wolff, "Banking and Sovereign Risk in the Euro Area," CEPR Discussion Paper No. DP7833, CEPR, 2010.

financial power to do so.[38] This situation happened first in Ireland in 2008 and subsequently in Spain in July 2012, when the government publicly affirmed its inability to rescue the country's banking system.

Soon it became clear that the situation was unsustainable, especially for Eurozone countries, which do not enjoy monetary sovereignty. Thus, European financial policymakers were confronted with the very trilemma described before. If they wanted to regain a stable European financial market, they had only two options: one was to break the process of European financial integration and return to a situation of financial autarchy in which foreign banks had to be licensed, regulated, and supervised by the host authority. This option would have guaranteed them full control over the financial stability of their own national financial system, although it would have not broken the vicious cycle between banks and the sovereign. However, this choice would have been catastrophic from a political perspective as it would have meant a reversal of the European integration process. The other option was much bolder as it envisaged the transfer of supervisory and crisis resolution power over European banks to a single European authority competent for supervising and resolving European banks. A common supervisory and resolution framework would have eliminated supervisory conflicts and prevented a sovereign from intervening to recapitalize a systemically important bank in distress. However, centralization would have entailed the quasi-total dismantling of national bank supervision, at least for Eurozone countries. As had occurred many times in European modern history, when confronted with a common problem, European policymakers chose the path of further integration.

On 25 June 2012, four European leaders – European Council President Herman Van Rompuy, ECB President Mario Draghi, Eurogroup President Jean Claude Junker, and European Commission President Jose Manuel Barroso – released a plan for the creation of a banking union among Eurozone states, to be complemented by a common EU framework for bank resolution.[39] This Banking Union had the objective of replacing national authorities in the supervision and resolution of Eurozone banks and creating a harmonized set of rules for dealing with bank in distress. As such, it was the most important economic governance reform since the creation of the Euro in 2000. Despite the intrinsic political difficulties in organizing such transfer of power, and the

[38] Martin Feldstein, "The Failure of the Euro: The Little Currency that Couldn't" (2012) 91 *Foreign Affairs* 105, p. 109.

[39] European Council: The President, "Towards and Genuine Economic and Monetary Union," Report Issued on 25 June 2012, Brussels 25 June 2012; European Commission, "Communication from the Commission to the European Parliament and the Council: A Roadmap towards a Banking Union," COM (2012) 510 final, Brussels 12 September 2012.

complexities of establishing a centralized authority with a potential range of action over more than 6000 banks, in less than 3 years this ambitious project became a reality.

At present the European banking architecture is organized under four pillars, two of which are exclusive to the Banking Union. Common to all EU members is a rulebook for all EU banks developed by the European Banking Authority. Eurozone countries, on the other hand, share: (1) a supervisory agency (the Single Supervisory Mechanism (SSM)), and (2) a common resolution authority (the Single Resolution Mechanism (SRM)) supported by a Single Resolution Fund. To these two institutions, which form the Banking Union, we must then add a fiscal backstop mechanism for Eurozone members under financial distress (European Stability Mechanism (ESM)).[40]

Centralization of regulation in the EU started long before the crisis, when the European Commission progressively acquired the competence for harmonizing financial regulation. However, because of the type of legislative instrument mostly used by the European Commission – the directive – allows room for substantial divergence in national law, dangerous loopholes and regulatory asymmetries arose across the single market. For this reason, in 2009 the European Banking Authority was entrusted with the power to formulate binding Technical Standards for all financial institutions operating in the European Union. The standards become law across the EU once the European Commission officially adopts them.

While regulation is harmonized across the EU, bank supervision differs between Eurozone and non-Eurozone countries. Since November 2014, the Single Supervisory Mechanism operating under the ECB has been responsible for the supervision of all systemically important Eurozone banks.[41] These are banks with more than 30 billion Euro in assets, or that represent more than 20% of the national GDP, or that have substantial cross-border activity, or that required emergency financing from Eurozone bailout funds. The SSM retains all the powers of a typical supervisory agency. These include the power to grant or revoke a license, monitoring and early intervention powers, and the right to authorize mergers and set prudential standards. In addition to the systemically important banks, the Single Supervisory Mechanism is also

[40] For an overview, see Danny Busch and Guido Ferrarini (eds.) *European Banking Union* (Oxford: Oxford University Press, 2015).

[41] For a good overview, see Eddy Wymeersch, "The Single Supervisory Mechanism or 'SSM,' Part One of the Banking Union," National Bank of Belgium Working Paper No. 255 (2014); Tobias Troger, "The Single Supervisory Mechanism – Panacea or Quack Banking Regulation? Preliminary Assessment of the New Regime for the Prudential Supervision of Banks with ECB Involvement" (2014) 15 *European Business Organization Law Review* 449.

indirectly responsible for the supervision of smaller banks, for which it shares the competence with the Eurozone national supervisory authorities, whose powers the Single Supervisory Mechanism (SSM) can replace if they do not comply with EU law. Non-Eurozone countries are not subject to the SSM and therefore retain sovereignty over banking supervision. However, they have the right to opt-in to the SSM if they chose.

Resolution is structured along similar lines to supervision. Since January 2016, the SRM has had the competence to resolve systemically important Eurozone banks based on the EU-wide Single Rulebook, including the 2014 EU Bank Recovery and Resolution Directive.[42] Similar to supervision, the SRM works alongside national resolution authorities, which are still competent for smaller banks. The decision-making process is co-shared by the Single Resolution Board based in Brussels, which takes the final decision based on the inputs from the European Commission and the ECB. An important asset in the hand of the SRM is the Resolution Fund: a 55 billion Euro fund managed by the SRM that serves to provide financing for the restructuring of financial institutions. It is important to note in this regard that the Resolution Fund cannot be used to bail out a bank in distress, but only to provide a maximum of 8% of the financing need of the bank. As with bank supervision, in non-Eurozone area countries the resolution powers rest with the competent national authority.

The ESM was the response of European authorities to the sovereign debt crises spreading around Europe. Born out of the ashes of two previous instruments – the European Financial Stability Facility and the European Financial Stabilization Mechanism – the ESM provides a fiscal backstop for sovereigns. Unlike the Single Supervisory Mechanism and the SRM, the ESM is not, formally, an agency of the European Union but rather a separate international organization created by Eurozone countries outside the purview of EU law.[43] The ESM is endowed with firepower of 500 billion Euros, which it uses for two main functions. One is to provide a financial backstop to sovereigns that are experiencing a financial crisis and do not have enough liquidity to bail out their banks. In this regard, the ESM can complement the Resolution Fund

[42] Chen Chen Hu, "The Recovery Framework in the BRRD and Its Effectiveness" (2015) 26 *International Company and Commercial Law Review* 10; Michael Schillig, "Bank Resolution Regimes in Europe – Part I: Recovery and Resolution Planning, Early Intervention" (2013) 24 *European Business Law Review* 751; Michael Schillig, "Bank Resolution Regimes in Europe – Part II: Resolution Tools and Powers" (2014) 25 *European Business Law Review* 67.

[43] Bruno de Witte and Thomas Beukers, "The Court of Justice Approves the Creation of the European Stability Mechanism Outside the EU Legal Order: Pringle" (2013) 50 *Common Market Law Review* 805.

using the Bank Recapitalization Programme. The second function is to provide emergency financing to sovereigns in fiscal difficulties, a function that is now explicitly prohibited by EU treaties.

The European Banking Union represents the most advanced example of centralization in financial policy. Yet, despite the great accomplishments of the European regulators, the architecture for financial stability in the Banking Union does not break the vicious link between banks and sovereigns and does not eliminate completely the risks of financial nationalisms. Centralization, as it is now, is not sufficient. To work effectively, the Banking Union needs to be extended further to comprise other tools. The critical missing element is certainly a Single Deposit Insurance scheme to complement the SRM. Deposit insurance is a fundamental tool to address a banking crisis because it insulates depositors from financial risks. If we think that, on average, they represent around a third of the bank's liabilities, and that all their credits are short-term, we can realize the role of deposit insurance in maintaining financial stability. Since the competence to manage and finance the deposit insurance scheme is left at the national level, there is still the risk of cooperation problems between national supervisors on the one hand, and between them and the European supervisors, on the other, over the level of contribution of each party. National supervisors may tend to minimize the problems of their own banks and live off the ECB's liquidity support to reduce the expenditures of the deposit insurance fund. On the other hand, knowing that the fiscal burden would fall on nation states, the European agencies may transfer a higher share of the burden to national authorities. Moreover, provided that the solvency of the deposit insurance scheme is a factor in the decision of depositors to choose one bank over another, a system of national deposit insurance funds financed by local banks would reinvigorate the sovereign–bank loop and enhance solvency risks. In this regard, Gros and Schoenmaker have argued that the history of deposit insurance in the United States before the creation of the Federal Deposit Insurance Corporation in 1914 shows that only the diversification of funds and the detachment of the fund to a particular area can reduce the insolvency risks of deposit insurance funds.[44]

Unfortunately, the creation of a common deposit insurance will imply a legal obligation of fiscal solidarity on the Banking Union members, some of which are explicitly against this idea. The biggest political objection is that a common fund would essentially force national taxpayers to underwrite the

[44] Daniel Gros and Dirk Schoenmaker, "European Deposit Insurance and Resolution in the Banking Union" (2014) 52 *Journal of Common Market Studies* 529, p. 539.

assets of weak and unstable foreign banks subject to crony capitalism.[45] As I will explain later in the chapter, fiscal solidarity is perhaps the biggest limit to centralization in finance.

7.4. CENTRALIZATION: NOT FOR EVERYONE

The European Union represents a unique case in the panorama of international organizations because of the persistent political commitment of its members toward "more Europe" and the sophistication of its institutional architecture. For all other countries, the question over the feasibility and efficiency of a global or regional financial organization remains. In this regard, despite the merit of some of the arguments for a decrease in national sovereignty, only rarely does centralization in finance actually work.

Centralization is extremely effective when it helps already established international organizations in achieving economies of scale. The clearest example is, in my view, the attribution of supervisory and crisis resolution powers to the European monetary and financial authorities that we have discussed. When the proposal for the Banking Union was launched in 2012, European states could count on an already established and well-oiled institutional architecture that already encompassed the power to set financial regulation in the hands of the European Commission, the monetary policy functions in the hands of the ECB, and the very powerful dispute settlement system with the Court of Justice of the European Union at the center of it. Another good example is the recent attribution to the IMF of surveillance powers on Systemic Stability and global imbalances. Given its broad membership, its already existing powers on monetary surveillance, and its expanding work on fiscal and financial matters, there is no doubt, in my view, that the IMF is best placed to monitor global macro-financial trends.[46] The IMF is indeed in the unique position of being able to access the data and monitor the financial and macroeconomic policies of most countries, a condition that gives the Fund the best view on global monetary imbalances.

As I will elaborate further in Chapter 10, I believe that centralization of adjudicatory functions – i.e. the creation of international courts – would be useful in some areas of finance such as sovereign debt and cross-border banking resolution. The creation of specialized international dispute-settlement mechanisms dealing with very narrow areas of financial law bears fundamental

45 Hans-Werner Sinn, "The European Banking Union?," *Project Syndicate* (13 June 2012).

46 As a matter of fact, one of the first post-crisis reforms concerned the expansion of the IMF's work on macro-financial stability.

sovereignty costs. Furthermore, it implies the non-negligible transactional costs of negotiating the procedural and substantive rules according to which the courts would operate. Yet, despite these sunk costs, these institutions would address long-standing coordination problems and increase states' compliance with international financial law while using only relatively limited resources. For instance, courts could be embedded within already existing organizations such as the Financial Stability Board or the IMF/World Bank that have demonstrated expertise on these topics. Those organizations would be able to offer expert opinions and supply data. Alternatively, the dispute-settlement mechanism could simply be attached to an already existing arbitration court while operating according to its own rules. In both cases, the real day-to-day costs of running the dispute-settlement system would be negligible if compared to the costs of establishing an international organization *de novo*, not to mention the benefits they would bring to international cooperation.

For many other aspects, however, centralization is an impracticable policy. Leaving the sovereignty and political costs aside, one of the biggest hurdles to supranational transfers of powers in finance is the enormous running costs that such an organization requires. Supervision and resolution are resource-intensive tasks that require the use of vast amounts of specialized employees and a constant direct access to banks. One could only imagine the gigantic organizational structure that a single global or regional banking supervisory authority would require, and the difficulty of matching different political and economic sensibilities into the same organization. Eurozone countries could do it only because of their long history of tight financial and monetary cooperation, and only the larger banks are subject to the SSM's oversight. Secondly, centralization in finance requires an extremely close collaboration between national monetary authorities, if not the presence of a monetary union. Because macro-prudential regulation must necessarily follow the national financial and macroeconomic cycle, it would be impossible to hand this task over to the supranational supervisor, unless there is an already very tight level of financial and economic integration. Thus, it would be indeed very difficult for the common financial authority to coordinate supervision or regulation if the national central banks of the participating countries had radically different approaches to macro-prudential regulation. Moreover, centralization in finance without centralization of monetary policy could make the provision of emergency liquidity assistance extremely complicated, as the national central bank might refuse or forbear to protect a local interest.

Finally, because crisis resolution requires the use of public money, states might object to transfer taxpayers' money to an institution that would eventually use them to maintain financial stability in other countries. This issue bears fundamental legal, political, and economic implications that deserve further discussion, which I provide in the next section.

7.5. THE "PROBLEM" OF FISCAL SOLIDARITY

Free capital mobility is the quintessential feature of global finance; the blood that keeps the global financial system alive and function. Sovereign borrowers can access new sources of capital to make their economy function; cross-border banks are able to raise capital where it is cheaper and move assets from one part to the other of the bank's group to lend where it is more profitable; corporations can list their shares or borrow from the markets that offer the best conditions. Thus, in the private sphere of global finance, dominated by investors and banks, the main regulatory objective is to reduce the barriers to capital mobility to create a global financial system in which financial firms can operate across borders and channel capital where it is more profitable. Yet, when it comes to global financial governance, the area of international finance that deals with public policies to maintain financial stability, moving public money abroad becomes an almost insurmountable problem.

The centralization of financial stability functions into a single supranational authority necessarily requires also the establishment of a centralized mechanism to channel and distribute public funds across the financial system in support of financial stability policies. This may sound strange when we think that after the global financial crisis the use of public money to support financial stability has been increasingly seen unfavorably by commentators and policymakers; a stance that ultimately became the philosophical underpinning of bail-in reforms across the world. However, despite global regulators' willingness to minimize governments' interventions in financial markets, the use of public money to maintain financial stability can never be absolutely avoided. In the context of bank resolution, public interventions may be necessary to bail out a failing bank, as a collateral for the bank's refinancing operations, to guarantee the bank's liabilities, or for any other operation in support to the bank in resolution. When the bank crisis is systemic or during a critical economic downturn, the resolution fund must be accompanied by a fiscal backstop. In a liquidity problem, lender of last resort or other type of emergency lending operations are the main tools that central banks use to keep alive a financial institution short of cash. Depending on the type of deposit insurance protection scheme chosen, deposit insurance relies on the participation of the government as a guarantor for the banks' funding of the scheme or as a direct contributor to the deposit insurance fund.

When those functions are transferred to a supranational agency or authority, it logically follows that the financing of those operations must necessarily come through the direct financial contributions of the members, except for the liquidity support that can be financed by expanding the central bank's balance sheet. Depending on the tool considered, those financial contributions are then pooled in a common fund that uses the assets to finance the operations of the agency in support of its statutory functions. The logic is not dissimilar from any other government contribution to a supranational agency, such as the UN or the World Bank, which then uses those funds to pay for their running costs and carrying out their mandates. However, the financial stability operations described before differ substantially from any other activity usually done by a government or an international organization. First, the level of financial support required to all members to address the risks of financial instability is much higher than any other budgetary contribution to make an international organization work. If we think that the bailout of the Irish financial system by the Irish government in 2008–10 cost around 268% of the Irish GDP, and the bailout of two UK banks by the UK government cost 18% of the UK GDP, we can imagine the size of the fund.[47] Second, the general public does not see those interventions as the protection of public good – although one could easily make an argument in this sense – but as the protection of a failed private enterprise; hence, as a wasteful use of public money.

The fact that those enterprises that receive the financial support could be located in a different state makes the fiscal transfer very difficult to be accepted from a political perspective.[48] Fiscal solidarity – the transfer of fiscal resources from once state to another – is one of the most contentious elements of economic governance and, usually, one of the last components to be added to the architecture of economic integration. Fiscal solidarity usually exists in fiscal unions or federal states, where taxes are collected centrally and the funds are then distributed to the various states according to their needs. Not surprisingly, even in the European Union, where an embryo of fiscal solidarity exists to support economic development projects in disadvantaged regions, fiscal solidarity is explicitly banned when it comes to sovereign financing.[49] The absence of fiscal solidarity in the EMU Treaty was indeed probably the most important

[47] Cornelia Woll, *The Power of Inaction: Bank Bailouts in Comparison* (Ithaca, NY, and London: Cornell University Press, 2014), p. 32.

[48] Fritz W. Scharpf, "Economic Integration, Democracy and the Welfare State" (1997) 4 *European Journal of Public Policy* 18; David McKay, "The Political Sustainability of the European Monetary Union" (1999) 29 *British Journal of Political Science* 463.

[49] Treaty on the Functioning of the European Union, Articles 123 and 125.

hurdle to a swift solution of the Greek sovereign debt crisis, as it prevented the ECB from bailing out Greece.

The reason why fiscal solidarity is so politically controversial, including in economic unions with a high level of economic integration, is because it presumes a very high level of political integration.[50] Fiscal solidarity is the very last dividing line between an economic union and a political union. Fiscal transfers are mostly funded with taxes collected at the local level whose proceeds are then put into a common pool. How much taxes shall citizens and firms pay, and how to use and distribute public funds are political issues that every government has to decide taking into consideration the interests of its citizens, which then are called to judge on their correct use through different means of political participation.

Municipal taxes are usually negotiated at the local level, and the funds collected are usually spent to finance local projects on which politicians will be evaluated. Likewise, corporation taxes or income tax are usually negotiated as part of a nation-wide electoral deal to finance public expenditures of national interest. Hence, there is a direct link between fiscal solidarity and democracy that makes it very difficult to finance projects that do not directly benefit those who pay for it and who can exert the necessary control on the use of the funds. Because of this political bond, governments will be reluctant to agree to fiscal transfers unless they perceive that the total national welfare gains arising out of the use of the supranational fund will be higher than the costs.

We can understand the problem better by referring to the principal–agent model discussed in Chapter 2. Governments have a mandate from their citizens to deliver a level of public goods that is at least equal to or higher than the costs in terms of taxes. When a government agrees to fiscal solidarity, it must accept that the return for its constituency may be lower than the costs, especially for those states that do not benefit from the use of the funds. The major implication of this is that fiscal transfers can be accepted only when citizens can directly influence the level of fiscal imposition or the use of the public funds, and exert an ex-post control over the use. In sum, supranational fiscal transfers necessarily require a parallel transfer of democratic power at the supranational level. This equation holds increasingly true the higher the level of fiscal transfers.

Hence, international fiscal transfers to finance common resolution funds, deposit insurance schemes, or to bail out a defaulting sovereign are politically

[50] Federico Lupo-Pasini, "Economic Stability and Economic Governance in the Euro Area: What the European Crisis Can Teach on the Limits of Economic Integration" (2013) 16 *Journal of International Economic Law* 211.

acceptable only when the taxpayers have a direct control on the policies that have contributed to the situation of emergency that necessitates the intervention of the funds. Clearly, a Canadian taxpayer would not subscribe to a common resolution fund to bail out a financial institution located in Mexico when it does not have any power to shape and influence financial supervision there. Similarly, it will be very difficult to agree to a principle of fiscal solidarity in the EMU treaty, when European citizens cannot exert any democratic control over economic or fiscal policy in the country that receives the solidarity. Professor Charles Goodhart and Professor Dirk Schoenmaker succinctly expressed this concept as "he who plays the piper calls the tune."[51]

If we apply a top-down approach to regulatory and political integration, a common deposit insurance and bank resolution funds presumes a common supervisory agency in charge of monitoring the bank as well as a common regulatory framework. This is precisely why, after the Eurozone crisis, European policymakers found it necessary to accompany the Single Supervisory Mechanism with an SRM.[52] Similarly, a common fiscal backstop to bail out insolvent states or to ease the restructuring process necessarily requires a very high level of supervision over economic policy formulation and implementation at the national level. The higher the level of intrusion over economic sovereignty, the higher will be the fiscal transfer allowed. In a federal state, for instance, municipal or state bankruptcies are financed through direct fiscal support from the federal budget. In certain countries, a government can appoint temporary administrators that look after the budget of the city or region.

The European Union's experience during the crisis is particularly revealing of the difficulties in creating a common European financial safety net financed directly from the states' budgets.[53] The reason why European Union treaties do not envisage an obligation of fiscal solidarity among the members is to contain the moral hazard that such an obligation would create and, more generally, to incentivize a fair degree of competition among the members. The fear was that states may be incentivized to defer important but politically difficult economic reforms or to indulge in fiscal profligacy knowing that a national budget default would be matched by an immediate fiscal transfer from Brussels. When Greece and other Eurozone peripheral countries were at the verge of default, the ECB could not save them because of the prohibition of fiscal solidarity contained in the EU treaties. The situation was

[51] Goodhart and Schoenmaker, above note 35.

[52] Gros and Schoenmaker, above note 44.

[53] Lupo-Pasini, above note 50, pp. 231–48.

aggravated because all states belonged to the Eurozone and thus did not have the monetary sovereignty required to increase the interest rate or devalue the currency. This led to a stalemate for months that was solved only by bypassing the European Union treaties. EU members then agreed to establish an intergovernmental organization outside the official perimeter of EU law – the ESM – and to finance it with public funds. The political process to create the ESM was fraught with difficulties as "virtuous" Eurozone countries were reluctant to contribute to a mechanism that was meant to bail out "less virtuous" members. In many of those countries, political parties were adamant in opposing any form of fiscal solidarity that would benefit peripheral states. However, because of the systemic risks that a government default in the Euro area would have created, and the monstrous political pressure under which government were subject to, it was decided to establish this mechanism and endow it with 500 billion Euro. In exchange for the ESM, it was agreed that all participating governments had to agree to the Fiscal Compact and sign a Memorandum of Understanding that outlined all the economic reforms to be implemented under the watchful eye of the ECB, the European Commission, and the IMF – the three institutions called in to evaluate the financial situation of the requesting member. Although the fiscal solidarity principle that underpins the ESM is not backed with a direct transfer of democratic control, the level of intrusion over the economic sovereignty of the requesting member is nonetheless extremely high, also considering that the size of the fund is "only" 500 billion Euro.

To conclude, the direct relationship between fiscal solidarity and democratic control makes it extremely difficult to establish a common fund to finance financial stability policies across borders. This is especially so given the enormous size that a credible common deposit insurance fund or a bank resolution fund would entail. It would be safe to say that the higher the size of the pot, the deeper must be the level of political integration. Not surprisingly, fiscal solidarity in sovereign debt is present only in federal states. Fiscal solidarity in international financial governance can exist only when taxpayers can exert some sort of control over financial policymaking or fiscal policymaking in the countries that are entitled to benefit from the fund. This control does not necessarily need to be the right to vote in local elections, but it could entail a common regulatory framework or supervisory agency that unifies the regulatory and supervisory playing field.

7.6. CONCLUDING REMARKS

The trilemma offers a succinct and useful picture of the tradeoffs at the core of international financial law. However, only in few and extreme circumstances can its precepts be usefully adapted into real policy actions. It is true that global financial stability can be achieved only by constraining the policy space of national authorities or by tackling the transmission channels of financial instability. However, the internalization of the externalities of domestic polices does not necessarily require the reduction of financial sovereignty, the creation of a centralized supervisory bulldozer, or the balkanization of the global financial systems along national lines.

In my opinion, the inefficiencies in the governance of international finance are also the result of the inefficient allocation of rights and obligations among different international actors, and the inability of international law to take into account the political economy dynamics of government actions, such as the principal–agent or time-consistency problems. In a rational-based theory of international law, states respond to punishments and incentives like any other subject. Consequently, the problems of financial instability can be solved by increasing the role of international law in preventing the externalities of a state's action, and by allocating, more efficiently, rights and obligations among different actors.[54]

I will discuss this in the next three chapters.

54 Eric A. Posner and Alan O. Sykes, *Economic Foundations of International Law* (Cambridge, MA and London, England: Harvard University Press, 2012); Eric A. Posner and Alan O. Sykes, "Efficient Breach of International Law: Optimal Remedies, 'Legalized Noncompliance,' and Related Issues" (2011–2012) 110 *Michigan Law Review* 243, p. 248; Trachtman, above note 1.

8

Compliance and Global Coalitions in International Finance Law

The last few chapters have showed the logic of financial nationalism behind the action of financial authorities, and the consequences that this carries for the global financial system. Under certain circumstances, financial nationalism is simply the logical consequence of the absence of international law or the protection of national interests. Sometimes, however, the problems of financial nationalism discussed in this book are problems of non-compliance. In certain cases, the non-compliance is obvious; the clearest example is when states refuse to comply with hard laws enshrined in international treaties or international contracts, as in the case of sovereign debt. In other cases, however, the non-compliance is subtler as it would not by itself qualify as a violation of the law. For instance, the failure to abide by soft-law agreements, albeit legitimate from an international law viewpoint, nonetheless entails a de facto violation of a pact that carries substantial costs for the non-violating partner. In both cases, non-compliance carries substantial long-term costs for the global financial system that must be offset.

At the center of the compliance problem in international finance lies the question of soft law. The large majority of the legal instruments disciplining international cooperation in financial policy are framed as non-binding agreements. Yet, while in certain areas of financial policy soft laws undoubtedly contribute to the problems of financial nationalism, in others they seem to function perfectly. A question therefore arises as to why states cooperate in certain areas of financial policymaking and not in others. To answer this question it is necessary to explain what drives compliance in international finance. The mainstream literature on soft law in international finance offers a narrative of compliance in which the weaknesses of the law are always offset by institutional or market mechanisms.[1] By focusing only on institutional or market discipline, this literature, however, ignores two fundamental points. First of all, under certain circumstances, markets will favor a strategy of financial nationalism rather than cooperation. When a cross-border bank fails the sovereignty costs of compliance augment exponentially, and so does the pressure on supervisors and national regulators to seek a national solution to the crisis. Secondly, the sovereignty costs attached to the compliance with home–host arrangements and cross-border crisis-resolution policies are much higher than those of international financial standards. Hence, the theory of compliance that explains international financial standards so well does not work when it comes to other areas of financial policymaking. A new comprehensive theory is thus needed.

A new legal theory of compliance will have to look at three fundamental issues. First, it needs to explain what drives states' behavior. More specifically, it should explain under which conditions a state will be more likely to coordinate its policy with partner states and more likely to defect. Second, it needs to explain how the law can help in modifying the behavior of the actors involved – the home and the partner states – to induce compliance. Third, it needs to develop a set of legal mechanisms that will increase the likelihood of compliance. In this theory of compliance, I will address these three points and test the theory on capital adequacy standards for bank, cross-border banking resolution, and sovereign debt. I argue that at the core of the principal–agent problem in international finance there is an asymmetry in the level and attribution of rights. Foreign stakeholders do not have any voice in the regulatory and decision-making process of foreign regulators, although they suffer the instability arising from domestic policies. Thus, the only way to counter the behavior of national regulators in promoting their own interests is to attribute rights to foreign stakeholders, by granting them standing and the power to retaliate. I will then develop this theory further in Chapters 9 and 10, where I will discuss its practical applications.

[1] Mario Giovanoli, "A New Architecture for the Global Financial Market: Legal Aspects of International Financial Standard Settings," in Mario Giovanoli (ed.) *International Monetary Law: Issues for the New Millennium* (Oxford: Oxford University Press, 2000), pp. 3–59; Chris Brummer, *Soft Law and the Global Financial System: Rule Making in the 21st Century* (New York: Cambridge University Press, 2012); Chris Brummer, "How International Financial Law Works (and How It Doesn't)" (2011) 99 *Georgetown Law Journal* 257; Chris Brummer, "Why Soft Law Dominates International Finance and Not Trade" (2010) 13 *Journal of International Economic Law* 623.

8.1. THE BRIGHT AND DARK SIDES OF SOFT LAWS IN INTERNATIONAL FINANCE

Unlike other areas of international economic law such as international trade or investment, international finance law is largely based on the partial or total absence of legalization.[2] The level of legalization varies across three different dimensions, which are to be present for proper international law to exist: obligation, precision, and delegation. First, states must not choose whether to abide by international laws or not, their application being simply compulsory. Second, the laws must be detailed and precise enough to guide the behavior of states toward a specified goal. Third, in the event of non-compliance with the laws, the non-violating party can delegate the adjudication of the dispute to an impartial dispute-settlement mechanism that interprets the laws and imposes fines.

With the exception of the international trade or investment rules dealing with market integration in financial services, the entire body of international agreements that aim at coordinating financial policies is non-binding. Scholars have identified such norms as *soft laws* to distinguish them from the harder laws of international law.[3] There are various types of soft laws. The most-cited examples are international standards and guidelines for regulators, such as the Basel Accords or the International Organization of Securities Commission (IOSCO) principles for securities regulators, or recommendations from international financial institutions, and reports. To these, we should add also the Mutual Recognition arrangements on securities regulation, bilateral Memoranda of Understanding (MoU) on cross-border banking supervision or resolution, and the various Basel Committee agreements on banking supervision, all of which are particularly important in the context of the present analysis.

[2] On the concept of legalization, see Kenneth W. Abbott and Duncan Snidal, "Hard and Soft Law in International Governance" (2000) 54 *International Organization* 421; Kal Raustiala, "Form and Substance in International Agreements" (2005) 99 *American Journal of International Law* 581; Miles Kahler, "The Causes and Consequences of Legalization" (2000) 54 *International Organization* 661; Beth A. Simmons, "The Legalization of International Monetary Affairs" (2000) 54 *International Organization* 573; Judith Goldstein and Lisa L. Martin, "Legalization, Trade Liberalization, and Domestic Politics: A Cautionary Note" (2000) 54 *International Organization* 603; Kenneth W. Abbott, Robert O. Keohane, Andrew Moravcsik, Anne-Marie Slaughter, and Duncan Snidal, "The Concept of Legalization" (2000) 54 *International Organization* 401.

[3] There is a vast and burgeoning literature on soft law in finance. For a good overview, see Giovanoli, above note 1, pp. 3–59; Brummer, *Soft Law and the Global Financial System*, above note 1; Brummer, "How International Financial Law Works," above note 1; Brummer, "Why Soft Law Dominates," above note 1.

The absence of a system to adjudicate financial disputes is another peculiar feature of the public international law of finance. I will discuss adjudication in the next chapter, but it is worth mentioning a few issues here. The absence of adjudication is probably most visible when it comes to international regulation or cross-border banking resolution. For instance, none of the various Transnational Regulatory Networks (TRNs) in finance provides a dispute-resolution mechanism. Hence, in the presence of a violation of a financial standard, such as the refusal to adopt a certain capital adequacy standard or to abide by the commitments to share data as prescribed in the Memorandum of Understanding, there is no legal remedy available to ensure compliance. However, also in the context of sovereign debt restructurings, which do rely on domestic courts and ad hoc negotiations, the absence of an institutionalized international adjudication mechanism has often prevented the quick and safe solution of an underlying sovereign debt problem.

Even though informality is a constitutive element of most international financial law, the impact of soft laws on international cooperation and financial stability is equivocal insofar as only in certain areas of financial soft-lawmaking do states seem to violate their soft obligations. The difference is most visible in the compliance rate with prudential standards, on the one hand, and cross-border bank resolution, on the other.

8.1.1. *Prudential Standards*

The regulatory outputs of TRNs can be roughly divided into three different types of regulatory instruments: best practices and regulatory guidelines, peer-review observations, and information-sharing agreements. The most important among these three instruments are undoubtedly regulatory best practices and guidelines, which are de facto the only example of international financial regulations. These instruments directly propose the best regulatory strategy for various areas of financial regulation such as capital adequacy, exposure limits, central counterparties, or payment systems. The level of precision of those best practices varies greatly, from very detailed guidelines whose domestic implementation across the members does not differ greatly, to very broad statements of principles whose general and far-reaching scope of application allows a much wider regulatory divergence.

In striking contrast with other aspects of international law, successful international cooperation in financial standard-setting (more specifically, best practices and guidelines) was achieved in spite of the non-binding character of those standards.[4] More specifically, national regulators decided voluntarily to adopt and comply with those standards even though no official penalty was attached to their violation. For instance, various authors have indeed demonstrated that most of the Basel Committee on Banking Supervision members have adopted and implemented Basel I and Basel II standards.[5] Furthermore, research by the BIS, Financial Stability Board (FSB), and IOSCO has shown that to a large extent states implement their financial standards and guidelines.[6]

The compliance of states with soft standards puzzles the analysts, as it seems to counter the logic that sees legalization as the only real incentive for states to enter into international agreements and comply with them. After all, why negotiate a complex set of rules if there is no guarantee that all parties to the agreement will implement them? The law and political science literatures have offered theories that explain the success of soft standards. One of the most prominent theories focuses on the general role of soft law in international governance, and it was first formulated in the context of political science research. This theory is not specifically focused on finance, but it tries to develop a consistent theoretical framework able to explain all aspects of soft law. Abbott and Snidal have developed a general theory of soft law, arguing that the absence of binding requirements typical of soft law enhances the possibility of bargains.[7] This theory thus looks at soft law as a mean to facilitate international agreements. The reason is that, in absence of the fear of retaliation and without any threat to lose reputation by not complying with a norm, regulators will be more incentivized to agree on a certain regulatory framework. The absence of sovereignty costs, typical of soft law, will essentially allow states to enter into the agreements without the costs of exit. Furthermore, Abbott and Snidal argue that soft agreements are easier to negotiate, as they do not require lengthy negotiations.[8] Finally, soft laws do not require the establishment of

4 Narissa Lyngen and Daniel Tarullo, however, argue that the adoption of the new Basel III rules shows problems of implementation. See Daniel K. Tarullo, *Banking on Basel: The Future of International Financial Regulation* (Washington, DC: Peterson Institute for International Economics, 2007); Narissa Lyngen, "Basel III: Dynamics of State Implementation" (2012) 53 *Harvard International Law Journal* 519.

5 Daniel E. Ho, "Compliance and Soft Law: Why Do Countries Implement the Basel Accord?" (2003) 5 *Journal of International Economic Law* 647, p. 649; Bryce Quillin, *International Financial Co-operation: Political Economics of Compliance with the 1988 Basel Accord* (New York: Routledge, 2008).

6 See, for instance, the periodical reports released by the BCBS. See BCBS, "Progress Report on Implementation of the Basel Regulatory Framework," Basel Committee on Banking Supervision (October 2016).

7 Abbott and Snidal, above note 2.

8 *Ibid.*

a formal institutional infrastructure to oversee compliance with the norms. It does not entail the creation of a dispute-settlement mechanism or the establishment of a centralized organization to which states transfer their power. This theory, however, is largely focused on explaining the popularity of soft law, and it does not address why states nonetheless abide by the soft norms in spite of their soft and non-binding character.

8.1.2. *Cross-Border Banking*

Cross-border banking supervision presents an entirely different picture when it comes to compliance. Standards and agreements on information-sharing between supervisors are one of the oldest objectives of international cooperation pursued by TRNs. Historically, the most important among them is the *Basel Concordat* and the *Minimum Standard for the Supervision of Cross-Border Banking Groups*, to which we should now add the *Principles for Effective Supervisory Colleges*, all of which have been issued by the Basel Committee on Banking Supervision. Their goal is to provide guidelines to supervisors on how to cooperate in the supervision of a cross-border bank. The effective cooperation between national supervisors however largely takes place at the bilateral level through MoUs on supervisory cooperation and resolution. According to most MoUs, financial authorities are expected to cooperate with each other to supervise cross-border banks and, when agreed in the MoU, to intervene to resolve them. Among the duties that supervisors must perform are data sharing, inspections, and imposition of fines and penalties. The ultimate goal is to enable national regulators to access the data of the parent or host financial institutions that are not under their direct supervision, but that are nonetheless important from a systemic point of view. More advanced and modern MoUs also deal with the adoption of Lender of Last Resort (LOLR), the location, type, and amount of the total loss-absorbing capacity, and some other resolution measures to sustain the stability of the bank group during resolution.

MoUs on cross-border bank supervision and resolution, like financial standards, are based on soft norms and lack a dispute-settlement mechanism. Cooperation is therefore fundamental to maintain global banking stability. The principle of home-country control indeed relies on the willingness of home authorities to maintain the stability of their home banks in all their foreign operations and, on a subordinate level, on the willingness of the host country to collaborate. In order to be effective, cooperation needs to be based on absolute trust between the two supervisors, and on the commitment by the home supervisor to do whatever it must to maintain the stability of the bank's foreign operations. At the same time, however, MoUs are constructed on a logic of "constructive ambiguity," which grants authorities a broader space for maneuver during the crisis. The absence of specific and detailed instructions allows supervisors and resolution authorities to intervene with non-orthodox strategies or simply not to intervene at all. In more general terms, the constructive ambiguity of those agreements permits supervisory authorities to tailor their intervention to the specificity of the bank in crisis. Moreover, the lack of a predetermined regulatory framework with clear obligations prevents moral hazards on the side of banks, which might take excessive risks if they know in advance the authorities' response to their crisis.

As I argued in Chapters 3 and 4, despite the regulatory efforts in streamlining supervisory coordination, the recent crises and other experiences in cross-border supervision have shown that, in various circumstances, states do not abide by their commitments and leave their partner countries alone in the crisis, with consequent negative impacts on global stability. The absence of legalization inherent to MoUs and cross-border banking arrangements increases the proclivity of supervisory authorities to pursue a logic of financial nationalism during a crisis, and hence have a direct impact on global financial stability. There are two problems in particular that arise from the use of soft law in a situation of home–host coordination. The first is the absence of any mechanism to force compliance, which is a natural consequence of the absence of an *obligation* to comply with soft agreements.[9] Indeed, when entering into a soft-law arrangement, states retain full legal control over their domestic policies, and are therefore able to regain the policy space whenever they deem it necessary. Given the sovereignty costs that are attached to the strict application of home–host arrangements in a crisis – which in turn increases the chances of defection – the use of soft laws ultimately incentivizes the violation of the rules by both sides. For instance, the home country can legitimately refuse to report data to the host authorities or, more generally, it can adopt non-cooperative policies maximizing domestic interests to the detriment of the host country's stability. At the same time, the host country can decide to boycott the agreement and ring-fence the foreign bank's assets.

Second, the logic of constructive ambiguity and the absence of any compliance mechanism attached to the MoUs encourage the use of unilateral actions on both sides. This ultimately leads to pre-emptive stability wars whereby supervisors are incentivized to violate the agreement first, believing that the other is about to do the same. In the absence of effective compliance

[9] See Abbott and Snidal, above note 2, p. 401.

mechanisms, national regulators cannot know what their partners' regulatory strategies might be. For example, in anticipating and fearing that the partner's strategy will be the adoption of a non-cooperative approach to a banking crisis, a partner may similarly adopt a non-cooperative strategy in order to protect itself. The behavior is, in this case, no different from that analyzed in the context of cross-border bank resolution. A cross-border banking crisis is likely to lead to a tit-for-tat situation in which each regulator will only care to prevent the worst outcome for itself.

As some authors have noted, the use of soft law is inherently unfit to address enforcement problems like the ones posed by home–host arrangements, as they inevitably lead to the adoption of prisoners' dilemma strategies on both sides.[10] In the absence of compliance mechanisms, national regulators have strong incentives to protect domestic stability and to boycott cooperation whenever the costs of compliance outweigh the benefits in terms of domestic welfare. In a banking crisis, where national supervisors have to take into account their national interests first, the use of soft law therefore guarantees a cheap exit from the international agreements.

8.2. THEORETICAL LOOPHOLES IN THE SOFT LAW'S NARRATIVE

Given the striking differences in the level of compliance with non-binding international financial standards and MoUs, a question arises as to why regulators and supervisors abide by certain agreements and not others. Since the 1990s, the question of compliance has become one of the hottest topics in the international law literature.[11] One particular stream of the burgeoning

[10] Pierre-Hugues Verdier, "Transnational Regulatory Networks and Their Limits" (2009) 34 *Yale Journal of International Law* 113, pp. 125–6; see, on the same issue, albeit not focused on financial law, Jack L. Goldsmith and Eric A. Posner, *The Limits of International Law* (New York: Oxford University Press, 2005); Andrew T. Guzman, *How International Law Works: A Rational Choice Theory* (New York: Oxford University Press, 2008); Robert E. Scott and Paul B. Stephan, *The Limits of Leviathan: Contract Theory and the Enforcement of International Law* (New York: Cambridge University Press, 2006); George Norman and Joel P. Trachtman, "The Customary International Law Game" (2005) 99 *American Journal of International Law* 541.

[11] Abraham Chayes and Antonia Handler Chayes, "On Compliance" (1993) 27 *International Organization* 175; Charles Lipson, "Why Are Some International Agreements Informal?" (1991) 45 *International Organization* 495; Guzman, above note 10; Abram Chayes and Antonia Handler Chayes, *The New Sovereignty: Compliance with International Regulatory Agreements* (Cambridge, MA: Harvard University Press, 1995); Kenneth W. Abbott, "Modern International Relations Theory: A Prospectus for International Lawyers" (1989) 14 *Yale Journal of International Law* 335; Kenneth W. Abbott, "International Relations Theory; International Law, and the Regime Governing Atrocities in Internal Conflicts" (1999) 93 *American Journal of International Law* 361; Andrew T. Guzman, "A Compliance-Based Theory of International

literature on compliance in international law looks at the relationship between the absence of legalization – commonly intended as the absence of hard and precise norms, and an impartial mechanism to settle disputes – and state behavior. Considering the coordination of international finance structured over the absence of a legalized regulatory framework, the question of compliance with international financial agreements has recently become a hot topic also in the legal financial literature.[12] Based on the relative success of financial standards as a regulatory coordination mechanism, the literature on international finance developed a set of theories that explain why states chose soft norms as a coordination tool, and why they comply with them.

8.2.1. *Institutional and Market Discipline*

Brummer and other scholars have developed a theoretical framework to address this precise question. According to Brummer, in spite of the soft character of international financial norms, standards can benefit from powerful informal mechanisms that ultimately induce states to stick to their commitments. The first such mechanism is reputational discipline. International financial standards are negotiated by national regulators in specialized fora – the so-called Transnational Regulatory Networks. According to this theory, the decision of not complying with a standard might reduce the future negotiating credibility of regulators among their peers.[13] The second mechanism relies on the role of the International Monetary Fund (IMF) or the World Bank as a watchdog of international finance. Both organizations monitor the financial stability of their members as part of their broader statutory goals. In doing so they provide reports in which they analyze, among other things, the compliance with international financial standards, such as the Financial Sector Assessment Program mentioned above. According to Brummer's theory, a negative evaluation might reduce not only the reputation of the state among its peers but, more importantly, it will affect negatively its market reputation. In certain circumstances, especially in the framework of IMF law, the availability of sovereign financing might be linked to the respect of certain financial standards.[14]

Law" (2002) 90 *California Law Review* 1823; Beth A. Simmons, "Money and the Law: Why Comply with the Public International Law of Money?" (2000) 25 *Yale Journal of International Law* 323; Harold Hongju Koh, "Why Do Nations Obey International Law?" (1997) 106 *Yale Law Journal* 2599.

[12] See, Brummer, "How International Financial Law Works," above note 1; Ho, above note 5.

[13] Brummer, "How International Financial Law Works," above note 1.

[14] Giovanoli, above note 1; Brummer, *ibid.*

A second mechanism is market discipline. Here, the assumption is that private investors would look favorably at the presence of a certain regulatory standards as a signal of a sound financial system to invest in. In this context, the decision of not complying with international financial standards might send a bad signal to foreign investors and thus reduce the overall appeal of the country as an investment destination. Hence, rather than receiving bad ratings, and thus suffering a crisis of confidence, states are often willing to sacrifice their regulatory freedom.[15]

The existing theories of soft law so far described present a compelling account of the powerful mechanisms available to address the softness of financial law. However, the theories base their narrative only on one aspect of financial policy: prudential standards. The legal literature has failed to examine in detail the question of compliance with the other two major (and neglected) aspects of finance: supervision and crisis resolution. When the same theories are tested on these two other areas of international finance, they reveal fundamental theoretical flaws, which have been further highlighted in the recent crises.

8.2.2. *Reputation in Cross-Border Banking*

Reputation is recognized by the legal and political economy literature as a formidable compliance tool. The basic premise of Guzman in his theory of reputation is that the reputation of a state as a good partner is dependent on its actual behavior. Consequently, a state that fails to obey its legal commitments will be seen as an unreliable partner and might be marginalized by the international community.[16] The most immediate consequence is that a state, abiding by its commitments, will be perceived as a reliable partner by other states and, thus, be able to reduce the negotiating costs of cooperation.[17] Indeed, similar to private institutional investors, states will demand a high interest when entering into a commitment with an unreliable partner.

In the context of international finance, however, the theory of reputation takes a further twist because it does not concern only state–state interactions, but rather the interaction between states and investors. The power of international institutions and investors in driving compliance is Brummer's

[15] See also, Thomas Oatley and Robert Nabors, "Redistributive Cooperation: Market Failure, Wealth Transfers, and the Basel Accord" (1998) 52 *International Organization* 35.

[16] Guzman, above note 10, p. 34.

[17] *Ibid.*

fundamental insight into the theory of compliance in finance.[18] Brummer argues that the real reputational costs deriving from a violation of international financial standards result from institutional or market sanctions, which will de facto expel the violating country from the financial system. However, while the theory of reputation works with regard to prudential regulation and, generally, for the regulatory apparatus for domestic financial stability, there are serious doubts of its effect in the context of cross-border banking policies and global stability. There are three main issues in this regard.

First of all, as argued by Guzman, the role of reputation as a compliance tool is greatly reduced when the stakes at issue are large. More precisely, the higher the sovereignty costs, the smaller the role played by reputation in ensuring compliance.[19] As will be discussed more in depth below, there is little doubt that, while conformity with international prudential standards demands certain sovereignty costs, these are nonetheless limited to the potential loss of competitiveness of domestic banks.[20] On the contrary, maintaining global stability in a cross-border banking crisis entails fundamental sovereignty tradeoffs. The examples of Fortis Bank and Iceland show that providing a fiscal backstop to maintain global stability abroad is politically difficult, to say the least.[21]

Furthermore, the effectiveness of reputational mechanisms is directly proportional to the number of states involved in the agreement. Reputational sanctions rely on the belief of the wider global society that a certain behavior, as described in the norm, is beneficial to the wider community. In this framework, the degree of openness of the treaty matters, because the more members, the wider reputational stakes at play will be, and consequently the stronger will be the societal push for compliance.[22] Cross-border banking

[18] Brummer, *Soft Law and the Global Financial System*, above note 1; Brummer, "How International Financial Law Works," above note 1; Brummer, "Why Soft Law Dominates," above note 1.

[19] Guzman, "A Compliance-Based Theory" above note 11, p. 1883.

[20] See David Andrew Singer, *Regulating Capital: Setting Standards for the International financial System* (Ithaca, NY: Cornell University Press, 2007); David Andrew Singer, "Capital Rules: The Domestic Politics of International Regulatory Harmonization" (2004) 58 *International Organization* 531; Stavros Gadinis, "The Politics of Competition in Financial Regulation" (2008) 49 *Harvard International Law Journal* 447.

[21] Federico Lupo-Pasini, "Economic Stability and Economic Governance in the Euro Area: What the European Crisis Can Teach on the Limits of Economic Integration" (2013) 16 *Journal of International Economic Law* 211.

[22] For instance, Steven Nelson shows that the violation of Article VIII of the IMF Articles of Agreements dealing with international payments (a mixed hard norm with soft compliance mechanisms) corresponds to a reduction of sovereign ratings. See Steven Nelson, "Does Compliance Matter? Assessing the Relationship between Sovereign Risk and Compliance with International Monetary Law" (2010) 5 *Review of International Organization* 107.

resolution is by its nature a bilateral matter in which only few national regulators play a role, usually the home and host regulators. Therefore, the violation of a bilateral MoU cannot put regulators under the same level of pressure they would experience under a multilateral agreement.[23]

Secondly, it is questionable whether the violation of an MoU would reduce the reputational capital of the violating country among private investors. The standard theory of compliance relies on the role of markets as controllers of financial stability. It assumes that states are willing to trade some of their sovereignty and comply with the agreements in exchange of the investment and financing benefits.[24] The concept is not dissimilar from the basic political economy of international investment treaties whereby states accept adoption of a minimum standard of treatment for foreign investors to increase their attractiveness to foreign investors.[25] In this context, the belief by investors and international institutions that a certain conduct is harmful is of fundamental importance in using reputation as a compliance tool. Only if the global community considers a certain conduct harmful, and only if the states consider foreign capital essential for their own welfare, will the state be induced to comply with the agreement.

Crucially, however, there is little data in support of the theory that the violation of a cross-border banking arrangement leads to a lower volume of capital inflows. Paradoxically, from a private investor viewpoint, the fact that a national financial authority chose to act unilaterally in a cross-border banking crisis would only signal a strong attitude of national regulators to maintain a stable domestic financial system. Institutional investors will certainly not punish a state that preserves its domestic finances. Investors are profit-maximizing entities focused only on the stability of the country where they invest. Moreover, the fact that home authorities do not use taxpayers' money to bail out banks might even increase the credibility of the home country in the eyes of investors. For instance, the Icelandic authorities motivated their unwillingness to pay depositor protection schemes to English depositors because of the consequences on the level of fiscal resources in Iceland.[26] Hence, the welfare

[23] See also Guzman, above note 10, pp. 63–4.

[24] Brummer, *Soft Law and the Global Financial System*, above note 1; Brummer, "How International Financial Law Works," above note 1; Brummer, "Why Soft Law Dominates," above note 1.

[25] Zachary Elkins, Andrew T. Guzman, and Beth A. Simmons, "Competing for Capital: The Diffusion of Bilateral Investment Treaties, 1960–2000" (2006) 60 *International Organization* 811; Eric A. Posner and Alan O. Sykes, *Economic Foundations of International Law* (Cambridge, MA, and London: Harvard University Press, 2012), pp. 288–97.

[26] Case E-16/11, *EFTA Surveillance Authority* v. *Iceland*, 2011, EFTA Court, 28 January 2013.

cost of complying with crisis-resolution arrangements would not produce the return in rating and investment that is present in the case of prudential regulations. Quite the opposite, in the context of crisis-resolution policies, where the more a state is willing to preserve its domestic interests, the higher the return will be in terms of market reputation.

The third major problem with the theory of reputation concerns the issue of transparency. A core assumption of this theory is that markets and institutions are aware of the substantive obligations in each soft-law arrangement, so that they can evaluate whether the arrangement is beneficial or not to the domestic and global stability of each state. Furthermore, only by knowing the content of the agreements will the market and institutions be able to participate as controller of the compliance of the state. Transparency is therefore the main and only mechanism for the society to oversee the compliance with the norms and to exert its role as controller. However, in the context of cross-border banking resolution and supervision the bilateral agreements between regulators are not publicly available in order to contain moral hazard.[27] Even assuming that institutional investors would price the compliance with crisis-resolution agreements, they will never be able to do it without knowing the procedural aspects of intervention.

8.3. A POLITICAL ECONOMY THEORY OF COMPLIANCE FOR INTERNATIONAL FINANCE

To address the problems in the previous theories, it is in my view necessary to articulate a new and different theory of compliance that encompasses the entire spectrum of international financial law, from soft standards, to cross-border banking, to sovereign debt. In line with the previous chapters, in developing my theory, I will adopt a legal and economic approach, in which states are considered as rational actors interested only in maximizing their own stability as well as their own welfare.

At the outset, it is useful to clarify again that international finance cannot be modeled as a single policy area. Prudential regulations, cross-border banking supervision and resolution, and sovereign debt present fundamentally different policy and legal challenges with regard to compliance. Prudential regulations are closer to the Battle of the Sexes game, as they mainly involve the incentives to cooperate, rather than the interests to defect.[28] In contrast,

[27] Indeed, even the central bank does not have a regulatory framework that guides the provision of liquidity, and it keeps the decision secret.

[28] Verdier, above note 10, p. 124.

cross-border banking policies predominantly involve enforcement problems, and as such they are much closer to a classical Prisoner's Dilemma game in which the dominant decision is not to cooperate.[29] This tendency is supported also by the fact that, in game-theoretical terms, financial crises are single games with no repetitions. Hence, the soft legal arrangements and the reputational compliance mechanisms that work so effectively for international financial standards cannot be replicated to ensure global stability in an international banking crisis. Sovereign debt presents unique compliance problems as the borrowing state has very strong incentives to access financial markets as well as to defect from the debt contract. Despite the asymmetry of legal power between the sovereign borrower and private creditors, it is precisely the long-term interest of states to access international financial markets that gives creditors the power to retaliate against the borrower in the event of its default. The threat of market access therefore counters the legal shield of sovereign immunity and resets the balance of power between the two parties.[30]

8.3.1. *The Political Economy of International Finance*

Financial stability policies entail distributive choices that necessarily penalize certain groups while favoring others. For instance, bailouts require the vast use of taxpayers' money to keep a financial institution afloat,[31] and bail-ins sacrifice the rights of equity holders and junior bond-holders, while capital adequacy standards reduce the profitability of firms.[32] At the domestic level, states will naturally choose a level of stability that balances the need to minimize risks with the concurrent need to minimize the impact of financial regulations on domestic welfare. The optimum level of domestic stability is, in this context, the result of a domestic political equilibrium between different domestic interest groups.[33] Each of those groups has an interest in driving the policy of the regulator toward its objective. Banks will try to lobby for a regulatory

[29] *Ibid.*, pp. 125–6.

[30] Rohan Pitchford and Mark L.J. Wright, "On the Contribution of Game Theory to the Study of Sovereign Debt and Default" (2016) 29 *Oxford Review of Economic Policy* 649.

[31] There is a huge literature on the issue of taxpayers' money in bailouts. See Adam J. Levitin, "In Defense of Bailouts" (2011) 99 *The Georgetown Law Journal* 435.

[32] Tarullo, above note 4.

[33] For more in general on the political economy of international finance, see Edmund J. Malesky, "Interest Group Politics," in Gerard Caprio Jr. (ed.) *Handbook of Safeguarding Global Financial Stability: Political, Social, Cultural, and Economic Theories and Models* (London: Elsevier, 2013); Pierre-Hugues Verdier, "The Political Economy of International Financial Regulation" (2013) 88 *Indiana Law Journal* 1405.

framework that would guarantee high profits, while depositors and unsecured creditors will try to push for more stability.[34]

However, if we move to the international level the situation gets more complicated. International financial standards, home–host arrangements, and sovereign debt contracts can be pictured in terms of a tradeoff between domestic stability and global stability. The protection of global stability achieved by the compliance with high capital adequacy standards and by the home supervisory intervention in the host country entails fundamental costs in terms of domestic welfare. The core assumption of global financial policy is that regulators are bound to a principal–agent relationship with their domestic depositors–citizens. This means that, whenever regulators have to choose between protecting the interests of their principals over the protection of other subjects – for instance, foreign depositors – they would naturally choose the former. The most immediate consequence is that, whenever the protection of global stability imposes a loss in terms of domestic welfare, states will be less likely to comply with the norms.

In a bi-country setting, the distributive choices that are inherent to financial policies are more difficult to address. For instance, I have explained above that in a banking crisis the protection of domestic stability sometimes requires the disbursement of a vast amount of resources, especially in the form of capital injections in the context of bailouts. In a single-country model, domestic authorities will choose a level of disbursement that maximizes domestic stability and minimizes the use of taxpayers' money.[35] The same can be argued with regard to bail-ins, in which the tradeoff is between domestic stability and creditors' losses. However, if an international agreement places the burden on one country only – usually the home country – to maintain the stability of the bank's consolidated structure, be it through a bailout or the bail-in of the bank's local creditors, this country would suffer a net domestic welfare loss. Indeed, it would have to provide direct or indirect fiscal transfers to foreign depositors or banks. The ultimate outcome is that while global stability increases, domestic welfare decreases. In this situation, as we argued before, home authorities do not have any incentive to comply with their home–host arrangements.[36]

[34] Verdier, above note 10, pp. 132–43; on the political economy of economic policy, see Mancur Olson, *The Logic of Collective Action: Public Groups and the Theory of Groups* (Cambridge, MA: Harvard University Press, 1965).

[35] Levitin, above note 31.

[36] Martin Schüler, "Incentives Problems in Banking Supervision: The European Case," ZEW Discussion Paper No. 03-62 (2003), available at ftp://ftp.zew.de/pub/zew-docs/dp/dp0362.pdf.

The political economy problems posed by the principal–agent model are by no means limited to cross-border banking resolution, but they extend to the whole set of financial policies. Let's take the case of capital adequacy rules for banks. Capital adequacy standards for financial institutions also imply a distributive choice between different groups. Banks will clearly find high capital buffers unprofitable and will try to push for their reduction, whereas depositors and taxpayers, which see the benefit of capital rules in reducing the moral hazard of banks and protecting financial stability, will push for their adoption.[37] When capital adequacy rules are negotiated at the international level, however, the distributive choices are fundamentally different. A higher capital adequacy ratio will put domestic banks in an uncompetitive position against less regulated foreign entities. If the choice of national regulators is to favor competiveness over stability, they will likely not agree to harmonize their capital adequacy rules.[38]

When the first Basel Accord was negotiated in 1988, Japanese banks dominated the international banking market. Unlike their American counterparts, they could leverage on a lower level of mandatory equity capital and on the commitment by the Japanese government to intervene heavily in the domestic banking market to restore financial stability in the event of a crisis.[39] Various authors reported that, if the United States had not threatened to revoke the license to Japanese banks, the Japanese authorities would have never agreed to follow the Basel capital adequacy rules.

In a sovereign debt contract, the borrower enters into a long-term agreement with its creditors in which it commits to repay the principal and the interest at a particular date. The benefits of the sovereign debt contracts are enjoyed by those who have borrowed but not by those who will repay it. This is due to the fact that over the life of the contract, the willingness of the government in charge to repay the debt might change. In the most extreme scenario, the ruling government in charge at the moment of repayment might simply repudiate the contract by claiming that it had been made by a previous totalitarian government without any benefits for the population, as in the case of odious debt. In most cases, an economic downturn makes it more difficult or even impossible for the government to service its debts – either the principal or the interest – when they fall due. In both circumstances, the most immediate

[37] Admati and Hellwig have proposed the imposition of a 100% capital adequacy ratio to contain the risk proclivity of banks. See Anat Admati and Martin Hellwig, *The Bankers' New Clothes: What's Wrong with Banking and What to Do about It* (Princeton, NJ: Princeton University Press, 2013).

[38] Singer, *Regulating Capital: Setting Standards*, above note 20, pp. 59–61.

[39] *Ibid.*, pp. 59–61.

interest of the government is to protect its own citizens by refusing to comply with the contract, as doing so would entail an overly burdensome financial cost for the country. Sovereign defaults nonetheless impose substantial costs on creditors, which may have to suffer liquidity problems or even insolvency problems, if their exposure toward the sovereign is too high. Depending on the volume of outstanding debts and their concentrations among financial institutions, a sovereign default could transmit global financial instability to other countries where the creditors are located.

These examples show that, in the absence of hard law and compliance mechanisms, compliance would arise only when the welfare costs of global stability do not exceed the costs that the same measure requires to ensure domestic stability. More specifically, domestic regulators are willing to accept a welfare reduction only to the point that it maximizes domestic stability. Any higher level of intervention to protect global stability requires a reduction in domestic welfare not matched by an increase in domestic stability. In this last situation, home regulators do not have any incentive to intervene and they will choose to forbear, thereby creating an externality for partner countries.

8.3.2. *Attribution of Rights and Global Coalitions*

It logically follows that, in the absence of external mechanisms, compliance is the exception and not the rule. How do we achieve compliance, then? The standard legal and economics answer to this question argues that in the absence of a central enforcer of international law, compliance can only arise when the gains for defection are lower than for compliance.[40] Hence, to induce compliance it is necessary to sanction the non-cooperative behavior of the violating states by putting the penalties against defection to a level whereby the welfare cost of non-compliance will be higher than its benefits. In essence, a theory of compliance needs to discourage selfish breach and promote only efficient breach. In this context, the role of international law is thus to create an efficient and legitimate legal framework in which either the partner states or third-party enforcers are entitled to exert efficient retaliation against the violators. In my view, any regulatory mechanism for compliance relies on two different elements. The first element is empowerment of foreign stakeholders who have an interest in the state's compliance with the agreement. More specifically, foreign states or private actors must be put in a

[40] See Posner and Sykes, above note 25, pp. 126–39; Alan O. Sykes, "International Law", in A. Mitchell Polinsky and Steven Shavell (eds.) *Handbook of Law and Economics, Volume 1* (London: Elsevier, 2007), p. 767.

position whereby they are able to monitor the compliance with international obligations of other states. In essence, we must make sure that foreign stakeholders can have a voice over the domestic policies of other countries. The attribution of rights through international treaties is often the easiest way to give a voice to foreign stakeholders. For instance, international investment treaties give investors a set of rights to protect them against the arbitrariness of host states, while international trade agreements give states a complex set of market access and non-discrimination rights that ensure the maintenance of a level playing field in international markets among national firms.

Under certain circumstances, however, the attribution of rights is not necessary as foreign stakeholders are already in a position of power over the state. For instance, in the context of international finance, markets are often in a position of power over the sovereigns whenever they are able to move assets or when they can refuse to provide financing to a sovereign in need of liquidity. The second element is the creation of a dispute-settlement system that uses those rights to threaten retaliation in the event of non-compliance. Thus, in the event of a breach, the law authorizes states or other entities the power to adopt retaliatory measures or to impose penalties up to a level that would induce compliance. As was explained previously, both customary international law as well as the World Trade Organization (WTO) Agreements and Bilateral Investment Treaties set specific penalties to discourage violations.

The role of international law in promoting compliance has been recognized by the law and economics literature.[41] One of the various explanations of the positive role of hard law posits that international law facilitates the implementation of international commitments that might be difficult to obey without the threat of retaliation. According to this theory, governments that cannot credibly make commitments because of the resistance of powerful lobbies enter into binding international agreements to make sure that in the event of crisis foreign interest groups will counterbalance their domestic lobbies against compliance. The ultimate goal is to reduce the likelihood of government officials under the pressure of powerful lobbies seeking short-term political gains

[41] Posner and Sykes, *ibid.*, at 250; Sykes, *ibid.*, p. 767; Posner and Sykes, *ibid.*, at pp. 20–4; Norman and Trachtman, above note 10; Jeffrey L. Dunoff and Joel P. Trachtman, "Economic Analysis of International Law" (1999) 24 *Yale Journal of International Law* 1; Joel P. Trachtman, *The Economic Structure of International Law* (Cambridge, MA, and London: Harvard University Press, 2008); Joel P. Trachtman, "International Law and Domestic Political Coalitions: The Grand Theory of Compliance with International Law" (2010–2011) 11 *Chicago Journal of International Law* 127.

and reneging on long-term interests.[42] For instance, Posner and Sykes,[43] point out the example of international trade, in which domestic groups favoring liberalization are chronically weak and dispersed.[44] Thus, a state enters into a binding framework to make sure that, in the event of a crisis, the overwhelming power of protectionist trade groups would not derail the free-trade policy stance of the country. Another example is international investment. Most of the international investment law and policy literature agrees that investment agreements serve to reduce the discretion of the host government in regulating foreign capital in their territory. By making credible commitments to the international community, host authorities reduce the cost of capital and thus attract more investment.[45]

Increasing the rights of foreign actors is, however, not enough to ensure compliance. In my view, it is of fundamental importance to give the rights to the most appropriate titleholder. Political science has argued that a state is not a monolithic structure, but the result of composite interests of many different actors with different policy preferences and varying degrees of political influence.[46] Therefore, domestic politics plays a fundamental role in shaping the foreign policy of a country. As Trachtman said: "there is no unified, ex ante national interest. The national interest is the result of a domestic political process, taking into account opportunities and risks in the international 'market.'"[47]

The role of domestic policy has been mostly theorized with regard to the decision to enter into an agreement. However, more recently political science scholarship has analyzed the role of interest groups in the decision to comply

[42] Eric A. Posner and Alan O. Sykes, "Efficient Breach of International Law: Optimal Remedies, 'Legalized Noncompliance,' and Related Issues" (2011–2012) 110 *Michigan Law Review* 243, p. 250.

[43] *Ibid.*, p. 250.

[44] See Giovanni Maggi and Andres Rodriguez-Clare, "The Value of Trade Agreements in the Presence of Political Pressures" (1998) 106 *Journal of Political Economy* 574; Robert W. Staiger and Guido Tabellini, "Do GATT Rules Help Governments Make Domestic Commitments?" (1999) 11 *Economics and Politics* 109.

[45] Elkins, Guzman, and Simmons, above note 25; Jeswald Salacuse and Nicholas Sullivan, "Do BITs Really Work? An Evaluation of Bilateral Investment Treaties and Their Grand Bargain" (2005) 46 *Harvard International Law Journal* 67; Kenneth J. Vandevelde, "The Economics of Bilateral Investment Treaties" (2000) 41 *Harvard International Law Journal* 469.

[46] Helen V. Milner, *Interests, Institutions, and Information: Domestic Politics and International Relations* (Princeton, NJ: Princeton University Press, 1997), p. 11; Jeffrey Legro, "Culture and Preferences in the International Cooperation Two-Step" (1996) 90 *American Political Science Review* 118; Andrew Moravcsik, "Taking Preferences Seriously: A Liberal Theory of IR" (1997) 51 *International Organization* 513.

[47] Trachtman, "International Law and Domestic Political Coalition," above note 41, p. 131.

with an agreement.[48] Foreign interest groups have a powerful role in shaping the decision of a state to comply or not with a norm. Indeed, they can reset the original balance between compliance and non-compliance by using penalties that reduce global welfare in the violating state. Joel Trachtman has developed a theory that explains how domestic and foreign interest groups ally to shape the decision of a state to comply or not comply.[49] According to Trachtman's theory, when the domestic and foreign interest groups share the same policy agenda, they can ally to push the regulators toward their positions. In the context of finance, the mechanisms they could use to induce compliance are peer-pressure and reputation, market discipline, bad ratings, threat of capital outflows, and institutional discipline through reduced official lending and institutional pressure. Therefore, the role of international law is to enable the mobilization of those interest groups that have the greatest impact on the welfare of other states.[50] Indeed, some actors will be more prone to exert their rights than others. Hence, the correct attribution of rights to the most appropriate foreign stakeholder will rebalance the equilibrium between the domestic groups favoring compliance and the foreign interest groups.

8.4. GLOBAL COALITIONS IN INTERNATIONAL FINANCE

After having introduced briefly the theory of compliance, it is now time to test it on the various areas of finance. As I said before, international prudential standards show a high degree of compliance, while cross-border banking supervision and crisis resolution, on the contrary, are often subject to defection during crises. Sovereign debt sits somehow in the middle as contentious debt restructurings represent a minority of the overall debt transactions. In light of the theory of compliance provided earlier, I argue that the reason why these policy areas present such remarkable differences lies in the different attribution of rights to foreign stakeholders. On the one hand, the domestic interest groups favoring defection against prudential standards are offset by the powerful role of foreign investors, which can retaliate by moving their capital out of the country. International soft law exerts a fundamental role in this regard, as it mobilizes foreign investors through the use of ratings and institutional pressure. On the other hand, cross-border banking-resolution agreements fail to mobilize those foreign interest groups that might favor compliance, thereby

[48] Xinyuan Dai, "Why Comply? The Domestic Constituency Mechanism" (2005) 59 *International Organization* 363, p. 4.

[49] Trachtman, "International Law and Domestic Political Coalition," above note 41.

[50] *Ibid.*

leaving the decision to comply only in the hands of domestic politics. I will now explain in more detail.

8.4.1. *Prudential Regulations*

The political economy account of international financial standard provided by the political science and legal literature can be broadly conceptualized as a tradeoff between two competing objectives: stability and competition.[51] This theoretical approach falls within the much broader and well-debated issue of regulatory competition in a global market,[52] but has been recently studied by various commentators in the context of international financial regulation.[53] The conflict between the two objectives originates from the main assumption that lax financial regulations, such as a lower level of capital[54] or less stringent reporting rules, increases the competitiveness of domestic firms against their foreign counterparts, but at the same time reduces financial stability. At the national level, the decision to adopt international financial standards – which promote more stringent regulations – will necessarily entail a fight between two different interest groups: depositors and financial institutions. Local banks want lower standards to enhance their competitiveness, while domestic depositors want higher standards to reduce the risk of a financial crisis.[55]

From a rational choice perspective, and absent external factors, the ultimate decision by regulators will be based on pressure exerted by different groups and by the broader industrial policy of the country. Provided that regulators will eventually choose to adopt those standards, in absence of compliance mechanisms, national regulators will nevertheless be constantly tempted to defect. Political economy theory has demonstrated that highly centralized industries such as banks and financial institutions have more lobbying power

[51] The literature on this topic is vast, as it falls within the broader topic of regulatory competition. A good overview of the issue and the related literature is provided in Gadinis, above note 20.

[52] Howell E. Jackson, "Centralization, Competition and Privatization in Financial Regulation" (2001) 2 *Theoretical Inquiries in Law* 649; Joel Trachtman, "Regulatory Competition and Regulatory Jurisdiction" (2000) 3 *Journal of International Economic Law* 331; Gerard Hertig, "Regulatory Competition for EU Financial Services" (2000) 3 *Journal of International Economic Law* 349.

[53] Jeffrey A. Frieden, "The Politics of National Economic Policies in a World of Global Finance" (1991) 45 *International Organization* 425; Howell E. Jackson and Eric J. Pan, "Regulatory Competition in International Securities Markets: Evidence from Europe in 1999 – Part I" (2000) 56 *The Business Lawyer* 657; Singer, *Regulating Capital*, above note 20.

[54] Singer, *ibid.*

[55] *Ibid.*

than dispersed groups such as depositors.[56] Domestic banks would probably prevent regulators from adopting stringent standards. However, foreign interest groups have the opposite interest: that the state sticks to its commitments and implements the higher standards. Foreign financial institutions indeed do not want to be put at a domestic disadvantage, while foreign investors probably require a stable and sound financial system to invest. To sum up, if we analyze the battle for compliance from an international perspective, foreign financial institutions and investors share with domestic depositors the need to promote compliance, while local banks are left alone in their desire to lower standards.

Without an alliance between foreign interests (foreign regulators and investors) and domestic groups (depositors), the decision of a country to agree to the Basel Accord will be difficult, as regulators will probably suffer the powerful lobby of domestic banks. However, if properly structured, international law can help in mobilizing foreign interest groups to rebalance the political economy equilibrium in favor of compliance. In the case of prudential standards, the ratings of private rating agencies as well as the reports of international financial institutions exert this function as they can sanction the behavior of a state and thus mobilize foreign interests.[57] Private investors as well as other states will rely on those reports and ratings, and they will exert their power to drive the compliance. Investors might pull out their capital, while foreign regulators might refuse to cooperate on other regulatory issues. National regulators, of course, still retain the right to defect. However, while in the short term this strategy might work, in the long term the risk of a financial crisis will induce lower ratings and thus reduce the overall investment inflows. The decision of a foreign agency to suspend the negotiation of an agreement following the violation of a standard by the partner country, or the decision of private investors to pull their capital out, are, by all means, a form of institutionalized retaliation legitimized and encouraged by the law.

When a country suffers a welfare loss because of the implementation of financial standards (as in the case of Japan), the incentives to deviate are therefore offset by an equal level of social retaliation by the international financial community. Furthermore, even if compliance will temporarily decrease profitability, the decrease in welfare will soon be rebalanced by an increase of investment inflows driven by the good ratings of financial institutions and market actors. Since compliance with prudential standards is essentially a self-interested policy, then the simple threat of capital outflow and institutional discipline will suffice. However, when the welfare losses of compliance

[56] Malesky, above note 33.

[57] Brummer, *Soft Law and the Global Financial System*, above note 1.

are much higher, as in the case of cross-border banking, the costs of retaliation are not enough to induce compliance.

8.4.2. *Cross-Border Banking Resolution and Home–Host Arrangements*

The case for hard laws is particularly clear when it comes to cross-border banking and home–host arrangements. In a banking resolution authorities are confronted with a dilemma between the need to protect economic stability and the concurrent need to limit government intervention or creditors' losses. In a purely domestic setting, the political economy conflict is between banks and insured creditors, on the one side, and taxpayers/subordinated creditors, on the other. According to various authors, regulators will decide to bailout or to bail-in a bank – rather than proceed with a normal insolvency – whenever the benefits of the resolution will outweigh the costs for the broader society.[58] Indeed, it is well demonstrated that systemic banking crises often have disastrous economic effects on GDP growth.[59] However, in a cross-border banking crisis the situation is different.

The lack of fiscal solidarity is one of the main issues of the home–host cooperation problem. It is very visible in the context of a cross-border bank **bailouts** and **home–host deposit protection arrangements**, in which case the main problem is the behavior of the home authorities. In a home–host arrangement the home country and the host country swap their jurisdiction on the supervision and protection of the home bank's foreign operations, mostly with regard to branches. This means that the host country partially relinquishes its power over its domestic stability, while the home country extends its jurisdiction across-border. In the event of problems in the parent bank's foreign operations, the home authority has to incur some extra costs to maintain financial stability. However, as demonstrated in Chapter 4, the home country does not have any gains from maintaining domestic stability abroad. Using domestic taxpayers' money to bailout a foreign financial institution, to protect foreign depositors – or conducting the bail-in of the bank group through the parent holding company, for that matter – will simply decrease domestic welfare without any return in terms of domestic stability. Taxpayers in the home country will clearly oppose any fiscal disbursement to save the foreign operations of the bank, because this would mean that domestic taxpayers' money would be

[58] Dirk Schoenmaker, *Governance of International Banking: The Financial Trilemma* (Oxford: Oxford University Press, 2013), p. 25.

[59] See Charles Kindleberger and Robert Z. Aliber, *Manias, Panics and Crashes: A History of Financial Crises* (New York: Palgrave, 2011).

used to maintain stability abroad. The preferable option for home authorities is not to comply with the MoU and abandon the bank's foreign operations. The literature on home–host arrangement is replete with cooperation failures. A recent example is the refusal of the Icelandic authorities to protect the Icelandic banks' depositors in England and the Netherlands.

The only groups that are interested in ensuring compliance are host-country depositors, bank's creditors, and host authorities. However, they are unable to exert their influence on the home supervisor because they do not have any legal and political rights in the home jurisdiction. The MoU swapped supervisory powers but it did not include a parallel transfer of rights. Host-country depositors are principals without any control on the agent (the home-country regulators). In the case of forbearance or mismanagement, depositors are unprotected. In this situation, it would be necessary that either the partner state retaliates by suspending its own concessions, or foreign investors are mobilized to punish deviations by pulling out their capital. However, neither of these situations would naturally happen. The foreign interest groups that are naturally interested in having the home authorities comply do not have any power to do so: host supervisors cannot retaliate; investors are not interested in exerting their pressure; and foreign interest groups cannot be mobilized to exert their pressure because they do not have any right to do so. To solve this problem, it is necessary to increase the rights of those interest groups that are subject to the foreign supervisor. Only then will they be able to exert the level of pressure necessary to offset the natural incentive of the home authorities to defect. This could be done by giving some of them standing in international courts, and by instituting a remedial system to compensate them.

In a **cross-border bank bail-in** cooperation problems are different as they mainly involve the non-recognition of the bail-in by the foreign authorities. In a bank bail-in, the main objective is to recapitalize the bank through the write-down and the conversion of the bank's liabilities as opposed to a bailout. From a political economy viewpoint, bail-ins do not divide opposing interest groups on their nationality, but rather on their participation, or not, in the resolution of the bank.

On one side of the fence, the group that has the greatest interest in carrying out the bail-in is the taxpayers where the bank is located, which have the interest in resolving the ailing bank without the use of public money. In a cross-border dimension, this group is represented by the resolution authority that is competent for initiating and coordinating the resolution action. On the other side of the fence are the bank's creditors and shareholders, who will lose some or all their investments in the bank. Hence, it is safe to argue that they will constitute the main opposition to the resolution authority competent for conducting the bail-in. This group, however, may not necessarily reside in the same territory. The liabilities subject to bail-in are sometimes distributed in different parts of the bank group, depending on whether the group is very centralized with a holding company at the top, or decentralized with each subsidiary financially independent. Furthermore, depending on the size of the losses, the bail-in of the liabilities could bear some negative consequences for the stability of the market where the creditors are located. This means that the host-authorities, where the liabilities are located, might object to the resolution action of the foreign resolution authority.

The question then, is which group shall deserve a voice in the procedure. To make the bail-in effective and guarantee global financial stability, it is absolutely necessary to ensure that the market perceives the resolved bank as safe and that the legal positions of the bank's creditors are certain. Irrespective of the resolution approach chosen for the bank group – either the Single Point of Entry or the Multiple Point of Entry – international cooperation between national resolution authorities and courts is absolutely necessary. Among the most important common actions required by the home and host needs are the provision of emergency liquidity assistance to the bank in resolution, the correct implementation of the write-down and conversion of liabilities, and the forced continuation of derivatives contracts. All these actions require a level of legal cooperation that might involve statutory changes. Alternatively, a bail-in requires the legal cooperation of the jurisdiction competent for the debt contracts subject to bail-in and the derivatives. This could be a third country where the bank does not have any actual operation. In certain legal systems, the conversion of the liability conducted by a foreign authority could violate some basic principles of law and, thus, may not be recognized as valid by the local courts.

In this situation, the resolution authority conducting the bail-in is the one that risks the most in the event of a non-recognition of the bail-in action by the other authorities. If the resolution is not carried out with the cooperation of all authorities, the ailing bank may be subject to a disorderly and costly resolution. For this reason, it is necessary to have the resolution recognized and carried out in all jurisdictions where the bank operates without giving rise to unnecessary legal disputes. In order to increase the pressure toward non-cooperative authorities, it would be necessary to establish a system of international legal entitlements whereby resolution authorities have the right to demand the compliance of the partner authorities in recognizing and carrying out the resolution. This is the idea behind the "statutory" system of mutual recognition of resolution action proposed by the Financial Stability Board in 2015.

This system of legal entitlement should, ideally, rest upon a mutual recognition agreement that sets the obligations of each authority during the resolution of the bank group, and a dispute-settlement mechanism that gives them standing before an international court. Creditors, on the other hand, should not be given additional rights beyond what they have been already granted according to domestic law. Because bail-ins necessitate the (forcible) cooperation of the creditors subject to bail-in and the holders of the derivatives contracts that are overridden, it would be unsafe to allocate them any direct rights over the resolution. Creditors' battles in courts could postpone the recovery of the bank and ultimately make the resolution uncertain.

8.4.3. *Sovereign Debt*

Sovereign debt presents very different problems compared to financial standards or cross-border bank resolution. When we look at sovereign debt defaults and restructurings through the lenses of the economics of international law, three salient international cooperation problems come to the forefront of the legal debate. The first one is how to use international law to reduce the likelihood of sovereign defaults and increase good fiscal governance. The second concerns the role of international law in preventing non-cooperative debt restructurings by the sovereigns, which becomes relevant if the state has indeed defaulted on its debt. The third problem is how to prevent jurisdictional arbitrage by holdouts and, consequently, how to provide an efficient restructuring for both creditors and sovereigns. Each of these problems involves different global coalitions, which in turn changes the potential role of international law.

With the level of sovereign indebtedness skyrocketing among developed countries, the prevention of sovereign defaults and the encouragement of good fiscal governance are necessary to avoid future systemic crises of the likes of Greece or Argentina. The political economy of sovereign indebtedness can be understood with reference to the time-consistency problem discussed in Chapter 5. On the one side, there is the actual borrowing government, which has the interest to get credit to finance immediate fiscal outlays. The government can rely on the older streams of the population which will not bear the fiscal consequences of the repayment, such as reduced welfare spending or less generous pension systems. On the other side, there are the actual creditors who lend to the government. The creditors rely on the support of the younger generations, who are nonetheless less reliable as they might not fully understand the long-term implications of their government's borrowing. In terms of legal rights, creditors do enjoy a legal right to be repaid. However, as I will explain below, their private contractual right suffers from many limitations and is not always effective as sovereigns are protected by international law.

Nonetheless, markets are able to exert substantial pressure on the sovereign to prevent strategic defaults. They do so by threatening to pull their capital out at the first sign of a crisis and by closing market access for the future. The threat of retaliation, however, is limited as not all creditors holding the debt security at the moment of the default are able to exert market pressure on the sovereign to prevent the default. Creditors are in a position of structural disadvantage over the sovereign, as they have already performed the lending part of the debt transaction, and can only hope to receive the principal and the interest when they fall due. Unless creditors are institutional investors in the business of lending to sovereigns, and hence to refuse lending, they will not be able to exert any pressure on the sovereign. In this situation, non-institutional investors are the weakest party, together with the future generations. Given the time-inconsistency problem, it is impossible to create an alliance between them.

However, creditors could be helped in monitoring the borrower by international institutions, which have a long-term mandate to monitor fiscal stability. For instance, creditors could be helped by the IMF or the World Bank in monitoring fiscal sustainability, by transferring retaliatory power to the IMF. In the European Union, fiscal sustainability is the competence of the Commission, which oversees the economic conditions of the member states and imposes fines, in case of violation of the EU public budget laws. This is complemented, of course, by rating agencies, which periodically advise on the sustainability of sovereign borrowers. Another way is to link sovereign debt borrowing to bilateral investment treaties and create a fiscal committee composed of representatives of the two governments to discuss informally the status of each other's finances. This option is, however, very difficult to be implemented as it may encounter political opposition.[60]

The sovereign immunity problem arises only if the government has indeed defaulted on its debts and refuses to cooperate with the creditors. By noncooperation, I mean a hostile stance of the sovereign against creditors that ultimately leads to a prolonged battle over the restructuring or, in a worse scenario, the repudiation of the debts. The general protection offered by sovereignty to debtor nations shields states from any responsibility toward the international community. Sovereigns are essentially free to bypass any international legal obligation they might have toward their partners and foreign financial markets. Moreover, the protection of fiscal sovereignty increases the proclivity of policymakers to take up a socially excessive level of debt and adopt unsustainable polices. In this situation, the relative efficiency of market

[60] The new generation of Investment Agreements explicitly excludes sovereign debt from the purview of the agreement. See the European Union–Vietnam Free Trade Agreement.

pressure as a compliance mechanism cannot be considered as a substitute for the serious loopholes of international law. Without the threat of legal remedies or fines that are present in a normal commercial bankruptcy, sovereigns lack the normal incentives to comply with their obligations.

In a sovereign default, the creditors and the sovereign are on opposite sides. It is precisely at this moment that creditors should make their voice heard by suing the sovereign in court that has jurisdiction over the debt contract. Creditors can do so by suing the sovereign in the court with jurisdictional competence over the contract, but the enforcement of the court order lacks effectiveness. As discussed earlier, the sovereign can legitimately refuse under international law to repay the debt by hiding the assets in its territory. In Coasian terms, the allocation of rights is not efficient as it encourages the sovereign to adopt a hostile stance against the creditors, which in turn increases its moral hazard in fiscal policy. Reducing the legal protection of the sovereign and increasing in parallel the international legal rights of creditors under international law would certainly rebalance the situation. In Chapter 10, I will discuss the role of an international bankruptcy court for a sovereign and how it could address this problem.

The question of jurisdictional arbitrage and holdout has very different dynamics compared to the two earlier problems as, in principle, it does not involve cooperation problems between the creditors and the sovereign, but only between creditors. However, if holdouts adopt an aggressive litigation strategy based on jurisdictional arbitrage in creditor-friendly and strategic jurisdictions, they could create substantial problems to both the borrowing sovereign as well as the other creditors. In this situation, the creditors as well as the borrower have a substantial interest to cooperate in avoiding the holdouts blocking the entire debt-restructuring procedure or the servicing of the debt. On the other side of the fence, creditor-friendly jurisdictions have an interest in hosting the legal dispute as this could incentivize creditors to denominate the contract under local law and use the services of local courts. The coordination problems between the two groups are similar to Battle of the Sexes games as they require the initial effort from borrowers and creditors to locate the dispute in a neutral court that protects both. This is precisely the logic behind the sovereign debt-restructuring mechanism and an international bankruptcy court for sovereigns.

8.5. CONCLUSION

This chapter has discussed the problem of compliance in international finance. The central argument is that the current regulatory framework based on soft law is unable to ensure compliance, as it does not take into account the powerful sovereignty costs attached to the maintenance of global stability in a cross-border setting. Therefore, the last element of an efficient international regulatory architecture for financial stability must necessarily be a reliable compliance mechanism that reduces the proclivity of national regulators for defection and guarantees obedience to the laws.

In the next two chapters I will develop further this argument by proposing the adoption of binding bilateral agreements on financial policies and market access – the Regulatory Passports – and the use of dispute-settlement mechanisms to adjudicate financial disputes.

9

A Different Path to Financial Integration: Regulatory Passports

So far, we have discussed the challenges of cooperation in international financial policies. Yet, regulation and policy cooperation is only one part of the broader regulatory architecture of global finance. The legal framework that enables and entitles financial institutions, investors, and consumers to access a foreign financial market is the other essential element of the global financial architecture. The way international law regulates the integration of financial market directly influences the incentives of financial authorities to cooperate on financial policies and, thus, it bears fundamental implications for the maintenance of global financial stability.

The current international financial system has developed over the years on three parallel regulatory fronts that have rarely come close to meeting. First, we have what could be called the "regulatory convergence agenda," which we have discussed earlier and which has developed through informal cooperation in Transnational Regulatory Networks (TRNs). In institutions like the Basel Committee on Banking Supervision (BCBS), financial regulators have engaged through a parallel exercise in regulatory coordination on standard-setting and supervision that has resulted in numerous bilateral cooperation agreements on various areas of financial policy, and a large set of regulatory instruments such as Basel III or the Key Attributes. The objective of the regulatory convergence agenda is not to integrate markets but to increase their resilience to internal and external shocks by leveling the regulatory playing field in each country. Crucially, cooperation and regulatory convergence in financial policies relies on the soft power of TRNs, and on non-binding regulatory instruments, which do not entail any international rights or obligations and do not entitle regulators to launch disputes.

On a completely different area of financial law, we have what could be called the "financial liberalization agenda," which has developed over the years through bilateral, regional, and international treaties promoting the dismantling of regulatory and administrative barriers to the movement of capital. Financial liberalization is the process whereby financial institutions and consumers can move capital freely across borders, and offer and consume financial services in another jurisdiction. The process of financial liberalization rests on the application of a few bedrock norms on non-discrimination, investment protection, capital mobility, and market access that are contained in most economic integration treaties with a financial services component, such as the World Trade Organization General Agreement on Trade in Services (the GATS),[1] preferential Free Trade Agreements, or most International Investment Agreements. Crucially, those treaties contain hard obligations for their signatories that: (1) give legitimate expectations that the treaty parties will comply with their international obligations; (2) allow the non-breaching party to launch a dispute against the breaching party through one of the various adjudication mechanisms; and (3) provide remedial mechanisms that ought to punish the violating party and discourage non-compliance.

Finally, we have the area of sovereign financing, which functions on an actually very limited body of public international norms and mostly relies on market negotiations and private contractual mechanisms as do all other private international financial transactions. As explained in Chapter 5, this public–private partnership does not always work, as states can easily refuse to cooperate with creditors, while holdouts can forum-shop to block a restructuring.

The three regulatory regimes exist independently of each other. This means, for instance, that the decision to grant market access to foreign banks is totally separate from considerations on the actual regulatory cooperation with foreign banks' authorities. The reasons that can be assumed to be behind this regulatory asynchrony are multiple. First, the three regulatory regimes have developed at different times. For instance, the law on sovereign debt developed much earlier than that on financial standard or trade integration. Given the absence of an already established international regulatory platform on which to embed debt policy, much of the law developed through private contractual commitments. This, however, does not explain fully why regulatory

[1] General Agreement on Trade in Services, 15 April 1994, Annex 1B, in the Marrakesh Agreement Establishing the World Trade Organization and the substantive multilateral agreements attached thereto, 15 April 1994, in World Trade Organization, *The Results of the Uruguay Round of Multilateral Trade Negotiations: The Legal Texts* 355 (1999), [hereinafter, The Legal Texts] available at www.wto.org/english/docs_e/legal_e/legal_e.htm.

cooperation and financial liberalization, which both developed between the late 1980s and the 1990s, have not progressed hand-in-hand. Another plausible explanation is that in most countries the actual competence on sovereign financing, standard setting, and market access or investment protection belongs to very different ministries. In trade and investment policy, the competence for negotiating agreements mostly rests with the Ministry of External Trade or the Ministry of Investment. International financial policy negotiations are mostly done by the actual agencies in charge of each sector, such as the Central Bank, the securities regulators or the bank supervisory authority. Finally, the issuance of sovereign debt and the actual fiscal policy are the competence of the Ministry of Finance.

Internal turf wars between different ministries are not unusual in most countries; one could safely argue that the desire to protect each authority's statutory competence has ultimately made regime convergence more difficult. Finally, we must not underestimate the turf wars between international organizations that were actually present until the global financial crisis. For instance, rumors have it that the failure to embody financial regulation into the GATS is due to the stiff opposition of the International Monetary Fund (IMF) and the BCBS, which feared losing jurisdiction on financial policy to the World Trade Organization (WTO). Indeed, the GATS Annex on Financial Services was negotiated in the early 1990s within the broader Uruguay Round of trade negotiation that created, among other things, a very well-designed and effective dispute-settlement system, the Dispute Settlement Mechanism. The incorporation of financial standards into the GATS would have enabled litigation on financial standards. Consequently, this would have led to a major shift in jurisdictional power on financial standards to the WTO and, indirectly, to the various national Ministries of Trade that lead the organization.

Yet, the failure of the financial policy community to include cooperation on international financial standards and policies in the financial integration agenda led to the creation of an asymmetric global financial system in which market access rights were protected under international law, while financial policies remained preserved as national prerogatives. This asynchrony between the global scope of financial markets and the national scope of financial policies is one of the fundamental reasons behind the dangers of financial nationalism. In an interconnected global financial system where market integration is protected under international law, globally suboptimal domestic financial policies can generate systemic risk and spread it across the network.

The goal of this chapter is to challenge the wisdom of this asynchronized international regulatory architecture. I will instead propose a different regulatory approach to financial integration based on the use of Regulatory Passports. According to this mechanism, the rights of firms and investors to trade or in a foreign jurisdiction will be subordinated to – and be accompanied by – the adoption of binding bilateral agreements on financial policies between the home and host regulators. I will demonstrate that by leveraging on the desire of states to access foreign markets and reap the benefits of international capital, regulatory cooperation on financial stability can be enhanced and made more resilient to financial nationalisms.

9.1. THE LAW OF FINANCIAL INTEGRATION

Financial integration did not come as a natural event, but as the result of the coordinated efforts of national regulators to open their borders to foreign capital and to allow financial institutions to operate across borders. Financial liberalization was part of a broader policy agenda to create an international economic system in which factors of production could freely move across borders with the minimum amount of impediments and with the highest level of protection.[2] Standard economic theory suggests that financial internationalization brings many benefits to the liberalizing country.[3] An open capital account allows the inflow and outflow of capital and, coupled with trade in financial services, achieves an extension of the domestic market. Consumers can access credit from financial institutions located in other countries, open foreign bank accounts or invest abroad. Financial institutions are able to access a wider market, thereby achieving economies of scale and increasing profits. Investors can enjoy a wider choice of products and choose the most profitable ones.

The process of financial integration was not conducted in isolation from the law. On the contrary, to be effective, it needed the establishment of system of

[2] Rawi Abdelal, *Capital Rules: The Construction of Global Finance* (Cambridge, MA: Harvard University Press, 2007); Barry Eichengreen, *Globalizing Capital: A History of the International Monetary System* (Princeton, NJ: Princeton University Press, 2008); Barry Eichengreen, *Global Imbalances and the Lessons of Bretton Woods* (Cambridge, MA: MIT Press, 2007).

[3] A good literature review on the benefits of financial openness is provided in Masamichi Kono and Ludger Schuknecht, "Financial Services Trade, Capital Flows, and Financial Stability," Staff Working Paper ERAD-98-12, World Trade Organization (1998); John Williamson, "Whether and When to Liberalize Capital Account and Financial Services," Staff Working Paper ERAD-99-03, World Trade Organization (1999); Masamichi Kono, Patrick Low, Mukela Luanga, Aaditya Mattoo, Maika Oshikawa, and Ludger Schuknecht, "Opening Markets in Financial Services and the Role of the GATS," WTO Special Study, World Trade Organization (1997).

rights bestowed on capital-exporting nations and foreign investors.[4] Financial integration is promoted by a complex set of norms enshrined in international treaties that increase the scope of financial markets and provide the necessary conditions for financial institutions and investors to be treated fairly and equally when operating abroad. Such norms have the ultimate effect of enabling financial institutions and consumers to provide or consume financial services in a jurisdiction that is not their own. In the presence of financial integration, banks can set up branches and subsidiaries in another country to offer deposits and provide lending to local customers; companies can list their shares in a foreign stock market; financial intermediaries can trade and buy financial products denominated in foreign currency, or buy sovereign bonds of another government. Crucially, the political economy bargain that supports the process of financial liberalization is based on a mutual exchange of concession between states, which grant each other market access and non-discrimination rights.

The achievement of market integration requires a great deal of regulatory and political convergence because it requires the dismantling of all the national regulatory and administrative barriers that de jure or de facto impede or discourage the free movement of capital or prevent the provision of financial services in another jurisdiction.

From a historical viewpoint, the regulatory process enabling financial integration started with the amendment of Article IV of the IMF Articles.[5] When the United States decided they could no longer sustain the burden of US$–Gold parity, Article IV was reformulated to grant the members of the International Monetary Fund the freedom to choose their preferred exchange rate arrangements. The reformulation of Article IV was a fundamental step toward financial integration, as it allowed states to liberalize capital flows.[6] The new world of exchange rate flexibility immediately opened for traders the possibility to buy and sell foreign

[4] On this point, see Alan O. Sykes, "Protectionism as a 'Safeguard': A Positive Analysis of the GATT 'Escape Clause' with Normative Speculations" (1991) 58 *The University of Chicago Law Review* 255, at pp. 274–8; Alan O. Sykes, "Public versus Private Enforcement of International Economic Law: Standing and Remedy" (2005) 34 *The Journal of Legal Studies* 631; Warren F. Schwartz and Alan O. Sykes, "The Economic Structure of Renegotiation and Dispute Resolution in the World Trade Organization" (2002) 31 *The Journal of Legal Studies* 179; Joel P. Trachtman, "International Law and Domestic Political Coalitions: The Grand Theory of Compliance with International Law" (2010–2011) 11 *Chicago Journal of International Law* 127.

[5] Articles of Agreement of the International Monetary Fund, 22 July 1944, 60 Stat. 1401, 2 UNTS 39, *as amended effective* 20 March 2014 [hereinafter the IMF Articles].

[6] See Dani Rodrik, *The Globalization Paradox: Democracy and the Future of the World Economy* (New York: Norton, 2011).

currency, and more importantly, to hedge on foreign exchange risk.[7] The early 1970s accordingly witnessed a constant surge in cross-border capital flows, which brought financial internationalization back to center stage. Exchange rate flexibility was, however, not enough to internationalize financial systems. To achieve this goal, it was necessary to enable financial intermediaries, such as banks, insurance companies, or investment firms to operate across borders. To achieve this objective, policymakers relied on three different regulatory strategies: (1) financial services trade liberalization, (2) free capital mobility, and (3) investment protection.

Free movement of capital is probably the backbone of financial liberalization – the element, in absence of which, financial integration would simply be impossible.[8] It consists of the freedom to move financial assets across borders. This takes place through international transactions of real and financial assets between a resident and a non-resident of a particular country.[9] Free capital mobility is not subject to a cohesive and centralized regulatory framework. The OECD Code of Liberalization of Capital Movements (hereinafter, the OECD Code on Capital Movement, or simply the Code) is the only agreement dealing specifically with capital account liberalization.[10] The OECD Code on Capital Movement offers a regulatory platform that promotes the liberalization of the capital account.[11] Unlike other instruments, the Code focuses on specific capital transactions, thereby covering capital transactions made by non-residents and those made by residents, as well as on their underlying payment and transfers. Furthermore, the Code applies to both inflow and outflow of capital.[12] Free movement of capital is also regulated as a necessary condition for investment protection under International Investment Agreements (IIAs), and as an element of financial liberalization under the GATS.[13]

7 See Kern Alexander, Rahul Dhumale, and John Eatwell, *Global Governance of Financial System: The International Regulation of Systemic Risk* (Oxford: Oxford University Press, 2006), p. 22.

8 Barry Eichengreen, *Capital Flows and Crises* (Cambridge, MA: MIT Press, 2004).

9 Federico Lupo-Pasini, "Movement of Capital and Trade in Services: Distinguishing Myth from Reality Regarding the GATS and the Liberalization of the Capital Account" (2012) 15 *Journal of International Economic Law* 79, p. 586.

10 Organization for Economic Co-operation and Development, Code of Liberalization of Capital Movements (2013) [hereinafter, the OECD Code on Capital Movement].

11 See OECD, *OECD Codes of Liberalization: User's Guide*, Organization for Economic Co-operation and Development (2008); OECD, "Forty Years' Experience with The OECD Code of Liberalisation of Capital Movements," Organization for Economic Co-operation and Development (October 2002); IMF, "The Experience of the OECD with the Code of Liberalisation of Capital Movements" (1999) 1 *Current Developments in Monetary and Financial Law* 28.

12 Respectively, OECD Code on Capital Movement, Article 7(c), and Article 7(b).

13 Lupo-Pasini, above note 9.

Free trade in financial services, on the contrary, gives to financial institutions the right to offer their services to customers located in another country. The regulatory instrument that promoted financial opening more than any other is the WTO GATS.[14] Besides providing for a regulatory platform that enables the general liberalization of trade in services, the GATS also propelled the liberalization of financial services.[15] Article XVI of the GATS gives countries the right to access another member's financial market, according to the Schedule of Concession of that member. WTO members exchange with each other market access commitments, which, in principle, bind the member to the same level of market opening and regulatory treatment throughout the life of the treaty.[16] Hence, once a member has liberalized its banking sector, foreign banks can set up branches or subsidiaries in the national territory, or provide a service to local consumers on a cross-border basis. For instance, they give loans or accept deposits. The GATS also establishes a complex regulatory framework that prohibits discrimination between members and promotes a level playing field between domestic and foreign firms. It does so by encouraging the dismantling of the various regulatory and administrative barriers that might hinder cross-border financial services trade. The regulatory framework for financial liberalization set out in the GATS has been replicated at the bilateral or regional level in various Free Trade Agreements dealing with financial services liberalization.[17]

The third pillar of financial integration is investment protection. This objective is promoted mainly by IIAs, which we briefly discussed in Chapter 5.[18] The goal of IIAs is partially different from the GATS and the OECD Code, as the large majority of them do not focus directly on integrating financial

[14] For an overview, see Sydney J. Key, *The Doha Round and Financial Services Negotiations* (Washington, DC: AEI Press, 2003).

[15] The normative framework of the GATS does not discipline specifically financial services trade – although it does contain norms that specifically target certain issues pertinent to financial services – but rather, it contains a general legal framework that, in principle, applies to all services sectors.

[16] The GATS offers a minimum level of market opening. However, states are free to further liberalize unilaterally.

[17] Pierre Sauvé and Martin Molinuevo, "Architectural Approaches to the Treatment of Trade and Investment in Financial Services in Selected Preferential Trade Agreements," in Mona Haddad and Constantinos Stephanou (eds.) *Financial Services and Preferential Trade Agreements: Lessons from Latin America* (Washington, DC: The World Bank, 2010).

[18] On this issue, see Federico Lupo-Pasini, "Monetary Policy Measures in Investment Law: The Uneasy Relationship Between Monetary Stability and Investment Protection," in Thomas Cottier, Rosa Maria Lastra, Christian Tietje, and Lucia Satragno (eds.) *The Role of Law in Monetary Affairs* (Cambridge: Cambridge University Press, 2014).

markets.[19] On the contrary, the goal of IIAs is to support cross-border investment through the imposition of a minimum regulatory standard related to the protection of foreign investment.[20] Crucially, the foreign investment they protect (which in essence is capital movement) is not only foreign direct investments (FDI), but also portfolio flows, such as purchase of securities, stocks, domestic and sovereign bonds, as well as other intangible financial assets, and the making and receipt of loans. Although IIAs deal primarily with the post-establishment phase of international investment, they nevertheless have become the most powerful tool for capital account liberalization. Once foreign investors have moved and invested their capital in the host country territory, they enjoy a complex set of rights, which entitles them to be treated fairly during the investment phase, and move the assets out of the country.[21] Thus, host countries are in principle prohibited from restricting capital outflows, and imposing measures that would reduce the profitability of the investment. The regulatory coverage of IIAs is extremely vast and it extends in principle to all the administrative, regulatory, and political measures adopted by the host country authorities that might affect the life of the investment. In the context of finance, it could cover the adoption of financial regulations, the implementation of crisis-resolution policies (such as bail-in, bailout, and insolvency procedures), the imposition of capital controls, as well as virtually any measures dealing with sovereign debt.

The financial liberalization agenda was extremely successful in promoting and sustaining financial market integration. With the notable exception of China and India, in a period of less than 20 years, most WTO members committed to maintain open financial markets to provide fair and equal treatment to foreign investors. Lifting the administrative and regulatory impediments to international finance is not however sufficient to make an international financial market work. For this to be possible regulatory and

[19] Giorgio Sacerdoti, "The Admission and Treatment of Foreign Investments Under Recent Bilateral and Regional Treaties" (2000) 1 *The Journal of World Investment* 105; Ignacio Gomez-Palacio and Peter T. Muchlinski, "Admission and Establishment," in Peter T. Muchlinski, Federico Ortino, and Christoph Schreuer (eds.) *The Oxford Handbook in International Investment Law* (Oxford: Oxford University Press, 2008).

[20] See August Reinisch (ed.) *Standards of Investment Protection* (Oxford: Oxford University Press, 2008).

[21] Abba Kolo and Thomas Walde, "Economic Crises, Capital Transfer Restrictions and Investor Protection Under Modern Investment Treaties" (2008) 3 *Capital Market Law Journal* 154; Abba Kolo, "Transfer of Funds: The Interaction between the IMF Articles of Agreement and Modern Investment Treaties: A Comparative Law Perspective," in Stephan Schill (ed.) *International Investment Law and Comparative Public Law* (Oxford: Oxford University Press, 2010).

supervisory cooperation is necessary. Yet, despite its consistent body of rules to promote and sustain market integration, neither the GATS, nor the OECD Code, nor IIAs contain rules to preserve market stability. On the contrary, they make it extremely clear that policies aimed at regulating financial markets or protecting financial stability are to be excluded from the scope of the agreements.

9.2. THE ECONOMICS OF CARVE-OUTS

The key to understand the regulatory strategy for financial integration stems from its total disconnection with the question of regulatory cooperation, and why it matters for global financial stability. These are a few provisions that are invariably contained in all international trade and investment agreement with a financial services component: the so-called "financial carve-outs."

The pursuit of financial globalization posed a fundamental challenge to the quiet implementation of domestic policies and to the very protection of financial stability.[22] Squaring globalization and national autonomy has never been easy. From environmental protection to human rights, policymakers have found it hard to accept the necessary loss of national political power that comes with closer integration.[23] In the context of finance, however, the debate was somehow more complex owing to one specific factor: the belief that closer financial integration would inevitably lead nation states to a permanent condition of financial instability. The history of finance and recurring financial crises unquestionably demonstrated that financial globalization exposes domestic economies to far more dangerous risks than free trade.[24]

[22] For a good overview of the literature on financial liberalization and sovereignty, see Erik Helleiner, "Sovereignty, Territoriality, and the Globalization of Finance," in David A. Smith, Dorothy J. Solinger, and Steven C. Topik (eds.) *States and Sovereignty in the Global Economy* (New York: Routledge, 1999).

[23] On the relationship between sovereignty and globalization, see Joel P. Trachtman, "L'Etat, C'est Nous: Sovereignty, Economic Integration and Subsidiarity" (1992) 33 *Harvard International Law Journal* 459; Anne-Marie Slaughter, "Sovereignty and Power in a Networked World Order" (2004) 40 *Stanford journal of International Law* 284; Helen Stacy, "Relational Sovereignty" (2003) 55 *Stanford Law Review* 2029; Saskias Assen, *Losing Control: Sovereignty in an Age of Globalization* (New York: Columbia University Press, 1996); John H. Jackson, "Sovereignty-Modern: A New Approach to an Outdated Concept" (2003) 97 *American Journal of International Law* 4; Kal Raustiala, "Rethinking the Sovereignty Debate in International Economic Law" (2003) 6 *Journal of International Economic Law* 841; Wenhua Shan, Penelope Simons, and Dalvinder Singh (eds.) *Redefining Sovereignty in International Economic Law* (Oxford: Hart Publishing, 2008).

[24] Charles Kindleberger and Robert Z. Aliber, *Manias, Panics and Crashes: A History of Financial Crises* (New York: Palgrave, 2011).

In a world where global capital flows could easily determine – for good or for bad – the destinies of a country, financial sovereignty was believed to be the ultimate safeguard against financial instability.

These beliefs influenced the regulatory framework for international trade and investment, which resulted in a difficult compromise between market integration and regulatory autonomy. The national control over domestic policy formulation allowed states to satisfy national policy interests and protect their domestic stability. Therefore, whenever the two objectives entered into conflict, the protection of regulatory autonomy usually prevailed. The protection of national interests is achieved through various legal mechanisms, which invariably structure financial, fiscal, and monetary policies as sovereign prerogatives. The most important among these legal mechanisms are carve-outs.[25] In international trade or investment treaties with a financial services component, it is common to see clauses that explicitly exclude domestic economic policies from the scope of the application of the treaty. The most-discussed among such clauses is Article 2 of the GATS Annex on Financial Services – most commonly known as the "prudential carve-out." Given its importance and the fact that it has been replicated almost word-by-word in all international agreement with a financial services component, it is worth quoting it in its entirety:

> Notwithstanding any other provisions of the Agreement, a Member shall not be prevented from taking measures for prudential reasons, including for the protection of investors, depositors, policy holders or persons to whom a fiduciary duty is owed by a financial service supplier, or to ensure the integrity and stability of the financial system. Where such measures do not conform with the provisions of the Agreement, they shall not be used as a means of avoiding the Member's commitments or obligations under the Agreement.

Another such clause results from the combination of Articles 1(3)(b)–(c) of the GATS and Article 1(b) of the GATS Annex on Financial Services that excludes monetary and other macroeconomic policies from the ambit of application of the GATS. With the progressive shift of trade rule-making away from multilateralism and toward regionalism, carve-outs are now present in all Free Trade Agreements with a financial services component. Over time,

[25] There is a vast amount of literature on carve-outs. Among the most representative contribution are: Lazaros E. Panourgias, *Banking Regulation and World Trade Law: GATS, EU and "Prudential" Institution Building* (Oxford: Hart Publishing, 2006); Mamiko Yokoi-Arai, "GATS" Prudential Carve Out in Financial Services and its Relation with Prudential Regulation' (2008) 57 *International and Comparative Law Quarterly* 613; Regis Bismuth, "Financial Sector Regulation and Financial Services Liberalization at the Crossroads: The Relevance of International Standards in WTO Law" (2010) 44 *Journal of World Trade* 489.

the sophistication of the Annexes on Financial Services contained in Free Trade Agreement has increased. For instance, the Transpacific Partnership Agreement (TPP Agreement) heavily innovates the regulatory apparatus for trade in financial services in terms of coverage of actual services as well as in the regulatory treatment, which comprises among other things data-sharing requirements, transparency, and regulation of innovative financial products. At the same time, the sophistication of prudential carve-outs has increased. The TPP Annex on Financial Services contains four different carve-outs dealing with prudential measures, monetary stability, and international payments, as well as money laundering.[26]

In the realm of international investment policy, carve-outs are a more recent addition. The old generation of IIAs was mostly focused on foreign direct investment, and only later on IIAs did start to protect portfolio investments, such as loans, stocks and shares, and debt obligations. As we have seen in Chapter 5, even without sector-specific financial carve-outs, regulatory autonomy was nonetheless partially ensured by the presence of necessity clauses, which if interpreted broadly still enabled governments to exclude regulatory policy and crisis management actions from the scope of agreements. In the last generation of IIAs, financial and sovereign debt carve-outs are a constant feature. For instance, in the Chapter on Trade in Services, Investment, and E-Commerce of the proposed *EU–Vietnam Free Trade and Investment Agreement* there is an Annex on Public Debt that specifically excludes debt restructurings from the coverage of the Agreement. The clause states:

> No claim that a restructuring of debt of a Party breaches an obligation under Section 2 [Investment Protection] may be submitted to, or if already submitted, be pursued under Section 3 [Resolution of Investment Disputes and Investment Court System] if the restructuring is a negotiated restructuring at the time of submission, or becomes a negotiated restructuring after such submission.[27]

A similar clause is contained also in the Investment chapter of the TPP Agreement,[28] which however, allows in principle litigation on sovereign debt as long as the claimants demonstrate that the default constitutes an unlawful expropriation and is not subject to a debt restructuring.[29]

[26] Trans-Pacific Partnership Agreement, Chapter 11, Article 11.

[27] Free Trade Agreement between the European Union and the Socialist Republic of Vietnam, Chapter 8, Annex on Public Debt.

[28] Trans-Pacific Partnership Agreement, Annex 9-G, Public Debt.

[29] Trans-Pacific Partnership Agreement Annex 9-G(1).

9.2.1. *Protecting Regulatory Autonomy*

Carve-outs operate to create a separation of jurisdiction between two broad regulatory goals: economic integration, and regulatory or policy autonomy. While economic integration falls under the rules of the treaty, financial or monetary stability is subject to a decentralized jurisdiction that is subject to national sovereignty. The role of carve-outs is therefore to distribute and assign regulatory power on economic stability, leaving full control over economic stability to home states. Therefore, with the caveat that such measures "shall not be used as a means of avoiding the Member's commitments or obligations under the Agreement,"[30] states are essentially free to devise whichever policy they deem appropriate to achieve their stability objectives. Even if the measure undermines another member's entitlements under the GATS, or if they hurt the financial position of a foreign investor this would still be the case.

Carve-outs give much policy space to states on financial stability matters, which members use to adopt a wide variety of policies. First, a member can adopt monetary and financial policies aimed at influencing the volume, destination, and composition of capital flows.[31] Capital controls are undoubtedly the most discussed measures in this regard. The use of controls benefits the states adopting them, but it undermines partner countries' economic integration entitlements. Indeed, controls reduce the freedom of investment and capital mobility normally enjoyed by foreign investors and traders. Second, and more importantly, states are free to regulate and sometimes discriminate when they need to. Examples of such measures are infinite. The local authorities might refuse or limit banking licenses to foreign firms; they might put equity caps on foreign investors; require the use of local management teams; or impose stricter prudential standards. Hence, while the domestic measure satisfies a domestic stability concern, it nevertheless reduces partner countries' entitlements to market access or capital mobility and, ultimately, financial integration.

Third, states are free to discriminate between domestic and foreign firms in the context of crisis-resolution policies. Discrimination between local and foreign banks might occur in all stages during a crisis. Often national supervisory authorities intervene to stabilize markets by rescuing failing financial institutions or by providing emergency liquidity assistance. In doing so, financial authorities sometimes distinguish between local

30 GATS Annex on Financial Services, Paragraph 2(a).

31 See Jonathan D. Ostry, Atish R. Ghosh, Karl Habermeier, Luc Laeven, Marcos Chamon, Mahvash S. Qureshi, and Annamaria Kokenyne, "Managing Capital Inflows: What Tools to Use," IMF Staff Discussion Note SDN/11/06, International Monetary Fund (2011).

financial institutions and foreign financial institutions by privileging the local institutions.[32] Discriminatory bailouts were particularly acute during the recent crisis, when supervisors refused to bailout or to provide emergency liquidity assistance to foreign-invested banks.[33] Finally, in the event of a insolvency of a cross-border bank, those financial authorities that apply the territorial approach to insolvency (for instance, the United States) follow a legal regime that specifically favors local over foreign creditors.[34]

The large majority of the literature on the relationship between capital mobility and financial stability sees the separation between integration goals and prudential or monetary concerns as a fundamental and necessary feature of the global financial system.[35] This view is, probably, largely informed by the experience of emerging economies in dealing with situation of financial and monetary distress. It is not unusual to see countries adopt capital controls to deal with surges of capital inflows or to protect balance of payments during a monetary crisis.[36] Without emergency safeguards, of which carve-outs are one example, governments would risk being sued in international courts for the actions of their central banks. More commentators now agree on the view that despite the costs to international investors in terms of capital mobility or financial returns, the imposition of *temporary* emergency measures to counter monetary instability achieves a globally optimal regulatory goal. The measure is indeed no different than the suspension of depositors' contractual rights to withdraw their funds during a forced bank holiday. In both cases, the

[32] The issue was, for instance, discussed in the investment dispute *Saluka* v. *Czech Republic*. See *Saluka Investments* BV v. *Czech Republic*, Partial Award, IIC 210 (2006), 17 March 2006, Permanent Court of Arbitration.

[33] Anne van Aaken and Jurgen Kurtz, "Prudence or Discrimination? Emergency Measures, The Global Financial Crisis and International Economic Law" (2009) 12 *Journal of International Economic Law* 859; Bart De Meester, "The Global Financial Crisis and Government Support for Banks: What Role for the GATS?" (2010) 13 *Journal of International Economic Law* 27; Thomas Cottier and Markus Krajewski, "What Role for Non-Discrimination and Prudential Standards in International Financial Law?" (2010) 13 *Journal of International Economic Law* 817.

[34] For a good overview of the legal problems affecting cross-border bank resolution, see Rosa Maria Lastra (ed.) *Cross Border Bank Insolvency* (Oxford: Oxford University Press, 2011); IMF, "Resolution of Cross-Border Banks – A Proposed Framework for Enhanced Coordination," International Monetary Fund (2010); Basel Committee on Banking Supervision, "Report and Recommendations of the Cross-Border Bank Resolution Group," Bank for International Settlements (March 2010).

[35] See, for instance, Kevin Gallagher, *Emerging Markets and the Re-regulation of Modern Finance* (Ithaca, NY: Cornell University Press, 2014).

[36] See, IMF, *The Liberalization and Management of Capital Flows: An Institutional View* (14 November 2012).

long-term costs of instability largely outweigh the short-term pain of capital controls.

Yet, it is impossible not to see that the protection that financial regulators receive from carve-outs is quite exceptional and puts finance on a very different footing from all other industrial sectors.

9.2.2. *Carve-outs and Global Systemic Risk*

The protection of financial sovereignty ensured by carve-outs created an ambiguous situation in which financial integration was regulated and protected, but policies to maintain market stability remained excluded. The legal framework on financial integration offered by trade and investment law ultimately encouraged the creation of a global financial system in which states enjoy all the benefits of financial integration without bearing its costs in terms of better global financial governance.

The question then is: shall regulatory cooperation be a necessary prerequisite to financial integration? In this regard, if there is a lesson that recent financial crises have taught us, it is that regulatory cooperation cannot be left out of the picture unless states are prepared to live with the constant danger of cross-border spillovers and systemic risks. In a global financial system, financial interconnectedness necessarily demands the presence of a system of rules that is able to control the transmission of instability from one side of the financial system to the other. Hence, the only option to sustain the stability of the global financial system is therefore to push for more regulatory cooperation. We can appreciate this argument if we look at the role of the law in a domestic financial system. Given the interconnectedness between firms, supervisory and licensing rules limit participation in the national financial market to only those financial institutions that satisfy basic criteria of soundness and stability.

Given the interconnectedness of financial institutions and the logical proclivity for spillovers and systemic risk, banks must bear the costs of their participation in an interconnected financial network. In order to participate within the network, they need to comply with stringent disclosure or prudential rules, and allocate part of their assets to limit liquidity or solvency risk.[37] If a bank fails to comply with the minimal prudential rules, thereby triggering systemic consequences, the most immediate reaction from the supervisory authorities

[37] On the role of prudential regulations in internalizing the externalities of banking, see David T. Llewellyn, "Role and Scope of Regulation and Supervision," in Gerard Caprio Jr. (ed.) *Handbook of Safeguarding Global Financial Stability: Political, Social, Cultural, and Economic Theories and Models* (London: Elsevier, 2013), pp. 451–64.

is to isolate the bank from the wider financial network. Supervisory authorities would then withdraw the bank's license and impose extremely high fines on management.

When we move to the global financial system, however, the philosophy changes drastically. According to trade and investment law, a state is able to participate in an integrated financial network as long as it agrees to open its own market to foreign firms. However, no member is required to follow rules of conduct that would minimize the costs of its poor domestic stability policies on its partner countries. Similarly, no member is required to coordinate its financial policies with other members – for instance, by signing a Memorandum of Understanding on cross-border banking supervision and resolution. Of course, states are in principle free to refrain from integrating their markets with countries that do not satisfy the minimum criteria of stability. They also are, in principle, free to demand supplementary conditions that would reduce the risk of instability. For instance, Article VII of the GATS and Article 3(a) of the GATS Annex on Financial Services allow the use of recognition agreements. Furthermore, during negotiations, a state could request its negotiating partner to level up its regulatory standards. However, both instruments are voluntary measures, whose adoption is left to the negotiating power of each signatory. If what really matters is market access, states will clearly be incentivized to reduce regulatory barriers, not to erect them. Exporting groups will naturally demand the removal of stringent prudential or supervisory rules in the foreign jurisdiction. Certainly, they will not beg to be subject to a more costly and burdensome regulatory framework. Hence, states will be induced by the strong lobbying pressure of exporting firms to reduce whatever regulatory and supervisory barriers they might encounter.[38]

The regulatory framework for financial integration is still based on an old era of finance, in which government failures and global systemic risk did not play a major role. The main objective of the international trade and investment agreement dealing with financial services is to achieve financial integration with minimal interference on the regulatory freedom of states. To protect states' financial sovereignty, those treaties give them the utmost freedom when it comes to financial and monetary stability policies. Whether those policies will ultimately transmit global systemic risk is not really an issue for international law. Members can still resort to prudential carve-outs to adopt more stringent standards or impose capital controls to safeguard their own

[38] Eric A. Posner and Alan O. Sykes, *Economic Foundations of International Law* (Cambridge, MA and London: Harvard University Press, 2012), p. 263.

domestic stability in the event of a crisis.[39] But they do so at their own expense. International law certainly does not do anything to prevent such systemic risk from arising, and certainly does not punish the member that created such risk. The political economy bargain at the basis of the international trade and investment law is therefore outdated to cope with the problems of global systemic risk. It does not incentivize members to consider the external implication of their domestic financial and monetary policies, or to internalize the global effects of their domestic policies.

By leaving financial policies outside the scope of the agreements, carve-outs break the economic logic of trade and investment integration that views the rights of market access and investment protection as fundamental tools to enhance good governance. Without the pressure to adopt globally efficient prudential standards or to cooperate on financial policies, states are not responsible for the instability originating from their financial policies or for the otherwise negative externalities of their conduct, while still being able to enjoy the benefits of financial integration. International trade and investment law have turned the bargain on financial integration upside-down. It was like giving the right to use public roads to car drivers without first ensuring the presence of a traffic code. This would incentivize drivers to drive carelessly, ignore the interests of other drivers or pedestrians, and ultimately lead to accidents.

To conclude, the separation between market access and domestic stability policies described above and the general exclusion of domestic stability policies from any international legal scrutiny is a dangerous combination. The law has created the "road" for economic interdependence without imposing the "traffic rules" to ensure its stability. States are free to set their own economic agendas, even though it will not be sustainable in the long term, and crucially, even if it might cause negative repercussions to partner countries. States are relatively free to opt out from the obligations set in international economic integration treaties, even if it causes a loss to partner countries. They can also adopt domestic stability policies that, when producing spillovers, might undermine partner countries' domestic stability. The law focuses only on enabling states to protect their domestic stability, by giving them the widest possible policy space. By doing so, however, it does not encourage them to take into account the external effects of their policies.

This philosophy is inefficient from a stability viewpoint, because it distorts the incentives of states to internalize the externalities of their domestic

[39] Yokoi-Arai, above note 25.

policies and to price correctly their participation in an integrated economic system. In a world where global systemic risk is a real possibility, states should be encouraged to adopt the safest and strongest regulatory framework, not to dismantle it. Furthermore, given the proclivity of contagion brought about by financial integration, the right to participate in an integrated financial system should be granted only when the state demonstrates its intention to have in place a regulatory and policy framework that minimizes global systemic risk.

9.2.3. *Some Recent Developments*

Some recent developments in preferential trade agreements might change this course, as a few treaties have been indeed equipped with clauses that push for stronger regulatory coordination on financial standards. For the first time, EU Free Trade Agreements and the TPP, the mega-regional agreement originally meant to liberalize trade between ten American and East Asian countries, set a very tenuous link between regulatory cooperation on financial standards and market access in financial services. For instance, the prudential carve-out of the EU–Vietnam Free Trade and Investment Agreement states that:

> Each Party shall make its best endeavors to the extent possible to ensure that internationally agreed standards for regulation and supervision in the financial services sector and for the fight against tax evasion and avoidance are implemented and applied in its territory.

Similarly, according to Article 11.12 of the TPP, a party can recognize autonomously, through harmonization, or by an agreement with another party, the prudential measures of another party. This clause should not be interpreted narrowly to encompass only prudential regulation such as capital adequacy or disclosure standards, but be intended to cover a broader range of measures, including supervisory arrangements for banks and clearinghouses, as well as resolution actions.[40]

It is probably too early to assess whether these timid developments indicate a clear direction toward the incorporation of financial policies in financial integration agreements. The current formulation of those clauses is very far from suggesting a movement toward the inclusion of financial standards in regional trade agreements. Both clauses do not grant any rights as they are indeed construed as mere suggestions for regulators; this prevents them from being used in a dispute. Yet, they indicate that trade negotiators and financial

[40] Transpacific Partnership Agreement, Article 11.12.2.

regulators are now aware of the need of ensuring cooperation on financial policies alongside the actual financial market integration.

9.3. REGULATORY PASSPORTS

To achieve a stable, and yet integrated, financial system it is therefore necessary to shift from a regulatory framework that privileges market opening toward one that ensures market resilience and compliance. To do so, it is necessary to put regulatory cooperation at the forefront of the financial integration agenda. One possible solution is to eliminate carve-outs and integrate financial standards and home–host supervisory agreements into international agreements with a financial services component. This would make states, wishing to integrate their financial system, more wary of the need of ensuring proper regulatory coordination.

Yet, international trade and investment agreements are probably too complex and cumbersome to deal with the complexities of international financial integration. First, as I will explain at the end of this chapter, the multilateral reach of the GATS is inherently in conflict with the problems of regulatory coordination, which require a narrower approach. Second, the regulatory machinery of international trade and investment agreements, which is tailored for market access and investment rights only, is simply not made for the specificities of financial policies. Rules on subsidies (if ever included in an agreement), fair and equitable treatment, transparency, and non-discrimination could easily enter into conflict with the particular needs of financial supervision.

A tailor-made approach to financial integration – an approach that guarantees both regulatory cooperation and market integration – is thus needed. One way to achieve this goal is to make market access rights for foreign firms and traders conditional on the adoption by the home and host financial authorities of a binding regulatory framework that addresses what the two authorities consider essential regulatory and supervisory aspects of cross-border finance. The regulatory rationale is to raise the price for the participation of financial institutions into the global financial system. Thus, only those institutions whose parent authorities accept to be bound by the regulatory and supervisory standards agreed in the agreement will be allowed to access a foreign market. Once the home/exporting country obtains the passport, the home firms and traders can then operate in all host jurisdictions that have signed the Passport agreement. I name this technique *Regulatory Passporting*.

Under this mechanism, if an exporting state wishes its domestic firms and traders to have access to a foreign financial market, it must first attain a financial Regulatory Passport granted by the importing/host state or by a regional authority. Only when the state subscribes to the regulatory requirements set in the Passport agreement can its domestic firms thus access the foreign markets. At the outset, it is essential to say that the Passport does not necessarily need to be an overarching agreement covering the entire spectrum of financial policies. On the contrary, sector-specific agreements could be signed between securities regulators, bank supervisors, or insurance supervisors. The Regulatory Passport, which is a binding international agreement, could envisage the adoption by the exporting/home state of core regulatory instruments to be agreed between the states parties to the agreement, such as capital adequacy and money-laundering standards, agreements on supervision and crisis resolution, and cooperation on frauds and market integrity. However, the same concept could be easily used to address regulatory concerns in sovereign debt, or even monetary policies; for instance, by inserting rules on budgetary transparency and fiscal sustainability. Thus, by putting regulatory cooperation as a condition for market access, the Regulatory Passport aims at incentivizing states to cooperate on financial policies. This will thus ensure that states will price correctly their participation in an integrated financial system.

9.3.1. *Essential Characteristics*

The idea of strengthening financial cooperation is not new. At the outset of the recent financial crises, some authors suggested integration of the Basel Accords into the various agreements promoting financial integration. For instance, Eva Hüpkes,[41] quickly followed by other finance specialists,[42] suggested signing a "New Concordat" and to integrate it into the GATS. The IMF similarly proposed in 2009 the adoption of a Code of Conduct on financial stability by national financial authorities covering prudential regulations, crisis resolution and home–host supervisory arrangements.[43]

The Regulatory Passport is based on a similar concept. Let us now see how it should work in practice. In this regard, the Regulatory Passport is a binding agreement between financial authorities of different countries that

[41] Eva Hüpkes, "Rivalry in Resolution: How to Reconcile Local Responsibilities and Global Interests?" (2010) 7 *European Company and Financial Law Review* 216.

[42] Stijn Claessens, Richard Herring, Dirk Schoenmaker, and Kimberly Summe, "Safer World Financial System: Improving the Resolution of Systemic Institutions," Geneva Reports on the World Economy 12, International Center for Monetary and Banking Studies and Centre for Economic Policy Research (2011), pp. 99–101.

[43] IMF, "Initial Lessons from the Crisis," International Monetary Fund (6 February 2009).

deals with: (1) the licensing and regulatory treatment applicable to firms and traders originating from one of the parties to the agreement; (2) the regulatory, supervisory, and (if agreed) also fiscal cooperation between the parties in matters of financial policy; (3) the settlement of disputes between the parties and the remedies available for violation of the agreement. Under the Regulatory Passport, firms authorized in the territory and under the law of one of the parties will be guaranteed market access and national treatment in the territory of the other parties, based on the condition that the competent national financial authorities have agreed to cooperate on financial policy. One of the key characteristics of this mechanism is its inherently preferential nature, which means that firms originating from countries that are not granted the Passport will be subject to different market access conditions and regulatory treatments.

Let us imagine three states wanting to further integrate their banking sector. According to my proposal, the states would subordinate their concession on the entry of foreign banks to the adoption in each state of equivalent (not necessarily identical) prudential regulations, highly developed supervisory arrangements, and agreed rules on crisis resolution. For instance, they could negotiate common rules on macro-prudential supervision, a binding burden-sharing arrangement for financial institutions, and common rules on deposit insurance. Whenever one of the members is found to be in violation of those rules (for instance, by refusing to implement a bail-in action on behalf of the partner supervisor), it would be automatically subject to the disciplinary actions set forth in the agreements. Similarly, if a fourth state would like to join in, it would be required to adopt the same rules. This approach is similar to the European Union's accession policy. If a state wants to accede to the EU, it must adopt the whole body of EU law: the so-called *acquis communautaire*.

The Regulatory Passport is essentially a very sophisticated Mutual Recognition Agreement that goes beyond the recognition of domestic regulation by including an additional regulatory and supervisory cooperation component. Mutual Recognition Agreement are essentially neutral instruments, in the sense that they can be used to level up the playing field or to level it down. The only requirement is that the two states agree to recognize each other's regulatory framework as adequate as a condition for accessing the foreign market.[44] In a classical mutual recognition framework, however, there is a risk of race-to-the-bottom as the host country does not have any particular surveillance power over the home country's regulatory and macroeconomic policies.

[44] Marguerite Bateman and Cynthia Beyea, "Mutual Recognition: A Step toward Greater Access to Global Market" (2008) 15 *The Investment Lawyer* 67.

Secondly, classical Mutual Recognition Agreements (MRAs) are quite limited in their coverage. Indeed, they are mainly used for securities regulations with regard to securities offering and disclosure.[45]

Yet, if properly corrected and managed, MRAs can achieve substantial regulatory convergence and lead to a race-to-the-top in stability policies. The EU Equivalency program discussed in Chapter 6 and the US Substituted Compliance program show the potential of mutual recognition to achieve race-to-the-top in regulatory coordination.[46] The SEC program, in particular, is very different from any other mutual recognition agreements insofar as it required the almost equivalent securities rules among the members and a stringent monitoring mechanism to prevent races-to-the-bottom.[47] In 2008, the United States and Australia signed an MRA[48] whereby each country contemplates the exemption of foreign stock exchanges and broker dealers from the application of domestic laws.[49] The US–Australia arrangement is, qualitatively, a very sophisticated MRA. First of all, it is a bilateral arrangement between like-minded regulators with similar regulatory philosophies. This means that the risk of races-to-the-bottom and regulatory competition were almost eliminated. Secondly, the two regulators agreed to meet periodically to reassess the regulatory compatibility and to share information on regulatory updates and possible problems. More importantly, the two regulators agreed to increase supervisory cooperation by allowing host supervisors to conduct inspections in the home territory, thereby reducing the "home-country risk."

Mutual Recognition shows that the appeal of market access can be used as a formidable tool to level up the regulatory and policy standards for financial stability, because it can force countries that are interested in accessing a particular market to coordinate their policies in that direction. The Regulatory Passport is based on the same philosophy. The difference is the regulatory

45 Pierre-Hugues Verdier, "Mutual Recognition in International Finance" (2001) 52 *Harvard International Law Journal* 55; Kalypso Nicolaidis and Gregory Shaffer, "Transnational Mutual Recognition Regimes: Governance without Global Government" (2005) 68 *Law and Contemporary Problems* 263.

46 Howell E. Jackson, "Substituted Compliance: The Emergence, Challenges, and Evolution of a New Regulatory Paradigm" (2015) 1 *Journal of Financial Regulation* 169; Alexey Artamonov, "Cross-border Application of OTC Derivatives Rules: Revisiting the Substituted Compliance Approach" (2016) 1 *Journal of Financial Regulation* 206.

47 Ethiopis Tafara and Robert J. Peterson, "A Blueprint for Cross-Border Access to U.S. Investors: A New International Framework" (2007) 48 *Harvard International Law Journal* 31.

48 Mutual Recognition Arrangement between the United States Securities and Exchange Commission and the Australia Securities and Investments Commission, together with the Australian Minister for Superannuation and Corporate Law.

49 Bateman and Beyea, above note 44.

framework that has to be agreed upon, which in the case of the Regulatory Passport is much wider. In a Regulatory Passport, the home and the host must agree not only on the equivalency of each other's prudential or disclosure rules (depending on whether the Passport deals with banking, securities, etc.), but also on all those issues that are necessary in a cross-border financial context. These include common supervisory rules for international financial institutions, central counterparties (CCPs), and traders, rules on cross-border resolution, location of liabilities, and so forth. Moreover, being Stability Passports binding agreements, they are equipped with a dispute-settlement mechanism. I will discuss this aspect in the next chapter.

One of the fundamental characteristics of the Regulatory Passport is that it links market access rights and regulatory cooperation duties. This means that the right of home firms and traders to access the host market is conditional on regulators' compliance with regulatory and supervisory rules. This aspect is critical for the success of the Passport, because the violation of regulatory cooperation rules could entitle the non-violating country to specific remedies, which might include the imposition of fines, the suspension of foreign firms' licenses, or even the revoking of market access rights.

9.3.2. *The Possible Content of the Regulatory Passport*

The SEC Substituted Compliance program and the EU Equivalency program are limited to securities offerings and, therefore, insufficient for tackling the complex regulatory problems discussed in this book. However, they shed a useful light on the possibility of using market access as an incentive to promote better financial governance. Since the Regulatory Passport is purely a regulatory and policy coordination mechanism – an empty box that can be filled with any content – it can be easily adapted virtually to each of the topics discussed in this book. The Regulatory Passport can indeed be tailored to the specific level of financial integration desired – from a simple agreement on prudential regulation, up to a binding code of conduct on monetary policies. One of the benefits of the Regulatory Passport is indeed the flexibility it offers to each state in terms of regulatory coordination. Without imposing a single platform on each state, it can allow the highest degree of flexibility and thus be adapted to the specificities of each integrated financial market.

Banking and securities regulations could be one of the obvious topics addressed in a Regulatory Passport. For instance, home and host supervisors could agree on the adoption of similar capital adequacy standards for banks and insurance firms, or disclosure rules for corporate issuers. While regulatory coordination could be achieved also by any mutual recognition agreement, the uniqueness of the Regulatory Passport is its ability to link market access concessions to more complex cooperation issues. In this regard, the Regulatory Passport could deal with those policies that are historically subject to compliance problems such as supervision, enforcement, and resolution. At present home–host supervisory coordination on banking is subject to non-binding bilateral cooperation agreements based on the BCBS standards, Memoranda of Understanding (MoUs), Supervisory Colleges and Crisis Management Groups.[50] None of these mechanisms, however, is able to address the dangers of the principal–agent problem.[51] As shown in Chapter 3, supervisory authorities often refuse to carry on their commitments by refusing to allow inspections or by transmitting data. Problems of cooperation on inspections and evidence arise also in the field of securities supervision. If home–host supervisory cooperation was embedded in the Passport, the refusal of one of the two supervisors to carry on its commitments would constitute a violation of the Passport agreement and, therefore, could entitle the non-violating party to suspend or revoke the license of the foreign banks or traders.

Resolution is also a potential area of cooperation to be tackled in regulatory passports, especially in the light of the new statutory powers of resolution authorities. International bail-ins are very complex procedures, which in order to work require the cooperation of various authorities some of which are not involved in Crisis Management Groups: supervisors, regulators, and courts. There are thousands of issues to consider before triggering a bail-in, including the location and amount of bail-in liabilities, the treatment of foreign creditors, the availability of emergency liquidity, not to mention the systemic risk implication of the resolution. If a foreign authority or a court refuses to recognize and implement the bail-in decision of its partner, the entire resolution procedure might be in jeopardy. Without a binding comprehensive agreement in place that tackles the critical aspects of the resolution, the refusal of one authority to cooperate does not carry any legal consequences. Alternatively, if cross-border resolution rules were to be included in the Regulatory Passport, their violation would trigger the disciplinary actions set in the agreement. This would probably minimize the compliance risks and encourage more cooperation. Besides bail-in rules, the two partners could also include in the passport burden-sharing arrangements which discipline the level of fiscal intervention

[50] Duncan Alford, "Supervisory Colleges: The Global Financial Crisis and Improving International Supervisory Coordination" (2010) 24 *Emory International Law Review* 57.

[51] The College of Supervisors did not have any power over national supervisory authorities in EU law, which could easily disregard the College's suggestions. See Tobias H. Troger, "Organizational Choices of Banks and the Effective Supervision of Transnational Financial Institutions" (2013) 48 *Texas International Law Journal* 177, p. 207.

required by each national authority in the event of a bail-out and the procedural mechanisms of intervention.[52] A common and binding framework in which each authority knows in advance the behavior of its foreign partner would not only reduce the panic faced by supervisors during the frantic hours of a bank collapse, but would also avoid the risks of national solutions arising from the principal–agent problem, and the consequences in terms of global instability.

9.3.3. *Beyond Regulation: Macro-stability Issues*

Sovereign debt could also be subject to a similar regulatory framework. In Chapter 5, I argued that the root of the problem of sovereign defaults is the behavior of debtor countries. If macro policies are indeed the main cause of concern for foreign investors, what we need is a regulatory framework that prevents defaults rather than addressing them. Since the current mechanisms of international law are deficient in constraining the borrowing behaviors of governments, the adoption of a Regulatory Passport focused on sovereign debt policy could help in this context. For instance, the Passport could refer to the IMF or the OECD Code for the regulatory treatment accorded to portfolio investment or contain new rules. The mechanism will be similar to that applied to banking or securities. Before allowing their investors to buy sovereign bonds from a foreign country, the investors' parent authorities should make sure that the host country is bound to a proper regulatory framework that reduces the likelihood of default.[53]

Furthermore, the underlying treaty could contain rules that constrain the borrowing discretion of policymakers or increase fiscal transparency.[54]

[52] Charles Goodhart and Dirk Schoenmaker, "Fiscal Burden Sharing in Cross-Border Banking Crises" (2009) 5 *International Journal of Central Banking* 141; Dirk Schoenmaker, "Burden Sharing for Cross-Border Banks" (2011) 18 *Banco de Espana – Estabilidad Financiera* 31.

[53] At the outset, it is important to note that host countries are already subject to a rather stringent regulatory framework through the adoption of bilateral investment treaties. However, these instruments are in my view unsuited to regulate fiscal matters. First of all, they apply a regulatory framework that has been designed to protect the interests of FDI investors rather than those of portfolio investors. Indeed, the regulatory platform for international investment grew out of the customary international law on the treatment of aliens, and it still relies on vague standards of treatment and an ambiguous jurisprudence that, while rightly addressing the long-term problems of greenfield investment, is certainly not suited for the complexity of international finance.

[54] For a possible list, albeit focused also on budget and domestic fiscal policy, see Barry Eichengreen, Robert Feldman, Jeff Liebman, Jürgen von Hagen, and Charles Wyplosz, "Public Debts: Nuts, Bolts and Worries," Geneva Reports on the World Economy 13, International Center for Monetary and Banking Studies (2011), available at http://dev3.cepr.org/pubs/books/CEPR/Geneva13.pdf, pp. 15–31.

For instance, the Passport could require the adoption of a mechanism of check and balances in the national legislation, whereby for any given legislature, policymakers could borrow only up to a certain point. Borrowing limits could be inserted in the constitution or in a special statute.[55] If the two countries are particularly keen to increase their economic integration, they could set more stringent rules along the lines of the European Union's Stability and Growth Pact, which sets a limit in the debt–GDP ratio of EU members, beyond which the members are subject to disciplinary rules.[56] Secondly, the treaty could mandate the creation of contact points in which monetary and fiscal authorities could discuss the respective macroeconomic framework and the level of bilateral investment. Finally, portfolio investment treaties could be complemented by a sovereign debt-restructuring mechanism along the lines of those recently proposed by the IMF.[57]

The IMF or the OECD (for its members) would monitor the compliance with financial, fiscal, and other macroeconomic standards. Whenever a member is found in violation of such standards partner countries would automatically be allowed to suspend their concessions on market access and standards of treatment. Legally, the suspension of concessions would not be a form of retaliation, but rather a mechanism of preventive self-defense. By doing so, the IMF and the OECD would essentially rely on the regulatory platforms offered by international investment law as a way to induce compliance. This would also indirectly harden the soft norms contained in the IMF and OECD treaties.

9.4. THE POLITICAL ECONOMY OF REGULATORY PASSPORTING

To understand the benefits of the Regulatory Passport as a regulatory tool it is useful to turn briefly to the political economy of financial policies. As I have reiterated throughout the book, financial policies are subject to political bargains. In this situation, regulatory authorities are naturally incentivized to pursue their most immediate objectives, and to avoid painful, but necessary,

[55] *Ibid.*, p. 21.

[56] Fabian Amtenbrink and Jakob de Haan, "Economic Governance in the European Union: Fiscal Policy Discipline Versus Flexibility" (2003) 40 *Common Market Law Review* 1075; Jacques Delors, "JCMS 50th Anniversary Lecture: Economic Governance in the European Union: Past, Present and Future" (2012) 51 *Journal of Common Market Studies* 169.

[57] Anne O. Krueger, *A New Approach to Sovereign Debt Restructuring* (Washington, DC: International Monetary Fund, 2002); IMF, "Proposed Features of a Sovereign Debt Restructuring Mechanism," International Monetary Fund, 12 February 2003; IMF, "Sovereign Debt Restructuring—Recent Developments and Implications for the Fund's Legal and Policy Framework," International Monetary Fund (26 April 2013), available at https://www.imf.org/external/np/pp/eng/2013/042613.pdf.

structural reforms.[58] For instance, in the context of international capital adequacy standards, various authors have highlighted that capital adequacy rules are the result of a political bargain between the interest of banks, on the one hand, and the interest of depositors, on the other.[59] Furthermore, with regard to fiscal policy, experience had demonstrated that, in absence of political solidarity among different political groups and social cohesion, structural economic reforms are indeed difficult to implement.[60]

In such a situation, the absence of long-term vision of national political elites, coupled with the principal–agent relationship at the core of stability policies, will render extremely difficult a voluntary reduction of sovereignty and the pursuit of interstate cooperation. States will simply not accept any binding rule. The most immediate consequence of this theory is that financial nationalism is a rather appealing policy for politicians, in the same way that protectionism is appealing for international trade policy.[61] Thus, without mechanisms to counter this tendency, there is a risk that countries would sacrifice their long-term welfare goals for short-term political gains.[62] Hence, in a world where protectionism and discriminatory domestic regulations constitute a constant threat, it is necessary to adopt mechanisms that minimize such risk. International law achieves precisely such an objective.[63]

9.4.1. *The Lessons from International Trade*

The law and economics theory of international law posits that states enter into international binding agreements to address the externalities of unilateral actions.[64] Cooperation allows them to move from the non-cooperative Nash

[58] Trachtman, above note 4.

[59] Verdier, above note 45, at p. 66; David Andrew Singer, *Regulating Capital: Setting Standards for the International Financial System* (Ithaca, NY: Cornell University Press, 2007).

[60] To be effective, fiscal discipline requires painful labor market and welfare state reforms that would readily encounter political opposition, making them politically difficult to implement. McKay notes that, in the past, only national parties with strong political appeal could implement major welfare state reforms. See David McKay, "The Political Sustainability of the European Monetary Union" (1999) 29 *British Journal of Political Science* 463.

[61] Sykes, "Protectionism as a "Safeguard'," above note 4, p. 276.

[62] International investment agreements have a similar dynamic. Here the incentive for states to seize properties or to adopt regulation that disfavors foreign investors does not come from import industries, but from within the government. Expropriations, lack of transparency, and discriminations against investors are usually adopted in order to serve domestic interests (favor local industries in procurement practices, maintain the control of certain industries or areas, or more simply, a bias against foreign investors).

[63] Sykes, "Protectionism as a 'Safeguard'," above note 4, p. 276.

[64] Alan O. Sykes, "International Law," in A. Mitchell Polinsky and Steven Shavell (eds.) *Handbook of Law and Economics, Volume 1* (London: Elsevier, 2007); Posner and Sykes, above note 38.

equilibrium in which each state maximizes its own welfare to the detriment of the partner countries' welfare, toward a Pareto-efficient equilibrium in which states internalize the externalities of their domestic policies.[65] One strategy to offset the problem of non-cooperative policies (either financial nationalism or protectionism) is to mobilize export interests.[66]

The law and economics literature on international trade has demonstrated that in order to work, the international trading system needs to be construed upon the right of investors or exporters, rather than importers. Only the former will guarantee the necessary political weight to battle protectionism. Exporters and investors have usually a powerful lobbying voice with their own governments. By granting to states the rights to access foreign markets and be subject to a regulatory level playing field with local firms, international law essentially mobilizes the domestic political coalitions that favor market liberalization, while at the same time it neutralizes those groups that oppose cooperation.[67] In doing so, the law also allows the realignment of domestic political economy interests toward a positive long-term equilibrium, thereby discouraging the government from pursuing short-term political gains lured by powerful lobbying interests.[68] Not surprisingly, economic integration has been construed, at least outside of the European Union,[69] as the legalization of export and foreign investment interests.[70] The political economy bargain at the basis of international trade agreements is centered on a mutual exchange of concessions for market access – a *do-ut-des* in which the core element of the bargain is the enhancement of export and investment interests.[71] In investment treaties, the bargain is not market access itself, but rather investment protection.

65 Eric A. Posner and Alan O. Sykes, "Efficient Breach of International Law: Optimal Remedies, 'Legalized Noncompliance' and Related Issues" (2011–2012) 110 *Michigan Law Review* 243, p. 247; Eric A. Posner, "International Law: A Welfarist Approach" (2006) 73 *University of Chicago Law Review* 487; Sykes, *ibid.*; Jack L. Goldsmith and Eric A. Posner, *The Limits of International Law* (New York: Oxford University Press, 2005); Andrew T. Guzman, *How International Law Works: A Rational Choice Theory* (New York: Oxford University Press, 2008); Posner and Sykes, above note 38; Robert E. Scott and Paul B. Stephan, *The Limits of Leviathan: Contract Theory and the Enforcement of International Law* (New York: Cambridge University Press, 2006).

66 Sykes, *ibid.*; Posner and Sykes, above note 38.

67 Joel Trachtman more recently explained this methodology. See Trachtman, above note 4.

68 Sykes, above note 4; Posner and Sykes, above note 38.

69 In EU law, the bodies of norms that discipline the single market have direct effect in domestic legal systems. On the contrary, outside of the EU, trade and investment agreements do not have any direct effect in the domestic territory. Hence, legally speaking, consumers do not have any legal right to ask their government to reduce trade barriers.

70 Sykes, "Public versus Private Enforcement," above note 4, pp. 646–8.

71 Bernard M. Hoekman and Michel M. Kostecki, *The Political Economy of the World Trading System: The WTO and Beyond* (Oxford: Oxford University Press, 2012).

However, even in this case, the ultimate objective is similar: to enhance the opportunities for cross-border investment. From a legal viewpoint, the stability of the whole bargain is ensured by the fact that those domestic groups that are more interested in expanding the scope of the market – multinational banks and investment firms – are also the ones that are directly or indirectly granted market access rights.

Furthermore, international treaties and customary international laws have also the fundamental function of giving a signal to partner countries of the willingness of the states to abide by their commitments.[72] For instance, WTO laws give a signal to exporting countries that the importing state will maintain the tariff profile and the non-discriminatory domestic regulatory regime inscribed in the Member's Schedule of Commitments. Bilateral Investment Treaties, similarly, serve the fundamental purpose of giving investors the certainty that the host country authorities will maintain a specific regulatory regime favorable to international investment, as specified in the standards of treatment contained in the Treaty.

9.4.2. *The Economics of Passporting*

The mechanism of Regulatory Passport is based on the same rationale. It uses powerful lobbying interests to promote international cooperation. The only difference is that, here, the goal is global stability rather than simple market liberalization. Earlier, I demonstrated that the domestic groups that favor financial cooperation are usually not well represented in the political economy bargains that take place in domestic policy.[73] By linking market access to the adoption of a binding regulatory framework for financial stability, the Regulatory Passport mobilizes the domestic interests that are more likely to drive the behavior of the government toward financial cooperation: large financial institutions with strong export and investment interests. Since market access can be achieved only by agreeing to a binding regulatory framework that promotes financial stability – for instance, by virtue of a binding crisis-resolution regime or a code on sovereign borrowing – states will be forced to cooperate on financial matters. Thus, they will be forced to adopt global stability-enhancing policies. Essentially, the Regulatory

[72] Guzman, above note 65.

[73] The political economy of the Regulatory Passport is similar to that of free trade, to the extent that unrepresented lobby groups (citizens) join their cause with more powerful lobby groups (the exporters). See Sykes, above note 4; Schwartz and Sykes, above note 4; Trachtman, above note 4; Verdier, above note 45.

Passport leverages on the desire of states to access foreign markets in order to achieve regulatory cooperation. Home states are forced to internalize the social costs of their domestic stability policies, while at the same time, the law achieves the objective to price correctly the costs and benefits of participation in an integrated economic system. The reduction of sovereignty in exchange for the gains of economic integration prevents domestic politics from derailing long-term economic efficiency, as it shifts the political economy bargains from the national to the international level. Essentially, it provides an excuse for national authorities to lock in domestic reforms and to adopt long-term visions.

The Regulatory Passport is a Pareto-efficient policy, as it raises the level playing field of international finance without making any country worse off. Home and partner states will be bound to the same minimal level of protection of domestic stability, which ought to reduce the risks of global instability, while at the same time discouraging the pursuit of short-term domestic political interests. Exporters (not necessarily only financial services exporters) will provide the domestic political support for international agreements that will offer the political base on which government will be able to implement structural reforms. In doing so they will offset the lobby groups that oppose structural reforms or that promote more profitable lax financial regulation.[74] Indeed, any violation of the codes will mean reduced market access or the suspension of investment treaty rights.

One of the key elements of the Regulatory Passport is reciprocity. In its simplest form, reciprocity subordinates the granting of a particular benefit or penalty by one state to another to the adoption of the same measure in the other state.[75] Reciprocity is, in its essence, a mutual exchange of benefits between states based on the adoption of a similar regulatory framework. Only those states that adopt such a framework and abide by their commitments can benefit from the positive externalities that arise from participation in the agreement. In the context of cross-border banking policies, reciprocity has a fundamental function in creating the incentives toward compliance and in leveling the playing field for financial stability. By subordinating the adoption of a particular regulatory platform for financial stability to the mutual adoption of the same framework in another country, reciprocity creates a closed regulatory area in which policies are coordinated. This, in turn, enhances the institutional underpinnings of financial integration, and incentivizes the

[74] Verdier, *ibid.*, p. 66.

[75] Robert O. Keohane, "Reciprocity in International Relations" (1986) 40 *International Organisation* 1.

adoption of the same measure by outside members, which wish to enter the "club." Indeed, it would be enough for a limited number of core members – whose financial markets are particularly attractive to foreign investors – to adopt the same regulatory framework to attract other non-core members. Moreover, by enabling states to suspend their commitments toward another state (be they market access, recognition, or direct support) in the event of non-compliance, reciprocity legitimizes retaliation.

9.5. THE DEMISE OF MULTILATERALISM IN FINANCE

Before concluding, it is worth spending some time on the logic of preferentialism in finance or, as some authors have called it, "minilateralism."[76] Moving from a market access-based integration model toward a stability-based model necessarily entails some costs. As Dirk Schoenmaker argued in his financial trilemma, achieving a stable, integrated, and sovereign financial system is almost impossible as one of the objectives must be necessarily given up.[77] Like many other regulatory approaches, while the Regulatory Passport tries to accommodate competing objectives, it inevitably gives prevalence to some. In this regard, it is unquestionable that the need to increase regulatory cooperation and compliance will inevitably demand the sacrifice of non-discrimination. More specifically, the Regulatory Passport will demand a certain reduction in the scope of financial markets and the sacrifice of multilateral and non-discriminatory integration promoted by the GATS, in favor of a preferential type of integration based on reciprocity and common rules among states with similar regulatory philosophies.

More than any other agreement, the GATS embodies a vision of international finance in which financial institutions from different countries are permitted to provide financial services across borders or in jurisdictions different from their own.[78] At the core of the GATS' mechanism for market expansion there is the Most Favored Nation clause (MFN) of Article II:2.[79] The

[76] On minilateralism, see Moises Naim, "Minilateralism: The Magic Number to Get Real International Action" (21 June 2009) *Missing Links, Foreign Policy Magazine Online*, available at http://foreignpolicy.com/2009/06/21/minilateralism/; Chris Brummer, *Minilateralism: How Trade Alliances, Soft Law, and Financial Engineering Are Redefining Economic Statecraft* (Cambridge: Cambridge University Press, 2014).

[77] Dirk Schoenmaker, *Governance of International Banking: The Financial Trilemma* (Oxford: Oxford University Press, 2013).

[78] Eric Leroux, "Trade in Financial Services under the World Trade Organization" (2002) 36 *Journal of World Trade* 413.

[79] Cottier and Krajewski, above note 33.

MFN is one of the oldest principles of international economic law, dating back to the eighteenth century.[80] This clause prohibits WTO members from negatively discriminating against other members with regard to any benefits granted by WTO law.[81] In essence, whenever a member grants to another trading partner a more favorable concession on market access or domestic regulations, the same concession must be automatically extended to all the other WTO members. As such, the MFN is a formidable tool to promote progressive trade liberalization. Members have the option to derogate from the MFN. For instance, a state can a priori exclude certain regulations from the coverage of Article II;[82] or it can lawfully engage in regional or preferential integration only with certain members under Article VII.[83] However, like for the other non-discrimination rules, this option is voluntary and subject to the negotiating power of each state. Multilateralism is the default rule in the GATS, and its main objective.

There is no doubt that non-discrimination worked – and still works – very well for international trade in goods, and other services. However, it is questionable whether it is an appropriate regulatory principle for financial integration. More explicitly, it is doubtful whether it is safe to indiscriminately extend market access concessions to states whose financial systems do not offer enough guarantees of stability. In a world in which global systemic risk is a very realistic possibility, a state would be selective as to which financial systems it would want to integrate with. The regulatory system set up in the GATS, however, does exactly the opposite. Once a state has opened its borders to the financial institutions of another member, it must automatically extend the concessions to the firms of all other members. Foreign firms can enter its market unchallenged, and domestic firms can go abroad and engage in meaningful business in other jurisdictions. It is true that states retain wide discretion

80 Hoekman and Kostecki, above note 71, p. 27.

81 William Davey and Joost Pauwelyn, “MFN Unconditionality: A Legal Analysis of the Concept in View of its Evolution in the GATT/WTO Jurisprudence with Particular Reference to the Issue of ‘Like Product’,” in Thomas Cottier and Petros Mavroidis (eds.) *Regulatory Barriers and the Principle of Non-discrimination in WTO Law* (Ann Arbor, MI: University of Michigan Press, 2000), pp. 13–50.

82 According to Cottier and Krajewski, ninety-three members (counting EC12 as one) have sought legal cover for 491 measures under such exemptions. See Cottier and Krajewski, above note 33, p. 360.

83 Martin Roy, Juan Marchetti, and Hoe Lim, “Services Liberalization in the New Generation of Preferential Trade Agreements (PTAs): How Much Further than the GATS?,” WTO Staff Working Paper No. ERSD-2006-07, World Trade Organization (2006); Mona Haddad and Constantinos Stephanou (eds.) *Financial Services and Preferential Trade Agreements: Lessons from Latin America* (Washington, DC: The World Bank, 2010).

with regard to their domestic regulations. For instance, they can require foreign firms to comply with their own domestic rules, thereby retaining the right to refuse a license if the foreign bank does not meet the requisite standard.[84] However, domestic regulations cannot insulate against government failures in the home country of the foreign financial institutions entering the domestic market. For instance, the host (importing) state cannot prevent a macroeconomic crisis in the parent state from negatively impacting the liquidity or the solvency of the foreign bank operating in its territory. The importing state can lawfully require foreign banks to abide by its prudential regulations, but it cannot request the parent's central bank to follow a certain monetary policy. Once the importing state accepts foreign banks in its territory, it automatically accepts the broader macroeconomic and regulatory framework of the parent country.

Given the problems with the MFN when it comes to financial coordination, preferentialism is probably the best option. The reason has to do with efficiency and the natural proclivity of states to focus on certain markets versus others. First, it would be impossible to have all countries agree on extremely detailed regulatory policies that would in most cases require substantial policy changes. In this extreme hypothesis, there would not be any difference between my model and the full centralization advocated by other scholars. Furthermore, an identical regulatory framework would prevent regional blocs tailoring the regulatory framework to the specificities of the market, and hence, it would be inefficient. Various studies indeed point out that different regulatory regimes might increase overall efficiency, as they permit each jurisdiction to tailor its regulation to the specificities of the market. This is in essence the principle of subsidiarity that is widely used in federal states.[85] Secondly, since the Regulatory Passport requires a higher level of cooperation between supervisory authorities, it would be practically impossible to meet and coordinate actions among dozens of regulators.[86] Third, it would be useless for a country to bind its regulatory and macro-stability policies without having a real market access interest in that country. The Regulatory Passport finds its strength in the

[84] On domestic regulations, see Margareta Djordjevic, "Do mestic Regulation and Free Trade in Services: A Balancing Act" (2002) 29 *Legal Issues of Economic Integration* 305; Panagiotis Delimatsis, *International Trade in Services and Domestic Regulations: Necessity, Transparency and Regulatory Diversity* (Oxford: Oxford University Press, 2008).

[85] For a good overview of the benefits of regulatory competition, see Daniel C. Esty and Damien Gerardin, "Regulatory Co-opetition" (2000) 3 *Journal of International Economic Law* 235.

[86] Marc Levinson, "Faulty Basel: Why More Diplomacy Won't Keep the Financial System Safe" (2010) 89 *International Affairs* 76.

fact that it achieves a race-to-the-top in stability policies. Since the main goal of states that engage in Regulatory Passport is to access a particular foreign financial market, integration will logically follow the regionalization strategies of multinational financial institutions. The regionalization of finance in different homogeneous blocks could, in turn, drive up the competition for the best regulatory framework, and thus increase efficiency.

10

Dispute Resolution

Unlike other areas of international economic relations, international finance does not rely on an international adjudicatory mechanism to settle regulatory or financial investment disputes. For instance, there is no international financial court to adjudicate sovereign defaults or to facilitate debt restructurings.[1] Similarly, outside of the European Union, there is no institutional mechanism to settle conflicts between home and host supervisors over the resolution of a cross-border bank, or to mediate between regulators on the adoption of financial standards. Until now, financial disputes between regulators have been solved behind the curtains of Transnational Regulatory Networks, within Supervisory Colleges, or through cross-retaliations such as the suspension of trade preferences or investment licenses.[2] There are reasons to believe that the current arrangements are not efficient. Not all disputes can be mediated successfully by Transnational Regulatory Networks (TRN)s or bilaterally through Colleges. When an agreed settlement is not possible, the solution of the dispute is simply left to pure power politics where the stronger regulator will impose its will upon the weaker regulator(s). Imagine, for instance, a disagreement over the resolution of a cross-border bank in which, given the urgency of the crisis, one supervisor has to do all the heavy lifting to protect its financial system while the other simply free-rides on its efforts. Or imagine the ring-fencing scenario discussed in Chapter 4. In both cases, supervisors cannot rely on any independent institution that is able to mediate between the parties, interpret the applicable law, and impose a solution or compensation.

[1] See Molly Ryan, "Sovereign Bankruptcy: Why Now and Why Not in the IMF" (2014) 82 *Fordham Law Review* 2473.

[2] One example is the 2015 WTO dispute between Argentina and Panama in which Argentina denied market access to Panama's firms as a retaliation against Panama's failure to comply with a number of rules on tax transparency and prevention of money laundering.

When the interests of international investors and traders are on the line, the absence of an institutional avenue to channel complaints becomes even more challenging. At present, firms and private individuals, which are adversely affected by the action of a foreign regulator or supervisor, can either litigate in local courts or use one of the dispute-settlement mechanisms available under international law, provided that they enjoy standing. None of those options is efficient, though. Local courts can be biased, especially when the rule of law is not fully developed. Sometimes regulators are protected by a legal regime that makes it difficult for firms to challenge the decision of regulators. International courts, on the other hand, are often unable to deal with the complexities of financial regulations, as they have to adjudicate based on a body of laws – international investment, World Trade Organization (WTO), or public international law – which is simply not made to address the legal and policy rationales of international finance.

Adjudication is a core function of any legal system. The last element of an efficient international regulatory architecture for financial stability necessitates a reliable compliance mechanism that reduces the proclivity of national regulators to pursue a logic of financial nationalism and guarantees obedience to international law. Discussing the underlying logic of a dispute mechanism for international finance is the objective of this chapter. The law and economics literature has analyzed the role and design of courts in all their implications, from the logic of litigation to the independence of judges.[3] It is not the purpose of this chapter to apply this complex analysis to international financial courts as this endeavor could easily occupy an entire book in itself. In this chapter, rather, I will focus on two aspects that bear particular importance for our analysis of financial nationalisms: standing and remedies. Rules on standing and remedies are critical elements in the functioning of courts as they decide who has the right to initiate a dispute and what can be reasonably expected as a consequence of a positive judgment by the court. This in turn influences the level of external pressure to which national regulators will be subject when applying international financial laws or formulating financial policies. Hence, if properly crafted, rules on standing and remedies have the

[3] See William Landes, "An Economic Analysis of the Court," in Gary S. Becker and William M. Landes (eds.) *Essays in the Economics of Crime and Punishment* (New York: NBER, 1974); Richard A. Posner, "An Economic Approach to Legal Procedure and Judicial Administration" (1973) 2 *Journal of Legal Studies* 399; Robert Bone, *The Economics of Civil Procedure* (New York: Foundation Press, 2002); Robert Cooter and Daniel Rubinfeld, "Economic Analysis of Legal Disputes and Their Resolution" (1989) 27 *Journal of Economic Literature* 1067; Andrew Daughety and Jennifer Reinganum, "Economic Theories of Settlement Bargaining" (2005) 1 *Annual Review of Law and Social Sciences* 35.

potential to act as counter-incentives against a logic of financial nationalism. After having explained the economics of standing and remedies, I will then look briefly at how adjudication could be applied to sovereign debt, international standards, and cross-border banking resolution.

10.1. LITIGATING INTERNATIONAL FINANCE

Given the soft law nature of international cooperation in financial regulation, the international financial law literature has rarely discussed the question of dispute settlement design.[4] After all, how can litigation be possible without an underlying existing system of rights and obligations? In the absence of an international financial court, a veil of mystery surrounds international financial disputes. Yet, litigation does have a place in international finance, albeit in very different forms than in other areas of international affairs. More precisely, the settlement of financial disputes is carried out through one of these three main mechanisms: informal consultations, domestic litigation, and international courts. Yet, none of them is actually fully efficient in addressing the problems discussed in this book.

When it comes to addressing international regulatory or supervisory conflicts, informal consultations behind the scenes are, undoubtedly, the main tool to address disagreements. These consultations are done bilaterally, within Colleges of Supervisors, or within existing TRNs. Given the secrecy surrounding them, it is difficult to strike a correct picture of the way international financial conflicts are resolved and what are the deals behind them. Most of the time international regulators do find a common position either by agreeing to some form of regulatory concessions or by threatening retaliation. Take the case of the famous threats launched at Japan by the UK and the US regulators during the negotiation of the 1988 Basel Accord on capital adequacy. Given the reluctance of Japan to agree on a common standard, the UK and US threatened Japan with withdrawing the license to operate from Japanese banks.[5] Yet, relying on this informal system is sometimes inefficient, as regulators could remain stuck for years in lengthy and painful wars of attritions that only disrupt markets. For instance, the EU and the United States refused, for almost 5 years, to agree on a common position on derivatives regulation; a situation

4 Bing Gu and Tong Liu, "Enforcing International Financial Regulatory Reforms" (2014) 17 *Journal of International Economic Law* 139, at pp. 168–72; Financial Markets Law Committee, "Coordination in the Reform of International Financial Regulation: Addressing the Causes of Legal Uncertainty" (February 2015).

5 See David Andrew Singer, *Regulating Capital: Setting Standards for the International Financial System* (Ithaca, NY: Cornell University Press, 2007).

that forced international traders to operate in only one of the two regimes.[6] Moreover, when a banking crisis strikes, as in the case of the *Banque Fortis* collapse, experience suggests that relying on negotiation alone will be fruitless, as the urgency of the moment requires a rapid response. It is precisely in these circumstances that supervisory authorities will decide to drop the benefits of cooperation in favor of a national approach.

International conflicts do not occur only between regulators but can arise also between foreign financial institutions, on one side, and regulators on the other. The history of financial crises over the last 30 years repeatedly reports episodes of forced nationalizations, ring-fencing measures and capital controls, or fire sales of foreign banks at below market prices. In the absence of binding international agreements that protect them against unfair treatments or abuses, international firms, traders, and creditors can only litigate under local law and in domestic courts.

Domestic litigation can actually be a strategic option for international investors favored by conflict of law rules.[7] The jurisprudence of international financial law that is taught in law schools has mostly been built on cases adjudicated under New York or England and Wales law, which guarantee a structured, stable, and well-developed system of law.[8] Yet, relying on local courts is not free from risks. First, financial authorities operate under statutory frameworks that give them a broad leeway in dealing with banks or traders. For instance, in the context of crisis-resolution policies, central banks and supervisory authorities have broad intervention powers that rely on the authorities' perception of risk and are difficult to challenge in court.[9] Second, local courts might be in one way or another biased against foreign institutions, thus giving prevalence to local interests however perceived. This risk is particularly acute in jurisdictions where the rule of law is not well developed or where national interests are more protected. Third, national courts might not have the expertise required to adjudicate complex financial disputes potentially worth billions of dollars.[10]

6 See Chapter 6.

7 See Annelise Rise, "Managing Regulatory Arbitrage: A Conflict of Laws Approach" (2014) 47 *Cornell International Law Journal* 63; International Chamber of Commerce, "Unilateral Jurisdiction Clauses in International Financial Contracts," Position Paper 470/1248rev (August 2015).

8 See Colin Bamford, *Principles of International Financial Law* (Oxford: Oxford University Press, 2015).

9 See, for instance, the recent dispute between international bondholders and the Portuguese financial authorities on the resolution of Banco Espirito Santo.

10 Jeffrey Golden, "Judges and the Systemic Risk in the Financial Markets" (2013) 18 *Fordham Journal of Corporate and Financial Law* 327.

The issue has become particularly relevant owing to the widespread use of standardized clauses in financial contracts. Derivatives contracts are, for the large part, based on standard clauses such as the International Swaps and Derivatives Association (ISDA) Master Agreement. As some authors have argued, those standard contracts are actually replacing international treaties as they are used by traders all over the world, from New York to Vietnam.[11] Yet, until very recently, there was no international court competent for interpreting them. This created substantial legal risks for traders, as differing contractual interpretations by national courts could create confusion in the jurisprudence and lead to financial chaos. To tackle this particular issue, the financial community has pushed for the creation of an arbitral tribunal specialized in private financial disputes, which was eventually established in 2012 in The Hague. As the name suggests, the Panel of International Market Experts in Finance (PRIME) is an arbitral tribunal that can count on a roster of leading experts in finance able to offer specialist knowledge on complex financial contracts.[12] Although it does not deal with state–state or investor–state disputes, PRIME is nonetheless the only specialist tribunal in finance able to create a stable jurisprudence on financial contracts, thereby offering a safe harbor to investors that choose it as the competent court of the contract.

Finally, regulatory disputes can be litigated in international courts under public international law. Indeed, despite the lack of a hard regulatory framework for finance, other areas of international economic law are increasingly helping investors to find a legal anchor to their claims. First, as we saw in the *EFTA* v. *Iceland* case, litigation in international courts is not unusual between members of regional organizations with substantial financial market integration, such as the European Union or the EFTA. This option, however, is available only when financial cooperation is regulated through a binding body of laws.

Outside that, Bilateral Investment Treaties are increasingly becoming a land of last resort for international firms that have been affected by regulatory actions. Since the *Fedax* v. *Venezuela* case in 1997,[13] the first reported investment dispute over a financial asset, there have been 59 disputes litigated under international investment law that primarily deal with the financial sector. The majority of them focus on similar claims: (1) expropriation in the context of a sovereign debt restructuring or default; (2) loss of share value during a privatization; (3) unfair/discriminatory treatment against foreign institutions during

[11] *Ibid.*
[12] See http://primefinancedisputes.org.
[13] *Fedax N.V.* v. *The Republic of Venezuela*, ICSID Case No ARB/96/3.

a resolution; (4) and the imposition of currency or exchange controls. WTO law and the General Agreement on Trade in Services (GATS) in particular have become another battleground for financial litigation as well. Despite the presence of carve-outs that exclude prudential measures from the scope of the GATS, the Dispute Settlement Body has adjudicated two major disputes on finance: *China – Electronic Payment Services* in 2012,[14] and *Argentina – Financial Services* in 2015.[15] The latter in particular is the first case dealing with the adoption of regulatory measures in financial services.

The increased reliance of international traders and financial institutions on investment law, and the timid surge in financial services litigation under WTO law shows that the narrative of international financial law as a lawless area is no longer reflecting reality: regulatory actions are indeed challenged. When regulatory conflicts cannot be solved, international courts fill a legal void. The question is whether non-specialized courts should take this role. I think this is not desirable. Neither international investment law nor WTO law are capable of addressing the complexities of regulatory actions in finance. Let us just imagine the complexity of administering a cross-border bank bail-in with thousands of debt claims to be adjudicated under different choice-of-law regimes and the pressure to achieve a swift resolution for the bank in distress. Giving creditors the right to pursue litigation under investment law for the violation of a fair-and-equitable treatment or non-discrimination standards would create undue distress on resolution authorities, which would be bound by rules of action that have very little to do with the logic of financial stability. It is not surprising that recent Free Trade Agreements exclude financial services from investment–state arbitration and subject them only a specialized mediation mechanism.[16]

Yet, it is undoubted that a need for some form of adjudication in finance exists. Hence, the best solution is to adjudicate financial regulatory actions under specialized courts competent in interpreting cooperation agreements, understanding the complexity of a debt restructuring, and able to mediate regulatory disputes on financial standards. The next sections will explain, from a legal and economics perspective, what a system of adjudication can do to address the problems of cooperation in international finance.

[14] *China – Certain Measures Affecting Electronic Payment Services* (DS4113), WTO Panel Report (adopted on 31 August 2012).

[15] *Argentina – Measures Related to Trade in Goods and Services* (DS453), WTO Panel Report and Appellate Body Report (adopted on 9 May 2016).

[16] United States Trade Representative, Transpacific Partnership Agreement – Financial Services.

10.2. ADJUDICATION AND COMPLIANCE

Courts exert very critical functions in the life of international agreements. By providing an institutional avenue where parties can settle their disagreements, courts prevent dangerous tit-for-tat situations from escalating out of control. Dispute-settlement rules allocate adjudicatory power between other national and international courts thereby guaranteeing a uniform interpretation of the law and avoiding national biases. Moreover, courts also provide a fundamental interpretative function that allows the law to evolve over time and to adapt to changed circumstances.[17] All these functions are essential in any legal system. In the context of our analysis, however, adjudication becomes particularly important for its role as a compliance tool.

Without external constraints, states are incentivized to pursue a logic of financial nationalism which may ultimately increase financial instability. As a result, the role of international law is to drive states' behavior toward a global Pareto-optimal solution. In the previous chapters, I have argued that one of the core features of financial nationalism is the violation of international agreements, whether in the form of soft or hard laws. Attributing rights to the correct titleholders could increase the pressure on states to internalize the externalities of their actions. The adoption of Regulatory Passports may help in this regard, as regulators and firms that rely on specific international rights will demand that foreign financial authorities comply with them. However, allocating rights and obligations alone will not be enough to guarantee compliance as the level of external pressure that international law creates is sometimes not enough to offset the logic of financial nationalism. A law that cannot be enforced lacks the strength necessary to drive the behavior of the actors that are supposed to comply with it. This is particularly true when the costs of compliance outweigh its gains, or when the internal pressure coming from specific lobbies for non-compliance is too much to bear for regulators. To be effective, this system of international legal entitlements must be accompanied by an adjudicatory mechanism that gives standing to the titleholders, interprets the law, and legitimizes retaliation when the law is violated. As Prof Trachtman acutely argued, only if rights can be litigated and enforced, is the law made formally binding.[18] In this situation, an adjudicatory system equipped with a retaliatory mechanism can serve as a very powerful compliance tool able to drive states toward a particular outcome.

[17] See Joel Trachtman, *The Economic Structure of International Law* (Cambridge, MA: Harvard University Press, 2008), pp. 208–71.

[18] *Ibid.*, p. 249.

The international relations and international law literatures argue that international dispute-settlement mechanisms provide a fundamental role in driving states' compliance with international law.[19] The conventional wisdom holds that the remedial system that usually goes alongside the adjudicatory function of international courts raises the costs of deviating from international law.[20] Most international dispute-settlement systems envisage a set of remedies to punish the violating party. These can range from the order to offer monetary compensations or damages, the elimination of non-conforming measures, or the imposition of specific retaliatory actions such as tariff increases or suspension of licenses. By increasing the cost of non-compliance with international law, the use of remedies within an established dispute-settlement system discourages states from violating the law and, therefore, enhances the power of international law in driving states' behavior toward the socially optimal. In addition, international courts increase the reputational losses from non-compliance with international treaties.[21] First, international courts can authoritatively interpret the law and adjudicate on whether a state has indeed breached the agreement. Second, given their role as guardian of the law, courts act as a megaphone to the wider international community in condemning a state's illegitimate behavior. This in turn damages the reputation of the violating state, which might be prevented from engaging in international treaties with other states in the future. It is not surprising, then, that states sometimes refuse to become members of international courts.[22]

10.3. THE ECONOMICS OF STANDING IN INTERNATIONAL COURTS

The literature on law and economics, international law, and international relations has developed a consistent body of research on the design of courts.

[19] Robert E. Scott and Paul B. Stephan, *The Limits of Leviathan: Contract Theory and the Enforcement of International Law* (New York: Cambridge University Press, 2006); Andrew T. Guzman, "A Compliance-Based Theory of International Law" (2002) 90 *California Law Review* 1823; Beth A. Simmons, "Money and the Law: Why Comply with the Public International Law of Money?" (2000) 25 *Yale Journal of International Law* 323; Harold Hongju Koh, "Why Do Nations Obey International Law?" (1997) 106 *Yale Law Journal* 2599.

[20] Jack Goldsmith and Eric Posner, "The Limits of International Law" (2005) 84 *Foreign Affairs* 2; Andrew Guzman, *How International Law Works: A Rational Choice Theory* (New York: Oxford University Press, 2008); Eric Posner and Alan O. Sykes, *Economic Foundations of International Law* (Cambridge, MA: Harvard University Press, 2012), pp. 126–38.

[21] Kenneth Abbott and Duncal Snidal, "Hard and Soft Law in International Governance" (2000) 54 *International Organization* 421, at pp. 427–30; Laurence Helfer and Anne-Marie Slaughter, "Why States Create International Tribunals: A Response to Posner & Yoo" (2005) 93 *California Law Review* 899, pp. 934–5.

[22] Andrew Guzman, "The Cost of Credibility: Explaining Resistance to International Dispute Resolution" (2002) 31 *Journal of Legal Studies* 303.

In the next two sections I will discuss, in particular, two elements that are critical to the context of our study: rules on standing and remedies.

Every act of life bears some sort of consequences on others. The violation of a contract, the commission of a tort, or unlawful administrative decision, all bear some direct or indirect negative externalities. A question that arises, then, is whether all those who suffered as a consequence of the violation of the law shall be entitled to launch a legal dispute against those who are allegedly responsible for it. Standing rules serve to filter the individuals that have an interest to litigate against another party, thus separating those whose legal entitlements deserve judicial protection from those whose attachment to the dispute is not strong enough to be worth the costs of adjudication.[23]

In the context of international law, standing rules are somehow more complex than in domestic law. In an international dispute, the range of subjects potentially affected by the violation of an international norm is inevitably more diversified than in a simple domestic dispute. These could encompass other states, individuals, firms, international organizations, or even NGOs. Moreover, because the right to launch a dispute puts the defendant (a state) and the claimant (a private actor or a foreign state) on a position of parity, standing rules give the claimant the power to influence the defendant's future behavior: to set the agenda.[24] In the context of international politics, this could give rise to tensions between the traditional proclivity of states to settle their affairs through diplomatic means and the rising globalization of commerce, which inevitably puts the interests of firms at the forefront. A question necessarily arises as to what extent a particular dispute shall be best left to political bargains between the parties or litigated in court. In this regard, the level of access to international courts mainly affects the standing of private actors. Contrarily, states will always retain the power to pursue the matter through diplomatic means, even if they have the right to launch a formal

[23] The literature on standing is mostly focused on the domestic aspects of standing in public law. See Eugene Kontorovich, "What Standing Is Good for" (2007) 93 *Virginia Law Review* 1663; Michael C. Jensen, William Mackling, and Clifford Holderness, "Analysis of Alternate Standing Doctrines" (1986) 6 *International Review of Law and Economics* 205; Cass R. Sunstein, "Informational Regulation and Informational Standing: Akins and beyond" (1999) 147 *University of Pennsylvania Law Review* 613; Richard J. Pierce Jr., "Is Standing Law or Politics?" (1999) 77 *North Carolina Law Review* 1741; William Fletcher, 'The Structure of Standing" (1988) 98 *Yale Law Journal* 221; David A. Logan, "Standing to Sue: A Proposed Separation of Powers Analysis" (1984) 37 *Wisconsin Law Review* 59; Stephen L. Winter, "The Metaphor of Standing and the Problem of Self-Governance" (1988) 40 *Stanford Law Review* 1371.

[24] Robert O. Keohane, Andrew Moravcsik, and AnneMarie Slaughter, "Legalized Dispute Resolution: Interstate and Transnational" (2000) 54 *International Organization* 457, p. 462.

dispute. For instance, around two thirds of international trade disputes are settled through bilateral consultations before the formal dispute-settlement procedures kicks in.[25] Hence, a standing rule open to private parties necessarily implies the inefficiency of state–state adjudicatory mechanism. Whereas states can bargain over a large multitude of issues – for instance, accepting a military deal to compensate a commercial loss – private parties have no options but to litigate. Having said that, it is important to note that an open standing rule will bear implications on the decision of a state to accede to a treaty and on the scope of the treaty itself.[26]

Because standing rules influence the level of pressure to which regulators will be subject, they have the potential of influencing their future behavior. This is why they are fundamental in the context of international cooperation. In Chapter 8, I argued that in order to overcome the principal–agent problem and ensure compliance it is necessary to increase the level of pressure that foreign actors exert on national regulators to a point equal to or higher than that exerted by domestic stakeholders. International law does so with regard to international financial standards by empowering international financial organizations to monitor the compliance of their members to the rules. However, this does not occur with regard to supervision and crisis resolution. To ensure that national authorities will be forced to abide by their commitments it is therefore necessary to develop a regulatory framework that effectively mobilizes foreign interest groups and legitimizes efficient retaliation.[27]

When we move to the issue of compliance, the presence of a centralized dispute-settlement system helps to reduce the discretion of national authorities in the interpretation and application of the law.[28] It does so by channeling the political pressure toward compliance through a set of legalized institutional avenues available to those that have access to the courts. In the context

25 See J.G. Merrills, *International Dispute Settlement* (Cambridge: Cambridge University Press, 2011, 5th edn.), at p. 199; WTO, "Understanding the WTO: Settling Disputes," available online at https://www.wto.org/english/thewto_e/whatis_e/tif_e/disp1_e.htm.

26 On this point, see Trachtman, above note 17, p. 250.

27 On retaliation and compliance, see Anu Bradford and Omri Ben-Shahar, "Efficient Enforcement in International Law" (2012) 12 *Chicago Journal of International Law* 375; Guzman, above note 19; Brett M. Frischmann and James C. Hartigan, "Compliance Institutions in Treaties" (2011) 7 *Review of Law and Economics* 89; Alan O. Sykes, "Public versus Private Enforcement of International Economic Law: Standing and Remedy" (2005) 34 *The Journal of Legal Studies* 631. On state–state retaliation and reciprocity, see Francesco Parisi and Nita Ghei, "The Role of Reciprocity in International Law" (2003) 36 *Cornell International Law Journal* 93; Vincy Fon and Francesco Parisi, "Reciprocity-Induced Cooperation" (2003) 159 *Journal of Institutional and Theoretical Economics* 76; Posner and Sykes, above note 20, pp. 126–38.

28 Keohane, Moravcsik, and Slaughter, above note 24, p. 459.

of international law, standing is a crucial, but often underrated, element in the game of compliance. Indeed, by granting to one or more parties the right to bring the violating state to the court, the right of standing exerts a fundamental monitoring function. The right of standing gives to those who benefit from it a loud voice over the life of the treaty, and it can greatly influence its level of implementation as well as its evolution. Standing separates those who can set the agenda from those who can simply complain about it. It logically follows that, the more subjects are granted access to the court, the more a state is placed under strict scrutiny. Thus, the decision as to which subjects have the right to bring a complaint greatly influences the overall level of political pressure that each treaty party will be subject to.

Keohane and others identify the right of standing as along a continuum. On the one hand, a restrictive approach would grant standing only to the states that are party to the treaty. On the other hand, a more open approach would extend the right to bring a complaint to private parties that are directly affected by the treaty. I would personally add a third option: the initiative of an international organization. The three options vary fundamentally in terms of the political pressure that they might exert toward compliance, and with regard to the evolution of the treaty itself. In Coaseian terms, different standing rules measure the transaction costs that are attached to the implementation of the treaty.[29] A strict approach would make it extremely difficult for interest groups to push for compliance, as they would need to lobby their government to bring a dispute and convince it of the necessity to do so. On the contrary, a more open approach that grants standing to private parties might subject the states to innumerable "frivolous claims," and greatly reduce its regulatory and political space. This will ultimately lead to the suppression of the right to regulate, as the state will be forced to bargain with multiple parties with different interests. A more advanced route is, in my view, the attribution to the court or to an institutional organ, created by the treaty, of the right to bring autonomously to the attention of the court any violation of the treaty. The clearest example is probably, the right of the European Commission to initiate a dispute against a EU member state. Given the enormous political power that such an institution would exert, this option is probably available only to those states that are willing to engage in substantial political relations and sacrifice much of their domestic political space. As such, this option falls outside the political perimeter that is analyzed in this book and will not be discussed. The remaining options are therefore only the state–state dispute mechanism and the private–state dispute mechanism.

[29] *Ibid.*, p. 463.

The differences in standing rules are very visible in the context of international economic law. Alan O. Sykes recently conducted a comparative analysis of standing and remedies in WTO and investment law.[30] The two regimes have strikingly different standing options. On the one hand, the WTO Dispute Settlement Mechanism is available only to WTO member states, while international investment arbitration is historically open also to foreign investors. In spite of their differences both mechanisms are surprisingly considered extremely effective in adjudicating their respective disputes.[31] Sykes argues that each of the adjudicatory systems works because it fits the specific political economy underpinnings at the core of the applicable agreements. Let's take the example of investment agreements. The standard economics of investment treaties argues that the main goal of investment agreements is to reduce the cost of capital. By committing to a certain regulatory standard to foreign investors, the host government promotes itself as a safe investment destination. In this situation, the main targets of the host government's investment policies are not partner governments, but rather foreign investors. Hence, the commitment must be directed primarily toward them. Essentially, in the investment setting, importing nations benefit directly by giving a remedy for breach of the agreement to all investors because it shows the level of openness of the host country and thus reduces the cost of capital, which in turn increases capital inflows. As argued by Sykes, "The private right of action for compensatory damages facilitates this government-to-firm commitment in a way that a mere government-to-government commitment cannot."[32]

The main goal of a government in the context of a trade agreement, on the other hand, is not to import goods, but rather the opposite: to favor domestic export industries. Those industries will clearly have a hard time in lobbying foreign governments for market access, as the foreign government does not have any interest in attracting imports. Thus, by granting exporters market access and non-discrimination rights, trade agreements mobilize domestic export industries that will lobby for market access within their own governments. Given the powerful role of import-competing industries, governments will nonetheless have high incentives to cheat and increase market access barriers to protect domestic industries.[33] In this situation, giving the right of

[30] Sykes, above note 27.

[31] The WTO DSM has been often called the jewel in the crown of the international trading system; similarly, the surge in investment treaty arbitrations over the last two decades and their increasingly complexity of the cases brought testify on the efficacy of the investment dispute-resolution system.

[32] Sykes, above note 27, p. 645.

[33] *Ibid.*; Posner and Sykes, above note 20.

standing to private investors would not be efficient. Importing nations will not gain anything by simply giving standing to exporters without having market access concessions in return. In the trade setting, importing nations can benefit (indirectly) only by giving a remedy for breach of a trade agreement to foreign exporters, who are politically powerful in their home countries given their ability to induce their governments to offer reciprocal trade benefits in return. A second, and consequential, argument by Sykes holds that dispersed and weak industries will not bring substantial benefits to the regulators and politicians that push for a dispute. States have agreed to create a political filter whereby only strong and powerful industries can lobby their governments. How can the parties implement such a rule? The obvious way is to omit any private rights of action from their agreement. Because it is costly for the parties to bring enforcement actions themselves, they will bring actions only on behalf of exporters who offer sufficient political rewards in exchange.[34]

10.4. REMEDIES AND RETALIATION

In a perfect world, a binding regulatory framework would probably suffice to ensure smooth cooperation. However, in reality, even the use of hard laws is often not enough to guarantee the obedience to such rules. Under various circumstances, states will be incentivized to disregard their international commitments whenever the gains from defection are higher than those from compliance. As Andrew Guzman has argued, international law is a two-stage game in which states first negotiate commitments, and then decide whether or not to implement them.[35] To offset the logic of unilateral action, it is therefore necessary to rely on what Joost Pauwelyn calls "back-up enforcement":[36] a remedial system available to the non-breaching party, by virtue of which the violation to the rules will be met with the imposition of penalties and fines. The rationale of any efficient remedial system is to rebalance the welfare gains and losses between the parties by setting the level of punishment to a point where the costs of non-compliance will be higher than its benefits.[37] Both national and international law rely on remedies to discourage deviations from the law. However, the problem of compliance in international law is made more complex by the absence of a central authority that can legitimately

[34] Sykes *ibid.*, p. 645.

[35] Guzman, above note 20, p. 1846.

[36] Joost Pauwelyn, *Optimal Protection of International Law: Navigating between European Absolutism and American Voluntarism* (New York: Cambridge University Press, 2008).

[37] On the use of remedies in domestic law, see Steven Shavell, *Foundations of Economic Analysis of Law* (Cambridge, MA: Harvard University Press, 2004), pp. 387–471.

enforce the law. More specifically, since international law lacks the monopoly of legitimate power that is present in domestic law in the hands of the government, a state always has the option to violate international law or not to enforce the rulings of an international court.[38]

The strategies for compliance in international law must therefore go beyond the pure use of remedies. Absent a supreme enforcer, only states have the power to intervene to address the violation of international law, and in doing so they can only rely on their own power.[39] They do so through various legitimate mechanisms that have the ultimate goal of discouraging further violation and, when possible, to restore the situation to the *status quo ante*. As we have seen in Chapter 8, three major mechanisms enhance compliance: retaliation, reputation, or reciprocity. For instance, partner states can suspend their compliance with relevant international laws, or they can retaliate by adopting a similar or equivalent behavior.[40] The question of compliance in international law therefore boils down to a chess-game between states in which the violation of a commitment triggers a parallel reaction by partner countries. We can see various examples of how international law ensures compliance. In the context of WTO law, binding norms require states to maintain a certain policy stance toward partner countries. In the event of a violation of the WTO Agreements, and upon the dismissal of the request by the Panel to the breaching state to withdraw the measure, partner countries are allowed to retaliate by suspending their concessions toward the breaching member, thereby causing a welfare loss.[41] In the context of international investment law, the violation of an investment treaty by the host country allows a partner country's investors to bring the dispute to an investment tribunal, which would normally demand the payment of damages. The award would be recognizable in different jurisdictions and would allow seizing the assets of the party to satisfy the claim.

Having set the theoretical framework for compliance, then the question is to assess how this could be applied to cross-border financial issues. At the outset, one of the important benefits of giving standing to states is the wide array of measure that states can adopt to induce compliance. Indeed, they could retaliate on other banking policies, by denying access to foreign banks or ring-fencing assets. But, they could also decide to cross-retaliate on completely different issues, for instance, by suspending concessions. In light of

[38] Posner and Sykes, above note 20.

[39] Posner and Sykes, *ibid.*, p. 254. The fundamental essay on this subject is L.G. Telser, "A Theory of Self-Enforcing Agreements" (1980) 53 *The Journal of Business* 27.

[40] Guzman, above note 19, pp. 1860–72.

[41] Chad Bown and Joost Pauwelyn (eds.) *The Law, Economics and Politics of Retaliation in WTO Dispute Settlement* (Cambridge: Cambridge University Press, 2010).

the Regulatory Passport, which is by itself relying on market access as the main incentive for cooperation, the first available mechanism for compliance should be, in my view, the suspension of market access concessions for foreign financial firms. For instance, foreign securities firms would be prevented from listing in the local stock exchange, while banks or insurance firms could be denied the license to operate.

This strategy alone would, however, be ineffective in offsetting the strong sovereignty costs attached to international financial policies. First of all, the loss of market access is a powerful strategy only to the extent that the partner country is dependent on the foreign market as a source of economic strength. This would probably occur when the two financial markets are big enough to host a high number of firms, as in the case of the United States, Japan, or the European Union. Whenever the host country is not considered as a strategic market, however, the threat of market access would not suffice in inducing compliance. Secondly, the suspension of market access concessions implies a cost for the retaliating country also, as this deprives the host economy of precious capital inflows. Sometimes, when the host economy is much smaller than the home, therefore, the costs of retaliation will simply be too high to bear.[42] One of the strategies to offset this problem is to increase the number of players involved. Retaliation indeed works best in a multi-country setting. One possibility is to shift retaliation from the single country to the whole market. For instance, all the signatories of the Regulatory Passport could suspend their market access concessions to the non-complying member, so that it would de facto be excluded from the market. Another possible solution is to locate the dispute-settlement mechanism and the whole remedial system in an international organization – perhaps the Financial Stability Forum (FSB), the World Bank, the International Monetary Fund (IMF), or a regional organization – which would also be responsible for coordinating retaliatory actions. For instance, refusal to comply with the agreement could trigger the intervention of the IMF or the World Bank, which could refuse to provide financial assistance to the member or suspend it from the organization. This also means, however, that whenever the non-complying member can afford to rely on private financing or on its own resources, such conditionality would be completely ineffective. A further option is to exclude the non-complying member from the international organization. Now, there are different ways to do it. The participation of the FSB/ Bank for International Settlements (BIS) clearly brings substantial benefits to the member in political and economic

[42] This is a common problem for all retaliatory strategies.

terms (higher ratings, network connections, influence in policy formulation, etc.). These organizations could make the acceptance of the treaties mandatory for the members, and make the expulsion or the suspension of one of the members mandatory in the event of a violation. By doing so, the cost of the retaliation is shared by the global community rather than the member itself.

10.5. ONE OR MANY INTERNATIONAL FINANCIAL COURTS?

In the next sections, I will discuss how a dispute-settlement mechanism for finance could be designed. Before starting the analysis, however, it is worth spending a few words on the peculiarities of adjudication in international finance. When we look at international finance from the lenses of law and economics and political economy, it appears immediately clear that, compared to international trade, or investment, or human rights, international financial law is a more complex and multifaceted area of law in which a wider diversity of interests are at play.

International financial standards represent probably the most visible aspect of international financial law. Although standards are negotiated between national regulators alone, financial institutions and traders have substantial interests in their correct implementation. As I discussed in Chapter 8, market discipline can exert a powerful compliance function that prevents dangerous regulatory races to the bottom and renders adjudication less necessary. This means that there is less need to use international courts as compliance mechanisms. Rather, in the case of international standards, the main function of an international court would probably be to act as a focal point regarding the correct interpretation of the rules, so that regulatory homogeneity is guaranteed over time. A ruling of violation coming from a specialized court would be viewed by the community of regulators as having a higher level of legitimacy than one coming from an individual member. In addition, an international financial court could act as a mediator between different regulators when regulatory convergence proves challenging.

In the context of sovereign debt, the dynamics at play are very different. First, the legal relationship is between a state with full financial sovereignty over its territory and its assets, and a group of foreign investors with no real legal power of their own. The role of an international court in this case would be to bypass the bias of domestic courts toward the sovereign and to increase its accountability in the same way that international investment courts do with international investment agreements. Second, the interests toward compliance may differ even within the two broader groups. For instance, the interest of the younger generation to reduce the level of state indebtedness or to service the debt on time often conflicts with that of the political elite in charge and the older generation that benefits from the debt. Finally, in sovereign debt restructurings, most of the economic and legal problems come from creditor battles. The function of an international bankruptcy court in this case would be to coordinate creditors and to adjudicate on their claims, thus reducing the already high economic costs of debt restructurings for the defaulting state.

Cross-border bank insolvencies present a complex set of different problems – ranging from creditors' protection to supervisory coordination – that make them unique in international finance. In a cross-border bank insolvency or resolution, the stakes are necessarily very high given the size of the bank's balance sheet. Supervisors have tremendous incentives to adopt a nationalist stance that minimizes losses for its own constituencies, often without regard to the interests of foreign creditors. Financial courts will reduce the risk of conflicts in the resolution of a cross-border bank. This is particularly important now as the complexity of bank-resolution regimes and the costs associated with bail-ins will almost inevitably lead to disputes involving banks' creditors and supervisors. Furthermore, with the adoption of the bail-in tool, there is a high risk of creditors' battles similar to those taking place in sovereign debt restructurings. An international financial court specialized in cross-border bank resolution could prevent multiple litigations from arising in different parts of the world and would guarantee a uniform interpretation of the bank's debt contracts.

Given the different dynamics at play, it would be impossible to devise a common dispute-settlement mechanism able to deal with the entirety of international financial law: a global financial court. A solution that may work for cross-border bank resolution may not work for sovereign debt restructurings. Hence, it will be very unlikely for international finance to have a specialized court of the like of the WTO Dispute Settlement Mechanism. What is more plausible is a constellation of dispute-settlement systems with different structures, goals, and mechanisms tailored for the specificity of each area of finance law. These could vary along a continuum that starts with semi-formal consultation and interpretative mechanisms with non-binding force, and terminates with formal and binding dispute-settlement proceedings with the possibility of retaliations. For instance, disputes on regulatory standards, which necessitate a certain leeway in their domestic implementation, could be settled through semi-formal adjudication systems in which an independent expert could mediate on the application and different interpretation of the standards. On the other hand, sovereign debt disputes could be dealt with a more formal dispute-settlement system – perhaps, a court of arbitration – located at the IMF.

In the next sections I will briefly sketch some ideas on how a dispute-settlement system could be designed for these three areas of financial law. Given the lack of space, it will be inevitable to conduct a very approximate analysis that merely scratches the surface of the problems. Yet, I hope to offer enough food for thought for future research.

10.6. INTERNATIONAL PRUDENTIAL STANDARDS

The question in the case of soft standards is whether a dispute-settlement mechanism is necessary, and how it could be tailored for non-binding laws. In this regard, it is undoubted that incomprehensions or even disagreements among regulators might arise as well with regard to standards. Regulators might complain about their financial institutions being disadvantaged vis-à-vis other institutions located in a country that does not adopt the standards with the same stringency. Disagreements might arise with regard to regulatory standards that de facto discriminate against foreign firms or make their life unnecessarily difficult. If not controlled, those situations could lead to tit-for-tat retaliatory wars that might disrupt financial and political relations between countries. For instance, at the outset of the global financial crisis, the United States and the EU disagreed with regard to the allegedly discriminatory treatment of foreign branches,[43] and the different regulatory requirements for derivatives clearing.[44] Those kinds of disagreements are mostly solved bilaterally through negotiations, often under the auspices of a standard-setting body or the G20. Nonetheless, it would be useful to channel them under the umbrella of a formal dispute-settlement mechanism, which does not necessarily need to encompass a court of law and a set of fines.

This mechanism could be enshrined formally under the standard-setting organization competent of the standard or under the Financial Stability Board, which may assist with its expertise in mediation between the parties. The benefits of such a system are numerous. First, the dispute would be channeled and controlled under an impartial institution, thereby preventing dangerous escalations of the conflict. Second, the interpretative function of the standards offered by the institution would lead to the progressive creation of a body of norms that would clarify the correct application of the standards and

[43] See The Economist, "Global Banking: Inglorious Isolation" print edition (22 February 2014).

[44] Philip Stafford, "EU and US Fail to Agree on Derivatives Rules," *Financial Times Online* (7 May 2015), available at www.ft.com/intl/cms/s/0/ed0e5df4-f4c7-11e4-9a58-00144feab7de.html#axzz41YyUnRoov; Philip Stafford, "Quick View: Clearing up Differences," *Financial Times Online* (16 June 2014), available at www.ft.com/intl/cms/s/0/3ccba18a-f52d-11e3-91a8-00144feabdc0.html#axzz41YyUnRoo.

the rationale for their suspension or deviation. This interpretative function would carry long-term beneficial effects for all the parties involved, including third countries that are not party to the dispute but yet interested in implementing the standards. Often, small states do not have the power to stand up to a bigger player, especially when there is no binding law preventing it from violating the standards or abusing its position. An impartial dispute-settlement mechanism that clarifies the boundaries of application of the standards would allow third countries to free-ride on others' complaints without carrying the burden of launching an official complaint.[45]

Let us now see how standing rules might work for prudential standards. In this regard, there are three groups that have an interest in the formulation and implementation of the standards: the domestic regulator that implements the standards; the foreign regulators; and the financial institutions. The domestic regulator, when choosing a certain standard, will take into consideration the impact it has on its own financial system in terms of stability and efficiency, presumably after having considered the different interests at stake, including depositor's protection, credit creation, return on capital and so forth. The foreign regulator has, as its main interest, not to be put in a difficult situation with its own financial institution. Its main objective will be to preserve the competitiveness of its own financial institutions in the global financial market as well as global financial stability. Hence, it may not look favorably toward regulatory races to the bottom that put the stability of the global financial system in jeopardy or that increase artificially the competitiveness of foreign firms. In a global financial system, banks are mobile and, presumably, will favor a rule that guarantees high returns on investment and equity, and which is viewed as safe enough by the market from which it has to borrow. A loose prudential standard that is not perceived as safe by the market will make the bank that complies with it riskier in the long term. Hence, although the short-term interest of the bank will be to invest in a country that offers very low standards (and hence higher returns), its long-term interest is to comply with the standards that are considered safe enough by the market, but yet not too costly for the firm.

Among the two foreign actors that have an interest in the application or modification of the standards, only the foreign regulator is without a clear voice. In a global financial market, firms are mobile and their investments necessarily reflect the view of the market over a particular location/standard. The response of the market to an unsound standard will simply be to

[45] Scott Barrett, *Why Cooperate? The Incentives to Supply Global Public Goods* (Oxford: Oxford University Press, 2007), p. 82.

leave. The evidence on the implementation of capital adequacy standards so far seems to corroborate this argument; the risk of races-to-the-bottom in financial rule-making that were the main fear of commentators in the early 1990s ultimately proved to be wrong, as banks pushed for a race-to-the-top. Moreover, financial institutions can already challenge a regulation in local courts. Foreign regulators, on the other hand, do not have a real voice as they cannot extend their jurisdictional reach outside their border (the United States is clearly an exception to that) or force all foreign institutions to leave. Without real retaliatory power beyond that available within their jurisdiction, regulators have no choice but to accept another state's regulatory action. This is especially true for small states.

For this reason, a dispute-settlement mechanism for international standards should not, in principle, be open to financial institutions but only to regulators. Institutions might offer their views on the regulatory issue at stake, as they already do during the standard-making phase, but without a formal right to challenge a regulation. Regulators, on the other hand, do need a formal compliance mechanism to channel their doubts over a foreign regulatory standard. As explained before, financial regulatory networks of the likes of the Financial Stability Board or the Basel Committee on Banking Supervision already offer informal discussion fora that seemingly work very well. Nonetheless, I still see a rationale to formalize their role by hosting a transparent dispute-settlement mechanism. First of all, a formal dispute-settlement mechanism in which an independent expert mediates on a regulatory dispute will increase the negotiating power of small states against big ones. Second, third countries' regulators may join in as third parties when they have an interest in the issue at stake, similar to the WTO Dispute Settlement Mechanism. Third, the interpretative function of the mediation court will, over time, create and stratify a regulatory jurisprudence on the application or non-application of standards that will then be useful to other courts of law or regulators. This will reduce regulatory loopholes and prevent regulatory divergence over time.

10.7. CROSS-BORDER BANKING

Cross-border banking is particularly prone to conflicts. Examples include the application of discriminatory policies during the bank's licensing process, the incorrect implementation of agreed international prudential standards, refusals to share supervisory data or allow inspections, or legal standoffs during resolution. This latter issue, if not addressed, will probably become a critical loophole in the regulatory architecture of international finance. International bail-ins in particular present regulatory and legal complexities that are not found in any other areas of international finance. Resolution authorities may fight with other resolution authorities over the location of liabilities counting toward the total loss-absorbing capacity of the bank group. Conflicts may arise with regard to the closing of derivatives contracts or the conversion of liabilities booked in a foreign subsidiary, or with regard to the support of the parent toward a weak subsidiary. In the worst-case scenario, supervisory conflicts may end with the ring-fencing of the bank's foreign operations or its selling at fire-sale prices. During the bail-in, supervisors may fight with foreign creditors for the conversion or haircut of bailed-in liabilities located in another jurisdiction or subject to another law. This situation tragically mirrors the perennial creditors' battles during sovereign debt restructurings.[46]

The earlier section has demonstrated the positive benefits of standing in addressing the problems of compliance in international law, and generally, in enhancing international cooperation. There is no doubt that adopting a harder legal approach in cross-border banking arrangements would probably reduce the Prisoner's Dilemma situations typical of international financial policies. The high sovereignty costs and the political tradeoffs typical of cross-border banking policies definitely impact the capability and willingness of states to stick to their commitments and protect global stability. Extending to foreign groups the right to challenge the violation of an agreement would clearly put domestic regulators under stricter scrutiny, and thus enhance supervisory coordination.

For this reason, the FSB has suggested in the *Principles for Cross-Border Effectiveness of Resolution Actions* to establish in each country a legal framework for recognition that provides "a foreign resolution authority with legal standing to request recognition and enforcement."[47] The FSB proposal does not suggest the establishment of an international financial court competent to adjudicate the violation of the FSB standards, along the lines of the WTO Dispute Settlement Mechanism. On the contrary, it simply suggests the insertion, in the national resolution framework, of provisions that give foreign stakeholders the right to challenge the decision of a local resolution authority with regard to recognition. Although the FSB Principles do not mention it, the right of standing should be accompanied by a procedure that clarifies the ground for refusing the recognition of foreign resolution measures.

46 Federico Lupo-Pasini and Ross P. Buckley, "International Coordination in Cross-Border Bank Bail-ins: Problems and Prospects" (2015) 16 *European Business Organization Law Review* 226.

47 Financial Stability Board, "Principles for Cross-Border Effectiveness of Resolution Action" (3 November 2015), p. 11.

Allowing foreign resolution authorities to challenge decisions is certainly a step forward toward compliance. However, it is undeniable that addressing the compliance problem only through domestic procedures is not enough. Local courts will likely be biased toward their own countries and come under pressure from local regulators and stakeholders. Given the wide scope of the public policy exception that most cross-border resolution frameworks contain, it would be very easy to justify a non-complying policy. Moreover, the absence of a centralized dispute-settlement mechanism would give rise to dangerous interpretative differences that would de facto maintain differences in national resolution systems. Therefore, it would be wise to insert in domestic legislation a clause that refers disputes to an international administrative body, exclusively competent to adjudicate disputes relating to cross-border resolution. Given the prominent role of the FSB in coordinating cross-border resolution, the FSB would have an absolute advantage in hosting such a body.[48] The body would clearly need to act rapidly and rely on simplified procedures, compared to other international tribunals. Perhaps, it could rely on a decentralized and relatively informal structure, whereby a closed number of pre-selected panelists would adjudicate the dispute hosted by local arbitration chambers. The important issue is to guarantee impartiality and uniformity of the jurisprudence. Over time, this could give rise to a transnational jurisprudence over cross-border resolution that could guarantee homogeneity of judgments and basic common principles of law. This would certainly help in preventing unreasonable refusals of recognition and grant further certainty in this complex area of law. The question now is how to frame the adjudicatory system in a way that maximizes its potential in inducing compliance without impinging too heavily on the policy space of states in the management of their financial policies.

The most important question is to see which stakeholder shall have standing. As a starting point it is, again, useful to restate that the main goal of the standing rules in international financial law shall be to break the principal–agent problem. In a bi-country setting, there are three major players to whom the rights can be attributed: (1) the resolution authorities; (2) the banks; and (3) the taxpayers, who bear the direct cost of the crisis.[49] The allocation of the right of standing to one or all of the three actors determines the level of

[48] Gu and Liu advance a similar argument. See Gu and Liu, above note 4, pp. 168–72.

[49] On the political economy of cross-border banking and the different stakeholders involved, see Kathia D'Ulster, "Cross Border Banking Supervision Incentive Conflicts in Supervisory Information Sharing between Home and Host Supervisors," World Bank Policy Research Working Paper 5871, The World Bank (2011), available at http://elibrary.worldbank.org/doi/pdf/10.1596/1813-9450-5871.

pressure that partner regulators will be subjected to, and therefore the level of compliance. As a general rule, the right of standing should be given to the foreign stakeholder that will be in the best position to exert pressure on the foreign regulators. On the other hand, it is also true that too liberal standing rules might create hold-out problems that restrict or impede policy formulation in the home country by exercising veto power.[50] Moreover, we need to consider that bank resolutions necessarily require speed and legal certainly, otherwise the resolution will turn into a slow and painful death.

In my view, the most important function of a cross-border bank resolution court is to offer a quick mediation and adjudication mechanism to resolution authorities during resolution. The main coordination problem will concern the financing of the bank in resolution, and the recognition and implementation of resolution actions. Resolution authorities are the only entities with the statutory powers necessary to resolve the bank and the capability to assess the systemic and legal implications of the bank's resolution. Hence, resolution authorities shall enjoy standing to this court. The main benefit of an international court over the domestic procedure proposed by the FSB is that the former guarantees independence and a high level of expertise on cross-border resolution issues. The mediation court would base its judgment on Memoranda of Understanding (MoUs) on crisis resolution, and any other agreement that governs the cross-border bank-resolution process, such as the agreement establishing the Crisis Management Group or the Resolution College. For this to be effective, it would be necessary that the agreement contain a choice-of-court clause devolving the interpretation of the agreement to the FSB. Given the speed required in resolution, the mediation mechanism will have to be ready immediately and possibly be detached to regional mediation or arbitration centers.

The other option is to have an international court competent for cross-border bank resolution in which both creditors and resolution authorities can adjudicate the claim. As I said before, the history of cross-border banking crises is replete with examples of alleged discriminatory treatments, such as the bailout of Saluka by the Czech Republic authorities to the more recent bail-in of Banco Espirito Santo's bondholders by the Portuguese Central Bank. In this regard, giving standing to creditors would most definitely increase the pressure over resolution authorities during the procedure for a non-discriminatory approach. However, opening the dispute procedures to the claims of creditors may nonetheless be detrimental to the efficacy and credibility of the resolution

[50] See Kontorovich, above note 23, p. 1678.

itself, which has to be carried out quickly and with the utmost degree of legal certainty. Bondholders are a very wide and dispersed group comprising retail depositors and hedge funds. The experience of sovereign debt restructuring shows that coordination problems among creditors and their proclivity for litigation could easily lead to prolonged legal battles. In a cross-border bank resolution, this would probably result in a disorderly resolution.[51] Thus, it would be sensible to give only to resolution authorities the right of standing in an international cross-border bank insolvency court, and let authorities represent the concerns of their creditors. The problem of discrimination certainly exists, and in certain cases it has given rise to international disputes, but it has to be solved through domestic law or through international law. For instance, following the FSB *Key Attributes*' recommendation, all national resolution laws and Regulatory Passport shall insert an obligation of non-discrimination among creditors. Creditors discriminated will therefore have the possibility to litigate it in front of domestic courts, after the resolution has been completed, or ask their own authorities to raise the violation within the available international adjudication mechanisms.

10.8. AN INTERNATIONAL SOVEREIGN BANKRUPTCY COURT

The idea of an international adjudicatory system for sovereign debt problems is one of the current themes in the sovereign debt restructuring literature.[52] Formally starting with the proposal for an "International Debt Commission" launched by the Group of seventy-seven developing countries at the outset of the Peru crisis in 1977, and culminating in the United Nation General Assembly 2014 and 2015 resolutions proposing the creation of a "multilateral framework for sovereign debt restructuring processes," the idea of a bankruptcy court for sovereigns seems to many commentators the most logical solution to sovereign debt problems. Among the various proposals on the table, the most debated was certainly the IMF's Sovereign Debt Restructuring Mechanism launched in 2003 by the then IMF's Deputy Managing Director, Anne Krueger.[53] This proposal was undoubtedly the most comprehensive with regard to the issues that it wanted to address as well as the participation open to all IMF members. Even though the IMF's idea was not approved by its

[51] Lupo-Pasini and Buckley, above note 46, pp. 212–14.

[52] Kenneth Rogoff and Jeromin Settelmeyer, "Bankruptcy Procedures for Sovereigns: A History of Ideas, 1976–2001," IMF Working Paper WP/02/133 (IMF, 2002).

[53] Anne O. Krueger, "A New Approach to Sovereign Debt Restructuring" (IMF, 2002); International Monetary Fund, "Proposed Features of a Sovereign Debt Restructuring Mechanism" (IMF, 2003).

Board of Governors following the objection of some of the members as well as concerns of the private sector, it has nonetheless constantly been taken as the "model" in all subsequent proposals. It is not the objective of this section to comment on the pros and cons of the previous proposals. Rather, I would like to briefly look here at the law and economics of an international bankruptcy court to see in particular how it could work, and how it can address the problem of financial nationalism in sovereign debt.

The very first objective of this international court is to take sovereign debt litigation away from national courts and centralize it into a single international dispute-settlement mechanism. From a practical perspective, the transfer of adjudicatory power to an international court necessarily implies a parallel reduction of national jurisdiction over the sovereign debt contracts, even if these are subjected to national law. This could be done through the insertion of a choice-of-court agreement in the debt contract – probably the easiest solution – or through a formal surrender of national jurisdiction over sovereign debt disputes contained in the treaty that establishes the international court. The exclusive competence of the international court bears some fundamental implications. First, creditors cannot submit separate proceedings in national courts or challenge a vote on the restructuring proposal. For instance, a dissenting minority creditor that has been blocked by a supermajority in favor of a restructuring cannot appeal against the ruling in a domestic court. Second, once a ruling had been issued, it is automatically valid in all countries that have agreed to the jurisdiction of the court. Thus, once a decision is reached, this cannot be challenged in national courts.

Managing and coordinating the debt-restructuring process is certainly another critical function, and the objective of most proposals, including the IMF's. As explained in Chapter 5, creditor coordination problems are undermining the efficacy of debt restructurings. Collective Action Clauses alone, however, cannot address all the issues that inevitably arise in a sovereign debt restructuring, and therefore, need to be complemented by statutory solutions. Hence, like any national bankruptcy court, the international court would also have as one of its main functions to collect and verify creditors' claims in the function of the debt-restructuring procedure. Some creditors may object to another's entitlement, claiming the latter's dependence from the sovereign. Moreover, the court will have to oversee the voting procedures and enforce collective-action clauses. For this, it would be necessary that all sovereign debt contracts contain a collective-action clause that blocks opposing minorities and allows aggregation of claims, as recent sovereign debt contracts already do. Secondly, it will be necessary that all countries have subscribed to a sovereign debt-restructuring mechanism that specify the voting rights and the procedure used during a restructuring. If the states agree to renounce their jurisdiction over sovereign debt claims and devolve them to an international court, creditors will no longer be allowed to initiate separate proceedings in creditor-friendly jurisdictions. At the same time, it will be guaranteed that a single national judge could not block the repayment to all other creditors, thereby delaying excessively the sovereign debt restructuring. This will protect non-holdout creditors and allow the sovereign to restructure its debt promptly.

A sovereign debt court would interpret the rights and obligations arising out of the contract by applying the law of the contract, complemented by the use of international laws (including the treaty establishing the court) when necessary. In this regard, one of the first problems in the law of sovereign debt is the lack of a uniform jurisprudence on the interpretation of critical contractual terms as well as on the public international law of sovereign debt. *Pari passu* clauses, in particular, are known to be quite open to ambivalent interpretations as they have been subjected to conflicting analyses by national tribunals. Given their critical role in a debt restructuring, minimizing the risk of unorthodox legal analyses of the likes seen in the *NML* v. *Argentina* dispute is key.[54] A similar problem occurs also with regard to the interpretation of key norms of public international law such as necessity, force majeure, or the "odious debt" doctrine. Without any doubt, assigning to a single court the competence to adjudicate sovereign debt contracts will address the long-standing problem of diverging jurisprudence. Although the actual judges deciding on the disputes inevitably have different approaches to legal analysis, they must nonetheless take into account previous rulings, especially if they are issued by the same court. Over time this will give rise to a more certain and coherent body of jurisprudence, which will guarantee the legal stability required by the business community and reduce the risk of jurisdictional arbitrage.

One of the most contentious aspects of any sovereign debt court is the determination as to whether the sovereign default is to be blamed on external circumstances or fiscal mismanagement, or whether the debt is sustainable. For example, according to the failed 2003 IMF proposal for a Sovereign Debt Restructuring Mechanism, the tribunal would have first examined the admissibility of the restructuring request. Thus, the tribunal would have decided on whether the debt could be repudiated, or if it resulted from economic mismanagement. If not, the restructuring process could have gone forward. In essence, this would have occurred only in the case of inability to pay, rather

[54] Natalie Wong, "*NML Capital, Ltd. v. Republic of Argentina* and the Changing Roles of the Pari Passu and Collective Action Clauses in Sovereign Debt Agreements" (2014) 59 *Columbia Journal of Transnational Law* 396.

than simply unwillingness to pay.[55] Understanding the "economic truth" behind a sovereign debt problem might prove very difficult. For instance, judges may have to decide whether an economic crisis in a neighboring country had a direct impact on the fiscal sustainability of the defaulting sovereign. Establishing a causal link of this kind is extremely difficult as it requires a very high level of scientific certainty that might be complicated to achieve. Authors have debated at length whether a sovereign debt court or mechanism should look into the actual macroeconomic policies, and whether it should rely on the IMF's help for doing so.[56] As some authors argue, sovereigns naturally fear the loss of sovereign power that comes with increased scrutiny, and the alleged bias of the IMF against expansive fiscal policies or non-orthodox economic policies. Creditors also may oppose this increased scrutiny, fearing that it would reduce their rights to receive the full payment. In my view, some form of inquiry into the actual macroeconomic history of the debtor is necessary as it is precisely this function that would prevent sovereigns from indulging in fiscal profligacy or fiscal mismanagement. Despite its perceived bias, the IMF is the only actual organization with the organizational capabilities and skills to conduct this process. Fears of partiality are legitimate, but they could be addressed by increasing the independence of the audit task force; for instance, by having the macroeconomic analyses done by an ad hoc committee to which all parties to the dispute can nominate their independent experts.

Before concluding it is important to say that court is not a panacea for all the problems of sovereign debt. It is not the role of a court to monitor the fiscal sustainability of the sovereign or to intervene with early corrective actions in the same way that a resolution or supervisory authority would do with an ailing bank. Only in the European Union does such a system exist – the Fiscal Compact and the Stability and Growth Pact – but even in the EU it has proven to be extremely difficult to manage owing to the opposition of nation states.

[55] Krueger, above note 53.
[56] For the debate, see Ryan, above note 1.

Concluding Remarks

In this book I have analyzed the relationship between financial sovereignty, financial integration, and global systemic risk. The history of financial crises – and the recent history, especially – demonstrates that global financial instability cannot be viewed only as a product of market inefficiencies. On the contrary, instability sometimes originates from the unwillingness or inability of nation states to coordinate their financial policies toward a Pareto-efficient global equilibrium. This book argues that at the origin of most cooperation failures there is a fundamentally flawed approach to international financial law – a logic of financial nationalism that mainly protects the interests of individual states rather than the stability of the global financial system. The law carries much of the blame for this situation. It has failed to price correctly the tradeoff between the legitimate protection of national goals and the participation of nation states into an integrated economic system.

How can the risks of regulatory divergence and coordination failures be minimized then? I do not believe in the power of soft law or in the possibility of devolving financial regulatory or supervisory powers to a gigantic international financial organization. While these two strategies might work under certain circumstances, they cannot be pursued in many others. In my view, the solution to financial instability requires a legal approach based on binding international law. International financial law must therefore move from a logic of financial nationalism toward a logic of externality in which regulators are accountable under international law and rights are actually protected. Only by forcing states to internalize the externalities of their actions can regulatory and government failures be reduced.

The book draws greatly from the institutional economics literature on regulatory coordination and on the law and economics literature on international law. However, it advances them by focusing on the role of international law in reducing global systemic risk. This contributes also to the institutional economics debate on the most appropriate architecture for international finance by taking a completely new approach to regulatory coordination. It does so by focusing on the power of international law in creating the necessary incentives to maintain financial stability, and on the role of legalization as a compliance mechanism.

This book was written at a very interesting and dynamic moment in the history of financial regulation. After the shocks of two consecutive financial crises, regulators seem to have understood that the only way to maintain the current level of financial integration and protect financial stability is to adopt a more coordinated approach to financial policymaking. The Financial Stability Board is currently doing an extremely important job in promoting a more coordinated regulatory framework for financial regulation. Regulatory reforms have encompassed most of the important issues highlighted by the recent crises, from over-the-counter (OTC) derivatives reforms, to capital and liquidity regulation, to compensation practices. Cooperation on cross-border banking, in particular, has improved greatly owing to the efforts of the Financial Stability Forum (FSB) in pushing forward important reforms and convincing regulators of the need to cooperate.

Having said that, the real question is whether the current reforms will force nation states to switch from a logic of financial nationalism to a logic of externality. The recent regulatory reforms have certainly improved the level of coordination between national financial authorities and, hopefully, they will avoid some of the mistakes of past financial crises. However, it is too early now to say that the logic of financial nationalism will be abandoned once and for all.

From a European perspective, the situation looks much better, although not all risks have been erased. After the biggest reform in the history of financial policy in Europe – the creation of the Banking Union – and the adoption of the new EU legislation on bank resolution, the lures of financial nationalism are still present. The Italian government tried to oppose the application of the new EU bail-in rules in the resolution of Monte dei Paschi – the third largest Italian bank, and the continent's oldest – in favor of an "old-school" bailout. In 2015, courts in England and Germany refused to recognize and implement the resolution action of foreign bank authorities. Across the Atlantic, regulatory authorities have enhanced their cooperation on cross-border banking and securities regulation. After 4 years of war, EU and US regulators seem to have agreed to a common regulatory deal for derivatives regulation. The US Federal Deposit Insurance Corporation, the Bank of England, and the Single Resolution Board have started to cooperate closely on a compatible crisis-resolution framework. However, at present, it is still very unclear how such cooperation will play out in terms of common rules, and whether it will become the norm for all countries. Above all, it is still unclear whether a soft cooperative approach will withstand the pressure of a cross-border banking crisis.

Finally, a few words on sovereign debt. After more than 15 years, Argentina has solved the legal disputes with its creditors and regained access to capital markets. Greece, on the contrary, is still in the same position where it was before, engulfed in a messy restructuring that has only led to misery and resentment. It is impossible to predict when the world will witness another sovereign debt crisis and whether the adoption of Collective Action Clauses and other contractual mechanisms will prevent the ensuing of another Argentine-style sovereign debt litigation. What we can do is learn from the past mistakes and try to minimize the risks. International law can help with that.

Index